AGEISM IN WORK AND EMPLOYMENT

The first Stirling Professions and Management Conference was held in August 1993. Over 100 participants were drawn from the UK, Europe, Australasia and the USA, and 75 papers were presented. In July 1994 the Fourth Internationalizing Entrepreneurship Education and Training Conference (IntEnt94) was held, followed in August 1995 by a second conference on the theme of Professions and Management, and in July 1996 by the conference on Ageism, Work and Employment from which this book draws most of its papers. These conferences also attracted numerous international participants.

Over 100 papers from or chapters stimulated by these conferences have now been published, in seven co-edited and edited books. *The Professional-Managerial Class: Contemporary British Management in the Pursuer Mode,* co-edited by Ian Glover and Michael Hughes, was published in 1996, as were *Beyond Reason: The National Health Service and the Limits of Management*, effectively a sector case study of the main themes discussed in the previous book and co-edited by John Leopold, Ian Glover and Michael Hughes, and, from the 1995 conference, *New Relationships among the Organised Professions,* edited by Robin Fincham. In 2000 *Professions at Bay: Control and Encouragement of Ingenuity in British Management*, co-edited by Ian Glover and Michael Hughes, took many of the arguments from the three previous books on professions and management further. In doing so it contained three chapters not given at the 1993 conference, ten from it which were updated by or with help from their authors, and extended introductory and concluding chapters. Further books in Ashgate's Stirling Management Series include *Educating Entrepreneurs in Modern Economies*, co-edited by Peter Rosa, Michael G. Scott and Heinz Klandt, and *Educating Entrepreneurs for Wealth Creation*, co-edited by Michael G. Scott, Peter Rosa and Heinz Klandt, which were published in 1996, 1998, as were *Enterprising Capital*, by Simon Harris and Chris Bovaird, and *Performance Review in Local Government* by Rob Ball.

Ageism, Work and Employment, co-edited by Ian Glover and Mohamed Branine, contains twelve papers presented at the conference on that subject, five invited ones written subsequently, and substantial introductory and concluding chapters. A further three of the conference papers were published in a special issue, co-edited by Mohamed Branine and Ian Glover, of *Personnel Review*, on ageism, work and employment in July 1997, and another was published in the *Human Resource Management Journal* in 1998. The introductory chapter addresses various themes and contains a brief description of the contents of the remaining chapters, and draws a significant proportion of its content from a paper presented by Ian Glover to an Economic and Social Research Council seminar series on Age and Labour Markets in December 1997. The core arguments of this volume include the following: age discrimination affects people all ages, not just older ones; that ageism is a near-universal phenomenon, but some societies exhibit more constructive and thoughtful attitudes towards age and to relationships between the generations than others; that the terms 'ageing population' and 'demographic time bomb' are misleading because longer and on the whole healthier and wealthier lives are achievements to build upon and not problems to cope with; that employment, education, pension, health and welfare policies need to be co-ordinated better as well as developed in the light of economic and demographic change; that to expect employees and citizens of various ages to 'wait their turn', to 'fit in' or to 'make way' for others will increasingly be regarded as both economically constraining and ethically very dubious; and that while all ageism is bad, age discrimination should always be good.

Ageism in Work and Employment

Edited by
IAN GLOVER
MOHAMED BRANINE
Department of Management and Organization
Faculty of Management
University of Stirling

UNIVERSITY of STIRLING
INNOVATION and EXCELLENCE

Routledge
Taylor & Francis Group
LONDON AND NEW YORK

First published 2001 by Ashgate Publishing

Reissued 2018 by Routledge
2 Park Square, Milton Park, Abingdon, Oxon OX14 4RN
711 Third Avenue, New York, NY 10017, USA

Routledge is an imprint of the Taylor & Francis Group, an informa business

A Library of Congress record exists under LC control number: 00110694

ISBN 13: 978-1-138-73639-9 (hbk)
ISBN 13: 978-0-367-24915-1 (pbk)
ISBN 13: 978-1-315-18597-2 (ebk)

Contents

List of figures and tables

Notes on contributors

James Arrowsmith is a Research Fellow at Warwick Business School, Coventry, UK. Before joining the Industrial Relations Research Unit at Warwick Business School in the University of Warwick he was at the Manchester Metropolitan University where he conducted, with Ann E. McGoldrick, a major study of ageism in UK organizations. His research interests are in age discrimination, employment flexibility, pay and working time.

Colin Bottomley is involved in entrepreneurship teaching, consultancy and research with the Hunter Centre for Entrepreneurship at the University of Strathclyde in Glasgow. He spent some ten years with the Scottish Enterprise Foundation at the University of Stirling prior to establishing the Centre for Enterprise in Leicester. He had 20 years of industrial experience in the ceramics industry before he developed his academic career. He has been involved in establishing entrepreneurial businesses and maintains a strong interest in helping the development of such enterprises. It was through this work that an involvement of the problems of ageism in the workplace developed.

Philip H. Bowers is a Senior Lecturer in Business Economics at the Department of Business Studies, University of Edinburgh. His research interests focus on managerial economics of the service sector with particular emphasis on health service and railway reform.

Mohamed Branine is a Senior Lecturer and MBA Programme Director at Stirling University. He has studied, worked or taught in Algeria, Canada, China and the UK. His research interests are in international and comparative human resource management including the effects of economic reforms on employment policy in developing countries; global trends in flexible working and family friendly employment policies; and perceptions of age and gender in employment in different cultures.

Adelina Broadbridge is a Senior Lecturer in the Department of Marketing at the University of Stirling. She teaches on a range of undergraduate, postgraduate, distance learning and post experience programmes. Her research interests are in the field of human resources management in retailing. Some recent publications include: 'Retail Managers: Stress and the Work-Family Relationship', *International Journal of Retail and Distribution Management* (1999) and 'A Profile of Female Retail Managers: Some Insights', *The Service Industries Journal*, 19, 3, pp. 135-161, 1999.

Colin Duncan is a Lecturer in Industrial Relations in the Department of Business Studies, University of Edinburgh. He has published widely in the fields of pay determination and public sector management. His current research projects include a survey work investigating younger people's experience of ageism and their attitudes towards a range of age and employment issues; and a survey of current British trade union policies towards age-related matters in employment.

Graham Elkin is a Senior Lecturer and Head of Department of Management, University of Otago, Dunedin, New Zealand. After a career in Human Resource Management in Britain, he joined the University of Otago in 1983. He directed the Otago MBA programme for five years and has subsequently taught Human Resource Development and Organizational Behaviour. He practices as an Organizational Development consultant and has published three books, and many academic papers in the general Human Resource Management field.

Wendy Evangelisti is Sports Development Coordinator at the Centre for Physical Education and Sports Development at the University of Stirling. Her interests include the development, delivery and management of physical activity programmes for older adults. She established the SUPERS group for older exercise participants at the University of Stirling, which currently has over four hundred active members. She is a member of the Management Board of the European Group for Research into Physical Activity for the Elderly, and is a Churchill Fellow.

Ian Glover is a Lecturer and Director of the Doctoral Programme in the Department of Management and Organization at the University of Stirling, Scotland. He left home in 1959 and enjoyed varied experience of employment, study, research and policy-oriented consultancy for the British government. The latter was concerned with UK management quality and industrial performance and with related issues regarding higher education. Ian's main research interest is managerial work and occupations at home and abroad, involving the study of technical and social divisions of labour and related economic and educational issues. His interest in ageism flows directly from his interest in technical and social divisions of labour.

Jenny Hamilton is a Senior Lecturer at the University of Strathclyde Law School. She qualified as a barrister and solicitor in Australia. Her main areas of research are in the commercial law field with a particular interest in the regulation of the business environment. She has been awarded a number of research grants by the Carnegie Trust, and the Home and Health Department of the Scottish Office.

Peter Herriot is Associate Director of the Institute for Employment Studies, and visiting professor at the City University Business School and at the University of Surrey. His main interest is in career management and the changing nature of the employment relationship, and he is author (with Wendy Hirsh and Peter Reilly) of *Trust and Transition: Managing Today's Employment Relationship* (Wiley, 1998). Peter is an ardent European, and editor of the *European Journal of Work and Organization Psychology*.

David Jenkins is in his mid-seventies and has had his own management consultancy for nearly twenty years. He is an Oxford history and LSE law graduate with a wide variety of commercial and industrial management experience and he has also been an academic. He is the author of two books and numerous articles on management. See chapter 10 for more details of his career and experiences.

Lesley Mayne is a Research Fellow in the Centre for European Human Resource Management at Cranfield School of Management. She has played a key role on the Price Waterhouse Cranfield Project, a major European project focusing on strategic European human resource management practices. She has a number of years managerial experience in both the public and service sectors, mainly in leisure services. Areas of experience cover flexible working practices, the changing relationships between the personnel function and line management and more broadly on European human resource management.

Ann E. McGoldrick is a Senior Lecturer in the Department of Management at Manchester Metropolitan University, UK. Her research interests include ageism, equal opportunities, organizational change and flexible working practices. She has just completed a major study of ageism in work and employment with James Arrowsmith and she has written widely on the subject.

Alan Nichols is the Director of the Centre for Physical Education and Sports Development at the University of Stirling. He has interests in the relationships between fitness and health, both in children and in the elderly. He has been Chairman of the British Universities' Physical Education Association, and United Kingdom representative to the European Network for Sports Studies in Higher Education. He maintains a practical interest in the teaching and assessment of lifeguarding and swim teaching.

David Parsons was a visiting research fellow, when writing his chapter, in the Centre for European Human Resource Management at Cranfield School of Management and is now a partner of the HOST Consultancy Labour Market Intelligence Unit. He is the author of numerous major reports and papers on ageism in the European Union.

Karen Rodham is a Research Fellow at the Department of Psychiatry, University of Oxford. Dr Rodham worked previously as a lecturer at the Universities of Central Lancashire and Surrey where she conducted research on discrimination and ageism.

Darren J. Smith is currently employed as a Human Resources Adviser with New Zealand's Ministry of Education. Previously he conducted research in diversity management at the University of Otago, Dunedin, New Zealand.

Philip Taylor is a Senior Research Associate at the Cambridge Interdisciplinary Centre on Ageing at Cambridge University. He has been researching in the age and employment field for a number of years. He recently co-chaired a European Commission funded project developing models of best practice in managing older workers and developing local projects to assist older workers and employers. This was a follow up to an EC funded study which evaluated initiatives across the European Union which aimed to assist older workers and employers. He also participated in two other recent European studies in this area: an investigation of best practice in employers' policies and practices towards older workers and a study of public policy options (for the European Foundation for the Improvement of Living and Working Conditions and Eurolink Age respectively). He was also recently grant holder for an ESRC seminar series on age and the labour market.

Christine Tillsley is currently working with the Open University Business School in research consultancy capacity, conducting research on the relationship between age and employment. Prior to this she worked on disability issues, most recently in the voluntary sector and before this in the Department for Education and Employment (DfEE). Whilst at DfEE she was also, for some time, responsible for designing, commissioning and managing research on older workers.

Acknowledgements

The idea for this edited volume arose out of the international conference on Ageism, Work and Employment held at Stirling University in July 1996. We are grateful to all the participants in that conference who helped shape the debate and the content of first a special issue of the *Personnel Review* journal published in July 1997 and second this book which contains updated and new papers. We are particularly grateful to the contributors to this book including of course those who were unable to come to the conference but who wrote invited papers subsequently.

We would like to thank Anne Keirby and Maureen Mansell-Ward at Ashgate for their understanding, patience and support, and all the members of staff of the Department of Management and Organization at Stirling for their support and encouragement. We would also like to thank Pauline Beavers at Ashgate for her considerable help with past collaborations between our Department and her company.

Further special thanks are due to people whose varied forms of interest, support and help have contributed much to this volume: Nadiä Branine, Helen Gamen of Age Concern, Dorothy Grace-Elder MSP, Dr. Jerry Hallier, Jaqy Jacobs of Forties People, David Jenkins, Professor Peter Lawrence, Vera Livingstone, John MacDonald and Dr. Frances Moore of the Scottish Campaign against Age Discrimination in Employment, Phil Lyon, Pat Scrutton, Phil Taylor for his unfailing readiness to supply help and information and for his professionalism in general, Professor Alan Walker, Philip Walker of the Campaign Against Age Discrimination in Employment, Deanne Wentworth for her gallows and many other forms of humour, and also to each other for staying friends throughout all our work on ageism irrespective of all our other competing commitments.

Above all we are greatly indebted to the care, competence, dedication, hard work and patience of Pauline McBeath, Sharon Bowie and Hazel Gentles for their typing and formatting. Pauline, Sharon and Hazel all made tremendous efforts on our behalf at different times and the order of names simply reflects differences in the balance of their individual efforts between this book and their many other responsibilities.

List of abbreviations

BPC	British Printing Corporation
CEO	Commission for Equal Opportunities
COW	Campaign for Older Workers
CSO	Central Statistical Office
EC	European Commission
EITB	Engineering Industrial Training Board
EOC	Equal Opportunities Commission
EOP	Equal Opportunities Policies
EOR	Equal Opportunities Review
ESACEC	Employment and Social Affairs Council of the European Union
ESRC	Economic and Social Research Council
EU	European Union
FIFO	First In First Out
HRM	Human Resource Management
IDS	Income Data Services
ILO	International Labour Organization
IPD	Institute of Personnel and Development
IPM	Institute of Personnel Management
IPMNZ	New Zealand Institute of Personnel Management
IRS	Industrial Relations Services
LEC	Local Enterprise Company
LIFO	Last In First Out
MAGOW	Ministerial Advisory Group on Older Workers
MBA	Master of Business Administration
NEDO	National Economic Development Office
NIESR	National Institute of Economic and Social Research
OECD	Organization for Economic Cooperation and Development
OPCS	Office of Population Census and Surveys
PAYG	Pay As You Go
PDP	Professional Development Programme
SAEOA	South Australian Equal Opportunities Act
SAEOC	South Australian Equal Opportunities Commission

SEF	Scottish Enterprise Foundation
SERPS	State Earnings Related Pension Scheme
SMEs	Small and Medium Enterprises
TECs	Training and Enterprise Councils
TfW	Training for Work

We dedicate this book to those who endure ageism, and the true lessons of history

Precious Years[1]

It's all over now
No more summers in heaven
After World War Two wed
and a life of ups and downs

I see it now
precious in the paper
A young man and his bride
and someone to make time stand still

But now I know
and I don't want to believe it
Where does it leave you now
that the precious years are gone?

All things remain
to ignore and outlive you
from the man in the moon
to the green hills outside your door

Alone you came
so alone you must go now
There's no mountain on earth
can ever outlive your soul

But now I know
and I don't want to believe it
Where does it leave you now
that the precious years are gone?

I know you well
You'll be nothing but grateful
Never let it be said
they were spent in thoughtless ways

Warm winds blow
'cross the ties that bind forever
For a place in the sun
and for the heart of love a home

But now I know
and I don't want to believe it
Where does it leave you now
that the precious years are gone?

[1] From 'Searchlight' by Runrig (1989). Composed by Calum and Rory Macdonald.

Part I
Introduction

1 Introduction: the challenge of longer and healthier lives

Ian Glover and Mohamed Branine

Introduction

The formal study of ageism and of age discrimination in employment is largely a product of the 1980s and 1990s. It tends to be characterized by diversity of researchers' backgrounds and fragmentation between their areas of interest and also by neglect of a number of significant features and forms of the phenomena in question. In July 1996 a conference on Ageism, Work and Employment was held at the University of Stirling. It attracted researchers with backgrounds in economics, law, psychology and sociology and from business and management studies, comparative management, entrepreneurship, human resource management, international business, marketing, and physical education and sports studies. Three of the papers presented at the conference were among those published in a special issue of *Personnel Review* (Vol. 26, No. 4, 1997), another was published in the *Human Resource Management Journal* in 1998 and twelve of the conference papers, which have been revised, are among those in this volume.

Most academic and lay interest in ageism, work and employment is currently focused on the problems of older people and most of the contributions to the conference and to this book reflect this fact. However ageism is an intergenerational phenomenon which both affects and involves employable people of all ages, and we anticipate and expect that as interest in and knowledge of the subject grow, research and writing will become more cohesive. We also expect that age and its links with employment and work and its management will replace age*ism* as the main concern of researchers. Currently there are some quite transparent elements of rawness, narrowness and lack of sophistication in and around thinking about age, ageism, work and employment. For example the often rather irrelevant term elderly is still used more often than it ought to be.

In the rest of this chapter we do four things. First, in the first main section of it, we spell out our working definition of ageism along with the three most important aims of the book. In the second main section we discuss the nature and context of age discrimination by reviewing some relevant studies and ideas, mainly those that are related to labour markets, and we offer an idea for summarising them by describing the contrasting notions of commodification and greening. Then we focus on other aspects of ageism in work and employment, notably some of the links between age, politics and management; age, education and training; and age and employer initiatives. In the third main section we outline the organization and the contents of the sections and chapters of the book. Finally and in the conclusion to this chapter we briefly anticipate some of the arguments of the book's final chapter by looking forward to the development of more constructive understanding, policies and practices regarding age, work and employment than have usually been apparent hitherto.

A definition and the aims of the book

We define ageism as unconscionable prejudice and discrimination based on actual or perceived chronological age. It occurs whenever a person's age is erroneously deemed to be unsuitable for some reason or purpose. It can be used to the detriment of people of any age. Age discrimination is treated as a universal, highly variable and complex phenomenon affecting people everywhere and of all ages, not just older ones, and it is considered as occurring in all aspects of employment and human resource management, not only when people are recruited or when their employment is terminated by employers. It is often prevalent when jobs are either particularly scarce or plentiful, when employers tend to find it a convenient excuse for deciding not to develop or to discard staff, or for not employing people who lack 'obviously' suitable backgrounds in the first place.

In work and employment, we see age as variously associated with the kinds of image that employers, and work colleagues, want to present: the terms dynamic, experienced, lively, mature, sensible, smart, powerful, wise, and others, including the opposites of these, come to mind. Age can be involved with control of employee attitudes, behaviour and performance. It can be used positively to convey a sense of appropriateness and dignity to employees, to help match employee capacity and employee performance, in the exercise of discretion and the granting of autonomy, and in employee and organizational development. Age can also be used negatively and destructively. This happens whenever it is used to reduce the dignity of and the respect given to individuals, when performance evaluation is confused by inappropriate application of age-related opinions or information, when levels of autonomy and discretion, types of training provision and forms of work organization are not matched to age profiles in ways that optimise performance and development (Herriot and Pemberton, 1994).

Ageism is present at all stages of employment, not just in advertisements for posts, but also in organizational structuring, selection, deployment, task allocation, appraisal of performance and career planning, and in remuneration and employee benefits. It is present, too, in the selection or non-selection of individuals for particular kinds of training and development and in decisions about redeployment, promotion, demotion, termination and pension rights (Pilcher, 1996; Arrowsmith and McGoldrick, 1997; Itzin and Philipson, 1993).

In societies where people are living longer, healthier and wealthier lives, and when older people constitute higher proportions of populations, ageism against older people may become incompatible with general economic and social needs. Employers responding to demographic change can find themselves in the position of having to reconsider their recruitment, training and retirement policies whereby they can benefit from the knowledge and skills of all potential or existing employees regardless of age.

On the basis of our definition and our thinking about ageism we have organized this book to achieve three main aims. First, we seek to identify and discuss the nature and some of the main causes of ageism and age discrimination in work and employment in the UK and to a lesser extent elsewhere. Second, we aim to describe and explore the experience and practice of age discrimination in work and employment. Third, we aim to present, compare and contrast some of the main remedies which have been proposed and we do so the context of relevant economic, political and social trends.

Our main focus, as noted above, is on ageism and its effects on older employees, or would-be ones, although the chapters by Peter Herriot and by Karen Rodham are concerned with middle-aged and younger employees respectively. Discrimination against older people, say those over 40 and especially against those over 50 and 60, is currently much more prominent and the subject of much more public criticism than that against people between their middle to late teens and, say, their mid-thirties. Discrimination against young people with few or no qualifications has tended to be studied, but more often neglected, as an issue in its own right, partly because concerns about education and training tend to overshadow and to be confused with it. Also, discrimination against the young does not in general appear to have quite so final a quality as that against older people, until, that is, some of the young victims commit suicide as a result of being thwarted in their searches for adult roles and identities. In many countries older people, especially males, have lost their jobs both with and without the benefits of early retirement 'packages', and in many sectors younger people are no longer getting apprenticeships, training positions and junior types of job. Not least because both younger and older employees may be affected by ageist attitudes and behaviour, it is not usually helpful for one group to blame its misfortunes mainly on the other. Ageism is different from other 'isms' such as racism or sexism because it can affect anyone at one or more time in their life (see Bytheway, 1995).

Many of the more general arguments in this book are very relevant for understanding ageism directed at people of all ages and at all those in their twenties onwards whose employment experiences and situations help to turn them into 'chronological misfits' of one kind or another. The reason why discrimination against younger people has not been so highly publicized as that against older ones is the use of the widespread assumption that a cult of youth operates in some Western countries to the detriment, on balance, of older people, who therefore need more public support than younger ones do. In fact the cult of youth primarily means middle aged and older people acting immaturely and neglecting the responsible care and upbringing of the young so that it is the latter who suffer most, and the rights and welfare of their elders so that they also suffer. Younger people are, we emphasize again, major victims of ageism, especially if they are unqualified and unskilled (Mizen, 1995). Immaturity is the stigma most commonly misapplied to the young (Gadd, 1996). As noted, as unemployment amongst young people has grown in the UK, so have suicide rates, especially amongst males who feel unable to form adult identities (Furnham and Stacey, 1991).

Age is also often used against people - chronological misfits - if they have not 'achieved' certain levels of employment by particular ages, very often irrespective of the reasons, and also often in ignorance of valid alternative experiences which may be of great use to employers. The stigma of mental and physical decrepitude are normally misapplied to older people, resulting in feelings of rejection and atrophy of mental and physical powers (cf. Taylor and Walker, 1994; Pearson, 1996; Taylor, 1998). As people live longer and as a culture of early retirement becomes more entrenched millions of discarded, inactive, yet fit older people become an unnecessary burden on the active middle-aged and young. However ageism in all its forms 'creates a series of barriers to the achievement of individual potential. This is wasteful in terms of the optimum use of human resources and represents a source of injustice and social exclusion' (Walker, 1999: 7). Older people do, of course, tend to be more experienced and wiser, but physically weaker than younger ones. This means that it is those who ignore relevant strengths and who exploit relevant weaknesses, either out of fear or greed, or both, who deserve the most criticism.

Age discrimination in context

Contemporary patterns of employment have evolved out of industrialisation, which in the developed countries and some other ones has produced great wealth by historic standards. Largely as a consequence lives are considerably longer than they were 50 to 100 years ago, and in most industrial countries twice as long as they were in the eighteenth century, but most societies and employers have yet to adapt to this major demographic change. Ideally, employers should try to use and develop all of the abilities at their disposal creatively, but in reality short term economic and political factors and longer term disjunctions between technical and social divisions of labour interfere with the pursuit of the laudable aim. Thus in the latter case it is common for the wrong people to be doing the wrong jobs as members of the wrong occupations with the wrong skills and wrong education and knowledge with wrong expectations, attitudes, beliefs and motives, and so on. Social divisions of labour based on such task-irrelevant factors as age, gender and race interfere with the ideal technical/practical ones. Rigid and negative views of human potential often prevail with managers and employers failing to realise or acknowledge that failure to learn and succeed at performing tasks is due to lack of confidence or effort, not to a lack of ability or potential. They *suspect* diversity in employees' backgrounds when they should celebrate, enjoy, explore and develop it.

Partly because of rising levels of income and of general affluence, partly because of the disjunction between (ideal) technical and social (aspects which interfere with the ideal, like age, gender and race) divisions of labour, meaning that the wrong sorts of people staff inadequately designed jobs, individualistic and selfish chaos can prevail in and around workplaces. People tend to be more concerned with career than with achievement and work. There is considerable social mobility (in all directions) but it is at least as much a product of chaos and often unrelated change in work organization as it is of effort, ability and positive economic and social development (cf. Herriot, Hirsh and Reilly, 1998).

Affluence, selfishness and organizational chaos tend to breed careerism, and concern with status, income and power, at the expense of vocation and the lifetime development of useful specialist personal skill and knowledge (Sorge, 1978; Jackall, 1988). The notion of vocation can be appreciated by reading Dingley (1996) on the medieval guilds, apprenticeship, professions, universities, religion and society, and on Utilitarianism and Durkheim's views on moral and social integration in industrial societies.

Age is perhaps the last 'legitimate' general resort and/or final excuse for excluding people from and within employment. It is relatively easy for employers to use age to eliminate candidates from selection lists, partly because doing so is not yet prohibited by law. Also, and although the validity of the following is often very dubious in practice, there may be some justification in employers referring to such factors as inexperience, reduced energy or inadequate speed of response, when discriminating on the grounds of age.

Several researchers have tried to explain the issue of ageism in employment and work situations by using theories and concepts concerned with the operations of labour markets. These concern labour market segmentation, internal labour markets, the reserve army of labour, and labour market flexibility (see Laczko and Phillipson, 1991). Labour market segmentation theory is based on notions of inequality in the labour market and accounts for it at least partly in terms of differentiation based on gender, race, age, educational type and level, occupation, remuneration grades and so on (Laczko and Phillipson, 1991). Advocates of internal labour market theory note how older employees benefit from seniority-related pay and promotion, and do not have to compete with younger people for jobs in external labour markets, but if they lose their jobs it is difficult for them to find new employment, and they tend to experience long periods of unemployment. This is why during economic downturns older employees are often pressurized to leave their relatively highly paid senior positions, through early retirement, to be replaced by younger and cheaper counterparts. The third concept regards older unemployed and underemployed people as part of the reserve army of labour. According to this notion many older people are only employed when needed depending on the fluctuating demand for labour. Fourth and finally, it is also often argued that one effect of the use of different types of flexible working can be to move older employees from full-time positions, which are given to younger people, and to put them into part-time and temporary jobs.

Lay and academic concern with the possibly increasing net costs of having an older population has burgeoned since the 1970s in the UK (Arber, 1996). Debate has become increasingly sophisticated so that, for example, it has been linked to the thinking of such social theorists as Elias (1991) on childhood and adulthood and youth and old age in history, and Kumar (1995) on the slippery nature of our thinking about time and the life cycle in the context of discussions of modernity, postmodernity and so on. Laslett (1996) has depicted a 'new map of life' which takes account, especially, of a 'Third Age' from fifty onwards to the mid-seventies onwards, of hopefully rewarding activity following full-time employment.

Other and often wider aspects of age discrimination are discussed by Casey, Metcalf and Milllward (1997) who compared redundancy and early retirement practices in the UK, Germany and the USA, countries with different systems of education and training, industrial relations and social insurance. Clark and Anker (1990) reported research which indicated that job satisfaction tends to decline from a moderate level in the early and middle years of a career, probably as tournament mobility and extrinsic sources of stress are encountered, and then to increase steadily up to retirement. This suggests that age discrimination, at least that against older employees, is rarely constructive in anything but a very short term financial sense. Pritchard (1990, 1992) has long studied the links between rising rates of suicide and unemployment amongst young males, in the UK especially, since the mid-1970s. Pilcher's (1996) review article covers a remarkable amount of ground, mainly on younger as opposed to older unemployed people, but noting how both suffer because of their 'inevitably' marginal positions in labour markets. Taylor and Walker (1997) pointed to some of the reasons why employers discriminate incompetently and unfairly, such as political-economic ones, 'cultural lag' (society is slow to recognise the relevant problems), and the unattractiveness of much of the employment on offer to older and younger people and to middle-aged ones whose ages and backgrounds ostensibly make them unfit for the work that they aspire to. Taylor and Walker (1994, 1997; also see Thomson, 1996) have also emphasized, on numerous occasions, the links between age discrimination in employment and related issues of social welfare, education, training, intergenerational relations, and so on.

The above ideas which link age, work and employment issues to labour market practices can be summarized by using notions of commodification and greening which concern various relevant economic, political and social, cultural and legal trends (Branine and Glover, 1997). They are two opposed scenarios regarding age and employment in advanced industrial societies. We reject the not entirely irrelevant but very shallow notion of post-industrial society, given the growing output, ongoing development and increasing economic significance, of industry and/or manufacturing (see Cohen and Zysman, 1987; Daniels and Radebaugh, 1998; Glover, 1992; Glover, Currie and Tracey, 1998).

The commodification thesis suggests that competitive pressures and technical change conspire to produce the following situation. Younger people of working age tend to be perceived as lacking the skills and commitment to be employable except and on the whole in so called 'MacJobs' (and as students). People aged from around 25 to around 40 are the most employable: they tend to be fit, to have skills and knowledge, and to conform because they have mortgages and dependants. Those over 40 are thought to be less fit (and increasingly so) and also less compliant because they know too much about their organizational seniors and peers. They are also often relatively expensive to employ. After 40 (or even earlier) they find work and careers harder and harder to obtain. The alternative, and opposite, thesis is that of greening. Here, and as highly affluent societies bloom, the first third or so of typically long lives, say up to 30 years of age, is spent mainly in learning and self-discovery. The middle third, from around 30 to the late fifties, is spent in productive and usually rewarding employment. The final third, until the age of about 90 and/or the fourth age of often rapid decline preceding death, is mainly spent in social and civic activities and recreation, and in transmitting experience and culture to younger people (cf. Laslett, 1996). Thus learning is followed by doing, and doing by teaching. In reality commodification tends to be experienced by people at or near the lower end of the social scale, and greening by those towards or at the top, by the highly qualified and by those with occupational pensions. Growing affluence increases the possibility, but by no means the inevitability, that greening will be experienced by more people, and commodification by fewer. What is certain is that the two related ideals of young people with resources and freedom to develop into experienced and rounded people before complete engagement with their lives' work, and of older people from their late fifties to middle sixties onwards, enjoying two or three decades of good health, living active and influential lives, look increasingly achievable. Awareness of such issues and influences appears to have been somewhat lacking in, although certainly not throughout, UK society (see Hockey and James, 1993; and Robertson, 1997, on the 'moral economy of interdependence').

The notion of commodification suggests that the pursuit of material progress in a highly affluent, consumerist and advanced industrial society dominates employment and management and symbolizes a powerful propensity to use human resources ruthlessly *up* in an accelerating quest for greater efficiency, and it argues that in the context of a widely prevalent and amoral cult of youth older people are discarded for being relatively expensive to employ and ostensibly unable to learn and produce as efficiently as younger ones. According to this perspective, an employee is a commodity that can be bought and consumed only before its so-called sell by or use by date. Some employers apparently regard almost any time after someone is 40 and others regard the official retirement age as the use by date by which people are seen to become unable to learn, unable to adapt to change, unsuitable for making decisions, unmotivated and less productive. Studies of relevant attitudes and behaviour, including stereotyping, the use of age bars and age-related criteria in recruitment, in placement, appraisal, training, promotion, redundancy and retirement have been reported and discussed by Arrowsmith and McGoldrick (1997, also see Lyon and Pollard, 1997), on the generally very negative stereotypes of older employees espoused by relatively young MBA students/managers compared with those of older personnel professionals). Taylor and Walker (1994) reported surveys of employers and older workers, which explored policies and attitudes of the former towards the latter. They recorded the operation of a self-fulfilling prophecy: employers argued that older employees lacked appropriate skills and the latter lacked access to employer and official training. This notion of commodification also sees younger employees as products that have not yet reached their useful levels of competence and maturity. Younger employees are exploited for their energy and naiveté and paid relatively low amounts because they are perceived as lacking expertise and commitment, and unreliable as subordinates and employees. In this context, Herriot and Pemberton (1995) discussed the apparently 'permanent loss of the traditional notion of career' (p. xiii), due to economic forces and elaborated upon ways in which those affected did and could fight back. On age-related difficulties and abuses near or at the bottom end of the age scale, Lavalette (1994) discussed the prevalence of child labour in the UK, not all of it necessarily harmful to those so employed, but not always conducive to their educational and social development either.

The diametrically opposed ideal typical notion of greening suggests, on the other hand, that technical progress has produced such levels of material affluence that it is no longer necessary for people to work as many hours per day, days per week, weeks per year, and years in their lifetimes, and that older people in particular may prefer to work flexibly on a part-time, temporary or job sharing basis and to give up full-time employment so as to be able to engage in less physically demanding activities such as caring, civic, advisory and voluntary work as well as passing on their accumulated wisdom and enjoying their leisure time and travelling (also see Laczko and Philipson, 1991). In the most developed version of this notion, this phase of life may in many instances begin after individuals have chosen to continue in higher level full-time employment for some years after the average and mandatory ages of employment.

A slightly jaded but at least fairly realistic perception of employer behaviour would suggest that young employees are perceived as having energy but as being lacking in skills, knowledge and sense. They are relatively inexperienced but tend to be unreliable. The early middle aged are not cheap but they have energy, knowledge and skills, and because they tend to have career prospects and family and financial commitments, they tend to be reliable. Older employers tend to be expensive, reliable and competent. They are also often (especially if unpromoted or underpromoted) critical of managements. Thus they are expensive and they know too much and are threats, both politically and in terms of competence, to some of their seniors. The most popular suggestions for dealing with the kinds of dilemma which these phenomena involve have included legislation, education, and employer initiatives.

Age, politics and management

Political events and institutions and legislation may have considerable effects on relationships between age and employment. In the United States of America (USA) and in a number of European Union (EU) countries and elsewhere policies on ageism are relatively well established and laws are enforced with varying degrees of effectiveness, while in the UK and in many other countries policy makers have yet to confront the issue of ageism and employment with much more than exhortation. In the United Kingdom there have been a number of aborted attempts as well as a number of individual employer initiatives but there is no legislation, nor a clear and decisively effective national policy. Warr and Pennington (1993) found that more than two thirds of 1,140 employers favoured some form of legislation against age discrimination but that there was no general consensus about the form that it should take, and that others, instead, wanted a voluntary code to cover recruitment, selection, training and promotion. Similarly Hayward et al (1997) found that 74 percent of over 500 employers consulted preferred the idea of a voluntary code of employment practice. However such developments as the government's 'Getting On' campaign to encourage employers to employ older people and the 1999 budget announcement to extend the New Deal to those over 50, may all be 'important steps in the right direction' (Walker, 1999: 7).

Surprisingly, perhaps, employers tended to favour anti-age discrimination legislation, presumably because they realised the waste caused by the discrimination and the value of there being a 'level playing field' for it to be staunched. Taylor and Walker (1994; 1997) argued that the employment prospects of older people would not be enhanced by the educational approach which has hitherto been favoured by all governments. Employers tended to adopt relatively tactical and cautious approaches to the employment of older people and without governments giving a strong positive lead older less skilled workers would generally face a choice between lowly paid and low-skill jobs in services and unemployment.

In general, and not of course completely unnaturally, and in the absence of a strong social and political consensus to the contrary, economistic approaches to employee motivation appear to prevail amongst employers. Thus they tend to overemphasise the power of extrinsic rewards and to play down that of intrinsic ones. Promotion and career tend to be valued more than work and long-term achievement, and job-hopping between employers is tolerated and even encouraged while loyal high level performance is often taken for granted or seen as evidence of lack of initiative. In these respects employers and less competent and principled employees often of course, collude. Many employees have aspirations which are self-aggrandizingly and predatorily managerialist, valuing pay, power and status more than achievement and integrity, and which are liberally suffused with ageist assumptions.

There is nonetheless - irrespective of employee collusion - a definite sense in which age and appearance serve as employers' last major repositories of prejudice amongst employees, in the absence of a firm political lead. Prejudice and discrimination based on ethnic background and gender are forbidden by law, but age and appearance can still be used to eliminate candidates for employment, promotion and so on, without much fear of open and formal opposition, or consequences. We are adding the word appearance to age here because it is very often how old people look, rather than their actual chronological age, which influences attitudes and actions. The widespread and the deep-seated character of age-related prejudice and discrimination, although only that directed at older people, are dealt with in the volume edited by McEwen (1990), which includes material on ageism in social security, health care, retailing and voluntary service as well as in employment.

The collusion that we referred to in the two preceding paragraphs has, as two of its outcomes, injelitance and mediocrity. Injelitance is a mixture of incompetence and jealousy which can spread like a cancer whenever mediocre people collude monopolistically to appoint and favour people like themselves (Parkinson, 1958). Negative, down-market approaches to staffing and other aspects of employment tend to foster blind ambition, conformity, jealousy, and fear of ability and enthusiasm. Managers appoint and foster the careers of those who are unthreatening or who, in their opinions, make them look good. Mediocrity and injelitance tend to engender a devil's brew which can damage organizations severely, even destroy them.

In the absence of legislation there are several important even if at times obvious things that employers, policy makers and employees themselves may do to reduce age discrimination. Measures such as the encouragement of lifelong learning and training would encourage a culture of greater flexibility and equality of opportunity regarding career progression, and the removal of incentives for early retirement and the use of different employment policies could help to keep many experienced people in work. Some policies would favour part-time and other 'flexible' forms of employment and others would favour the continued employment into what used to be or still is regarded as old age, in influential and demanding posts.

Even if legislation exists prohibiting employers from stating age limits in recruitment advertisements and from discriminating on age grounds against staff openly as regards training, pay and promotion, it may not be easy to protect them from covert but equally damaging discrimination. It may be just as important and effective, as well as necessary, to raise awareness of the diversity and the value of people to employers, regardless of age, and to encourage everyone to think far more positively about the insignificance or otherwise of age-related attributes in the context of employment than they currently appear to. Opposing ageism is not just the responsibility of policy makers and employers but of everyone. This helps to bring us to relationships between education, training and ageism.

Age, education and training

Those who oppose the use of legislation usually advocate relevant education and training instead. Typically there are two parts to their argument. First, they contend that employers, employees and the general public should make themselves more aware of the problem of ageism and the potential of all people regardless of age. For example, in 1991 the Institute of Personnel and Development (then the Institute of Personnel Management) called upon its members to educate and train their employees, particularly those making employment decisions, about the employment and business implications of ageism. As Taylor argues in chapter 15 the issue of the legislative versus the voluntary approach was addressed seriously in a study of employers' attitudes and practices commissioned by the Conservative government in the mid-1990s when it was found that most employers preferred the voluntary approach (Hayward, Taylor, Smith and Davies, 1997) but there is no evidence that this option favours older people.

The second part of the argument is that learning through formal education and training should not stop at a certain age. Lifelong learning, it is argued, is for everyone. However older employees tend to be ignored or deliberately marginalised when it comes to training for employment and they are therefore prevented from keeping pace with relevant technical and other changes. Those who argue that older employees may have difficulties in adapting to new techniques and methods have little evidence to support their claims (Davies, Mathews and Wong, 1991) and there is a growing number of cases that have shown that older people are able to learn and to cope effectively if training is provided adequately and not patronisingly. Employers who provide continuous training for all their employees and who appreciate the value of energy, enthusiasm, and varying and effective combinations of experience and wisdom have taken the lead by introducing employment practices that promote equal opportunities and help to eliminate age discrimination. Growing numbers of such employers belong to the Employers' Forum on Age which was established by Age Concern in 1997.

Age and employer initiatives

It can be argued that neither legislation nor education will influence employers to be less prejudiced about their employees' ages if they are unable to envisage managerial and financial benefits. In such countries as France, Germany and Spain, where the governments have not only introduced laws against age discrimination but also introduced incentives to employers to employ older people, age discrimination still exists (Guillemard, Taylor and Walker, 1996; Weber et al., 1997). In the UK, where the government is in favour of an educational approach, people are also still discriminated against (see Taylor in this book). Therefore, and although they are very limited in number and often scope, too, employers' initiatives against ageism have been the most successful. In the UK, despite the absence of legislation, a number of organizations, notably B and Q, Tesco, Sainsbury's, British Telecom, IBM, and various regional and local authorities, have been reported, publicized and praised widely for their initiatives in employing people regardless of their age, or for targeting, as in the case of B and Q, older people (see Smith, 1990; Summers, 1990; Elliot, 1991; Pickard, 1999). Some organizations, mainly in retailing and catering, have been able, to some extent, to improve their customer relations, to reduce employee turnover and to respond to fluctuations in the demand for their goods or services by introducing less or non-ageist policies. It has been argued, perhaps a little uncharitably, that such employers are merely responding proactively to labour and other market pressures, rather than being benevolently proactive in promoting equal opportunities (Casey, Metcalf and Millward, 1997). But in general it is fair to conclude that there is very little evidence in the UK, for example, of many employers having strategies for the recruitment and retention of older staff, or having in place gradual retirement schemes or encouraging later retirement (see for example Taylor and Walker, 1994).

Parts and chapters of the book

After this introductory chapter which constitutes the first Part of the book, in Part Two the authors of the chapters explore the nature and causes of the problem. All of the chapters include attempts to define ageism and they all also discuss the main reasons for age discrimination as well as some of its social, cultural, economic and political implications. In chapter two Colin Duncan explores the concept of ageism and discusses the features of the early exit phenomenon and considers whether this trend can be attributed chiefly to age prejudices held by employers. He draws some useful conclusions concerning the efficacy of current and proposed policy responses. In chapter three Glover and Branine argue that changes in labour markets and thus economic forces, real and perceived, have been reducing both the quantity and quality of the work and employment available to older and other unfortunately aged people. At the same time too, technical development and the cult of youth, both of which are variously causes, features and products of mass affluence, have helped to legitimize rejection of much of whatever, in the form of achievement, experience, knowledge, skills and wisdom, older people have to offer. In doing so, they try to redefine ageism, review the broad phases of economic and societal development from pre-industrial times to the present day in order to detect some of the powerful links between rational modernist impulses and the tendency to value youth, and then begin to explore ways in which the extent and nature of ageism vary between societies. In chapter four Peter Herriot looks at the issue of ageism from a different angle, adopting a very critical approach to managerial discourse. He argues that the whole thrust of 'new is good, old is bad' revolves around the assumed importance and value of change, which is what much management thinking has always been concerned about. In chapter five, Ann McGoldrick and James Arrowsmith go further by examining the roles of objective and organizational level conditions and processes, as well as subjective stereotyping in determining age discrimination. The empirical study that they report shows how important both managerial stereotyping and organizational characteristics are as influences on the significance of age in employment. In chapter six, Philip Bowers discusses whether retirement is sustainable by pointing to the public finance implications of both pensions and health care costs and the burden of increased dependency on future generations. He focuses in his analysis on the potential effects on equities of positive and negative net cash flows into pension schemes. In doing so he reviews some of the recent work in the USA on this issue and provides a forecasting model to assess the likelihood of the cash flows into pension schemes becoming negative in the UK. His conclusions are quite optimistic as far as the UK is concerned. In chapter seven, Glover takes some of the arguments of chapter three further in exploring the international character of relationships between age, work and employment in different societies. The main conclusion that can be drawn from his lengthy discussion is that discrimination based wholly or partly on age is more likely to take a constructive form in societies in which people think and act openly and continually about how they renew themselves on the basis of their experience, and which show concern for people as individuals, and that these two practices are not always found together.

In Part Three the chapter authors offer and discuss evidence of ageism in work and employment. In chapter eight, Adelina Broadbridge examines the issue of ageism in retailing, first by considering some of the difficulties in defining older workers and when age discrimination occurs, and then by outlining some attitudes related to older workers and the effects that these can have on career development. She then uses evidence from a survey of retail companies to investigate the career development of retail managers in some detail, in ways which say great deal about how future research should develop. In chapter nine Karen Rodham takes a different approach by focusing on ageism regarding younger people in an institution of historically mixed ages. She starts by suggesting that some of the literature on ageism is itself ageist and then, by drawing from anecdotal evidence collected from colleagues and acquaintances, she describes and explores problems experienced by young academics as a result of ageism. Chapter ten consists of an interview with David Jenkins, a very successful and thoughtful management consultant in the eighth decade of his life, with wide-ranging experience of postwar British management. Jenkins' hard-nosed attitudes are very illuminating about the sheer thoughtless of much age discrimination. As far as legislation is concerned Jenny Hamilton in chapter eleven outlines the approach taken in the South Australian anti-discrimination legislation. After a review of relevant literature on ageism she describes the background to the legislation, explores the scope of anti-age discrimination provisions and its enforcement mechanisms, and then explains the approach of the courts to the legislation. By pulling few punches and by being open-minded, she tells us a lot about what legislation can and cannot do. In chapter twelve Darren Smith addresses some of the stereotypes which exist concerning older versus younger non-managerial employees in New Zealand businesses and argues, using data obtained from personnel managers, that such stereotypes are affected by the age and sex of respondents. His conclusions have clear practical implications for the management of age and employment. We then revisit the European Union where David Parsons and Lesley Mayne in chapter thirteen consider the issue of ageism in the labour markets and social policies of the EU member states. They start by stressing the importance of practical implications of ageism in Europe and then by drawing on evidence from a research project based upon an annual survey of organizational policies and practices in human resource management of organizations across the EU, they make comparisons between a number of countries. In chapter fourteen Graham Elkin provides an analysis of the relationship between the growing economy of New Zealand and its workforce. He explains the growing age dependency of the population together with the need to create new jobs and then considers and suggests approaches for changing attitudes to older people and their possible contribution to solving the problem of labour shortages.

In Part Four some of the remedies and potential approaches for dealing with ageism are suggested. The prospects for older people as well as the issue of ageism in political, social and economic contexts are also discussed. In chapter fifteen

Philip Taylor considers the issue of ageism in public policy by, first, reviewing developments in public policies towards older workers and then discusses the feasibility of the legislative versus the educative approach. He suggests ways in which public policies on age discrimination and older workers might develop and identifies areas where problems might arise. In chapter sixteen, Allan Nicols and Wendy Evangelisti argue for fitness for work in a society in which employers would eventually seek to employ healthier and fitter employees regardless of their ages. After identifying the demographic problem and the benefits of fitness they point out to the cost of illness and then conclude on the benefits of exercise and employment or employability. Thus they show how fit and healthy people of any age are capable of making productive contributions to society. In chapter seventeen Colin Bottomley provides some practical remedies to the problems of ageism and unemployment by describing the merits of a secondment-training programme that helps both older and younger people to get employment in small and medium-sized enterprises. Bottomley's emphasis on the practical value of cooperation between different generations has major implications for the concerns of this book, as we explain in chapter nineteen. In chapter eighteen Christine Tillsley and Philip Taylor provide a critical and rigorous review of some of the literature on age discrimination and identify what can be learned from approaches to the ageing of workforces in other countries, and then they suggest new avenues for research. Both this chapter and Taylor's earlier one, chapter fifteen, are invaluable for their emphasis on the need for so-called joined up government and policy making in this area.

In the concluding Part and chapter of the book we attempt to summarize the main issues that have been covered in this book, reconsider the debate so far and then offer ideas for future thinking, research and policy.

Towards a new philosophy for employment?

High affluence, associated with advanced industrial economies, has seriously weakened the ideologies of earlier industrialization, those of capitalism, socialism and pluralist democracy. Efficiency and consumption became overarching social goals, to be pursued by managers acting principally on their own behalf or at least in according with crude economic laws or vague social forces (Enteman, 1998). The resultant political and social order tends to be morally confused and ethically uninformed. Economic and social fragmentation at the national and local levels, at least, is connected loosely with advanced economic development and internationalization of information, finance, entertainment, education and of much production and trade and associated with very complex and elaborate technical and social divisions of labour (Ackroyd, Glover, Currie and Bull, 2000).

While the above tend to lead to moral chaos and often to exacerbate economic inequality, a more affluent and free, if also more unequal, social order than that of thirty years ago is one in which much positive change is possible. Fragmented work organization can be used, especially in a free social climate, for heterarchical (cross-organizational, horizontal) communication, networking and innovation on an unprecedented scale, to help foster increasingly diverse, creative and socially tolerant forms of employment and divisions of labour.

In a society in which deference is less and less often automatically given, competence and (perhaps less often) good nature are the main requirements for those seeking to earn authority. Older people, as Plato noted, are readily loved when they display the latter, and despised when they do not. The same point almost certainly applies to the young and to the 'chronological misfits' in their middle years (referred to above). The fluid situation described so far this section is potentially very conducive to creativity and diversity in employment.

An expanded life course, from apprenticeship to practice to guidance, or in other words, from learning to doing to teaching and recreation and relaxation, might result, hopefully, from the developments and possibilities discussed above. There would be revivals and expansion of notions of apprenticeship and of vocation and of elders giving guidance to the less experienced. Expertise and gender-free paternalism could re-form as a 'new' basis for authority at work and in employment and in general. Paternalism (or maternalism, whatever) should be based authentically on expertise and moral integrity, and not take one of the bogus (traditional, welfare or sophisticated) forms described by Wray (1996), and certainly not on chronological age as such, but it is also inevitably but loosely associated with age. It embodies several important feminine attributes. Patriarchy and matriarchy would be unpopular as potential general guides to action. Technique and vocation would be valorized: unpredictable ingenuity and craft would gain increasing respect, to some extent at the expense of rationally guided search behaviour and formal planning. Stable but flexible employment would be increasingly valued, competition and cooperation would be equally valued, and the notion of vocation would be revivified in both debate and practice.

In spite of some of the above, however, a static economic, political and social order - as opposed to a fairly stable one - is not what people strive for. Change and development might and should develop more of a circular, rather than a linear, quality, and benign playful experimentation should be encouraged, to make work and employment more efficient, pleasant and interesting. Employers need to be more, not less, discriminatory regarding age and employment, and to discriminate well, rather than badly. Discrimination occurs at every stage of employment and affects people of all ages. Some age discrimination, based on financial necessity and various specific features of employment, is justifiable. Much, however, is the result of confusion, ignorance, prejudice and selfishness. Increasingly diverse forms of work and employment and increasing affluence make age discrimination less and less necessary and desirable, however. Several policy implications - for education and training as well as for employment - which follow these arguments, are outlined.

- *Education* should have a both-and, rather than an either/or quality, so that it is explicitly both general and specialist, humane and useful, theoretical and practical, focused and diverse, traditional and experimental and the same in these ways for people from all backgrounds and of all perceived levels of academic ability. It should be lifelong and it should glorify and celebrate diversity. It should assume that most human beings inherit very similar levels of imaginative intellectual potential.

- *Training and Development* should never exclude individuals on to grounds of age (or any other normally irrelevant criterion), and they should be integrated with education and informed by the same assumptions and principles.

- *Sector-specific, tailor-made human resource management*: HRM should be about development more than about control and exclusion (although the latter do have their places in management and employment). Developmental HRM which is not sector-specific and tailor-made is both unworkable and disrespectful (Lyon, Hallier and Glover, 1998).

- *Health, welfare and mature citizenship*: Flexible and fair policies regarding age and employment need, to be practicable and sustainable, to be part of an integrated set of policies covering health, social security and economic, political and social, duties, entitlements, responsibilities and rights.

- *Research*: more studies of age-related aspects of employment of people of all ages are needed. The Commodification versus Greening hypothesis could be a broad framework for investigation. Researchers should be more aware of the very large and long-established US literature (for example, Binstock and Shanas, 1976). Sources which are helpful in thinking in broad terms about the issues include Hardy (1997), Holmes and Holmes (1995), Pilcher (1995), Vincent (1995), Glover and Branine (1997) and the chapters in Part Four of this book. Researchers should compare the varied uses, in employment, of different kinds of age: chronological; biological (physiological); psychological (intellectual capacity and capability, and emotional maturity); actual social (psychological age plus social experience, maturity and skills); attributed social (which is very often different from actual social age); and employment age (the combination of attributes relevant in employment such as particular skills, knowledge, experience, the helicopter quality, strategic vision and prescience).

References

Ackroyd, S.J., Glover, I.A., Currie, W.L., and Bull, S. (2000), 'The Triumph of Hierarchies over Markets: Information Systems Specialists in the Current Context', in I. Glover and M. Hughes (eds), *Professions at Bay*, Ashgate, Aldershot.

Arber, S. (1996), 'The age of ageing', *The Times Higher Education Suplement*, 23 August, 1996, p. 20.

Arrowsmith, J. and McGoldrick, A. (1997), 'A flexible future for older workers?', *Personnel Review*, Vol. 26, No. 4, pp. 258-73.
Biggs, S. (1993), *Understanding Ageing: Images, Attitudes and Professional Practice*, Open University Press, Buckingham.
Binstock, R.H. and Shanas, E. (1976) (eds), *Handbook of Aging and the Social Sciences,* Van Nostrand, New York.
Branine M. and Glover, I. (1997), 'Ageism in Work and Employment: thinking about connections', *Personnel Review*, Vol. 26, No. 4, pp. 233-44.
Bytheway, B., Keil, T., Allatt, P., and Bryman, A. (1989) (eds), *Becoming and Being Old: Sociological Approaches To Later Life*, Sage, London.
Bytheway, B. (1995), *Ageism*, Open University Press, Buckingham.
Casey, B. Metcalf, H. and Millward, N. (1997), *Employers' Use of Flexible Labour*, Policy Studies Institute, London.
Chisholm, L., Buchner, P., Kruger, H-H. and Brown, P. (1990) (eds), *Childhood, Youth and Social Change: A Comparative Perspective*, The Falmer Press, London.
Clark, R. and Anker, R. (1990), 'Labour force participation rates of older persons: an international comparison', *International Labour Review*, No. 129, pp. 255-71.
Cohen, S.S. and Zysman, J. (1987), *Manufacturing Matters: The Myth of the Post-Industrial Economy*, Basic Books, New York.
Daniels, J.D. and Radebaugh, L.H. (1998), *International Business*, 8th edition, Addison-Wesley, New York.
Davies, D.R., Matthews, G. and Wong, C.S.K. (1991), 'Ageing and Work', in C.L. Cooper and I.T. Robertson (eds), *International Review of Industrial and Organization Psychology*, Vol. 6, pp. 149-211, Wiley, Chichester.
Dingley, J. (1996), 'Durkheim, professions and moral integration', pp. 155-70, in I. Glover and M. Hughes (eds), *The Professional - Managerial Class: Contemporary British Management in the Pursuer Mode*, Avebury, Aldershot.
Elias, N. (1991), *The Society of Individuals*, (Schröter, M. (ed.), translated by Jephcott, E.), Basil Blackwell, Cambridge MA.
Elliot, H. (1991), 'Holiday firm to recruit over-50s', *The Times*, 3 January 1991.
Enteman, W.F. (1993), *Managerialism: The Emergence of a New Ideology*, Wisconsin Press, Madison, WI.
Fogarty, M. (1975), *Forty to Sixty: How We Waste the Middle Aged*, Centre for Studies in Social Policy, London.
Fry, C.L. (1980) (ed.), *Aging in Culture and Society: Comparative Viewpoints and Strategies*, Praeger: New York.
Furnham, A. and Stacey, B. (1991), *Young People's Understanding of Society*, Routledge, New York.
Glover, I. (1992), 'Wheels within wheels: predicting and accounting for fasionable alternatives to engineering', in G. Lee and C. Smith (eds), *Engineers in Management: International Comparisons*, Routledge, London.

Glover I. and Branine, M. (1997), 'Ageism and the labour process: towards a research agenda', *Personnel Review,* Vol. 26, No. 4, pp. 274-92.

Glover. I. A., Tracey, P. and Currie, W. (1998), 'Engineering our future again: towards a long-term strategy for manufacturing and management in the United Kingdom', in R. Delbridge and J. Lowe (eds), *Manufacturing in Transition*, Routledge, London.

Guillemard, A.M., Taylor, P. and Walker, A. (1996), 'Managing an Ageing Workforce in Britain and France', *The Geneva Papers on Risk and Insurance*, No. 81, pp. 469-97.

Hardy, M. (ed.) (1997), *Studying Ageing and Social Change*, Sage, London.

Hayward, B., Taylor, S., Smith, N., and Davies, G. (1997), *Evaluation of the Campaign for Older Workers*, The Stationary Office, London.

Hockey, J. and James, A. (1993), *Growing Up and Growing Old: Ageing and Dependency in the Life Course*, Sage, London.

Holmes, E.R. and Holmes, L.D. (1995), *Other Cultures, Elder Years: An Introduction to Cultural Gerontology*, Sage, London.

Institute of Personnel Management (1991), *Statement on age and employment*, IPM, London.

Jackall, R. (1988), *Moral Mazes: Inside the World of Corporate Managers*, Oxford University Press, Oxford.

Jefferys, M. (ed.) (1989), *Growing Old in the Twentieth Century*, Routledge, London.

Kumar, K. (1995), *From Post-Industrial to Post-Modern Society*, Basil Blackwell, Cambridge, MA.

Laczko, F. and Phillipson, C. (1991), *Changing Work and Retirement: Social Policy and the Older Worker*, Open University Press, Milton Keynes.

Laslett, P. (1996), *A Fresh Map of Life*, Weidenfeld and Nicolson, London.

Lyon, P., Hallier, J. and Glover, I. (1998), 'Divestment or investment? The contradictions of HRM in relation to older employees', *Human Resource Management Journal*, Vol. 8, No. 1, pp. 56-66.

Lyon, P. and Pollard, D. (1997), 'Perceptions of the older employee: is anything really changing?', *Personnel Review*, Vol. 26, No. 4, pp. 245-57.

Noller, P. and Callan, V. (1991), *The Adolescent in the Family*, Routledge, London.

Parkinson, C. Northcote (1958), *Parkinson's Law or the Pursuit of Progress*, John Murray, London.

Pickard, J. (1999), 'Grey areas', *People Management*, 29 July, pp. 31-37.

Pilcher, J. (1995), *Age and Generation in Modern Britain*, OUP, Oxford.

Smith, M. (1990), 'IBM offers work after retirement', *The Financial Times*, 13 August 1990.

Summers, D. (1990), 'Register for recruiting retired people launched', *The Financial Times*, 25 November 1990.

Sorge, A. (1978), 'The management tradition: a continental view', in M. Fores and I. Glover (eds), *Manufacturing and Management*, HMSO Books, London.

Taylor, P.E. and Walker, A. (1994), 'Ageing Workforce: Employers' Attitudes Towards Older People', *Work, Employment and Society*, Vol. 8, No. 4, pp. 569-91.

Victor, C.R. (1994), *Old Age in Modern Society*, Chapman and Hall, London.

Vincent, J. A. (1995), *Inequality and Old Age*, UCL Press, London.

Walker, A. (1999), Breaking down the barriers on ageism, *Professional Manager*, Vol. 8, No. 3, May, p. 7.

Warr, P. and Pennington, J. (1993), 'Views about age discrimination and older workers' in P. Taylor, A. Walker, B. Casey, H. Metcalf, J. Lakey, P. Warr. and J. Pennington (eds), *Age and employment: policies, attitudes and practice*, Institute of Personnel Management, London.

Weber, T., Whitting, G., Sidaway, J. and Moore, J. (1997), 'Employment policies and practices towards older workers: France, Germany, Spain and Sweden', *Labour Market Trends*, pp. 143-48.

Part II
The problem and its causes

2 Ageism, early exit, and the rationality of age-based discrimination

Colin Duncan

Introduction

The recent elevation of the phenomenon of 'ageism' to the realm of public and political discourse derives chiefly from the trend in most industrialized economies towards 'early exit' of older workers from the labour market. This trend, along with recent demographic projections, has led to concerns over longer term social, welfare and budgetary consequences. Such concerns underlie current initiatives that seek to persuade employers to jettison ageist assumptions and employment practices. The message to employers has been that discrimination against older employees is not only socially unjust but also irrational and damaging in commercial terms, a view invariably promoted through reference to growing evidence that negative stereotypes typically held by employers regarding the productivity and other supply-side characteristics of older workers are, in general, quite erroneous.

This chapter first explores the concept of ageism, in view of its relatively recent arrival on the social agenda and continuing ambiguities surrounding its meaning. The discussion traces the evolution of the term and considers whether the concept of ageism, as developed by academic gerontologists, can be regarded as the same phenomenon now said to be influencing the labour market. The next section discusses some features of the early exit phenomenon, and the section which follows considers whether this trend can be attributed chiefly to age prejudices held by employers. Following from this analysis the final section draws some conclusions concerning the efficacy of current and proposed policy responses.

The concept of ageism

Concern over age-related discrimination has a relatively short pedigree. In both Britain and the United States the roots of concern are often located in challenges to 'disengagement theory' and similar perspectives which dominated the work of gerontologists in the 1950s and 1960s, and which emphasized physical, psychological and social decline as the normal features of growing old. The ageing process from such perspectives portrayed an inevitable, mutual disengagement between the older person and society and implied a 'blame the victim' mentality towards explaining the poor social and material conditions associated with old age. This thinking was challenged from a variety of disciplinary perspectives that sought to promote more positive images of the ageing process and to demonstrate that the conditions of older age groups owed more to factors such as poor social provision, low incomes and enforced retirement than to biological or psychological decline.

According to the extended *Oxford English Dictionary* the term 'ageism' made its first appearance in the *Washington Post* in 1969 and was attributed to an American psychiatrist, Dr Robert Butler, who 'believes many of his Chevy Chase neighbors suffer from "age-ism"'. Then in the *Gerontologist* Winter 1969, Butler is quoted: 'we shall soon have to consider ... a form of bigotry we now tend to overlook: age discrimination or age-ism, prejudice by one group toward other age groups'. The same source attributes the first UK reference to the *Observer* colour supplement, 30 September, 1973. The first mention of the term 'ageist' anywhere in the English speaking world was in the *Daily Telegraph* in 1970. The dictionary invites comparison with the terms 'racism', which first appeared in 1936; 'racist' (1932); 'sexism' (1968); and 'sexist' (1965).

In the United States, the concept increased in popularity with the growth of such social movements as the Grey Panthers, reflecting 'its geneology [sic] as part of the impetus for civil rights, now recognized as a distinctive feature of the late 1960s' (Biggs, 1993, p. 85), but in Britain the term did not really enter popular vocabulary until the 1990s in the context of concern over early exit. For example, in 1980 Bytheway (1980) felt it necessary to challenge the view of ageism as 'just a joke'; and even by 1990 an edited text published by Age Concern that dealt with age-related discrimination was sub-titled 'The Unrecognised Discrimination' (McEwen, 1990).

The more recent association of the term with early exit trends has been accompanied by some shift in the focus of research from ageism, as it affects the welfare of the elderly beyond normal retirement age, (the so-called 'old-old'), to ageism as implied by labour market discrimination against (chiefly) men in their fifties and sixties (the 'young-old'). This division is broadly paralleled in the conceptualization of a new stage in the life course, the Third Age, that intervenes between a Second Age - characterized as one of maturity, productive work and child rearing - and a Fourth Age of final dependence, decrepitude and decline.

Butler was among the first to attempt to define ageism systematically, and his definition is still often quoted. It was defined (Butler, 1987, p. 22) as: 'a process of systematic stereotyping and discrimination against people because they are old, just as racism and sexism accomplish this for skin colour and gender'. Prior to the current vogue for distinguishing different categories of old age, the concept of ageism that evolved under this definition seemed chiefly informed by the conditions and experience of the 'old-old' beyond normal retirement age. Descriptions of ageism in this tradition usually include some or all of the following as its features:

1. Ageism represents and creates prejudices about the nature and experience of old age. Such prejudices and negative stereotypes are held by all age groups, including the elderly themselves. A crucial point in most accounts however, is that prejudice is *socially* rather than *biologically* determined and that it is the social construction of old age that is more damaging to the fortunes of the elderly than is the biological ageing process.

2. Ageism is not a new phenomenon and its history long predates capitalism as a form social organization. According to Scrutton (1990), negative views of old age that are embraced in dominant social ideas, chiefly originate from the high value that has always been placed upon physical strength. Prejudice thus reflects the loss of strength that is associated with old age. On the other hand, more positive images of old age, that have rested upon the value attached to experience, knowledge and wisdom, have declined along with the decline of custom, the acceleration of change and the loss of oral traditions: 'Civilisations which pass on their learning and experience verbally have to rely on older citizens to provide the vital link between generations. The development of writing and the widespread circulation of books undermined the importance of memory, thereby destroying one of the most useful social functions provided by older people' (ibid., p. 15).

3. Negative images of old age are instilled in almost all individuals by a process of socialization through language, religion, literature, the media and the theories and practices of the medical establishment and social services professionals. The result is fear and anxiety over the ageing process and our future ageing selves, which reinforces negative attitudes, encourages attitudinal distancing of the elderly from ourselves, and fosters a tendency to 'blame the victim'.

4. Such attitudes are also confirmed and reinforced by the phenomenon of 'structural ageism', which operates to determine the functions and rules of everyday life. For example, compulsory retirement enforces non-productivity, depresses social status, and promotes the idea of old age as a burden, leading also to officially sanctioned neglect of the elderly in medical, educational and social service provision.

5. Ageism thus leads to a perception of old age as some kind of disease or affliction. The elderly are stripped of their 'humanness' or 'personhood' and are also treated as a homogeneous mass, even though heterogeneity is argued to increase with age (Laslett, 1989). This reinforces the them/us mentality and fosters the belief that the ageing process makes independent action, participation and self-determination by the elderly in policy matters impossible.

6. The net effect is a manifestation of ageism in at least two forms, each denying an independent role for the elderly, but distinguished by charitable intent: as a form of patronising concern, where old age is associated with a denial of competence and freedom, thereby undermining independence and morale; and as a form of neglect and vilification, depriving older people of a secure status and role and denying them a fair share of resources.

In Britain, the work of Bytheway represents one of the few attempts to further develop and clarify the concept (Bytheway, 1995; Bytheway and Johnson, 1990). Here, Butler's definition is forcefully challenged on two main counts. First, the equivalence of ageism to sexism and racism is disputed on the ground that older people do not form an exclusive group, but one in which every individual will eventually become a member:

> The unique character of ageism in later life can best be conveyed by evoking the ideas of worlds in which we each over the course of a full lifetime slowly and consistently change from white to black, or from male to female; and conversely of worlds in which blacks and women have statistical life expectations of no more than 15 years. It is in this way that social responses to the ageing process and old people differ radically from those to gender and women and race and ethnic groups (Bytheway and Johnson, 1990, p. 33).

The authors seem keen to distance ageism from other 'isms', in part to establish its credentials as a form of oppression in its own right, in view of attempts by some to treat the concept as a sub-component of more salient oppressions, and by others to deny it any substance whatsoever: 'if ageism is perceived to be simply an idea formulated in the mode of sexism and racism, then it can be dismissed as being no more than joining a bandwagon' (ibid., p. 30). However, Itzin (1995) among others, while not disputing the distinctiveness of ageism, has argued that it has much in common with other oppressions such as sexism, which have developed through similar processes, and that it is helpful to recognize this. Moreover, she contends that many of Bytheway's examples of ageism relate to women and illustrate not just ageism but the combined impact of ageism and sexism.

Second, Bytheway takes issue with the use of the term 'old' in Butler's definition. 'Old age', it is argued, is in the nature of a social construct and does not exist as a specific condition arising from biological or chronological ageing. Rather, the ageing process should be viewed as a continuum and, as such, there is no logical border beyond which a condition occurs that can legitimately be labelled 'old age'. Thus such absolute terms (old age, elders, the elderly, the aged) are themselves ageist, in distancing the 'old' from the 'not old' and further encouraging 'them and us' thinking. He makes clear that he is not disputing that a process of physiological or biological decline occurs with age, but that this should be distinguished from the social phenomenon that forms the basis of the disadvantage and oppression of older people:

> You cannot deny that many [older people] are frail and that they have declined both physically and mentally ... Where ageism comes in is, in our pathetic attempts to be certain about the changes that come with age, in the assumption that they are all universal, in our efforts to distance ourselves from those who appear different, in our negative interpretations and in the consequential regulation of the social order ... If we are to be effective in challenging ageism, we have to recognize the significance of *difference* (Bytheway, 1995, p. 125).

However, the legitimate observation of absence of precision or substance to terms such as 'old age' leads Bytheway to a somewhat confusing train of thought in attempting to arrive at a definition considered more suitable than Butler's. He toys with the idea of defining ageism as being 'any unwarranted response to age' but rejects this on the basis that 'paradoxically' this conceptualization 'implies that we are all victims of ageism and that there is no oppression of one group by another' (Bytheway and Johnson, 1990, p. 32). Hence the authors' conception of ageism is clearly distinct from age discrimination *per se*. However, the basis for rejecting the latter as a definition is curious in that the criterion now adopted for constituting ageism - oppression of one group by another - seems to imply rather closer similarities between ageism and the other 'isms' than the authors were initially prepared to admit, even accepting that the oppressors may one day become the oppressed.

The authors continue: 'Although it complicates what should be simple, it seems appropriate to conclude that ageism is experienced both through the negative valuation of the ageing process throughout the life course, and through the consequential stigmatizing and institutional identification of 'special' groups on the basis of chronological age' (ibid., p. 33). In similar vein, the final definition arrived at considers ageism as:

> a set of beliefs originating in the biological variation between people and relating to the ageing process ... [that] ...'legitimates' the use of chronological age to mark out classes of people who are systematically denied resources and opportunities that others enjoy, and who suffer the consequences of such denigration - ranging from well-meaning patronage to unambiguous vilification (Bytheway and Johnson, 1990, p. 37; Bytheway, 1995, p. 14).

However, the composition of these 'special' groups or 'classes of people' remains unclear, as do the criteria by which they might be judged 'special'. It is unclear, for instance, whether this definition is meant to cover *all* groups or age categories subject to age-based discrimination, or just those accorded 'special' status on some unspecified ground. As such, the definition is most ambiguous, not least as to whether ageism should be confined in its meaning to age discrimination against older people, however the latter are defined. Bytheway seems to face both directions on this issue. On the one hand, he asserts (Bytheway, 1995) that 'we are all ageing, are all of an age and are all vulnerable to ageism' (p. 120), and that 'the ageism experienced by young people is the same phenomenon as that experienced by older people ...' (p. 13). On the other hand, components of his definition that refer to 'well-meaning patronage' and 'unambiguous vilification' seem to confine the definition to treatment meted out to those at least of retirement age and beyond.

Ageism in employment

Such definitional ambiguities seem to reflect some difficulty in extending the original concept of ageism to the field of employment, while maintaining its integrity. It is not clear that the concept of ageism, as described in its six features above, is the same phenomenon that is alluded to in analyses of early exit and other aspects of age-based discrimination in employment.

On the one hand it might be argued that there are many parallel themes in the literature that deals with the employment experience of older workers and that concerned with the treatment and experience of those of more advanced years. Negative stereotyping, undervaluation of ability and potential, denial of opportunities and reluctance to acknowledge the heterogeneity of older age categories are examples shared in common. In the case of older workers, however, it is rarely suggested that discrimination extends to a denial of 'personhood' or the assumption of a sub-human species. Nevertheless, this difference may be viewed simply as one of degree. For Bytheway, there would seem to be little difference, apart from one of misplaced emphasis on ageism in employment: 'Some ... think of ageism primarily as age discrimination in employment practices and that it affects people in their forties, fifties and sixties - they would be surprised if it were to be suggested that exactly the same phenomenon affected the lives of people in their nineties' (Bytheway, 1995, p. 105).

On the other hand it might be argued that while age discrimination in employment, including that implied by early exit trends, more evidently affects older workers, it is by no means a phenomenon experienced only by those in their fifties and sixties. Upper age bars in recruitment advertisements are often set around the 40 age mark, and training and promotion opportunities in many occupations tend also to diminish around this age (Taylor and Walker, 1993; Trinder et al., 1992). For some occupations, recruitment and career prospects are adversely affected at much lower ages. Moreover, age-related discrimination amongst women exhibits complex patterns that reflect the 'double jeopardy' of age and gender. In their local authority case studies, Itzin and Phillipson (1993) observed that at whatever age they were, women's age tended to be held against them, and that from line management perspectives 'women are never the right age' (p. 45). The adverse labour market experience of school-leavers and other young workers below 'prime age' (normally considered by employers to lie within the 25-35 age band) in terms of pay, employment and other working conditions (Blanchflower and Freeman, 1996) can also be judged as deriving in some part from age discrimination.

The presence of apparent age discrimination over such broad age ranges - indeed possibly affecting every age, even if more evident among older employees - begins to raise doubts as to whether ageism in employment can be considered the same beast as that once assumed to be largely confined to those over state retirement age.

It is certainly difficult to conceive of the victims as in any sense a minority group, when the age range of 'older workers' who experience age discrimination can extend over some three decades from just beyond 'prime labour age' to retirement. Moreover, there are signs that in employment policies, the association of the term 'ageism' with old age is beginning to loosen, and that ageism is sometimes being equated with age discrimination in a general sense. To date this is most apparent in the wording of voluntary codes directed at employers, and in employers' own equal opportunities codes. For example a code issued by the Institute of Personnel Management in 1991 made a number of recommendations with a view to reducing arbitrary age discrimination in general, rather than with respect just to older employees (IPM, 1991). Similarly, Itzin and Phillipson (1993), in their review of age-related employment practices in local authorities, cited some examples where ageism was being interpreted in the broader sense. For instance, Cleveland County Council's code of practice on ageism defined the term as 'prejudice, misconception and stereotyping which hinders proper consideration of an individual's talents, skills, abilities, potential and experience'. The code explained that age discrimination 'can affect people of all ages', but ...' consistently disadvantages older workers, young people and women returners' (p. 15).

The application of the term in the employment sphere differs from its traditional application in another respect, in that a distinction is often drawn between 'arbitrary' or 'unwarranted' or 'irrational' discrimination and that based upon commercial criteria. In other words, discrimination on the grounds of age becomes ageist only if such discrimination is guided by irrational prejudice or mistaken beliefs, rather than commercial exigencies, a distinction with no obvious counterpart in applications of the term outside employment. In recent government-backed campaigns against ageism in employment the message to employers seems to be that age discrimination against older workers chiefly falls into the former category and therefore is both irrational and commercially damaging. This viewpoint is assessed below with reference to the early exit phenomenon.

Early exit

In Britain and elsewhere the trend towards early exit from the labour market is often considered as *prima facie* evidence for increasing ageism in employment. The phenomenon of early exit has been described as 'one of the most dramatic economic transformations of labour markets in modern industrial economies' (Rein and Jacobs, 1993), and has occurred to varying degrees in all Western economies, irrespective of their institutional regimes (Kohli et al., 1991). The term refers to the trend towards withdrawal of older workers from employment during the years preceding state pensionable age, as illustrated for Britain in Table 2.1.

The figures show that the trend is most apparent in the case of older men, and, for those below 65, is especially noticeable from the 1970s onwards. The decline in activity of those above 65, on the other hand, is part of a longer trend that is usually considered as a different process from the early exit phenomenon. In Britain the

1980s nearly three-quarters of men aged 65 plus were still in employment (Laczko and Phillipson, 1991), and the subsequent progressive decline in this proportion to just 7.5 percent by 1994 chiefly represents the institutionalization of the life-course and emergence of the concept of retirement.

Table 2.1 : Economic activity rates (percentages) of older men and women in Britain 1951-1994

Age:	1951	1961	1971	1975	1981	1985	1990	1994
Men								
55-59	95.0	97.1	95.3	93.0	89.4	82.6	81.5	76.1
60-64	87.7	91.0	86.6	82.3	69.3	55.4	55.4	51.2
65+	31.1	25.0	23.5	19.2	10.3	8.5	8.7	7.5
Women								
55-59	29.1	39.2	50.9	52.4	53.4	52.2	55.0	55.7
60-64	14.1	19.7	28.8	28.6	23.3	18.9	22.7	25.6
65+	4.1	4.6	6.3	4.9	3.7	3.0	3.4	3.2

Source: Taylor, P. and Walker, A. (1995), 'Utilising older workers', *Employment Gazette*, April.

By contrast, the decline in participation of those below state pensionable age is a comparatively recent phenomenon that has been judged to be distinct from retirement in several respects. For both governments and those affected it has been mostly unplanned and unpredicted. Moreover only a privileged minority - those excluded from the labour market through early retirement or voluntary redundancy schemes on generous terms by their employer - tend to think of themselves unambiguously as retired. Other exit routes have included redundancy, dismissal, or retirement on grounds of ill-health, routes which are mostly involuntary but, in combination with recent labour market conditions in Britain and elsewhere, have effectively excluded older workers from further participation in the labour market. Rather than retired, the ambiguous status of such groups has been characterized as 'a generation in limbo' (Bosanquet, 1987).

For Britain, the trend is less apparent in the case of women, and for women in the 55-59 age band, activity seems to have increased slightly from 1971. However, a similar decline in the activity rates of older women is masked by a trend towards higher activity rates of women in general. The easiest way to disentangle these opposite and overlapping trends is to examine the employment participation of different birth cohorts of women over time. Such an exercise reveals a significant, if less marked, trend towards early exit among older women also (Trinder et al., 1992; Ginn and Arber, 1996).

Two further features of the early exit trend should be noted. First, the declining labour force participation rates of older workers cannot simply be viewed as a statistical consequence of demographic trends that are leading to a progressively ageing labour pool, with employers simply maintaining their traditional age balance. Not only has the proportion of older men who are economically active declined, but the *numbers* of men in employment aged over 55 have also fallen significantly, from 3.2 million in 1971 to 2.1 million in 1991. The corresponding reduction for women over 55 was from 1.7 million to 1.3 million, most of the fall being in groups over 60 (Trinder et al., 1992). Second, such trends cannot be wholly or mainly explained by changes in industrial structure, for example by a decline in the share of employment of industries that have traditionally employed relatively high proportions of older workers. Nor has early exit been confined to rapidly declining or 'troubled' industries but is taking place in almost every industry, including those that are growing in employment terms (Jacobs et al., 1991).

The causes of early exit

The debate as to the causes of early exit has focused on the relative role of 'pull' and 'push' factors. The former approach assumes that early exit is chiefly the result of social policies that have created attractive exit routes, while the latter assumes that early exit is driven by the evolution of the labour market and assigns a dominant role to the influence of high levels of unemployment. Kohli et al. (1991), in analyzing exit trends in seven countries, favour the 'push' explanation, assigning the major role to employer policies and economic conditions as the main driving forces. For example, the trend has been significant even in countries with restrictive public welfare regimes such as the United States, a country also with explicit legislation forbidding age discrimination. From this perspective, social policy may facilitate or inhibit exit trends, but does not represent the main driving force, with the state not so much instigating the process as reacting, in most cases, to ease the course of exit. Moreover, the authors argue that many institutional causes of early exit, including state or company early retirement schemes, are themselves motivated by 'push' factors. Often this has meant that state welfare arrangements designed for other purposes have been incorporated into pathways of early exit, and are now used not to deal with specific risks (such as unemployment or disability), but with the burden of a whole age group.

The relationship between the chief 'actors' involved in early exit processes (employers, the state, employees and their representative organizations), has been characterized as one of 'cooperative antagonism' (Kohli and Rein, 1991), where each actor seeks to contribute to the process of exit, but shift the burden of costs to another party. From the standpoint of governments, the motivation to collude in early exit programmes lay in macroeconomic considerations. Problems encountered by Keynesian economic regulation meant that policies of employment stimulation fell into disrepute, so that early exit (along with deferred entry) became one of the few remaining alternatives for aggregate labour market management. In Britain this was reinforced by a broad consensus that youth unemployment constituted the priority social issue which, in slack labour market conditions, justified job sacrifice on the part of older workers. Government measures that facilitated exit included the Redundancy Payments Act 1965 and the Job Release Scheme that operated between 1977 and 1988, as well as certain modifications to unemployment and other benefits. Similarly, British trade unions have supported the early exit path as a more acceptable option than redundancy or dismissal, especially if voluntary and financed by concessions from industry or the state.

For Britain and elsewhere the role of employers as the key actors in fostering early exit is usually explained by reference to the need to reduce headcount in a context of overmanning, changes in industrial structure and periodic recession. Processes of organizational restructuring, 'delayering' and other 'leaner and meaner' strategies required by competitive pressures and rapid technical change also contributed to the displacement of older workers. However, early exit was not just confined to reducing manpower. In both contracting and expanding industries employers also used early retirement selectively to alter skill mixes, reduce labour costs and overhaul human resource strategies (Guillemard and Van Gunsteren, 1991).

The process of antagonistic cooperation described above in favour of early exit evaporated in the late 1980s with the growing belief that society could not afford the mounting costs of early exit in the longer-term, and amidst warnings about a demographic time-bomb and impending intergenerational conflict (Johnson et al., 1989). In Britain, the shift in perspective was remarkably abrupt, as was noticed by the House of Commons Employment Committee in 1989 in an inquiry on the employment patterns of older workers:

> When we began to plan our inquiry, interest still centred on the development of schemes to ease older workers into early retirement. By the time we had finished taking our evidence there had been a dramatic shift of emphasis and there was growing discussion of ways in which older people could be persuaded to stay at work in order to offset the impending shortage of young workers. The pendulum has rarely swung so swiftly (House of Commons, 1989, para. 1).

This 'dramatic shift in emphasis' was broad-based, apparent in Government policy statements, policy positions adopted by the age lobby, and also evident among some employers, employees and their trade unions. One feature of the recession beginning in the late 1980s was its relative effect upon previously secure and relatively senior white-collar occupations in commerce and finance. Such groups added a powerful middle-class note of dissent that helped shift the perception of early exit from that of a necessary and socially acceptable means of coping with mass unemployment and structural change to a phenomenon deriving from age prejudice.

This new perspective has been largely endorsed in subsequent campaigns supported by the Government, the Carnegie Third Age inquiries, voluntary organizations and some employers, that are aimed at halting or reversing early exit trends. These seem to be built chiefly on the premise that early exit and other forms of age discrimination owe more to age prejudice on the part of employers than commercial criteria, and further, that such prejudice is not only irrational but commercially damaging. However, the commercial rationality of age discrimination is a topic that has been rather poorly explored, though from the point of view of framing policy options this issue would seem to be rather important. For example, if 'ageism' in employment can be shown to embrace rational commercial criteria, then present campaigns to persuade employers to reform their practices voluntarily are likely to achieve little.

The rationality of age-based discrimination

There are at least four ways in which the rationality of employer policies towards older workers might be classified, as illustrated in Figure 2.1 in matrix form: policies which discriminate against older workers and in so doing are commercially damaging (Box A); those which treat older employees unfavourably but which are rational in a commercial sense (Box B); policies which are favourably disposed towards older workers and which are again commercially rational (Box C); and policies that favour older workers but which might be judged irrational from a business perspective (Box D). If ageism is taken to mean age-related policies or practices that have no commercial basis, then these would be confined to boxes A and D. It is also possible that employers may pursue age-based policies that have a neutral or indeterminate effect on business performance, as represented by points E and F in the figure. Perusal of the literature suggests that employer policies are by no means confined, as is often supposed, to Box A.

Box A represents the current orthodoxy. Discrimination against older workers, not only with regard to exit policies but also with respect to recruitment and training restrictions, is deemed both irrational and commercial damaging. This view is currently so prevalent as to seem almost unchallengeable. It is the message that was promulgated by the Advisory Forum on Older Workers set up by the Conservative Government in 1992 to encourage employers to abandon age discriminatory practices, a body that include representatives of employers, trade unions, the Equal Opportunities Commission, Age Concern and the Institute of Personnel and Development. This initiative led to the Government publication, *Getting On*, that was sent to 165,000 employers in March 1994, advising them of the benefits of employing older workers and how to avoid discriminating against them. This was followed by a further Government booklet, *Too Old - Who Says So?*, in February 1995, which offered advice to older people about finding work, training and changing jobs, and which sought to boost their confidence. That ageism is bad for British business is also the central message of the Employers Forum on Age, launched in May 1996 to combat age discrimination. The Forum at its launch was composed of eighteen organizations, including British Airways, British Telecommunications, Marks and Spencer, the Post Office, J Sainsbury and W H Smith, with Howard Davies, the Deputy Governor of the Bank of England, as its chairman. The Carnegie Inquiries and continuing programmes have also promoted this message strongly.

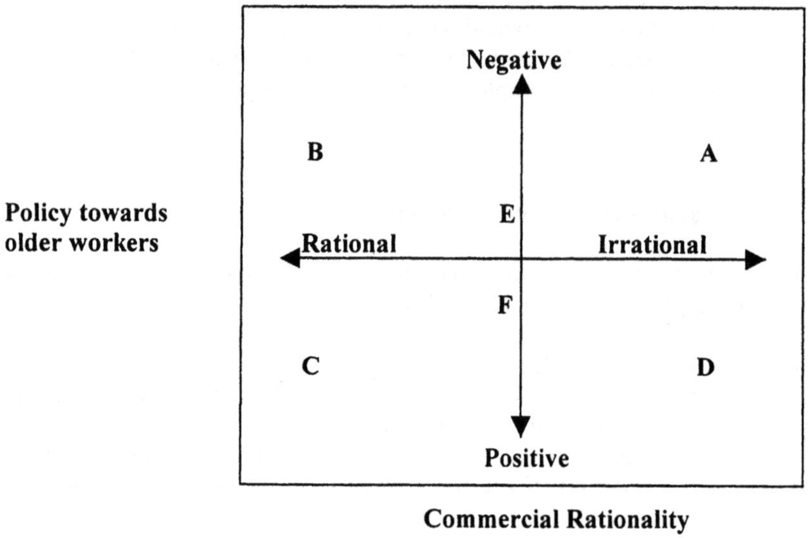

Figure 2.1: Typology of age-based employer policies towards older workers

The basis of this perspective lies in evidence of negative stereotypes underlying employer attitudes and practices towards older workers, stereotypes that endorse a deficit model of ageing and are held to have little basis in fact. In general older workers are thought by employers to be less productive, to have less relevant skills, to be resistant to change and new technology, to be less trainable, and to leave employment sooner so that training them to provide updated skills has a low rate of return (Tillsley, 1990; Taylor and Walker, 1993, 1995; Trinder et al., 1992). Accordingly they are discriminated against with respect to recruitment - as evidenced by the widespread use of upper age bars in job advertisements and other more covert forms of age filtering in recruitment processes - and in training and promotion opportunities, as well as exit policies. Upper age bars on recruitment, together with policies of early exit, mean that older workers who become unemployed remain so for longer periods, and often indefinitely. Such stereotypes have been challenged by some twenty-five years of industrial gerontological research, which seems to show that age is a rather poor proxy for performance, as illustrated in Figure 2.2 below. Accordingly, it is argued that ageism leads to sub-optimum use of human resources, including a poor return on investment in human capital, a sub-optimum balance between youth and maturity in labour composition and a narrowed pool of talent to draw upon in recruitment. Indeed, Trinder et al., (1992) found evidence of upper age bars being applied even in jobs where the generally perceived qualities of older workers (stability, reliability, low turnover, commitment, responsibility) should have been an advantage.

Other 'bad for business' arguments have included the view that early exit has resulted in important skill shortages and a loss of the 'collective memory' of organizations, with damaging consequences for business performance; and the view that along with the ageing of the population, older workers are increasingly necessary in that they better understand the needs of the market and may also be more suited at the customer interface. A further argument has been the contention that early exit has not always achieved even short-term cost-savings for companies, as compensation packages have sometimes exceeded salaries saved. The observation that employers rarely conduct a cost-benefit analysis of age policies has also led to the presumption of irrationality and prejudice in age-related employment practices. Worsley (1996) observed that few employers were even aware of the current age composition of their organizations.

Box B of Figure 2.1 above, concerns the implication that employers in most industrialized economies have been acting against their objective self-interests in displacing older workers seems intuitively unsound, and there are several grounds for arguing that early exit and other age-related policies may represent quite rational employer responses to macro-economic and competitive conditions. For example, Kohli and Rein (1991) argue that to focus only upon

1. Laboratory tests demonstrate that some abilities such as muscular strength, reaction times and some aspects of memory decline with age. But assessments of older workers on the job tend to show that, except where these particular abilities are especially important, experience may compensate.

2. Studies in the USA and Sweden have shown that in many situations older workers are as productive as younger ones provided they are not under stress; in particular they work better if they are part time.

3. In training, older people may be disadvantaged if training methods used for younger people are applied without modification. In particular, rote learning, or a fast pace of presentation may cause difficulties. Older persons can be equally successful provided training is geared towards their needs.

4. A person's performance is governed as much by their experience and skill as by their age. Experience compensates for many underlying changes, thus a range of experiences earlier is highly important to adaptability in the third age.

5. The majority of laboratory studies show that performance deteriorates with age in areas involving heavy demands on sensory and perceptual mechanisms; but in some areas older people seem to perform at about the same level as younger people in tasks requiring sustained attention and extended practice appears to reduce age differences.

6. Studies of technical 'knowledge based' jobs showed an inverted U relation with age, productivity peaking in the early 30s and declining after 55. Nevertheless, productivity of the oldest groups can still remain higher than the youngest groups.

7. Managerial performance as assessed by appraisal tests also shows some decline with age although one study showed that older and younger managers employed different decision making strategies and this was what produced differences in performance appraisal rating.

8. As age increases so does variability between individuals; averages become less representative: differences within age groups may be greater than those between groups. Therefore, chronological age should not be the sole criterion by which a person is assessed for employment purposes.

Figure 2.2: The effect of age on performance

Source: Grimley Evans, J. et al., (1992), *Health: Abilities and Well-Being in the Third Age,* Research Paper 9, Carnegie UK Trust, Dunfermline.

the work performance of older workers is to take too narrow a view of the employment contract. What must also be considered is that older workers usually earn more than comparable younger workers because of formal and informal seniority arrangements. They also enjoy a series of other seniority-based prerogatives making them less easy to move around or fire as the interests of the firm change, thereby representing higher transaction costs. Such observations support an efficiency wage model of the labour market with a life-time earnings contract consisting of sub-productivity earnings at the beginning and above-productivity earnings towards the end of work-life. Accordingly, it may be more profitable when job reductions are required for firms to terminate their older workers early. The fact that the cost of occupational pensions tends to increase as the formal retirement date approaches adds weight to such considerations, as does the general trend towards an ageing population and workforce which puts upward pressure on wage costs. In this context the absence of institutional practices which would make it possible to reduce the wages of older workers increases the likelihood of job shedding.

Pressures to substitute younger for older workers on cost grounds were enhanced, according to Standing (1986), along with the quest for greater flexibility in labour markets, itself a response to competitive pressures. One effect of growing flexibility has been an increase in the elasticity of substitution between different age groups:

> the movement away from lifetime, secure employment, the growth of narrow static jobs for which workers are interchangeable, and the growth of casual indirect forms of employment have all encouraged the substitution of other groups for older workers, or rather have increased the substitutability of different groups and the impact of relative costs and the external labour market (p. 336).

In this context, five specific costs are identified that militate against the employment of older workers in conditions of labour surplus and growing flexibility: *productivity costs,* arising from the tendency, however weak, for older workers to be less productive; *overhead costs,* arising from seniority-based pay systems; *protection costs,* arising from work arrangements designed to shield older workers from hazardous or arduous work or to lighten the burden on them; *adaptability costs,* where in some respects at least older workers are less flexible in their ability to adapt to change; and *motivational costs* which arise if a high ratio of older workers limits promotion opportunities and thereby adversely affects morale and general productivity. This last cost tends to increase in times of labour surplus and employment stagnation when older employees in particular are reluctant or unable to develop their careers through job-changing, so that over time the age profile of individual organizations can become dangerously skewed.

It has also been argued that older workers tend to be less well educated or educated in technologies that have long become obsolete, and thus are of less value to firms in times of rapid technological change. The cost of requalifying older workers may be higher than younger workers, not necessarily because they are less trainable but because younger recruits may partially possess such skills from outwith the firm. With respect to computer skills, for example, Johnson and Zimmermann (1993, p. 13) observe that: 'the socialization and acculturation processes experienced by children today, both at home and at school, mean that they grow up using and identifying with computer technology and so develop a competence which is unlikely to be achieved by more than a handful of 50-60 year olds'.

Other arguments used to confer some legitimacy upon apparent age bias, include the observation that older workers tend to be less mobile than younger groups; that in growing youth markets younger employees are required at the business/public interface; and that the recruitment of displaced older workers to relatively junior positions can undermine the position and authority of younger senior personnel. Upper age bars on recruitment and poor redeployment of displaced older workers may also reflect the presence of internal labour markets with ports of entry restricted to younger groups for succession planning purposes. There is also the point that in a context of required labour reductions early retirement policies may be more socially acceptable than forced redundancies, thereby minimizing industrial relations problems and maintaining organizational morale and hence productivity.

Moreover, in a period of almost continuous reorganization and restructuring by many businesses during the 1980s and 1990s, in responding to competitive pressures, it is possible that the greater experience and 'wisdom' of older employees may not have been valued positively by some employers. Such reform processes have invariably entailed decollectivization of employment relationships together with shifts towards more unitary management styles, as embraced for instance in HRM and performance management systems, approaches that seek to motivate through attitudinal restructuring via inculcating employees with corporate values, goals and culture. However, as Hallier, Glover and Lyon (1995) have argued, the judgements of longer-serving employees about such initiatives will be distinguished from those of younger workers in being based more upon their past treatment by management. Accordingly, older employees, especially if reared in a pluralist-collectivist tradition, will generally be more wary, less malleable and more likely to greet such initiatives with a measure of cynicism and resistance. Resistance to change on the part of older employees will be reinforced where they retain advantageous contractual conditions of service from older regimes. Accordingly, it may be simpler and cheaper for employers to retire off older employees than seek to alter ingrained attitudes and re-negotiate or buy-out employment contracts.

Finally, there are broader labour process perspectives that assign a certain rationality to age discrimination. The use of older workers as a contingent labour force or 'reserve army' to be drawn into and expelled from the labour force as and when conditions demand, has received some support from examinations of past trends (Tillsley, 1990; Laczko and Phillipson, 1991).

Examples of *Box C* policy approaches, where older workers are positively favoured on commercial grounds, seem mostly confined to those widely-publicised policies of firms chiefly in the retail and catering sectors (e.g. B&Q, Tesco, Sainsbury's, McDonalds, Thistle Hotels), which, in responding to labour supply difficulties, have found that recruiting from a pool of displaced older workers has secured certain commercial advantages in terms of reduced turnover, employee commitment, improved customer interface and public relations. However, it is unclear whether this approach can profitably be extended beyond 'non-standard' forms of manual employment and lower paid jobs in the service sector, where older workers have been found to be cheap and convenient.

Box D supposes the existence of policies favourable to older workers that might also inhibit business performance. As several commentators have argued a company's age mix is rarely informed by careful evaluation of organizational requirements, but rather seems guided by factors such as organizational culture or custom; or it may have evolved somewhat arbitrarily, influenced by such factors as past labour availability and firm-specific turnover rates. It therefore seems plausible that some firms will employ too many older workers relative to what might be judged an optimum mix, and thereby incur cost or productivity disadvantages of the sort identified under Box B above. In addition, the application of automatic formulae such as LIFO (last in first out) in redundancy situations, can favour older workers on the basis of customary rather than commercial criteria.

It is also plausible to suppose that differing policy approaches towards older employees may have an indeterminate or neutral impact on business performance. Trinder et al., (1992) refer to evidence showing that firms operating in the same product market with similar technology can have widely varying age profiles, some with predominantly young workforces and others with predominantly mature workforces, and there was no evidence to suggest that either age profile led to improved economic efficiency. Such differences might reflect again differences in company philosophies and management styles or, quite simply, differing degrees of age prejudice. This need not, however, imply that such companies could more easily be persuaded to adopt policies favourable to older workers. In terms of Figure 2.1, a move from points E to F would not necessarily be costless. A new age profile in favour of older workers could entail substantial initial set-up costs, including job redesign and new training approaches to allow older workers to maintain productivity. Firms might therefore be quite reluctant to move in this direction, especially if existing sources of labour supply are perfectly adequate. Revisions might also be required to deep-rooted corporate philosophies, beliefs and styles, and to elaborate human resource strategies underpinned by these, changes that are unlikely to be made in the absence of some clear financial inducement.

The typology represented in Figure 2.1 clearly oversimplifies matters and can be challenged on several counts. For example, different age policies are invariably applied to different categories of labour in any one firm. The existence of internal labour markets, for instance, can lead to quite different age policies as between manual and non-manual people or between core and peripheral employees, and policies can also vary according to gender. Moreover, as the discussion reveals, there is an ambivalence in employers' treatment of older staff: disadvantage with respect to recruitment, training and job displacement can coincide with relatively favourable treatment with regard to pay and other seniority prerogatives. Accordingly, it is difficult to judge in any clear sense whether a company's approach to older employees is predominantly negative or positive. Or again, defining ageism as prejudice unwarranted on commercial grounds is problematic. As with other forms of discrimination age-based employment policies can take a form that reinforces or exploits prejudices for economic gain. The use of older workers as a contingent labour force is an obvious example, as is prejudice towards older employees as a means of avoiding industrial relations difficulties.

However, the matrix is nevertheless helpful in indicating that a much broader and more complex range of employer approaches to older employees may exist than is often assumed by those seeking to combat ageism. Moreover, the model is useful in focusing attention upon where employers' policies might *predominantly* lie on this matrix, a matter of some import from a policy viewpoint. That employers' practices predominantly fall within Box A is invariably assumed but rarely demonstrated. Trinder et al., (1992, p. 55) represent this dominant view in asserting that 'there is no doubt that much age discrimination in employment is not justified'. However, for Guillemard and van Gunsteren (1991), Box B-type considerations explain early exit trends better. Indeed the authors argue that early exit, far from demonstrating greater age prejudice, may reflect a *decline* in the use of age-based criteria in employment policies; early exit can be viewed as denoting a shift from chronological age to functional criteria in determining retirement. Older employees are being laid off under present conditions not simply because they are old but because they are less useful or efficient, possibly, *but not necessarily*, as a result of ageing.

Conclusions

The concept of ageism was first coined to describe irrational prejudice towards older people, a prejudice born of fear of mortality and the ageing process. The extension of the term to the employment sphere is a relatively recent phenomenon, linked to an abrupt switch in public policy towards employment trends affecting older workers which have been apparent and indeed encouraged for at least two decades. While some parallels can be drawn between the experiences and treatment of the 'old-old' and the recent labour market experience of third agers, there are differences that go beyond those of degree. In particular, age disadvantage in employment need not wholly denote irrational prejudice, though this is rarely acknowledged in a climate where public policy objectives towards older workers seem to converge with those of the age concern lobby. This recent, somewhat fragile, alliance has reinforced a view of age discrimination in employment as both irrational and commercially damaging, a prognosis that is rarely challenged. The extent to which early exit and other employment conditions experienced by older workers simply reflect irrational prejudice is an issue that has as yet been poorly researched, but the consistency of such trends across national boundaries and in widely varying institutional and cultural contexts, suggests their substantial underpinning by rational employer responses to competitive pressures, technical change and changes in the macroeconomy. Indeed early exit trends may denote not so much an upsurge of ageism in employment but rather some shift from age-determined employment policies to age-neutral functional criteria as the basis for management decision-making, irrespective of how managers choose to rationalize such decisions.

If this view is accepted then policy initiatives may have unintended consequences. Present campaigns to persuade employers voluntarily to reform their attitudes and practices towards older workers are unlikely to have much impact in terms of halting or reversing early exit trends. Indeed, they may have the opposite effect if employers are called upon to justify the rationality of their current age profiles. In terms of Figure 2.1, the move may not be chiefly from Box A to Box C as policy makers intend, but possibly from Box D to Box B, were employers to become more sensitive to the relative cost and other disadvantages that can be associated with older workers. Legislative intervention that constitutes an effective challenge to irrational age prejudice could have a similar, if more dramatic, effect in that employers would then be compelled to focus upon the rationality of age-based policies.

Though the British Conservative Government consistently rejected the legislative path as neither 'practical nor beneficial' the Labour Party, when in opposition, undertook to 'consider comprehensive legislation on age discrimination similar to that currently applying to sex and race discrimination should they secure office'.

Apart from the possibility suggested above, that legislation could conceivably act to reinforce the labour market disadvantage of older workers, there are a number of other thorny issues touched upon in the discussion that would require some thought prior to embarking upon a legislative path. For example, it needs to be decided whether legislation should be confined to older age groups or whether it should be framed to challenge all forms of age prejudice. As argued earlier there would seem to be few grounds in principle for confining the concept of ageism to older age groups, though a recent review of international policies towards age-based employment practices revealed that most legislative initiatives were so confined, with Canada representing one of the few exceptions (Moore et al., 1994).

A broad-based approach would seem more sound on social equity grounds, providing scope to challenge discrimination against both older and younger workers and also the diverse patterns of age discrimination affecting women. However, given the distinctive nature of ageism as discussed earlier, where there is no clear oppressed group, where almost everyone might be considered as both perpetrator and victim, and where the sources of prejudice are deeply ingrained in human nature, broadly-framed legislation of this sort would seem to provide almost limitless scope for challenging employer practices. In particular, the concept of indirect discrimination, an important feature of sex and race discrimination laws, would seem especially hard to apply in any practicable manner to age matters where there is no clearly oppressed minority group. Fierce employer resistance is therefore likely, leading to poor enforcement or a restrictive legal framework as has been found in other countries. In Canada's case for example, the Supreme Court has ruled that while compulsory retirement is discriminatory, it is still legal.

On the other hand, confining the scope of anti-discrimination law to older age groups, while possibly more manageable, may be construed as inequitable and even sexist and may foster intergenerational tensions. Indeed recent evidence on trends in youth labour markets in OECD countries in the 1980s and 1990s suggests that young workers are equally deserving of protection in having been similarly marginalized and discriminated against in recent years. Despite a decline in the youth share of population, increased enrolments in school, and shifts in industry mix toward youth-intensive sectors, the wages of youths relative to adults fell and the employment rates of youths have declined sharply in Britain and other OECD countries (Blanchflower and Freeman, 1996).

Whatever legislative approach may be adopted it is almost certain to provide exemptions to protect commercial interests, and as the discussion has suggested the scope for defending age-based policies on commercial grounds may be broader than is often supposed. If British legislation is modelled along the lines of the US Age Discrimination in Employment Act 1967, then such exclusions are likely to be wide-ranging. Exemptions under this Act include: where age is a *bona fide* occupational qualification; where differentiation is based upon 'reasonable factors' other than age; where a decision is based upon observing a *bona fide* seniority system for benefits; or where employees are being disciplined or discharged for a 'good cause'. Legislative remedies so curtailed provide little prospect of altering age-based employment practices, even where these are built upon simple prejudice.

For these and other reasons, most commentators are doubtful that early exit trends will be reversed to any appreciable extent in the foreseeable future, irrespective of whether such trends are viewed as deriving from irrational prejudice or commercial exigencies. Moreover, in view of radical and abrupt policy swings in the past towards the employment of older workers (Tillsley, 1990; Laczko and Phillipson, 1991), the recent positive stance of governments towards older workers is by no means assured in the longer term. Worries about the demographic time-bomb and future dependency ratios already seem to be subsiding along with indications that in comparison to other OECD countries the economic and budgetary consequences of demographic and employment trends in Britain may be relatively benign (OECD, 1995). Accordingly, the employment prospects of older workers would seem rather grim, and their continuing exclusion from the labour market, especially if accorded some rational, commercial justification, may serve both to reinforce irrational age prejudices and traditional ageist attitudes, and to extend the victim base to a larger proportion of the older population.

It is this prospect that has fostered alternative policy responses, as manifested in the Carnegie programme and other initiatives, which entail the delineation of a new third age stage to the life course, and focus upon how third agers should be integrated into society through new social roles that do not necessarily contain a work element. One danger here is that social concern over ageism, that has been reinforced by the recent employment experience of older workers, may evaporate as third agers seek to distance themselves in self-image and life-style from the plight of 'old-old', a process that may undo the sense of solidarity recently generated between third and fourth agers. In the United States, this trend is already apparent in the intensity of prejudice by the younger, affluent and active older people against those who are frail and dependent (Marshall, 1990), and for Britain, Laslett (1995) detects a similar tendency in the offhand attitude of the Carnegie researchers towards fourth agers, indicating an apparent willingness to reinstate the distinctions and inequalities of traditional old age.

References

Biggs, S. (1993), *Understanding Ageing: Images, Attitudes and Professional Practice*, Open University Press, Buckingham.

Blanchflower, D. and Freeman R. (1996), *Growing into Work*, Mimeo, OECD, Paris.

Bosanquet, N. (1987), *A Generation in Limbo: Government, the Economy and the 55-65 Age Group in Britain*, Public Policy Centre, London.

Butler, R. (1987), 'Ageism' in *The Encyclopedia of Ageing*, Springer, New York.

Bytheway, B. (1980), 'Is Ageism just a joke?', *New Age 12*, Age Concern, London.

Bytheway, B. (1995), *Ageism*, Open University Press, Buckingham.

Bytheway, B. and Johnson, J. (1990), 'On defining ageism', *Critical Social Policy*, Vol. 27, pp. 27-39.

Ginn, J. and Arber, S. (1996), 'Gender, Age and Attitudes to Retirement in Mid-Life', *Ageing and Society*, Vol. 16, No. 1, January.

Guillemard, A. and Van Gunsteren, M. (1991), 'Pathways and their prospects: A comparative interpretation of the meaning of early exit', in M. Kohli, M. Rein, A. Guillemard, and H. Van Gunsteren (eds), *Time for Retirement: Comparative Studies of Early Exit from the Labor Force*, Cambridge University Press, Cambridge.

Hallier, J., Glover, I. and Lyon, P. (1995), *The Ageism Taboo in Human Resource Management Research*, Mimeo, Stirling.

House of Commons (1989), Employment Committee (Second Report), *The Employment Patterns of the Over-50s*, Vol. II, HMSO, London.

Institute of Personnel Management (1991), *Age and Employment: an IPM Statement*, IPM, London.

Itzin, C. (1995), 'Reviews' [of Bytheway, (1995)], *Ageing and Society*, Vol. 15, pp. 427-28.

Itzin, C. and Phillipson, C. (1993), *Age Barriers at Work*, Metropolitan Authorities Recruitment Agency, Solihull.

Jacobs, K., Kohli, M. and Rein, M. (1991), 'Testing the industry-mix hypothesis of early exit', in M. Kohli, M. Rein, A. Guillemard and H. Van Gunsteren (eds), *Time for Retirement: Comparative Studies of Early Exit from the Labour Force*, Cambridge University Press, Cambridge.

Johnson, P., Conrad, C. and Thomson, D. (eds) (1989), *Workers Versus Pensioners: Intergenerational Justice in an Ageing World*, Manchester University Press, Manchester.

Johnson, P. and Zimmermann, K. (1993), 'Ageing and the European labour market: public policy issues', in P. Johnson, and K. Zimmermann (eds), *Labour Markets in an Ageing Europe*, Cambridge University Press, Cambridge.

Kohli, M., Rein, M., Guillemard, A. and Van Gunsteren, H. (eds) (1991), *Time for Retirement: Comparative Studies of Early Exit from the Labour Force*, Cambridge University Press, Cambridge.

Kohli, M. and Rein, M. (1991), 'The changing balance of work and retirement', in Kohli et al. (eds), ibid.

Laczko, F. and Phillipson, C. (1991), *Changing Work and Retirement*, Open University Press, Milton Keynes.

Laslett, P. (1989), Memorandum submitted to the House of Commons Employment Committee, House of Commons (1989), op. cit.

Laslett, P. (1995), 'The Third Age, the Fourth Age and the Future', *Ageing and Society*, Vol. 15, pp. 436-47.

McEwen, E. (ed.) (1990), *Age - The Unrecognised Discrimination*, Age Concern, London.

Marshall, M. (1990), 'Proud to be old - attitudes to age and ageing', in E. McEwen. (ed.) (1990), ibid.

Moore, J., Tilson, B. and Whitting, G. (1994), *An International Overview of Employment Policies and Practices Towards Older Workers*, Research Series No. 29, Department of Employment, London.

OECD (1995), *Economic Outlook*, 57, June.

Rein, M. and Jacobs, K. (1993), 'Ageing and employment trends: a comparative analysis for OECD countries', in P. Johnson and K. Zimmermann (eds), *Labour Markets in an Ageing Europe*, Cambridge University Press, Cambridge.

Scrutton, S. (1990), 'Ageism - The Foundation of Age Discrimination', in E. McEwen (ed.), op. cit.

Standing, G. (1986), 'Labour flexibility and older worker marginalisation: The need for a new strategy', *International Labour Review,* Vol. 25, No. 3, May-June.

Taylor, P. and Walker, A. (1993), 'Employers and older workers', *Employment Gazette*, Vol. 101, No. 8, August.

Taylor, P. and Walker, A. (1995), 'Utilising Older Workers', *Employment Gazette,* Vol. 103, No. 4, April.

Tillsley, C. (1990), *The Impact of Age Upon Employment*, Warwick Papers in Industrial Relations, No. 33, Industrial Relations Research Unit, University of Warwick.

Trinder, C., Hulme, G. and McCarthy, C. (1992), *Employment: The Role of Work in The Third Age*, The Carnegie Inquiry into the Third Age, Research Paper No. 1, Carnegie UK Trust, Dunfermline.

Worsley, R. (1996), 'Only prejudices are old and tired', *People Management,* January.

3 'Do not go gentle into that good night': some thoughts on paternalism, ageism, management and society

Ian Glover and Mohamed Branine

Introduction

As most of our readers probably know, the first line of the poem by Dylan Thomas which forms part of our title and which was addressed to his dying father, is followed by

> Old age should burn and rave at close of day;
> Rage, rage against the dying of the light.

Our arguments in this paper are also mainly concerned with matters related to age, to being older rather than younger, and to the idea or ideal of living life to the full, in a society that to some at least, appears to be increasingly ageing and ageist.

In a nutshell, the problem or topic that concerns us is this. The most significant change in the labour markets of developed societies in general and that of the UK in particular, since the growth of the large-scale formal employment of ladies and the demise of semi-skilled and unskilled jobs in factories, is the recent growth in the number and proportion of employees and potential employees of mature years. Our lives are longer and healthier than in the past – the population has not so much been rejuvenating as 'juvenating', for it can seem alarmist, clumsy, insensitive and misconceived to say that it is ageing – *but* economic forces, real and perceived, have been reducing both the quantity and quality of the work and employment available to those aged over, say, 40. At the same time too, technical development and the cult of youth, both of which are variously causes, features and products of mass affluence, have helped to legitimize rejection of much of whatever, in the form of achievements, experience, knowledge, skills and wisdom, older people have to offer.

The situation or scenario just described is, at least on the surface, a very exclusionary and divisive one, with seemingly dire implications for relationships between the generations, economic well-being and the moral order. However the main assumption behind, and the main contention of, this paper, is that while the situation is indeed serious and damaging in many important respects, it is nonetheless one which contains very powerful seeds of its own destruction, and one that, on balance, ought to be perceived and approached as much more of an opportunity than as a threat. To help explain why we believe this, we now sketch out an outline of our argument while simultaneously describing the main contents of each of the following sections of the paper.

In the next, and second, section we emphasize our belief in the value of the broadest possible definitions of ageism and age discrimination. We argue that these phenomena can affect people of *all* ages and that ageism should be thought of in qualitative as well as quantitative terms, insofar as it has many causes, features and dimensions, and is a multifaced and multidirectional phenomenon and not merely a simple and unidirectional matter of youthful *angst* and impatience directed at the 'old'. Here we also emphasize the relevance of knowledge of life cycles and of divisions of labour and of all of the varied forms that they take.

In the third section, we suggest that through the broad phases of economic, societal and philosophical development from pre-industrial times to the present it may be possible to detect some powerful links between rational and modernist impulses and the tendency to valorize youth. We also suggest that as such impulses achieve their final flowering and also burn themselves out in the face of their own contradictions, social and economic relationships between the generations become temporarily very anomic and confused prior to the restoration of some sort of equilibrium.

Next, in our fourth section, we move on from considering ageism over time to tentatively exploring some ways in which its extent and nature vary between societies. Although this paper is written in the UK, principally about events in the UK and primarily for a UK audience, we wish to try to add some comparative breadth to hints at the historical depth that we hope is hinted at in the preceding section, so that the context of the UK's current experience is better understood. Thus we discuss the character and extent of ageism in individualist and collectivist cultures and consider a number of other hopefully relevant societal influences for ageism. We suggest that managerialism is the dominant ideology and political philosophy of our era and explore a little of its variety in relation to ageism. We briefly consider the relationship between order and ageism in different kinds of society.

In the fifth section we consider ageism and age discrimination in the UK and come to some perhaps surprisingly optimistic conclusions after a rather concerned, sceptical and even pessimistic discussion. After taking into account some of the most relevant recent demographic and economic changes we go on to criticise some relevant contemporary myths of the UK's relative economic decline and political and social strain and transition. These myths are those of post-industrial society, the lump of labour fallacy, and the demographic time bomb. The practice, extent, variety and experience of age discrimination in the UK are also discussed, as are some of the main economic, political and social consequences. We also identify some of the main vested interests, which stand to benefit from age discrimination, such as insurance companies and members of salaried occupations with long incremental scales.

Then we consider the future. Here we re-emphasise our point that chronologically older but physically younger, fitter and stronger population has to be though of as an opportunity rather than a threat. We make a few suggestions about how the roles and responsibilities of the generations might be re-thought, and we offer some other pointers to the future.

Ageism and age discrimination: the importance of clear and comprehensive definitions

We define ageism as the form of prejudice which abuses perceived chronological age in forming judgements about people, and age discrimination as acts based on such prejudice. Some such acts can be favourable as well as unfavourable in intent, and thus very likely to be patronising. We see them as acting in any direction, that is against younger or older people and against contemporaries who are deemed on the basis of inadequate evidence to possess and/or to exhibit desirable or undesirable age-based attributes.

As many writers have noted, age discrimination can indeed affect anyone, regardless not only of their perceived age, but also irrespective of their social background, gender, marital status, ethnic origin, or religious, political or other belief. When prejudice on some other ground such as one or more of the foregoing exists, as well as ageism, then its focus may be a victim of double or triple jeopardy or worse. In the contexts of employment and work it is not just a matter of making unwarranted assumptions based on age when people apply for jobs. It affects all aspects of employment and work, including the tasks that people are given to do, their training and development, promotion and termination, and so on. Thus someone who because of some dubious age-related judgement is given work below or above their ability, someone not sent on an important training course, or sent on another that signifies that their career is 'plateaued', or denied promotion because they are somewhat older or maybe embarrassingly more skilled or street-wise than their colleagues, or forced into early retirement – from one stand-point effectively killed off as a fully paid up member of society – will not be much happier, to say the least, than someone not selected for a job because of their age.

The importance of defining ageism in a broad and all-inclusive, in a qualitative as well as a purely quantitative a way as possible, was emphasized by Bythway (1995). Whereas definitions of a generation ago, which had restricted ageism to being a force acting against older people, had been useful for putting the notion on the political agenda, they were also 'inadequate and arguably ageist' themselves. Thus they accepted 'the old' or 'the elderly' as an objective, scientific, category whereas it was a 'cultural concept, a construction that has certain popular validity in sustaining ageism within societies that need scapegoats'. However, and like middle age, old age had 'no clearly identifiable beginning and ending' and it meant different things to different people. The terms 'elderly' and 'old age' were ageist because they lumped diverse individuals together on the basis of age, often as a preliminary to excluding them from being or doing something. By the same token therefore, all age bars were ageist. For Bytheway, 'ageing is a shared epxerience, [and] we are all subject to the fear and ignorance of ageism, and ... the power of ageism should be challenged in ways that promote a holistic and undivided view of "the whole of our lives". He also describes how anti-ageist intentions, actions and rhetoric could be embarrassing, naïve and patronising instead of rational and compassionate and sceptically so.

For Biggs (1993) ageism was a form of oppression 'arising from the social construction of older age' and it was important to understand and study it as such. Ageism tended to assume that older people were increasingly and inevitably passive and dependent on other members of society. Elders tended to be disenfranchised as functioning members of society, if not as voters, by more powerful younger people. For some other writers, ageism was not the same as 'adultism' (cf. Itzin, 1986), which oppressed younger people including children. It is true that most writings on ageism see it as a phenomenon of younger versus older people but we feel that this is unfortunate and that a separate category of 'adultism' or 'youthism' is unnecessary. Age, like bureaucracy, is both a pejorative and a technical term in practice, and to restrict the use of the term ageism to one 'end' of the life course seems likely to add to the confusion, fear and prejudice which already suffuse our thinking, as it has tended to do with bureaucracy.

If ageism is a matter of degree as well as of kind, and about relationships, and about the presumed (in) capacities and (lack of) potential for people, then knowledge and thought concerning the life cycle and divisions of labour have to be highly relevant for understanding it. Biggs (1993) argued that the very complexity of contemporary life embodies a constant danger of personal disintegration for most people. Social boundaries and realities changed constantly, meaning that life offered great variety and choice, but that many people were tempted to take refuge in superficial relationships and thus to distance themselves from genuine involvement. However people could adapt and renew themselves continually, although this meant keeping inconvenient parts of the whole self suppressed in order to create an impression of wholeness. This was bad for old people because their situation was virtually the only one in which one identity could not be exchanged for another, and in which personal disintegration was unavoidable and in some cases imminent. Most people reinforced their positive self-images by taking the (dreaded) situation of the very old as their point of reference. Most decisions about very old people were taken by younger ones with precisely this negative perception of the old condition, and it was generally agreed that it should be kept 'hidden'.

Old people wanted their final years to express the full meaning and significance of their lives, to provide a sense of integrity and achievement. However their physical dependence on younger people often meant that they were oppressed and their desires frustrated. Younger people often tried to encourage old people to engage in spurious activities in order to create a sense of 'normality'. The practical relevance of the past and present experiences of old people was often discounted by younger people because of the distasteful and threatening connotations of age. Old people often colluded with the assumption that they were no longer entitled to have their views accepted as much or as often as previously.

The situation was underpinned by the fear felt by younger people about their own ultimate fates. Older people could reinforce the negative aspects of their lives by allowing their capacity for understanding, reflection and wisdom to degenerate into rigid, conservative and controlling behaviour, treating others as (their) children. Negative perceptions of age were often reinforced further when younger people, especially those in the caring professions, acted 'prematurely' in such ways, sometimes tyrannising and demoralising those in their care.

Older people needed to approach death in a positive way, to acknowledge their future openly and to disengage from social interaction constructively by accepting their situations openly and using their experience, wisdom and remaining time to help and support the development of younger people. Unfortunately the latter's stereotypes of age too often dehumanised and marginalized their qualities. The mass media added to the problem by developing an image of 'positive ageing' in the form of perpetual active middle age and by actively denying the reality and the real needs of old people. However most older people themselves were gratified by learning, as they became older, that they and their lives did not change for the worse to anything like the degree that they had expected previously.

Health problems notwithstanding, older people often felt more adaptable, alert, capable, creative and wiser that ever, in general realistically so, and their self-confidence helped them to cope with negative stereotyping by younger people. As older people used their experience and reminiscences to make sense of their lives, any loneliness experienced by them tended to be caused by unsatisfying interaction with other people with different backgrounds, rather than with younger people, with whom it was perhaps surprisingly much more often possible to build mutually satisfying bridges. However the widespread belief that younger people are more productive and valuable members of society many made of them reluctant to interact meaningfully with older people. This rejection made older people frustrated and resentful and likely either to compete with or to exclude younger people. To compete with them, older people had to persist in pursuing middle-aged goals and to repress inconvenient parts of their older selves. The alternative was to accept a definition of oneself, by younger people, as having no value.

The power of the forces acting against older people is not merely economic. The idea that life has fixed stages is a near universal one, and in most respects of course, accurate. In literature, economic and social policies, religion, psychology, medicine, economics, work and employment, sociology and gerontology the idea of stages is taken for granted. The current salience of the 'Third Age' (50 to 74) as a candidate for positive treatment has stimulated some writers to point to a fourth one of total dependence and decay, whereby the increasing health and vitality of older but not aged people is emphasised, although sometimes at the expense of the latter. In general old age is thought of as if it were the final part of a long hill-walk, with early life being the climb, the middle years being those steady achievement on a plateau, or gentle (up, down, undulating) incline, and the older years ones of descent.

When considering the generation and experience of age discrimination it is vital to look beyond the lives of individuals and to consider the other, and in many respects much more powerful side of the equation: social institutions and systems. Among these, and in the context of work and employment, divisions of labour are central. Technical divisions of labour, those internal to places of work, ideally ensure that the right tasks are performed by the right individuals with the right kinds of knowledge and skill. Social divisions of labour, those external to places of work, such as those associated with social and educational background, age gender, race, religion, appearance, political affiliation, occupational and professional status, and so on, often interfere with the achievement of the ideal just described, as when someone is not promoted at work because they do not attend the same church or support the same sports as their bosses.

Ageism over time

We are confident enough for it to be a major suggestion or contention (we are unreservedly unsure which!) of our argument, that the modern project has *generally* tended to value youthful energy and rationality and to devalue elderly detachment and wisdom. In spelling out this part of our argument we assume the existence of five phases of economic, societal and philosohphical development in the West since the Dark and Middle ages: pre-modern, classical, modern, postmodern and the mature aboriginal or neo-aboriginal.

By pre-modern we mean the periods before the Renaissance and geographical discoveries of the fifteenth and sixteenth centuries. We suspect that in these times older people were variously marginalised and/or despised as economic burdens, or respected for their wealth and venerated for their wisdom, depending to a large extent on their economic situations, and less subtly than in subsequent periods. We take the classical period to be that from the sixteenth century or thereabouts until, and largely in the eighteenth and nineteenth centuries, industrialization, urbanization, republicanism and nationalism, not to mention democracy, became purposeful forces. Here the Renaissance and similar notion that humans might understand, tame and put to use the forces of nature was developing and starting to be put into effect. Reason, truth and the law, it was increasingly felt, would and should be used to make lives wealthier and more predictable and secure. In the so-called fine arts, for example, it was felt that representations of phenomena should correspond exactly to reality. Overseas exploration and expansion, commercial growth and technical developments in agriculture and manufacturing helped to increase standards of living and to encourage development of genteel and ordered attitudes and behaviour in the middle ranks of society.

The 'modern' era may be seen as corresponding very roughly to the more of less harsh and brazenly (in the eyes of many) industrial one, variously and according to more or less objective measures or historical interpretations of them, starting in the eighteenth, nineteenth or early twentieth centuries and ending – or not ending at all in the eyes of many – some time after the 1950s. Rising incomes, the growth of large-scale government and large-scale organization in general, more comfortable and civilised lives for the majority, meant generally greater resources for younger and older members of society alike. However when faced with the choice of providing for younger or older people, industrial societies have tended to choose the former because of their generally greater productive potential, in line with the Utilitarian maxim of the greatest good for the greatest number.

Modernist thought and practice have been suffused with the notion that most large-scale human problems are being solved through the application of 'science plus will', the latter in the form of decisive high-level provision of material resources, and their vigorous use (Kelly and Glover, 1996). In health care this has led to widespread investment in the fallacy that provision of sophisticated acute facilities and 'efficient' cost-conscious management of resources will produce healthier and longer lives, whereas it is higher incomes, healthier life styles and physical environments which tend more often lead to such desirable outcomes. In education it is associated with such dubious notions as that which argues that high rates of economic growth and high participation rates in post-school education go together, that 'mere' engineering and production are the 'easy' and 'dirty' ends of applied physics, and that management education is inevitably a civilising influence. However the main underlying characteristic of the modernist project or impulse is arguably that of 'digesting science' (Gellner, 1964).

By this we mean that it seeks to put to effective use the proudly rationalist modernist conceit, noted above, that science or reasons plus will and resources should solve almost any problem, while gradually coming to terms with its contradictions and limitations. This is or has been an arguably very noble impulse, and one with a great deal of mileage left in it, but it is not very tolerant, at least in the explicit sense, of human playfulness, idiosyncrasy or even of the unpredictable ingenuity central to all successful human action. It also tends to assume that genius rarely outlasts the first half of the average life span (Bytheway, 1995, chapter 2; Lehman, 1953). It is still expressed very powerfully through the diffuse managerialism that constitutes, according to Enteman (1993), the dominant ideology of the advanced industrial societies. For Enteman managerialism was an ostensibly value-free secular and non-moral ideology, one which ostensibly prioritised efficiency and which had replaced capitalism, socialism and democracy, none of which had functioned as its authors had intended. It was a creation of managers, for managers, filling the 'vacuum created by the fact that intellectuals have not created an alternative ideology which might have some more justification'.

If an intellectual were deliberately to begin to develop such an alternative ideology they might usefully start by drawing on the ideas of Durkheim (1933, 1957) and Dingley (1996) on pressing need of advanced societies to re-unify the economic, social and moral-religious spheres, to re-assert the primacy of society over the selfish interests and desires of individuals and groups; and those of Veblen (1921) on the moral emptiness on contemporary corporate life in the USA; of

George Orwell and perhaps even Karl Marx on how the unrestrained pursuit of individual happiness and pleasure leads directly to alienation in its most extreme forms; and of Sorge (1978) and Locke (1996) on Germany's and to a lesser extent Japan's rejection of American-style managerialism after 1945 (cf. also Albert, 1993). All of these writers, in one way or another, support the view that people are much more likely to fulfil themselves through what Sorge (1978) called 'the lifelong development of personal skills in a specialism', by genuinely educated people as defined by their awareness of their own limitations and humble and sceptical curiosity rather than by any formal qualifications that they might have, and rather than by the exercise of 'social skills', careerism and managerial self-aggrandisement. Here we have more than a hint that 'scientific', 'modern' managerialism is about the use and, if needs must, the abuse, of (sic) 'human resources' rather than about the self-development and self-expression of people, and that those 'resources' which may be readily depicted as obsolescent – when they may merely be creatively recalcitrant – may reasonably be discarded and replaced with more 'flexible' 'new blood' (cf. Hallier, Lyon and Glover, 1993).

The postmodern era which many writers think is now with us has often been depicted as starting with the near-simultaneous final flowering and dissolution of modernism. Thus for Crook et al (1992:10) premodern societies become modern through processes, central to the operation of modern societies, of differentiation, commodification and rationalization. Thus 'Modernization leads to society that is highly differentiated, with high levels of specialization and complexity, and highly organized with high levels of rationalization and commodification' (Leopold, Glover and Hughes, 1996:4). The two master processes of differentation and organization, the latter embodying rationalization and commodification, are taken to extreme levels in highly affluent, advanced, postmodern societies which have founded that 'science' is digestible, but only in part and with difficulty. The postmodern condition is one in which the contradictions of the one-sided modernist impulse become clearly unmanageable, in which top-down managerialism is no longer accepted, and perhaps beginning to be socially unacceptable. It is arguably one in which free and on the whole affluent individuals begin to perceive a need to rebuild the society and the moral order which economic progress and bureaucratic managerialism have hollowed out to an extent that threatens their existence. On the other hand it is not really '*post*modern'.

We have called the final stage, in effect our post-postmodern one, mature aboriginal or neo-aboriginal. The notion of the post-modern depends totally on that of the modern, a millennialist one which in some respects vaingloriously and fallaciously assumes that 'our age is like no other'. What philosophers and sociologists refer to as modern and postmodern consists of a number of complicated and interrelated developments of the last two hundred to three hundred years for which the simplest and by far the most accurate term is 'industrialisation'. These changes have been traumatic and tumultuous for millions of people; yet they have also generated enormous hope, satisfaction, wealth, comfort, pleasure and security for many more millions of others. Thus Snow (1964:25) was surely being sensible when he wrote that 'Industrialization is the only hope of the poor'.

These changes have clearly not ended and people surely now realise that the full development of existing industrial and related techniques, let alone the invention and development of new ones, is likely to take centuries. However we are also increasingly – or once again – aware of how finite our planet's resources and our own bodies, minds, needs and even our desires are. Sane adult people no longer aspire, if they ever did, to be immortal or to live lives which variously combine physical ecstasy, psychosocial and spiritual peak experiences and thrilling journeys of intellectual discovery, and no more. Aspirations may be becoming more 'modest': shelter, food, clothes, comfort, love, work, interesting leisure pursuits, some mobility, respect, peace and so on. Our use of the word aboriginal, which means more or less what it looks to mean, 'is based on our recognition of the inevitability finite character of the modern-postmodern project. Nature, for most practical purposes, will have been temporarily tamed (but never conquered). The pace of economic and social change will almost certainly decelerate because the possibilities for technical change are finite (Ackroyd, Glover, Currie and Bull, 2000). Human beings will recognise that (as ever) they face the old stark choice spelt out by Auden in his poem '1st September 1939' that 'We must love one another or die'. In using the term 'mature aboriginal' to describe the future, we are being optimistic. By posing an alternative, 'neo-aboriginal', we are hedging our bets, and we have shrunk, for obvious reasons of style and also in what is perhaps a typically conceited modernist fashion, from omitting an adjective or hyphen.

We hope that we have offered a broad context, albeit a rather speculative one, for Cole's (1992) assertion that contemporary attacks on ageism by magazine publishers and advertisers, designed to develop 'new positive images of old age [had] yet to confront the de-meaning of age rooted in modern culture's relentless hostility toward decay and dependency'. For Featherstone and Hepworth (1995:46), the result was a 'profound failure of meaning that currently surrounds the end of life' (Cole, 1986: 130) which leaves ageing and the 'third age' (the 'young-old') as 'an extended plateau of active middle age typified in the imagery of positive ageing as a period of youthfulness and active consumer lifestyles'. Such assertions about moral and social confusion surrounding age have recently been reinforced by the arguments, however patronising and out of touch they clearly are in some respects, of Anderson (1996) and colleagues, about the apparent contemporary lack of order, civility, gentility, politeness, manners and so on in the UK. The culprits for Anderson and his co-authors include Marxism and feminism, and the modernist youth culture or cult of youth, whereby old people no longer acted their age, but instead aped youth and in doing so colluded in the general lack of respect for achievement, experience and traditional, albeit really modern, values and standards of behaviour which had been developed over centuries to simplify and smoothe out everyday life.

Ageism in society

The observation that UK society since the 1950s has tended to separate, in some ways but not all, the economic sphere of life from its moral and social ones has virtually become a truism. A misreading of the economic runes has perhaps involved, a regression to the rugged individualism of nineteenth century Utilitarianism and liberalism, in an over-reaction against the expansion and internationalization of economic activity, whereas if the UK had gone with the flow our politics and economics would have emphasized a need for people to pull together against the more threatening external forces, not one for them to fight each other. The tendency for personal economic gain to be pursued at the expense, not only of moral and social values, but at its own selfishly destructive expense, is seen, as we have implied, in the cult of youth and its superficially paradoxical but in fact consequent disinvestment in the upbringing of the young and the neglect of both the wisdom and the physical welfare of the old. In the past the leaders of the major professions, meaning the church, the law and medicine, guided society. They did this through their knowledge and their concern for morality, wisdom, justice and the physical and social welfare of others. After communing with God about these things, they passed their knowledge down to the lower branches of their professions for society's use and benefit. The medieval guilds, which fostered the systems of apprenticeship that lasted until the disastrous and wide-ranging adoption in the 1950s and 1960s of already dating US and other management practices like company amalgamations and very large systemic scale mass production, were designed as much to produce good citizens as skilled craftspeople. For the last forty years the largely unbridled pursuit of management power and status, wealth, happiness and pleasure has only succeeded to a limited extent in the UK, and with considerable social costs, precisely because of the withering away of restraints on individual selfishness (Dingley, 1996). A society in which managements genuinely cared for employees and in which employees had come to respect the authority of management because it was based on genuinely superior expertise and wisdom would surely have performed far better economically, especially if more had been invested, earlier, in education, skill, and mutual understanding (cf. Reed and Anthony, 1992; Anthony, 1986).

The neglect of the young, for example by parents who believed that teachers, not they, should inculcate self-discipline into children, and who uncritically accepted every fashion that came from across the Atlantic, especially the over-valuing of the beauty and power of youth, has arguably been a recipe for growing crime in general and the abuse of vulnerable older people in particular. Other relevant aspects of such phenomena include the apparently growing reliance of young people on their peers as role models and their peer groups for social support and moral guidance, and the widespread and disturbingly shallow, not to mention decadent, obsession with 'image'.

These rather negative accounts of the two original individualistic Business Management cultures, those of the UK and the USA, need some modification. It is broadly true that German and Japanese employees and managers are less mobile between and more loyal to their employing organizations than Britons and Americans are. However the force of the cult of youth itself in the UK and the USA, as opposed to more general individualistic tendencies and habits, is fairly new and largely a product of post-war affluence. Moreover, there is nothing to stop societies which value the individual and which define ageism as a problem for individuals from taking it very seriously indeed. Also ageism could well be rampant in collectivist societies if it was felt in them that it served the general interest well.

Hampden-Turner and Trompenaars (1993: 90-91) reported the results of a survey conducted by Trompenaars who asked respondents in thirteen industrial countries about the value of hard work and achievement versus that of age and experience for success and respect in management. North American and European countries tended to emphasise the value of the former, and Pacific Rim countries – China, Japan and Korea – the latter. However Hampden-Turner and Trompenaars felt that the reported attitudinal differences were not very great, and that the long service, experience and maturity valued more in the East, and more in France, Italy, The Netherlands and Germany than in the USA, Australia, Canada and the UK, were associated with success there because the Japanese and others *made* them work. In other words and for example, the top ranks of Japanese companies, full of older men, were not 'littered with "dead wood"' (p. 91) because the Japanese took great care to make their system work by investing heavily in the development and supervision of such people and by making sure that they acted as mentors and teachers to younger employees. In the USA, on the other hand, young managers were expected to take their responsibilities very seriously and to work very hard. How a country's managers succeeded was less important than that they made the peculiarities and strengths of their national cultures work for them.

Comparisons between higher technical education and management development in Germany and Japan have normally shown how in Germany young graduate engineers are much more 'finished' and 'formed' when they start their careers than their Japanese counterparts. The latter's employers took far more responsibility for their early training and development than the Germans' employers had to. This involved significant differences in staffing and work organization. However in each case managements were very focused on the technical details of their work and that of their companies, very hard-nosed *and* able to see the wider picture. This has often been contrasted with management in the US and the UK, at least until the last five to ten years, when more detached, more arms'-length with regard to technical detail and work, and more overtly commercial and financial regimes and practices prevailed (cf. Glover, 1985; Locke, 1996a, 1996b).

Thus what seems to be important is gaining some measure of economic success is to find a way, one which works for oneself, one's organization or one's country. This means playing to strengths, not focusing too harshly on weakness while dealing with it if and as necessary, and normally avoiding extreme 'solutions' which can kill the patient(s). It acknowledges the interdependence of opposites, the fact that all ways of thinking and acting contain their own opposites, and are meaningless without them. Thus the barbarian and the civilised, the long-term and the short-term, the collectivist and the individualist, always co-exist, always compete, are always co-joined or locked and in opposition to each other, with one side of the equation in any given setting temporarily privileged and the other temporarily marginalised (Derrida, 1976, 1978, 1981). Similarly, scientific, activist, rationalist, 'Western' management thinking, dominant since early industrial times, probably since the seventeenth century, has emphasised analysis over synthesis, rationally-guided search behaviour versus unpredictable ingenuity, practical-minded Platonism, scientific and secular certainty versus the uncertain ambiguities of the sacred and of Renaissance humanism. Scientific rationalisation was part of the seedbed for the latter development of 'rational' management thinking and of instrumentally-activist managerialism in the West, especially but not only in its English-speaking parts.

The growing sophistication and breadth of management thinking and research can be seen in the ways in which they increasingly draw on historical knowledge of different societies. Thus the study of Japanese management has moved away from the making of such simple, not to say crude, distinctions as Japanese paternalism versus UK individualism, to deep study of the long-standing tensions and changes within complex societies. Wada (1995), for example, explained why the ageism which apparently followed the modernist, utilitarian emphasis on the work ethic and efficiency in the West, where the latter was reinforced by the development of age-stratified national education and welfare systems, did not develop much at all in patriarchal, benevolently paternalistic hierarchical Japan, where industrialisation was much faster and more centrally planned, and much more socially and politically conservative.

The significance of such writings in the present context, taken with our earlier discussions of self-aggrandizing managerialism, is that there is much that is accidental (and sometimes well-intended in every respect), and little that is inevitable about the ageism and age discrimination apparent in the UK now and recently. Thus Pilcher (1996), following Dex and Philipson (1986) and others, noted how there was a '"golden age" for interest in older workers' (Pilcher, 1996 : 172) in the 1950s and 1960s in the UK, when labour shortages were the norm. Bytheway (1995) discussed a number of paradoxes in contrasting the great political, legal, economic, social and medical power of some old people in the UK with the powerlessness of the majority who were in many respects quite erroneously perceived as burdens on society, and whom they routinely and often unwillingly and unnecessarily oppressed.

The current situation in the UK

In the UK as in most industrial societies the proportion of the population over 40 is on the increase and many of those over 55 find themselves, for 'ageist' reasons, forced to accept early retirement and compulsory redundancies (Reday-Mulvey and Taylor, 1996). However it is helpful to understand a little more fully the kinds of misconceived assumptions and thinking that have accompanied the ageism currently rampant in the UK, and which concern work and employment in particular and economic life in general.

One such idea is that of post-industrial society, a fatuous product of wishful thinking on the part of people brought up to despise work in manufacturing. Although it is true – because the work is largely mechanised and automated – that only about one in fifty of the UK labour work force works on assembly lines in manufacturing and well under one in ten inside a factory of any kind, about two thirds of all jobs can be described as 'goods-related', as dependent for their existence on manufacturing (Cohen and Zyman, 1987; Delbridge and Lowe, 1998). Thus apart from those within factories, many more jobs are 'upstream' of them, in market research, technical development, finance and so on, and many more, too, are 'downstream' ones, such as all those involving the distribution, sale, hiring, maintenance, repair and disposal of goods. And moving from production to consumption, we live in a highly and increasingly gadget-dependent 'self-service economy', in which all sorts of service once performed by and bought from other people are now done by privately owned machines, as in entertainment, transport, communicating information, washing clothes and many other activities (Gershuny, 1978; Gershuny and Miles, 1983). The idea and/or myth of post-industrial society is based partly on the notion of manual labour in fields, mines, workshops and factories, being increasingly replaced by the superficially more intellectual kind in services. It tends to assume that the need for physical effort at work is ever-diminishing, so that full-time labour can and should be increasingly reserved for the young, and with there being less and less need for older people to work at all.

Another relevant, influential and equally dubious notion is the 'lump of labour fallacy', which argues that there is only a fixed amount of work needing to be done at a given time. Apart from anything else, it is self-contradictory and amoral, because whenever part of a labour force is poor and unemployed, work is needed to increase their incomes, skills and employment opportunities. Also, and although globalisation is a seriously over-valued notion (Hirst, 1995), it is clear that we do live in an interdependent world containing great poverty and injustice, and it seems selfish as well as economically naïve to argue that there is a need for only so much employment to be available and for only so much work to be done at any time.

The equally dubious idea of the demographic time bomb is much less subtly connected with age discrimination. Here is it suggested that a populace largely consisting of under-twenties, self-indulgent early retirees and senile geriatrics is going to be kept together mainly by over-working the minority in employment, who are largely aged between 25 and 50. This supposed problem is exaggerated beyond anything that can be supported with statistical or other evidence. As noted, most people are living much healthier and longer lives than in the past, meaning that the employable population is much larger, and that we confronted, not with a threat, but with a great opportunity for people to have much more varied and fulfilling lives than was ever possible in the past. Unfortunately the thinking of many people is still locked into what might sensibly be described as an early twentieth century bureaucratic time warp. When the pension age was fixed at 65, very few people lived for many years after 70, and pensions were not the necessary burden that they may now become unless we flexibly adjust our rules about employment and retirement to match our achievement in producing so many strong and fit mature people in their sixties, seventies, eighties and so on. Thus we need to re-adjust our thinking about the life cycle and stop putting so much responsibility on to young shoulders, and allow young people more time to educate and develop themselves for a far wider and more complicated world than the one that their parents and grandparents grew up in. We also need to give more authority back, in considered and discriminating ways, to people of experience and achievement. We should go back to regarding growing older and wiser as life-enhancing achievements, not as threatening, ugly, useless and 'boring' things.

Also for the future, it would seem sensible to acknowledge and debate the parts played in ageist behaviour by and the needs of vested interests of every kind, including some affluent and some impoverished early retirees and the unemployed young, insurance companies with pension plans to sell, age-based groupings of managers, members of salaried occupations and professions with long incremental scales, and the beauty, fashion and entertainment and other leisure sectors. It is of course vital to make the physiological potentials and capacities of older and younger people more widely known (cf. Nichols and Evangelisti, 2000). It is also very important for as many people as possible to understand why age discrimination is not a minor issue or isolated phenomenon, and some of the reasons why it is sometimes mistakenly thought of as such. One danger is that we will continue to look on it simply as a problem and on old and young people as burdens and threats respectively, whereas in the factually correct words of a slightly mawkish popular song about children, *both* older *and* young people are 'the future'.

The market will ultimately resolve many of the issues that we have discussed. No-one is going to tolerate most of those aged over 45 being retired and living into their eighties and nineties, supported along with most of those under twenty-five, largely by people aged 25 to 45. But the issues will continue to blow up in our faces if we over-react to them by ghettoising the young through commercial exploitation and social and moral neglect and by trying to pacify older people with a mixture of early retirement and thinly disguised contempt. Moves towards practical solutions could include making more of the rights and responsibilities of young people co-equal, and by older people refusing to irresponsibly take sides, either as punitive authoritarians or trendy liberalisers. They should include a new recognition of the rather elementary fact that youth is primarily a time for learning, and that it is wrong to worship and to over-lavishly reward its beauty and strength, so that it is not wrong for the incomes of young people to reflect their inexperience, as well as being enough to allow them to live and develop. Similarly, older people with established and paid-for homes and independent adult children might sensibly be expected to make limited economic sacrifices as a consequence, and to adjust gradually to withdrawing from the labour force by working for fewer and fewer days per week until they are in their seventies, eighties or older. This is not to advocate inflexible and authoritarian, only more complicated and diverse, practices and rules concerning the dependence that grows as increasing numbers of increasingly diverse people grow older. It is to suggest that ideas about need, contribution and justice should start to play larger parts in our lives again, in the post-Thatcher Shock period of the UK's history. It is, also, to suggest that the transition from middle to old age should be turned into a more protracted, thoughtful and dignified one that it often currently is, with the forms of involvement in society or on its sidelines changing from hard work to a mixture of passing knowledge and experience on, work of a non-onerous (as individually experienced) character, and to relaxing, reflecting and resting. It most certainly implies the partial abolition of the notion of the old age pensioner and of permanent retirement as conventionally practised.

Two practical points concerning age discrimination should now be spelt out. First, it is not entirely fair, however tempting, to argue that it is unjust to expect an older employed person to 'make way' for a younger one as it is to expect someone from one ethnic group to give up their livelihood for someone from another, even if there is sometimes something very unpleasant, even mildly fascist, in the attitudes of some people to older as well as younger employees and managers. It is perfectly true that, in general, there are important, strong and statistically significant links between lack of ability and lack of years, that on the whole ability declines with youth, but as almost all of us know, the relevant tendencies are only very general ones! Not only is age, like youth, sometimes disabling, but there are also of course plenty of occasions when some of the age-related attributes of younger employees are preferable, for practical and entirely fair reasons, to those of older ones, and vice-versa. Second, when young managers baulk at the idea of supervising older staff, the solution is not to refuse to appoint (or promote) anyone unless they are younger than the managers are themselves. The solution may be training of the young managers, direct guidance and help from above, or even the occasional appropriate demotion or promotion. There is also a fair amount of evidence which suggests that older people can feel enlivened and encouraged and perfectly comfortable working as subordinates of younger people whom they have cause to respect and like. However the main thing is to openly confront and solve the relevant problems in all their glorious diversity and complexity, not to ignore them, to debate them endlessly, or worst of all, to institutionalise, exacerbate and 'manage' them with politically correct and inflexible bureaucratic rules.

Conclusion

We have argued that ageism affects people of all ages, and that age discrimination is always intertwined in various ways with life cycles and divisions of labour, and present in one form or another in most societies. In the present UK context and to many people it *appears* to be directed more against older people than younger ones, although it affects people of all ages considerably, and to be connected with modernist impulses, anomic divisions of labour and 'postmodern' economic, moral and social confusion. More generally, and in all societies, it tends to have strong links with managerialism, which is arguably the dominant economic and political ideology of the late twentieth century and of the putatively postmodern as well as the modern era. For the UK and its future, we regard ageism and age discrimination, cruel and incompetent as they so often are, nonetheless more as evidence of a number of opportunities, economic, political and social, rather than as very serious threats.

References

Aiken, L. (1978), *Later Life*, Saunders, Philadelphia.

Albert, M. (1993), *Capitalism versus Capitalism*, Whurr, London.

Anderson, D. (ed.) (1996), *Gentility Recalled*, London, The Social Affairs Unit.

Arber, S. and Ginn, J. (1991), *Gender and Later Life*, Sage, London.

Biggs, S. (1993), *Understanding Ageing*, Open University Press, Buckingham.

Bytheway, Bill (1995), *Ageism*, Open University Press, Buckingham.

Chapra, M.U. (1979), *The Islamic Welfare State and its Role in the Economy*, The Islamic Foundation, Leicester.

Chia, R. and Glover, I. (1995), 'Seven Dialectics of Modernism', paper presented at *the Second International Conference on Professions and Management*, Stirling, August 1995.

Cole, T.R. (1986), 'The "enlightened view" of aging: Victorian morality in a new key', in T.R. Cole and S.A. Gadow (eds), *What Does it Mean to Grow Old? Reflections from the Humanities*, Duke University Press, Durham NC.

Cole, T.R. (1992), *The Journey of Life: A Cultural History of Aging in America*, Cambridge University Press, Cambridge.

Crouch, C. and Marquand, D. (eds) (1993), *Ethics and Markets: Cooperation and Competition within Capitalist Economics*, Blackwell, Oxford.

Derrida, J. (1976), *Of Grammatology*, John Hopkins University Press, Baltimore.

Derrida, J. (1978), *Writing and Difference*, Routledge and Kegan Paul, London.

Derrida, J. (1981), *Position*, University of Chicago Press, Chicago.

Dingley, J. (1996), 'Durkheim, Professional and Moral Integration', in (eds) I. Glover and M., Hughes, *The Professional – Managerial Class: Contemporary British Management in the Pursuer Mode*, Avebury, Aldershot.

Durkheim, E. (1933), *The Division of Labour in Society*, Free Press, New York.

Durkheim, E. (1957), *Professional Ethics and Civil Morals*, Routledge, London.

Enteman, W.F. (1993), *Managerialism: The Emergence of a New Ideology*, The University of Wisconsin Press, Madison, Wisconsin.

Featherstone, M. and Wernick, A. (1995), *Images of Ageing: Cultural Representations of Later Life*, Routledge, London.

Featherstone, M. and Wernick, A. (1995b), 'Images of Positive Ageing: A Case Study of Retirement Choice Magazine', in M. Featherstone and A. Wernick (eds) (1995), op cit.

Gellner, E. (1964), *Thought and Change*, Weidenfield and Nicholson, London.

Gershuny, J. (1978), *After Industrial Society*, Macmillan, London.

Gershuny, J. and Miles, I.D. (1983), *The New Service Economy*, Frances Pinter, London.

Ginn, J. and Arber, S. (1996), 'Gender, Age and Attitudes to Retirement in Mid-Life', *Ageing and Society*, 16, pp. 27-55.

Glover, I.A. (1995), 'History and Saga in Management and Organization: Ford and Sloan, Amundsen and Scott, Franklin and Rae', paper presented to conference on *Dissent in Management Thought*, London, December 1995.

Hallier, J., Glover, I. and Lyon, P. (1993), 'The Ageism Taboo in Human Resource Management Research', paper presented to *the 1993 Annual Conference on the Labour Process*, Blackpool.

Hampden-Turner, C. and Trompenaars, F. (1993), *The Seven Cultures of Capitalism*, Doubleday, New York.

Hirst, P. (1996), 'Globaloney', *Prospect*, February 1996, pp. 29-33.

Hofstede, G. (1980), *Culture's Consequences*, Sage, Beverly Hills and London.

Itzin, C. (1986), 'Ageism Awareness Training', in C. Philipson, P. Strange and M. Bernard (eds), *Dependency and Interdependecy in Old Age*, Gower, London.

Jackall, R. (1998), *Moral Mazes: Inside the World of Corporate Managers*, Oxford University Press, Oxford.

Kelly, M. and Glover, I. (1996), 'In Search of Health and Efficiency: The NHS 1948-1994', in J.W. Leopold, I.A. Glover and M.D. Hughes (eds), *Beyond Reason: The National Health Service and the Limits of Management*, Avebury, Aldershot.

Lane, C. (1989), *Management and Labour in Europe: The Industrial Enterprise in Germany, Britain and France*, Edward Elgar, Aldershot.

Leopold, J.W., Glover, I.A. and Hughes, M.D. (1996) (eds), *Beyond Reason: The National Health Service and the Limits of Management*, Avebury, Aldershot.

Lehman, H.C. (1953), *Age and Achievement*, N.J. Princeton University Press, Princeton.

Locke, R.R. (1996a), *The Collapse of the American Management Mystique*, Oxford University Press, Oxford.

Locke, R.R. (1996b), 'The Limits of America's *Pax Oeconomica*: Germany and Japan after World War II', in I. Glover and M. Hughes (eds), *The Professional-Managerial Class: Contemporary British Management in the Pursuer Mode*, Avebury, Aldershot.

Moore, S. (1996), 'Takin' Out My Generation', *The Guardian*, 16 May 1996, p. 5.

Nichols, A. and Evangelisti, W. (2000), 'Fitness for work: the effects of ageing and the benefits of exercise', Chapter 16 of this book.

Pilcher, J. (1996), 'Transitions To and From the Labour Market: Younger and Older People and Employment', *Work, Employment and Society*, Vol. 10, No. 1, pp. 161-73.

Reday-Mulvey, G. and Taylor, P. (1996), 'Why Working Lives Must be Extended', *People Management*, 16 May 1996, pp. 24-29.

Reed, M. and Anthony, P. (1992), 'Professionalizing Management and Managing Professionalization: British Management in the 1980s', *Journal of Management Studies*, Vol. 29, No. 5, pp. 591-613.

Snow, C.P. (1964), *The Two Cultures and a Second Look*, Cambridge University Press, Cambridge.

Sorge, A. (1978), 'The Management Tradition: A Continental View', in M. Fores and I. Glover (eds), *Manufacturing and Management*, HMSO, London.
Taylor, P.E. and Walker, A. (1994), 'The Ageing Workforce: Employers' Attitudes Towards Older People', *Work, Employment and Society*, Vol. 8, No. 4, pp. 569-91.
Veblen, T. (1921), *The Engineers and the Price System*, Viking, New York.
Wada, S. (1995), 'The Status and Image of the Elderly in Japan: Understanding the Paternalistic Ideology', in M. Featherstone and A. Wernick (eds), *Images of Ageing: Cultural Representations of Later Life*, Routledge, London.
Worsley, R. (1996a), 'Only Prejudices and Old are Tired', *People Management*, 11 January 1996.
Worsley, R. (1996b), *Age and Employment*, Age Concern England, London.

4 The plateaued manager: the anatomy of an ageist stereotype

Peter Herriot

Introduction

Management rhetoric is always on the lookout for heroes and villains. Its heroes over the last few decades have been several, each candidate having to make way for the next as they turn out to have feet of clay. So in the 1970s, the heroes were the leaders of great corporations (Conger, 1989). But as many of the so-called excellent companies rapidly lost their pre-eminence, the front line workforce took their place as the golden boys and girls of the management press (Wickens, 1987). As the attraction of the Total Quality movement faded, so too did the image of the worker hero. Finally in the 1990s, the fashionable hero was the changemaker (Katzenbach, 1995), the young thruster who disregards procedures, challenges authority, and gets things done. It is hard to think where the next heroes will come from, as the gurus have trawled organisations from top to bottom for candidates already.

Villains have been fairly thick on the ground too. On the principle that we prefer to attribute our successes to ourselves but our failures to others, most villains have come from outside the organisational structure. We have blamed the unions for sabotaging our success (Kelly, 1990) and wily orientals for stealing our ideas (Ohmae, 1985). But apart from the usual references to lazy workers, the most frequent internal scapegoat has been the middle manager. Middle managers have been stigmatised as the wet blanket which prevents the vision and mission so brilliantly formulated by the Board from percolating down into the organisation. Or they stifle any good innovation from the shopfloor or the office for fear that it will decrease their power and lose them their jobs. The worst villain of all is the plateaued middle manager, and it is this stereotype that I will seek to examine in this chapter.

Before doing so, however, it is important to consider the process of *attribution* in a little more detail. Attribution refers to the psychological process of allocating a cause to an action or event. In its original formulation, the theory distinguished two sorts of attribution that we habitually make; internal attributions to the person, and external attributions to other people or other elements of the situation (Kelley, 1972). Subsequently it has been recognised that there are many other forms of attribution, for example, we may make an internal attribution either to ability or to effort (Weiner, 1985). However for the purposes of our discussion here, I will concentrate upon the simple distinction between internal and external attributions.

It is no accident that the popular management literature looks for heroes and, sometimes, villains to explain organisational success and failure. It is because this literature emanates mostly from the United States, a nation whose culture is particularly characterised by internal attributions of causality (Trompenaars and Hampden-Turner, 1993). In American culture, it is the individual who is responsible for what happens, and who has the capacity to change outcomes, provided only that they have energy and self belief. An internal locus of control is a desirable managerial characteristic (Rotter, 1966), and those who explain bad outcomes in terms of unavoidable external events are merely seeking to deflect the blame from themselves; so runs the internal attributional bias.

It is in this context that we should examine the stereotype of *the plateaued manager*. For here if anywhere is an example of an attribution to the person when an attribution to the situation would be a more reasonable account of causality. First I will trace the use of the stereotype in the academic literature, and then demonstrate that a situational attribution fits the facts far better. Finally, I will discuss in more general terms the use of this rhetoric in managerial discourse, with particular reference to its ageist assumptions.

The villain is identified

Ference and colleagues (Stoner and Warren, 1977) were the first to identify academically the plateaued manager as a villain. They assessed 55 American executives along two dimensions using unstructured interviews. These were their perceived likelihood of future promotion and their current performance. Using the 2x2 matrix so beloved of management writers, they identified four categories of executive: *stars*, who scored high on both dimensions; *comers*, high on promotion but low on performance; *solid citizens*, low on promotion but high on performance; and *deadwood*, low on both. Stars and comers are clearly upwardly mobile, whereas solid citizens and deadwood are plateaued. Comers are weak performers only because they have recently reached their current levels. Deadwood, on the other hand, are former solid citizens who have declined.

Already we have here the hint of villainy, but it was to be extended by Feldman and Weitz (1988). These authors redefined plateauing as follows: 'an employee may be considered plateaued if his or her likelihood of receiving further assignments of increased responsibility is low'. They attribute plateauing to six factors, as follows. These were individual skills and abilities: the individual is incapable of progressing further; individual needs and values: the individual does not want to progress further; lack of intrinsic motivation: the individual is not interested by his or her job; lack of extrinsic rewards: few salary rises or promotions, and perceived inequity; stress and burnout: the individual cannot take it any more; and slow organisational growth: the opportunities are not there.

To be fair to all these authors, not all of their attributions are internal, although it is noteworthy that it is the internal, personal reasons for plateauing that are more numerous and are adduced first. Managers themselves have a strong sense of being ahead of their career timetables, on time, or behind time, where timetable is defined by the grade you have reached by a certain age (Lawrence, 1984). Indeed, there is a marked tendency by older managers to believe that they are behind, when in fact they are not (as judged by the actual age-grade distribution). Apparently they underestimate the number of older people in particular grades (Lawrence, 1988). However, the concept of the deadwood plateaued manager had gained credence and entered into the academic vocabulary of management. With it came some legitimacy for the already prevalent assumption that deadwood by definition should be cut down and cleared out. It therefore fitted in well with the increasing contemporary requirement to downsize in order to cut costs. And it directed the attention of the cost cutters to a clearly defined category of persons so that they did not have to go through the difficult task of deciding why particular individuals should stay or leave. Membership of the category was often reason enough.

The real reasons for plateauing

Yet all the evidence we have points to other reasons than their own shortcomings for managers to become plateaued. There is of course the ludicrously obvious fact that nearly all *organisational structures* are pyramidic in shape, and therefore it is impossible for everyone to continue an upward progression until they leave or retire. It is far more likely that plateauing is the cause rather than the effect of low motivation and performance. The evidence shows clearly that the higher individuals are in the hierarchy the longer they remain in a particular job (Herriot et al, 1994). And the longer they remain in a job the less satisfied and the more bored they become (Herriot et al, 1996).

As we might expect, different organisational *business strategies* result in different career structures, and so in different levels of opportunity. Using Miles and Snow's (1978) well known categorisation of corporate strategies, a Defender organisation aiming to keep its share of a static market contained more plateaued managers in general and more deadwood plateaued managers in particular than did an Analyser (the latter both defends its existing markets and moves cautiously into new ones) (Slocum et al, 1985). Another structural predictor of how far up an individual will go is simply *organisational size.* There is much more potential progress to be made in larger organisations, not least because they are more likely to promote from within than are smaller ones (Dalton and Kesner, 1983). However, there is also evidence that the distance up the hierarchy that an individual will progress is predictable on the basis of events much earlier in their career within an organisation. Specifically, the longer they stayed in their first job (Rosenbaum, 1979), or at least their position after their first seven years in the organisation (Forbes, 1987), predicted how far up they would progress. The analogy drawn is with a tournament, where failure in an early round is fatal.

And of course, there are always *politics and patronage* as reasons for upward progression. Belonging to some functions is certainly more career progressive than belonging to others (Sheridan et al, 1990), and visibility in the shape of headquarters postings or high profile projects also helps (Nicholson and West, 1988). As for patronage, one does not even need a real patron to get ahead; to be perceived to have one is sufficient to boost one's reputation as a good performer (Kilduff and Krackhardt, 1994)!

So the evidence clearly refutes the stereotype of managers becoming plateaued because they are lacking in ability or motivation. There is a whole range of situational factors which are alternative explanations. However, it is of more importance and interest to ask why such rhetorical stereotypes are formed, and what functions they perform.

The justificatory function of managerial rhetoric

We may distinguish several functions served by managerial rhetoric (Herriot, Hirsh and Reilly, 1998). First comes the *aspirational*. This is in order to make clear to the rest of the organisation what it is that top management has decided should be their aim or aspiration. It is an easy and slippery slope from speaking in terms of what we would like to happen to speaking as though it is already happening, often by picking up on supposed advance indicators. And it is a further easy descent into believing this propaganda. From the statement of aspiration and intent, we have moved to an attempt at encouragement and persuasion, and from thence to self-delusion.

A second and related function is *presentational*. Those using rhetoric seek to persuade others by changing their perceptions of the situation. If employees construe the situation as one of hope and opportunity instead of one of uncertainty and threat, runs the logic, they will act accordingly. This reasoning is based on the well-established psychological principle of cognitive dissonance (Festinger, 1957). If there is a gap between our thoughts and our actions, we will seek to reduce it by changing one or the other. So if we have already changed people's perceptions as a consequence of the rhetoric, they will change their behaviour to reduce the dissonance (the discomfort they feel about the gap between their beliefs and their behaviour).

A third and final function is that of *rationalisation*, either of what has already occurred, or of what is presently going on. Such rationalisation can serve to help the actor by enabling them to make sense of the situation, so that, for example, the phrase 'emergent strategy' has been coined to describe reacting to changes in the business situation (Mintzbirg, 1994). It is also used by way of justification of managerial actions to others (Weick, 1995).

It is worth asking which rhetorical function is being served by the use of the plateaued manager stereotype. The evidence points towards the third and last of those I have described above: that of justification for actions being or already having been taken. The evidence is to be found in the content of the other rhetorics which surround its use. The first of these we may term the rhetoric of *the virtue of the new.*

Managerial rhetoric cleverly capitalises on our preferences for thinking in categorical, and often binary categorical, terms rather than in terms of trends and continua. So we have a plethora of pronouncements from gurus proclaiming the demise of one category and its replacement by another. The job is dead, announces one guru (Bridges, 1995); long live Me plc. Hierarchy is doomed, preaches another; chaos and anarchy rule OK (Peters, 1992). We are in the midst of the information revolution, alleges a third; the past is indeed history, a different era which has little in common with the future (Rifkin, 1995). Such transformational changes are presented as inevitable, and therefore whether they are in themselves good or bad for us, we must prepare for them and adapt to them. In order to help us do so, we must be persuaded that *new is by definition good and old is bad.*

Old habits and practices are bad, old structures and ways of working are bad, old products and services are bad. And by extension, so are those associated with these old things. And who may they be? Why, *old employees* of course, old in terms of service and therefore more likely to be older in terms of age too.

Association with bad old things leads to an assumption of hostility to good new things. Deadwood acts as a blockage, preventing its replacement by fruitful new branches. Any historical memory which warns on the basis of previous experience against a particular course of action is categorised as *resistance to change*, and only what is to be expected of old deadwood. Flexibility is to be found only in young shoots.

Such rhetoric is supported by the *culture* rhetoric. This makes the unitarist assumption that an organisation possesses a single culture (Keenoy, 1990), rather than subsuming several subcultures based on occupational groupings, organisational level, and the like (Van Maanen and Barley, 1984). Hence transformational change requires a change of culture: new beliefs, values, artefacts, and behaviour. Who are the representatives of the bad old culture? Why, by definition those who have been here a long time. They represent beliefs and values which must change. They will either change their beliefs and values by the end of the culture change programme, or they must go. For otherwise they are putting a brake on the change which we must pass through or perish.

Underpinning these justificatory rhetorics is their rational and scientific foundation: the rhetoric of *Human Resource Management* (Legge, 1995). Resources are what you own and use. You may husband them or you may use them up. But your aim is to rationally optimise their productivity so as to best achieve business objectives. Within this rhetoric it is entirely justifiable to cut out dead wood and cast it aside. Indeed, it is so self-evidently prudent that the annual reports of large companies boast on the same page about record profits and record downsizing (Galbraith, 1992).

What is being justified by the rhetoric?

The general rhetorical context of the specific deadwood plateaued manager rhetoric has pointed us towards the conclusion that its purpose is primarily *justificatory*. This is because the whole thrust of 'new is good, old is bad' is around the assumed importance and value of change itself. And change is what top management has sponsored in the recent past and continues to do so.

The last fifteen years have seen major changes in organisations. Some of these have been in response to demands for short term dividends for shareholders (Hutton, 1994), a pressure which leads to redundancies as the quickest way of cutting costs and showing good bottom line figures. The fact that over the longer term, such tactics have not enhanced profitability, or various other financial indices of success, has only recently been demonstrated (De Meuse, Vanderheiden and Bergmann, 1994; Cascio, 1994). Other changes have appeared to be fashionable, for example, the devolution of budgetary responsibility to smaller and smaller business units, or the wholesale adoption of a sequence of management fads which addressed the issues of the time. The question we need to ask is, *what particular organisational actions is the plateaued manager rhetoric designed to justify*?

One answer is at a fairly specific level of analysis. Whatever the reality of the historical record, it was generally accepted, at least after the second world war, that the jobs of managers and professionals were reasonably secure. Whilst operatives and office personnel did not assume their jobs were secure, those who had achieved management status not only believed they were, but also aspired to regular promotion and pay rises. The fundamental distinction in the organisational hierarchy was between management and the rest, and top management could rely implicitly on middle managers as their agents to implement policy. During the 1980s and early 1990s, downsizing occurred for middle managers and professionals as well as for the workforce. The danger was that top management would lose the loyalty, or at least the compliance, of the managers who remained after downsizing. The psychological divide, top management feared, would be between themselves and everyone else, and nothing would get implemented properly. Hence the use of the deadwood manager stereotype enabled them to *justify their actions to the survivors*. For it permitted them to scapegoat those made redundant as deadwood; then they could argue that it was only those who failed to add value who were being made redundant. Those who remained were still, of course, valued partners of top management and had a long term future in the company.

The second justification is at a more general level of analysis. If change programmes are promoted and pursued with the usual high-flown rhetoric, and if hopes and expectations for successful outcomes are encouraged, then *what happens when they fail to have the desired transformational effect*? Blame for the failure has to be laid somewhere. It is hard to blame the intervention itself for being inadequate, since part of the marketing hype used by the consultants has been the endorsements by famous CEOs of famous companies of how well Business Process Reengineering, Total Quality Management, Performance Related Pay and so on worked for them. It is not in top management's nature to blame themselves for choosing an inappropriate intervention, so their best plan is to agree with the consultants that it did not work on this occasion because it was not carried right through to the end. If it had been, then of course all the advertised benefits would have accrued. Then the search is on for a scapegoat, a villain to blame for this failure of implementation. What more obvious place to look than those who are generally responsible for implementing top management's decisions: middle managers?

At a yet more general level of self-justification, many top managers are insecure in their own power and authority. It has been argued that many conceive of real or imaginary threats to their positions (de Vries, 1994). They may react by attracting to themselves those who give them unconditional admiration, scapegoating any critic as personally disloyal. They may tolerate mediocrity and denigrate stars because the success of others reflects badly on them. They may seek to control everything and everyone so that nothing can get out of control and harm them. In all of these defensive manoeuvres, *they need people to blame*. In such situations of exclusion, middle managers are the ideal scapegoat, for they have not the power base to fight back.

The failure of the deadwood rhetoric

Whatever the reasons for the justificatory use of the plateaued manager rhetoric, it is very clear that this particular rhetoric has failed to convince. This is because *the actions of top management have evidently contradicted their rhetoric*.

First, employees have asked, if plateaued managers were such a liability, why is it that we see them back within a few weeks as consultants on much higher pay? Or why do they succeed in getting equally good jobs with our competitors? If these management fads that top management keeps on falling for are such wonderful things, why is it that every single one of them dies a death? Surely you cannot blame middle management every time? And if top management deserves respect and has the best interest of the organisation at heart, why do they award themselves huge benefits even when we are failing financially? Surely it is they and not plateaued managers who are failing to put their organisations' interests first?

In sum, there is major mistrust of top management, and it is due in no small measure to its use of rhetoric. Middle managers' subordinates and colleagues know at first hand how hard they work now that their numbers have been culled. Middle managers have never worked longer hours, nor been under such stress (Institute of Management, 1996). When rhetoric is at odds with employees' own experience, experience generally wins out and the motives of those responsible for the rhetoric begin to be questioned. When the purpose of the rhetoric is believed to be to justify their own mistakes, then both the integrity and the competence of the rhetoricians is in doubt. It is no wonder that the British have the lowest opinion of top management of any European country (International Survey Research, 1996).

But the demographic ageing of the workforce is gaining momentum (Employment Gazette, 1994). The increased number of women managers is making the old age-grade equation outmoded. And managers and professionals are predicted to become in greater demand in the labour market (Institute for Employment Research, 1994). So the boot will indeed be on the other foot. Instead of attributing to middle managers the responsibility for outcomes which are in fact the consequence of changing markets, technology, legislation and structures, and of their own difficulties in coping with these changes, top management may come round to eschewing such rhetoric in all its forms.

Instead, top management will need to concentrate on the regaining of the trust which they have dissipated over the last several years. They will take some public responsibility themselves for the low levels of morale and trust currently prevalent; make some specific deal, and then keep their side of the bargain come hell or high water; establish a reputation for trustworthiness by keeping several different deals; and come to identify with employees so that they can empathise with them and enjoy mutual respect (Kramer, Brewer and Hanna, 1996).

For unless trust is regained, employees will be unwilling to commit themselves to the career transitions which changes in the business environment will undoubtedly require them to make.

All this is a long way from the ageist stereotype of the deadwood middle manager. However, the history and uses of that stereotype, and its unfortunate consequences for its users as well as its sufferers, indicate that much managerialist rhetoric probably has the opposite effects to those intended. The fact that employees now fail to succumb to rhetoric, though, suggests that trust will be hard to re-establish.

References

Bridges, W. (1995), *Jobshift: How to Prosper in a Workplace without Jobs*, Nicholas Brealey, London.

Cascio, W.F. (1994), 'Downsizing: What do we know? What have we learned?', *Academy of Management Executive*, Vol. 7, pp. 95-104.

Conger, J.A. (1989), *The Charismatic Leader: Behind the Mystique of Exceptional Leadership*, Jossey-Bass, San Francisco.

Dalton, D.R. and Kesner, I.F. (1983), 'Inside/outside succession and organisation size: the pragmatics of executive replacement', *Academy of Management Journal*, Vol. 26, pp. 736-42.

DeMeuse, K.P., Vanderheiden, P.A. and Bergmann, T.J. (1994), 'Announced lay-offs: their effect on corporate financial performance', *Human Resource Management*, Vol. 33, No. 4, pp. 509-30.

Employment Gazette 1994, HMSO, London.

Feldman, D.C. and Weitz, B.A. (1988), 'Career plateaus reconsidered', *Journal of Management*, 14, 1, pp. 69-90.

Ference, T.P., Stoner, J.A.F. and Warren, E.K. (1977), 'Managing the career plateau', *Academy of Management Review*, Vol. 2, pp. 602-12.

Festinger, L. (1957), *A Theory of Cognitive Dissonance*, Harper and Row, New York.

Forbes, J.B. (1987), 'Early intraorganisational mobility: patterns and influences', *Academy of Management Journal*, Vol. 30, No. 1, pp. 110-25.

Galbraith, J.K. (1992), *The Culture of Contentment*, Houghton Mifflin, New York.

Herriot, P., Gibbons, P., Pemberton, C. and Jackson, P. (1994), 'An empirical model of managerial careers in organisations', *British Journal of Management*, Vol. 5, pp. 113-121.

Herriot, P., Hirsh, W. and Reilly, P. (1998), *Trust and Transformation: Managing the Employment Relationship*, Wiley, Chichester.

Herriot, P., Pemberton, C. and Hawtin, E. (1996), 'The career attitudes and intentions of managers in the finance sector', *British Journal of Management*, Vol. 7, pp. 181-90.

Hutton, W. (1994), *The State We're In*, Jonathan Cape, London.

Institute for Employment Research (1994), *Review of the Economy and Employment: Occupational Assessment*, University of Warwick, Warwick.

Institute of Management (1996), *Are Managers Under Stress?*, Institute of Management, London.

International Survey Research (1996), *Employee Satisfaction*, Tracking European Trends, London.

Katzenbach, J. (1995), *Real Change Leaders*, McKinsey, New York.

Keenoy, T. (1990), 'HRM: a case of the wolf in sheep's clothing?', *Personnel Review*, Vol. 19, No. 2, pp. 3-9.

Kelley, H.H. (1972), 'Attribution theory in social interaction', in E. Jones, D.E. Kanouse, H.H. Kelley, R.E. Nisbett, S. Valins, and B. Weiner (eds), *Attribution: Perceiving the Causes of Behaviour,* General Learning Press, Morristown NJ.

Kelly, J.E. (1990), *British trade unionism 1979-1989: change, continuity, and contradictions*, Work, Employment and Society, Vol. 4, pp. 29-65.

Kets de Vries, M.F.R. (1994), 'The leadership mystique', *Academy of Management Executive*, Vol. 8, No. 3, pp. 73-89.

Kilduff, M. and Krackhardt, D. (1994), 'Bringing the individual back in: a structural analysis of the internal market for reputation in organisations', *Academy of Management Journal*, Vol. 37, No. 1, pp. 87-108.

Kramer, R.M., Brewer, M.B. and Hanna, B.A. (1996), 'Collective trust and collective action: the decision to trust as a social decision', in R. M. Kramer and T.R. Tyler (eds), *Trust in Organisations: Frontiers of Theory and Research*, Prentice Hall, Englewood Cliffs NJ.

Lawrence, B.S. (1984), 'Age grading: the implicit organisational timetable', *Journal of Occupational Behaviour*, Vol. 5, pp. 23-35.

Lawrence, B.S. (1988), 'New wrinkles in the theory of age: demography, norms and performance ratings', *Academy of Management Journal*, Vol. 31, pp. 309-37.

Legge, K. (1995), *Human Resource Management: Rhetorics and Realities*, Macmillan, London.

Miles, R.E. and Snow, C.C. (1978), *Organisational Strategy, Structure, and Process*, McGraw-Hill, New York.

Mintzberg, H. (1994), *The Rise and Fall of Strategic Planning: Reconceiving Roles for Planning, Plans, and Planners*, Free Press, New York.

Nicholson, M and West, M.A. (1988), *Managerial Job Change: Men and Women in Transition*, Cambridge University Press, Cambridge.

Ohmae, K. (1985), *Triad Power*, Free Press, New York.

Peters, T. (1992), *Liberation Management: Necessary Disorganisation for the Nanosecond Nineties*, Alfred A. Knopf, New York.

Rifkin, J. (1995), *The End of Work*, Putnam, New York.

Rosenbaum, J.E. (1979), 'Tournament mobility: career patterns in a corporation', *Administrative Science Quarterly*, Vol. 24, pp. 220-41.

Rotter, J. (1966), 'Generalised expectancies for internal versus external control of reinforcement', *Psychological Monographs*, Vol. 80, p. 609.

Sheridan, J.E., Slocum, J.W., Buda, R. and Thompson, R.C. (1990), 'Effects of corporate sponsorship and departmental power on career tournaments', *Academy of Management Journal*, Vol. 33, No. 3, pp. 578-603.

Slocum, J.W., Cron, W.L., Hansen, R.W. and Rawlings, S. (1985), 'Business strategy and the management of plateaued employees', *Academy of Management Journal*, Vol. 28, pp. 133-54.

Trompenaars, F. and Hampden-Turner, C., (1993), *Riding the Waves of Culture*, Nicholas Brealey, London.

Van Maanen, J. and Barley, S.R. (1984), 'Occupational communities: culture and control in organisations', in B.M. Staw and L.L. Cummings (eds) *Research in Organisational Behaviour*, Vol. 6, JAI Press, Greenwich CT.

Weick, K.E. (1995), *Sensemaking in Organisations*, Sage, Thousand Oaks,CA.

Weiner, B. (1985), 'Spontaneous causal thinking', *Psychological Bulletin*, Vol. 97, pp. 74-84.

Wickens, P.D. (1987), *The Road to Nissan*, Macmillan, London.

5 Discrimination by age: the organizational response

Ann E. McGoldrick and James Arrowsmith

Introduction

Awareness of the potentially unfair and inefficient nature of age discrimination in employment has begun to increase in recent years. Employer organizations and managerial professional bodies have, for example, begun to adopt statements and codes on age. Yet in the present buyer's market for labour, age barriers have continued to be used extensively. This applies most obviously in respect of recruitment and selection procedures, although other HRM internal organisational decision making practices, including training and promotion, merit review. In addition, many older workers have been encouraged or selected to leave the workforce as part of the focused reaction to 'downsizing' pressures. Criticism has focused upon the costs to employers, state and individuals. Despite responses from some companies, particularly in the growing service sectors (Arrowsmith and McGoldrick, 1994), organizational response has been sufficient to the problem and the proportion of older people in the labour force has continued to decline. Understanding of the extent, patterns and potential use of age in employment policy, however, remains weak. Managerial stereotyping must be a consideration, with older workers remaining the 'last resort' for many jobs (Thompson, 1991). In this chapter we seek to go further by examining the role of objective, organizational-level conditions and processes, as well as subjective stereotyping in determining age discriminatory.

Official concern regarding the use of age in employment decision-making has increased (e.g. Employment Department, 1991, 1994; House of Commons Employment Committee, 1989, 1991) while it has been acknowledged that recessionary climates have reinforced the practice of age discrimination in recruitment, selection and redundancy practices (e.g. Trinder, 1991; Laczko and Phillipson, 1991; Dibden and Hibbett, 1993; McGoldrick and Arrowsmith, 1993). The costs to be incurred at all levels may well continue to rise as the potential labour force continues to undergo a process of ageing (e.g. Johnson and Falkingham, 1992; McGoldrick, 1992). Relatively small numbers of employers, however, have been ready to develop an integrated and proactive approach to the older worker in their human resource planning (e.g. NEDO, 1989; Casey et al, 1993). The proportion of older people in the labour force has continued to decline, particularly in respect of men (Taylor and Walker, 1997). By 1993 it was reported that only just over half of men in the UK aged 60 to 64 were economically active (Taylor and Walker, 1996). Experimental research supports the hypothesis that negative stereotyping relating to competence and personality traits of older workers is extensive (e.g. Rosen and Jerdee, 1989; De Micco, 1989) while laboratory and case study research contradict the negative assumptions made concerning older worker performance and motivation (e.g. Davies et al, 1991; Warr, 1993), job satisfaction and organizational commitment (e.g. Bourne, 1982), incidence of turnover and consequently training investment (e.g. Elias et al, 1987). The wasteful and short-sighted policies towards them nevertheless remain (Department of Employment, 1994), with procedures frequently operating at an impressionate level and the lack of real directives to introduce and implement realistic equal opportunities measures at higher management levels. Likewise formalised processes and procedures may be resisted by line managements.

Two main sources of data are used to illustrate the problems faced by older employees. The first looks at potential for entry to the labour market, outlining some of the major findings from surveys of national recruitment advertising repeated in four years between 1981 and 1993. This research investigated 'age filters' in careers at this critical stage of the organizational resourcing process, which may be associated with a received conjunction of prior experience and potential for further internal development in the favoured age groups. This has, of course, only been the 'tip of the iceberg', since further practices in respect of selection at this stage will again intervene in the filtration exercise adopted by many organisations. The second study therefore provides a more intensive view of current perceptions of older employees within UK companies. This relates to an ESRC survey on age and employment conducted with a sample of the Institute of Management membership, examining individual experiences and attitudes, as well as organizational policy and practice across the range of employment practices. The results show how important both managerial stereotyping and organizational characteristics are within the process of change in determining the significance of age in employment decision making. This leads to discussion of managerial views on age as an equal opportunity issue.

The survey of recruitment advertising

The survey was designed to systematically measure the extent and patterns in the use of age, direct and implied, in recruitment advertising. Although focusing only on the most explicit stage of resourcing in the external labour market, a survey of this type can be used to create understanding and enable conclusions to be drawn in relation to the use of age as a benchmark in the development and delimiting of careers. Further detailed examination of the qualitative data drawn from the sample also provided an explanation of the underlying rationale in the use of age as a discriminator.

Context of the enquiry

Several previous investigations undertaken in recent years indicated the existence of age discrimination in employment advertising, with potentially widescale effects for older job seekers. Naylor (1987), for instance, found that 41 percent of advertisements sampled in the 'Sunday Times' contained references to age, while 32 percent of advertisements in the Institute of Personnel and Development (IPD) house journal 'Personnel Management' similarly carried discriminatory criteria. A wider survey of posts advertised in national and local press sources (Tillsley, 1990) suggested that 11 percent and 9.5 percent of adverts respectively imposed barriers on the basis of age. Research for the Department of Employment also revealed that 11 percent of advertisements placed within Job Centres excluded older applicants, while staff also tended to reinforce this informally in respect of many posts (Jones and Longstone, 1990; Taylor and Walker, 1991). Similarly, an unpublished survey carried out by Reed Employment (1991) revealed that 19 percent of a sample of personnel managers and directors from technical and engineering companies confirmed that they imposed upper age limits in their own advertising or when briefing a recruitment agency. Some evidence also existed in respect of the parameters of the practice of age discrimination. An upper age limit in the period between 40 and 50 was found to be common. A survey by MSL Advertising revealed that 88.5 percent of advertisements which referred to age placed an upper limit at 40 years, with 9 percent stating 40 to 45 and only 2.5 percent utilising a higher age bar (Heaton, 1989). Naylor (1990) also found that over two-thirds of discriminating advertisements in the sources surveyed targeted the 30 to 40 age group.

The source in which the advertisement was placed likewise appeared to be of relevance. Rock (1987) found that while only 15 percent of advertisements in 'The Times' were age specific, 25 percent of 'Daily Telegraph' job adverts and 40 percent of 'Financial Times' entries indicated preferred age-range. The findings of Tillsley (1990) confirm this differential, demonstrating higher rates of age discrimination for 'The Times' than for 'The Independent', 'Daily Express' or 'Daily Telegraph', and a significantly lower occurrence in 'The Guardian'. The relationship with posts advertised was obviously of interest here. Both Naylor (1987) and Tillsley (1990) noted, in fact, that private sector post advertisements were far more likely to contain discriminatory reference on the basis of age than those for public sector employment; as were those for managerial and white-collar positions in comparison to advertisements for blue-collar jobs, suggesting linkage to perceptions of career orientated posts (Jolly, Creigh and Mingay, 1980). Finally, it was suggested that where advertisements were placed through an intermediary agency, there was greater likelihood of the operation of age limits than when they were placed directly by the employers.

A more structured examination of recruitment advertising was suggested, which could provide a direct comparative analysis over a substantial period and permit differentiation on a range of attributes. The years 1981, 1986, 1991 and 1993 were selected as suitable indicators of a twelve year time span, which could also be related to changing economic conditions. The investigation focused upon major national newspapers: 'The Guardian', 'Times', 'Independent', 'Independent on Sunday', 'Sunday Times' and 'Financial Times'. The Independent newspapers were, of course, not in existence in the earliest years. Overall, however, the sample was fairly evenly distributed amongst the different sources. The Institute of Personnel and Development Journal 'Personnel Management' was also surveyed in order to permit comparison of the results with previous surveys and to obtain a sample representative of the personnel and training profession itself. In addition it permitted the evaluation of the effect of IPD policy activity introduced in respect of age discriminatory practices on employment recruitment advertising in this significant house journal in later years.

While a specific focus was to assess the use of age bars in recruitment advertising, it was noted that inferences regarding age related qualities might also be important in signalling preferred response. An attempt was therefore also made to measure the extent of indicated preference for or against particular age groups by means other than a direct use of age limits (e.g. 'young person required/preferred'), or indication of specific experience requirements (e.g. 'graduate plus two years post qualification work experience'); possibly together with, for example, potentially age stereotypical language, an emphasis on development or training or an accordingly 'appropriate' salary indicator. Job characteristics may be relevant criteria for selection (e.g. 'up to date', 'familiar with modern techniques', 'to fit into a young team') or again may indicate pre-determination of required attributes which can be displayed across the range of ages. Personal qualities (e.g. 'energy', 'dynamism', 'ambition') are by no means the prerogative of younger aged individuals, although reference may infer to the reader of the advertisement that, whilst not been excluded, assumptions are being made in respect of the type of applicant anticipated. The potential interpretative dangers here, however, demanded a strict approach and accordingly, advertisements were assessed as 'inferred' discriminatory only on the strictest of criteria.

Evidence of discrimination

Overall almost a third (27.1 percent) of the advertisements carried a directly stated upper age limit for potential applicants as shown in Table 5.1. The figures also suggest that the extent of the practice may have increased through the 1980s but declined in the 1990s. On the basis of inferred preference for younger candidates, a further 9.3 percent of advertisements appeared to carry this message strongly, a practice which again appears to have grown over the years but started to decrease at the time of the latest investigation. In sum, 36.4 percent of recruitment advertisements sampled appeared to exclude or inhibit older applicants, although over the period explicit age discrimination diminished. On the other hand, over the entire sample only ten advertisements appeared to infer a preference for relatively older candidates and a further seven directly stated that age would not be a consideration in the assessment of the applications.

Table 5.1 : Upper age bar use and inferred preference by year

Year	N	Upper age bar Stated (n)	%	Upper age bar inferred alone (n)	%	Upper age bar either stated or Inferred (n)	%
1981	639	(245)	38.3	(32)	5	(277)	43.3
1986	1078	(477)	44.2	(77)	7.1	(554)	51.4
1991	874	(199)	22.8	(43)	13.8	(242)	27.7
1993	2167	(365)	16.8	(169)	10	(534)	24.8
x^2(p=)		(.000)		(.001)		(.000)	
Total	4758	(1286)	27.1	(321)	9.3	(1607)	36.4

Where upper age bars were most commonplace it was in the 30s and 40s age-bands, while the 20s and 30s tended to be the most popular ages for lower age bars. For discriminatory employers at least, the 'golden age' for potential candidates appears to be in the 28-37 year range. Variations in the use of age as a recruitment filter were observed according to a number of criteria. Upper age barriers were, for example, more commonly incorporated in private sector advertisements, where over a third had a stated upper limit (33.9 percent) and in total 42.3 percent indicated a preference for younger people. In fact, 96.5 percent of all advertisements which indicated this were placed by private sector firms. In the public sector the practice of age referencing also continued to decrease steadily across across the four time periods. While one in ten public sector advertisements carried an age ceiling in 1981, only 1.6 percent did so by 1993. Low usage applied on a sub-sector basis in respect of arts, health, education and social services, with industrial (40.1 percent) organisations applying them more frequently than service sector ones (29.8 percent) generally. The latter were, however, more likely to utilise inferred upper age bars (18.2 percent in comparison to 15.1 percent). In total almost half (46.1 percent) of advertisements identified as industrial organizations either stated or implied an upper age limit, as did almost two fifths (39.8 percent) of services sector organisations.

In terms of more specific occupational patterns two broad groups were identified. The primary discriminating group related to finance and insurance, where 39.3 percent of advertisements carried an upper age bar, business consultancy (38.1 percent), sales and marketing (36.7 percent), secretarial (32.2 percent), personnel (30.6 percent), general line management (27.0 percent) and training (26.0 percent). The second and less explicitly discriminatory group consisted of information technology and computing (17.1 percent), technical and engineering posts (16.5 percent), administrative and clerical jobs (14.4 percent), creative and media (12.1 percent), research and scientific posts (9.0 percent) and legal (7.0 percent) employment advertisements. Qualitative data suggested that the most direct age discriminatory occupations involved direct selling and business generation, causing jobs to be 'pitched' and identified with aggressively individualistic and essentially youthful characteristics. The latter set of occupations may be more generally characterised as credentials, with potential for assessment more clearly linked to predefined skills, qualifications and experience requirements, rather than general personality related characteristics.

In respect of occupational level, senior positions appeared more likely to carry explicit age limits. In advertisements for more junior white collar positions, however, there was more likelihood of an inferred preference for younger applicants. As might be expected, the stated upper age limit tended to increase with the seniority of the post although at all levels the majority of upper age bars were placed prior to the age of 50.

Table 5.2 demonstrates a further interesting distinction in the use of age criteria on the basis of the method of placement of advertisement. For the sample as a whole, advertisements placed by recruitment agencies or other intermediaries were more likely to carry such a reference. In addition, agency advertisements in which the company remained anonymous were more likely to refer to age than those in which the company was named. In total a quarter (24.5 percent) of all directly placed advertisements indicated a preference for younger people, whereas the figure was doubled for advertisements placed by an agency. While this may indicate imposition of categorisation for ease of delineation of suitable candidates for either agency or client preference, there are possible intervening factors. The majority of private sector advertisements (54 percent), for example, where distinction is more frequent, are placed via intermediaries in comparison to low public sector use (5 percent). There may also be greater representation of less ostensibly 'discriminatory' occupational categories within those placed directly by organisational recruiters. It is also possible that agencies are more likely to be used for early and later career positions, particularly, for example, for 'head-hunting'.

Table 5.2 : Method of placement and the use of age

Placement Method	Lower bar (n)	%	Upper bar (n)	%	Inferred (n)	%	Total (n)	%
Direct	(509)	18.5	(434)	16.1	(145)	6.4	(579)	4.5
Agency (anon)	(827)	46.6	(769)	43.9	(157)	15.6	(926)	59.0
Agency (named)	(73)	33.5	(70)	32.1	(15)	10.1	(85)	42.2
B.O. number	(9)	8.4	(9)	18.4	(4)	10.0	(13)	19.4

There were also major differences between the vehicles in which the advertisements appeared. 'The Guardian' maintained a consistently strong record over the years in terms of low proportions of both direct and inferred age discriminatory measures; which represents a mixture of the 'culture' of the newspaper, including a stated policy of discouragement, together with the nature of some of the sectors to which it is targeted. Significantly higher levels in other daily papers, the 'Sunday Times' and 'Financial Times', possibly reflect the level of posts advertised and therefore choice of more exclusive/expensive advertising mechanisms. The case of 'Personnel Management' is of particular interest, demonstrating significant progress over the period. This concurs with the adoption of the IPD statement on Age and Employment, with the journal 'People Management' introducing a policy from January 1996 not to accept recruitment advertising containing references to age.

Management attitudes towards older employees

The principal objective of the ESRC/Institute of Management survey was to investigate in detail issues relating to discrimination within UK companies. This included policy and practice towards older employees, managers' perceptions in respect of age and their experience of the use of age as an employment decision criteria. The study linked to Government initiatives to encourage employers not to discriminate on the basis of age but to recognise the neglected skills and abilities of older people. The 'Campaign for Older Workers', for instance, was introduced as early as 1993 and produced a series of publications aimed to provide information for organisations, recruitment agencies and employees (for example, the Department of Employment, 1994 and 1995), leading to further attempts to incorporate older employees.

Background to the study

There have been relatively few enquiries of employer attitudes towards older workers, with large gaps in our understanding and empirical knowledge relating to the use of age as a criterion in employment decision-making. Qualitative enquiry through case studies within specific organizations has indicated the widespread extent of negative stereotypes (Metcalf and Thompson, 1990). Institutional barriers (for example, salary cost, pensions, training payback) combine with attitudinal criteria to reinforce employer reluctance to recognise the potential contribution from higher age bands. A small number of quantitative studies have been carried out which provide guidelines for the way forward.

Concern regarding recruitment and retention characteristics in growth conditions led to a survey of 581 employers (Thompson, 1991), for example, which demonstrated that older workers were seen as a 'last resort' even under tight labour market conditions. The conclusion that stereotypical attitudes were widespread amongst managers was confirmed by a survey of 1140 personnel managers, indicating a tendency for those employers who were more positive still to continue to identify jobs considered suitable for different age-groups (Warr and Pennington, 1993). A further study of large organizations (Taylor and Walker, 1993) also suggested the extensive nature of age stereotyping, which was reinforced through follow-up interviews with a sub-sample of 100 firms. Although many managers claimed to recognise the qualities of older workers as employees, few had developed strategies to retain or attract them into employment (Taylor and Walker, 1995); while almost half indicated that age was a relevant and important consideration when recruiting staff. Likewise, greater priority tended to be given to the protection of jobs for younger people by both management and Trade Union representatives than towards the needs of older age-bands in the workforce (Taylor and Walker, 1996), leading to the potential utilisation of redundancy arrangements and early retirement schemes to solve 'downsizing' problems (Arrowsmith and McGoldrick, 1997).

Previous research in the current programme at Manchester Metropolitan University examined the response of HRM professionals through a survey of Institute of Management membership (Arrowsmith and McGoldrick, 1994), obtaining a sample of 1,700 responses. This again suggested the existence of age-related stereotypes and discriminating practices, indicating particular concern in respect of external recruitment and selection rather than in respect of the internal labour market. It strongly suggested that the focus for relevant policy in respect of older workers would tend to be concerned with more closely monitoring and responding to the changing demographic profile of the workforce, operating within the overall constraints of organisational change and restructuring (Arrowsmith and McGoldrick, 1996). To date our knowledge has related mainly to large organisations and personnel management attitudes. Sample size has at times been relatively small and sometimes focused more upon descriptive criteria rather than engaging in systematic detailed enquiry into key issues. One study of 221 Local Authority employers similarly found evidence of extensive negative stereotyping in respect of older workers (Itzen and Phillipson, 1993). Significantly, it draws attention to line management attitudes as a major area in need of investigation and to the frustration of progressive policy initiatives.

With the support of the ESRC, a collaborative project was set up in conjunction with the Institute of Management which would address management attitudes more generally rather than being confined to an HRM sample. A questionnaire instrument was established, based upon the evidence of focus group enquiries amongst membership and an extensive pilot survey in an individual branch. A random sample of 5,000 IM members was contacted on a national basis, with a response rate of 33 percent (N=1665), which equated well with previous IM surveys. The respondents were representative of current IM membership generally, which covers all sectors and types of organisational activity. In line with the membership profile, respondents tended to be male (94 percent) and over the age of 40 (88 percent). The majority were in senior or middle management roles, with approximately a third classifying their job as having cross-functional general management responsibilities and representing the range of organizational sizes (Arrowsmith and McGoldrick, 1996).

Figure 5.1 provides an overview model of the approach taken and the linkages determined between the various stages of investigation, suggesting the types of organizational and individual factors which were taken into account in questionnaire development, as well as major questions relating to age discrimination arising as a result of the study.

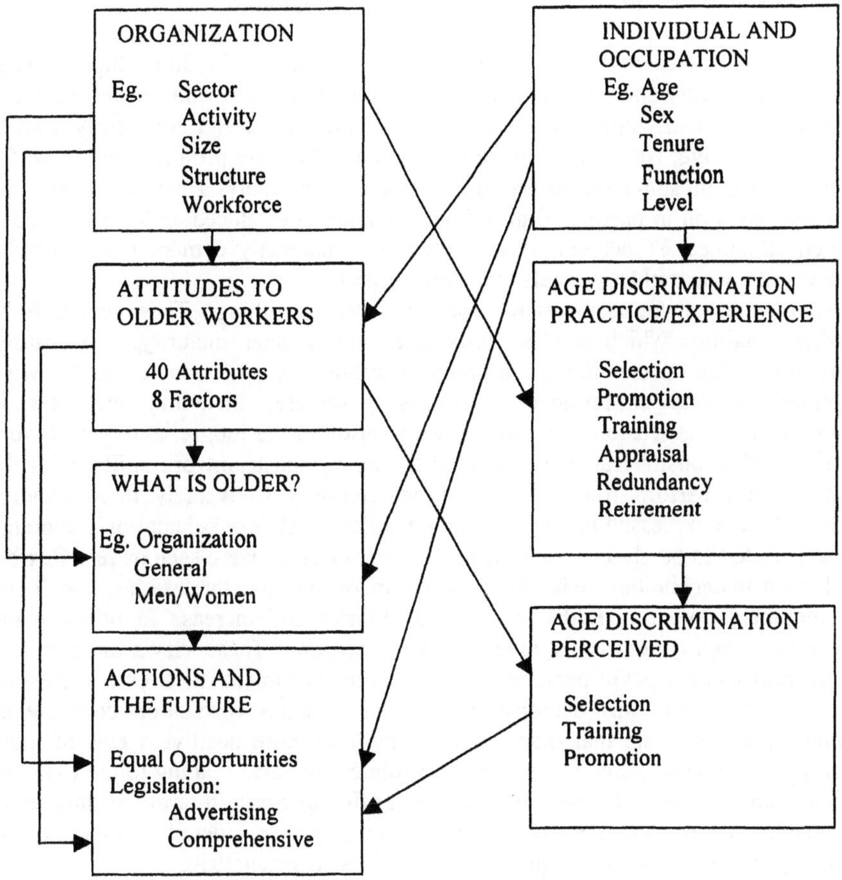

Figure 5.1: Attitudes towards older employees and age discrimination in employment

Attitudes towards older employees and age stereotyping

Managers contacted held strong views regarding the potential relationships between age, employability and performance, demonstrating an 'ambivalence' in respect of their evaluation of characteristics exhibited. Some attributes were clearly seen to increase with age, while others were considered to be more problematic. Table 5.3 presents this in summary in the form of a Factor Analysis across 40 criteria. Varimax rotation in pursuit of an orthogonal solution produced an 8 factor model, which explained 61 percent of variance. This succinctly demonstrates attitudes expressed towards older workers and stereotypes held.

Many employment attributes were seen to develop with age. These tended to be 'softer' qualities which can be associated with greater maturity. This placed particular value on the 'job commitment' exhibited by older employees, viewing motivational and commitment attributes positively; including increases in conscientiousness, customer service, loyalty, pride in the job, reliability and work quality. Other positive attributes related to coping and teamwork skills, with the confidence to perform roles whilst accepting authority. Conversely, more negative attitudes were expressed in terms of the potential of 'change orientation', although scores tended to be closer to the mean. Older employees were seen as less flexible and open to technology, with less interest in or aptitude for training and lower development potential. Reduced physical abilities and increase in primary and secondary employment costs added to this perception. These views did not vary significantly in respect of personal or organisational characteristics. One interesting outcome, however, was demonstrated by the Pearson correlation coefficients, which clearly indicate that older respondents hold more positive views of older workers in terms not only of their job commitment but also relating to their change orientation abilities and potential decrease in primary costs. In terms of qualitative evaluation, it was also interesting to note that managers considered the nature of the job in question, assessing the qualities required, fairly or unfairly:

> I would always prefer older people in a customer contact role.
>
> I tend to recruit older workers for routine jobs as they are much more stable.
>
> Older persons have an abundance of experience that enables them to avoid the pitfalls made by younger staff.

Likewise, chronological age may not be an appropriate predictor of abilities and behaviour and it may be appropriate to have a more balanced age mix:

> It is up to the individual and their attitude to life. You can be old at thirty.
>
> An organisation is healthier for a spread of ages, like a big family.

Table 5.3 : Factor analysis of attitudes to older workers

Factor	Factor loading	Univariate		Correlation: Age	
Variable	>.4*	Mean**	S.D.	Pearson Coeff	p=
Factor 1: JOB COMMITMENT				-.1681	.000
Quality of Work	.7319	2.95	1.01	-.1516	.000
Conscientiousness	.7315	2.82	0.97	-.1476	.000
Commitment to quality	.7302	2.87	0.98	-.1730	.000
Pride in job	.7298	2.68	1.13	-.1613	.000
Customer Service	.7218	2.80	1.03	-.1197	.000
Reliability	.7167	2.51	1.10	-.1299	.000
Loyalty to organisation	.6694	2.61	1.18	-.0943	.000
Work effort	.6342	3.38	1.02	-.1370	.000
Responsibility	.5883	2.56	1.06	-.0904	.000
Job satisfaction	.5630	3.29	1.18	-.1123	.000
Performance	.5284	3.46	0.96	-.1607	.000
Productivity	.5251	3.56	0.95	-.0993	.000
Efficiency	.5222	3.29	1.09	-.1314	.000
Motivation	.4724	3.55	1.13	-.1342	.000
Skills	.4432	2.78	1.10	-.0257	n.s.
Factor 2: CHANGE ORIENTATION				-.0867	.001
Openness to technology	.6842	4.69	1.03	-.1085	.000
Ability to learn	.6828	4.29	0.93	-.0336	n.s.
Interest in training	.6740	4.01	1.15	-.1123	.000
Potential	.5906	4.11	1.03	-.0621	.012
Trainability	5028	4.37	0.98	-.0102	n.s.
Adaptability	.4596	4.26	1.12	-.0998	.000
Performance	.4357	3.46	0.96	-.1607	.000
Ambition	.4292	4.48	1.09	-.0626	.000
Productivity	.4044	3.56	0.95	-.0993	.000
Factor 3: MATURITY				-.0044	n.s.
Coping under pressure	.6445	3.40	1.24	-.0801	.000
Teamwork abilities	.6004	3.38	1.14	-.0961	.000
Confidence	.5924	2.87	1.15	-.0463	.000
Responsibility	.5142	2.56	1.06	-.0904	.000
Acceptance of authority	.5036	3.31	1.28	-.0422	.000
Qualifications	.4656	3.63	1.21	-.0743	.000
Skills	.4319	2.78	1.10	-.0257	.000

Factor 4: ABILITIES				.0020	n.s.
Physical ability	.7407	4.76	.094	.0077	n.s.
Work speed	.6733	4.11	1.02	-.0611	0.14
Flexibility	.6589	4.16	1.27	-.1403	n.s.
Trainability	.5351	4.37	0.98	-.0102	n.s.
Adaptability	.4246	4.26	1.12	-.0998	.000
Factor 5: ABSENCE				.0388	n.s.
Sickness	.7790	3.99	1.04	.0554	.026
Short term absence	.7713	4.38	1.20	.0124	n.s.
Long term absence	.7355	3.88	1.20	.1119	.000
Accidents	.5085	4.23	0.87	.0679	.006
Turnover	.04064	4.43	0.88	-.0548	0.27
Factor 6: PRIMARY COSTS				.0775	.003
Wage costs	.8138	3.20	0.92	.0714	.004
Pension costs	.7241	3.11	1.00	.0543	.030
Factor 7: SECONDARY COSTS				.0132	n.s.
Insurance costs	.8548	3.53	0.95	.0008	n.s.
Benefit costs	.8311	3.44	0.95	-.0028	n.s.
Factor 8: MOVEMENT				.0775	.003
Energy	.6195	4.84	1.31	-.0048	n.s.
Turnover	.4348	4.43	0.88	-.0548	.027

What is older?

It was important to ask managers to specify the age at which they would describe an employee as 'older'. This used four measures, relating to male/female employees within the organisation the manager was familiar with and to a more generally applicable definition for men and women. From the overall results presented in Table 5.4 it can be seen that earlier research findings were supported.

Table 5.4 : Age at which organisational employee considered 'older'

Age in years	Men %	Women %
Under 40	2	8
40-44	11	17
45-49	15	16
50-54	35	34
55-59	21	15
60+	16	10
Mean	51	48

The categories of age, originally extracted as metric variables, produced a mode in the 50-54 age range. While consideration of age begins in the 40s, it becomes a much more important factor in the 50s. An interesting finding also occurs in respect of the differential relating to men and women, where mean ages differed significantly on measures investigated. Earlier ages were perceived as indicating 'older worker' status for women. The average ages were 51 and 48 years for male and female employees respectively. The defining female age was placed below 50 by 42 percent of those contacted in comparison to only 28 percent for male employees. Over a quarter of managers, in fact, regarded an 'older' female employee age as being under 45 years. Not surprisingly the effects of respondents' ages upon this perception are highly relevant. Differences also tended to be more pronounced where female employees were in a 'minority' or in a mixed sex workforce, which may indicate a possible interaction between gender and age issues, with women dropping back in career timetables if they temporarily left the labour force. It could also reflect the anticipated male oriented nature of the sample.

Age discrimination practice and experience

A further interesting facet of enquiry related to the extent to which managers had themselves used age as a discriminator in various types of employment decisions. In general the survey demonstrated the use of age barriers in respect of managers' own decision processes; with more extensive application in terms of recruitment and selection, rather than the internal operation of HRM practices relating to training and development, appraisal and promotion. Enforced organisational exit was a further area where managers identified age as a significant criterion (Table 5.5).

Table 5.5 : Age used in decision making

Type of decision	Age used		
	Yes %	No %	Not applicable %
Recruitment/selection	55	41	4
Redundancy/dismissal	32	55	13
Promotion	29	66	5
Training	25	72	3

Personal experience of discriminatory practices was examined to compliment these findings (Table 5.6), revealing that almost half (44 percent) of the managers believed that they have experienced a disadvantage as a result of their older age when applying for jobs, with a significant proportion also considering that promotion opportunities had been denied (24 percent). Comments made support the view that age may be more significant in terms of recruitment to an organization, rather than internal organizational processes which may be related to the greater need to rely on more general information at this stage. In internal processes it may be possible to utilise more objective and individual-related performance criteria. It should also be noted, however, that ageism may be felt by the relatively young. Being 'inside' the organization is seen as critical:

> There are fewer problems once within an organization. The problem is getting an opportunity to be considered if you are over 35.
>
> My experience of 'age prejudice', and that of most others I suspect, is not a denial of equal opportunity once inside an organization, it is the difficulty of getting an interview in the first instance - at the recruitment stage skills, abilities and experience appear to be secondary to age.

Table 5.6 : Personal experience of age discrimination

	Source of disadvantage					
Type of decision	Too old %			Too young %		
	Yes	No	Don't Know	Yes	No	Don't know
Job application	44	44	12	25	62	13
Promotion	24	67	9	30	60	9
Training	14	80	6	6	86	8
Appraisal	14	78	8	10	80	10
Redundancy	15	70	16	5	77	18

Further investigation revealed that female respondents were far less likely to state that they had personally discriminated on age grounds, probably being more aware of or sensitive to the effects of discrimination. Senior and top managers were considerably more likely to have used age as a discriminator, possibly having had more opportunity to so do and not feeling particular constraints in this respect. Managers in larger organizations emerged as more likely to have discriminated in terms of promotion, redundancy and dismissal.

The future?

A very significant outcome of the research relates to decisions in respect of organizational Equal Opportunities Policies (EOPs) and the case regarding legislative enforcement. Written company EOPs were reported by almost two-thirds of managers (63 percent) with public sector organizations more likely to do so. Managers, however, held very positive views of EO activity, reporting age discrimination as a moral (90 percent), business (73 percent) and mainstream managerial (62 percent) issue. They clearly indicated that this should be formally addressed in their own organizations, regardless of any legislative measures, assuming equal importance to more conventional areas of EO activity (Table 5.7). Managerial attitudes towards the relevance of legislative intervention are obviously of prime importance. Legislation was favoured by the majority of respondents at two levels. Firstly, in respect of the restriction of upper age limits in job advertisements (69.1 percent) and secondly, by the introduction of comprehensive employment protection (64.9 percent).

Table 5.7 : Comparison of age to other equal opportunities issues

Comparative Issues	Age		
	More important %	Equally important %	Less important %
Race	18	71	12
Sex	15	76	9
Disability	13	72	15

At the individual level, no systematic age difference was measured on either of the legislation issues. This might, for instance, reflect some scepticism amongst older respondents as to the likely efficacy of this process. Female respondents tended however to be more likely to favour legislation, significant only in the case of advertisements. The level of the respondents' jobs, however, revealed marked contrasts, with top managers (Board or Senior Executive levels) being significantly less likely to favour either type of legislative measures. The factor score breakdowns also demonstrated some linkages between attitudes towards older employees and desire for Government action against discrimination.

Reasons for support or opposition to legislation are of interest. The case in favour was argued in respect of individual and organizational criteria, as well as in terms of fairness and efficiency. There was nonetheless a recognition that age legislation alone could not be the solution and that it could be potentially problematic and complex:

> I feel strongly that it is morally and commercially just as indefensible as discrimination on the grounds of sex, race and/or disability.
>
> Age discrimination results from an obsession with 'bright young people' and is one of the UKs major social evils, as well as an incredible waste of potentially highly productive and motivated resources.
>
> I am strongly in favour of legislation against age prejudice - my older employees are my best!
>
> There is a problem of age discrimination but there are also legislative problems that do not exist with race and sex: e.g. what is old?; many older employees want the early retirement provisions; many older workers accept age in the working environment; older people work differently.
>
> Legislation will have little meaning because companies will still operate with upper and lower age limits but on an informal basis.

In HRM terms age may be a relevant consideration in decisions. In terms of its relationship to experience, physical ability and family circumstances. Thus it may serve as a justifiable source of information for the employer, particularly in the recruitment stages. Legislation could also be counter productive 'window dressing', which might be prejudicial to younger people's employment, while also reducing the opportunities for desired early retirement and the potential for individual choice of career goals:

> I believe age ranges are sometimes necessary in recruitment. In order to ensure specific applications and to avoid timewasting all round, the age range is included in the job advert. I see this as open, honest and effective management - not age discrimination. I would be most concerned if I was not permitted this flexibility because of legislation.
>
> I am fifty and am seeking a new job on impending retirement. I find it useful to know from advertisements the age group sought, otherwise I can waste a lot of time making useless applications for jobs.
>
> Earlier retirement should be across the board in order to cope with the lack of opportunities for graduates and school-leavers.
>
> Clearly young people with family obligations, say between 25 and 45 years should have priority.

In addition to being problematic and potentially ineffective, some managers suggested that legislation on the basis of age might also be unnecessary. Is it possible that demographic, economic and industry changes could combine with the need for the qualities which more mature workers can contribute? Might this be the means to change employer attitudes towards older people within the labour force, whilst still leaving opportunity for individual choice of career pattern? There was some evidence of optimism here:

> Many organizations are consciously recruiting older people. As the birth rate drops the situation will take care of itself; i.e. organizations will have to look to older people.
>
> Demographic changes are making it imperative for organizations to recruit and train older people, although they are using age to streamline senselessly.
>
> The younger population is shrinking, in both numbers and quality. The skills gap is becoming serious. Market forces will override age and sex. I believe that the millennium could become the age of the 'Greys'.

Conclusions

Managerial ambivalence

The comments of the managers are the best way to begin to explain the 'age at work' paradox:

Convenient indicator: This relates to potential stereotypes held. Age may be a convenient indicator of a number of personal characteristics. It may be used as a proxy for expected attributes, experience, physical abilities or family circumstances. Younger recruiters, in particular, may use this type of association:

> Age is not a consideration when I'm dealing with a known person or group of people. However, when seeking a new contact with no recommendation, age would influence my judgement as to the suitability of the person or persons being considered.
>
> Until I had more direct experience of working with older people over the last 3-5 years I would have assumed older people were less flexible or willing to change. In fact I have discovered that they are more prepared, willing and understanding of the need for change and are happy to put forward positive suggestions.

Ageism in society: It may be that ageism in employment is related a wider set of negative cultural values and attitudes towards ageing and older people. Recessionary times may have accentuated this:

> Ageism is not limited to the employment environment ... following the sixties older people came to be regarded as no longer respectable by virtue of their seniority.
>
> The eighties trend to turn away form the experienced, mature workforce has been short-sighted. The 'yuppie' movement was shallow.

Existing age profiles: HRM professionals must evaluate existing age profiles and the management of succession planning, which may be a legitimate consideration:

> There is a need to have a relatively smooth age profile for career progression, pension funding and general organizational vitality.
>
> Age is important if there is a requirement for long term development.
>
> As a stable organization we face a problem of ageing together - 75 percent are over 40. We would like a better spread of ages, but expect to reduce number rather than recruit staff over the next five years.

Age 'fit': Age barriers may also arise as a result of management preference to recruit younger subordinates, which may develop monitoring responsibilities or keep power/authority lines clear:

> In my experience it is the mature managers who tend to discriminate against older potential recruits. This is possible because older potential recruits are more experienced and more capable than the interviewing manager.
>
> The biggest obstacle is the trend to a younger aged executive and senior management who are uncomfortable with the idea of recruiting people who are older than themselves.

Change and job requirements: The nature and demands of the job in question may be affected by the pace of change and the response to work intensification:

> Younger people may be advantaged if they are in possession of the most up to date qualifications and relevant skills. This might particularly apply in relation to new and/or rapidly expanding technological fields, where the recency of full-time education for the young can give them a headstart.
>
> Many employers are looking more and more to younger employees as layers of management are cut away leaving heavier workloads and longer hours to those left. It is believed that the younger managers will be more prepared to take this on lower pay.
>
> Managers are informally expected to work 70 hours to be making any sort of contribution. This does have a 'burn out' effect in respect of retention of middle management.

Cost: When recruiting, the cost of employing an older worker may be seen as a consideration, particularly if related to seniority pay and benefit structures:

> I have witnessed older, experienced accountants being got rid of and replaced by inexperienced younger accountants purely on a financial basis.
>
> Younger employees are taken on because they are cheap.
>
> The experience and stability that the more mature employees can offer is discarded because the younger are cheaper.

The comments above suggest the need for a re-evaluation of the 'older' employee by management generally and a more open attitude towards appropriate incorporation into the organization. Current discriminatory practices may be counterproductive, not only to individuals, but to future business HRM resourcing. Moreover, as policy concern continues to increase in respect of the balance between the ageing population and the burden this places upon the state and in terms of pension benefits and health care (Bowers, 1996), it is imperative that the potential of the older worker is reviewed, addressing the ambivalence which employers demonstrate. The opposing views spelt out to explain this more widely (Branine and Glover, 1997) do not lead to optimism for the immediate future, particularly when considering the differential in response between personnel professionals and line management. The political debate regarding the suitability of legislation or a voluntary approach through the developing codes of practice (Taylor and Walker, 1997) remains, with consideration at EU level essential (McDonald and Potton, 1997). Further understanding at the organizational level is also essential if discrimination on the basis of age is to be fought effectively.

Note

The support of the Economic and Social Research Council (ESRC) is gratefully acknowledged. Part of the work was funded by the ESRC award number R000221527.

References

Arrowsmith, J. and McGoldrick, A.E. (1994), 'The Future Resourcing of the Service Sector', in C. Armistead (ed.), *The Future of Services Management,* Kogan Page, London.

Arrowsmith, J. and McGoldrick, A.E. (1994), 'Older Worker Employment: Towards a Model of Organizational Practice', Paper Presented to the British Academy of Management Conference, University of Lancaster, September.

Arrowsmith, J. and McGoldrick, A.E. (1995), 'Expectations of Labour Market and Policy Developments: Effects on the Employment of Older Workers and Potential for Flexible Working Practices', British Academy of Management Conference, Sheffield, September.

Arrowsmith, J. and McGoldrick, A.E. (1996), *Breaking the Barriers: a Survey of Managers Attitudes to Age and Employment,* Institute of Management, London.

Arrowsmith, J. and McGoldrick, A.E. (1997), 'A Flexible Future for Older Workers?', *Personnel Review,* Vol. 26, No. 4, pp. 258-73.

Bourne, B. (1982), 'Effects of Ageing on Work Satisfaction, Performance and Motivation', *Ageing and Work,* Vol. 5, No. 10. pp. 31-47.

Bowers, P.H. (1996), 'Is Retirement Substainable?', Paper Presented to the *'Ageism, Work and Employment'* Conference, Stirling, July, and chapter six of this book.

Branine, M. and Glover, I. (1997), 'Ageism in Work and Employment: thinking about connections', *Personnel Review,* Vol. 26, No. 4, pp. 233-44.

Casey, B., Metcalf, H. and Lakey, J. (1993), 'Human Resource Strategies and the Third Age: Policies and Pratices in the UK', in *Age and Employment Policies, Attitudes and Practice,* Institute of Personnel Management, London.
Davies, J.A., Matthews, G. and Wong, C.S.K. (1991), 'Ageing and Work' in: C.L. Cooper and I.T. Robertson (eds), *International Review of Industrial and Organisational Psychology,* Vol. 6, Wiley, Chichester.
De Micco, F.J. and Reid, R.D. (1988), 'Older Workers: A Hiring Resource For The Hospitality Industry, *Cornell HRA Quarterly,* Vol. 29, No. 1, pp. 56-61.
Department of Employment (1991), *Equal Opportunities Training for Older Workers,* Department of Employment, Sheffield.
Department of Employment (1994), *Getting On: The Benefits of an Older Workforce,* Department of Employment Group, London.
Department of Employment (1995), *Too Old - Who Says? Advice for Older Workers,* Department of Employment Group, London.
Dibden, J. and Hibbet, A. (1993), 'Older workers - an overview of recent research', *Employment Gazette,* Vol. 10, No. 6, pp. 237-48.
Elias, P.K., Elias, M.F., Robbins, M.A. and Gage, P. (1987), 'Acquisition of word-processing skills by younger, middle-age and older adults', *Psychology and Ageing,* Vol. 2, No. 4.
Heaton, S. (1989), 'The Grey Discriminator', *Industrial Society Magazine,* June, pp. 7-9.
House of Commons Employment Committee (1989), *The Employment Patterns of the Over-50's,* Vol. 11, HMSO, London.
House of Commons Employment Committee (1991), *Recruitment Practices,* Vol. 1, HMSO, London.
Institute of Personnel Management (IPD) (1993), *Statement on Age and Employment,* London, IPM.
Itzen, C. and Phillipson, C. (1993), *Age Barriers at Work: Maximising the Potential of Mature and Older People,* METRA, Solihull.
Johnson, P. and Falkingham, J. (1992), *Ageing and Economic Welfare,* Sage, London.
Jolly, J., Creigh, S. and Mingay, A. (1980), *Age as a Factor in Employment,* Research Paper No. 11, Department of Employment, London.
Jones, A. and Longstone, L. (1990), *A Survey of Restrictions on Job Centre Vacancies,* Research and Evaluation Branch Report No. 44, Department of Employment, London.
Laczko, F. and Phillipson, C. (1991), *Changing Work and Retirement: Social Policy and the Older Worker,* Open University Press, Milton Keynes.
McDonald, F. and Potton, M. (1997), 'The Nascent European Policy Towards Older Workers: Can the European Union Help the Older Worker?', *Personnel Review,* Vol. 26, No. 4, pp. 293-306.
McGoldrick, A.E. (1992), 'Europe's Disappearing Workforce: Current Response and Future Needs', Paper presented to the Conference Studies in the New Europe, Birmingham, April.

McGoldrick, A.E. and Arrowsmith, J. (1993), 'Recruitment Advertising: Discrimination on the Basis of Age', *Employee Relations,* Vol. 15 No. 5, pp. 54-65.
Metcalf, H. and Thompson, M. (1990), *Older Workers: Employers' Attitudes and Practices,* IMS, Brighton.
National Economic Development Office (NEDO) (1989), *Defusing the Demographic Timebomb,* NEDO, London.
Naylor, P. (1987), 'Age in Perspective', Paper presented to the Institute of Management conference, Harrogate, October.
Reed Employment (1991), *Survey of Personnel Managers and Directors of Technical and Engineering Firms,* Unpublished Report.
Rock, S. (1987), 'Age: Discrimination's Last Frontier?', *Director,* September.
Rosen, B. and Jerdee, T.H. (1989), 'Investing in the Older Worker', *Personnel Administrator,* Vol. 34, No. 1, pp. 70-74.
Taylor, P. and Walker, A. (1991), *Too Old at 50? Age Discrimination in the Labour Market,* Campaign for Work, London.
Taylor, P. and Walker, A. (1993), 'Employers and Older Workers', *Employment Gazette,* August, pp. 371-78.
Taylor, P. and Walker, A. (1996), 'Combating Age Discrimination in Employment: education versus legislation, *Policy Studies,* Vol. 16, No. 1, pp. 51-61.
Taylor, P. and Walker, A. (1997), 'Age Discrimination and Public Policy', *Personnel Review,* Vol. 26, No. 4, pp. 307-18.
Thompson, M. (1991), *Last in the Queue? Corporate Employment Policies and the Older Worker*, IMS, Brighton, Sussex.
Tillsley, C. (1990), *The Impact of Age on Employment,* IRRU, University of Warwick, Coventry.
Trinder, C. (1991), *Older Workers and the Recession,* Institute of Employment, Brighton, Sussex.
Warr, P. (1993), *'Age and Employment',* in M.D. Dunnette and L.M. Hough (eds), *Handbook of Industrial and Organisational Psychology,* Vol. 4, Consulting Psychologists' Press, Palo Alto.
Warr, P. and Pennington, J. (1993), 'Views About Age Discrimination and Older Workers', in *Age and Employment: Policies, Attitudes and Practice,* Institute of Personnel Management, London.

6 Is retirement sustainable?

Philip H. Bowers

Introduction

This chapter considers the effect of an ageing population on the UK economy. While recognising the burdens created on social security and hence taxation, it stresses the problems likely to be created by the increased consumption of an ageing population and the potential for difficulties in the capital markets.

A larger retired population could be expected to consume without producing, which might be expected to require government intervention to balance the economy to avoid inflation. The elderly population might need to sell assets to finance this consumption, and so some means would need to be found to ensure that the capital markets did not lose value to such an extent as to cause a crisis. Neither of these problems looks to be overwhelming in the UK context taken on its own, but other OECD countries will both have lower future support ratios,[1] and a faster decline in support ratios; they may face these difficulties in the next century. In the UK context, the present policies chosen to resolve these issues will entail increased disparity in the incomes of retired people, and there may well be an unacceptable old-age poverty problem. Raising the retirement age seems unlikely to provide the solution. It may be that partial retirement is the best approach, with the burdens of care borne by the retired population itself.

Policy concerns in relation to population ageing

The linking of the state old age pension to prices rather than incomes, and the ever-tighter targeting of income support, will help to reduce the burden of an ageing population on the working population. However, such moves clearly make the retired population who have only the state old age pension considerably worse off. The present trends in occupational pensions appear to indicate a ceiling of about 50 percent of the population benefiting from occupational pension schemes, and a further 30 percent who will have private pensions (Johnson, Disney and Stears 1996, pp. 9-13). These figures mask the high proportion (around 70 percent) of men, particularly in the age groups between 44 and 54, who have one of these pensions, and the much lower proportion of women (around 40-45 percent) who have them. The personal pension coverage is much more highly concentrated on the younger age groups, with 40-45 percent of both men and women between the ages of 20 to 30 having such pension arrangements. Also there is disquiet about the adequacy of many of these pensions. A large portion of the population remains reliant on state provision, however, and these will suffer from the lowering of state aid.

The other area of concern is that the burden of health care for an elderly population will become insupportable. This is clearly a possibility if health care costs are strictly related to age. Present estimates are based on costs per person for each age group multiplied by the forecast number of people in the age group. However, if in general health costs are related to the costs of the last months of life rather than to age in itself, the above calculation would overestimate costs. It neglects the fact that there will be a smaller proportion of the population in the older age groups near death, and thus health expenditures will be more nearly constant than expected. Hills (1993, p. 58) shows that even without this possible overestimate, demographic change will cause less of an increase in health care costs per head than that which was experienced in the period since 1946. One of the most important concerns has been that of the provision of long-term care for those elderly people who need care but not constant medical treatment. This is at present provided either privately, if people have assets worth more than £10,000, or within the community but with full government support if they have less than this figure. The sense of inequity and the distress related to losing life savings for those who have been thrifty, and concern for both the adequacy and the cost of community care have made this a serious issue. It seems possible, however, that part-retirement could both increase the incomes of pensioners and provide the care at reasonable cost. This will be taken up in the final section of the chapter.

It has been pointed out (Börsch-Supan, 1990) that in the German context and, to a lesser extent, in the USA, the increase in elderly population also creates significant problems for the housing market because of the unwillingness of pensioners to move from family homes and hence their over-consumption of space. This, along with the increasingly fissile nature of family relationships, is likely to increase the requirement for housing units. Whether the ageing of the population is the most significant variable in the UK context, however, is open to question, particularly in view of the large number of people who move on retirement.

Recent work in the USA has stressed the interrelated themes of reduced savings rates attributable to a well-funded elderly population (Gokhale, Kotlikoff and Sabelhaus, 1996) and the possibility that pension funds will move into deficit, and hence will cease to be a source of savings. This may cause a fall in asset values (Schieber and Shoven, 1994). This chapter will consider some of the implications of these lines of discussion in the UK context and compare this to the situation in the USA.

Consume as you go

At any particular time, the working population has to provide for its own dependants, because goods are consumed close to the time when they are produced and services exactly at that time. Thus if a population is ageing, it implies an increasing burden on those in work to provide for this consumption, or impoverishment of the retired. The only way in which this can be alleviated is by the investment which each generation makes in physical and human capital such that the increased production required from the working population is made easier. As a higher level of production is possible from any one group, this may solve the problem of providing sufficient products and services for consumption but a mechanism still has to be found to give property rights to the retired population so that they have a claim on the national product.

In the context of an agricultural society, this claim stems from the ownership of land until death so that the children benefit from the capital asset and in return support their parents. Such a system leaves a major problem for the landless in the developing countries now, as it did in Britain in the past. In an industrial society, the same process occurs if the parents own a share of capital either as investments in the stock market or as sole owners or partners in an enterprise. For those who have subsisted by virtue of wage labour, however, there is no such claim on resources. In the past, where industry was based essentially on artisanal work, people worked on until infirmity prevented them. As pay was on the basis of piece-work, older and slower workers simply had reduced incomes. Once the production line became important, however, an older worker unable to keep up with the speed of the line slowed the whole line and thus reduced everybody's production rate. Under these circumstances the older worker became a liability and retirement had to be invented. This need to get rid of the slower worker parallels the need to provide work for the younger workers in periods of recession. It is thus no accident that pension provision has expanded in these periods. As wages were frequently so low that adequate savings for retirement were impossible, the state intervened to provide a minimum level of pension. Furthermore, as pointed out by Hannah (1986, p. 8), the likelihood of early death for the poorer worker was sufficiently high to discourage the use of meagre earnings to purchase insurance for old age. The first of these government interventions was by Bismarck in Germany and according to Myles (1989, pp. 30-31) this was to engender loyalty to the paternalistic state and to prevent the rise of Socialism. Lloyd George's 1908 Pensions Act marks the start of the state pension in this country. Similar state interventions followed, notably in the USA with the Social Security Act in 1935, under the influence of the Depression and the need to provide an exit route for older workers from the labour market, so that younger people might have chances of jobs. Both Myles (1989) and Hannah (1986) provide fascinating accounts of the backgrounds to the evolution of pension coverage and the political and social battles surrounding it.

The initial aim of these pension Acts was to provide a minimum subsistence income for those who had been unable to make savings, without significantly reducing the incentive to save, thereby keeping the burden of taxation to a minimum while avoiding the scandal of starvation of elderly workers forced to retire by the capitalist system. The tensions are obvious in this position, which at once recognises the moral obligation to provide a pension and yet provides only the bare minimum for subsistence. Subsequent developments, therefore, have been towards more generous state pension provision. In the UK this took the form of both increased basic pension allowances (though this has now been reversed) and the State Earnings-Related Pension Scheme (SERPS) which was paid for by contributions from employers and employees. Both SERPS and the basic pension have always been Pay As You Go (PAYG), that is to say, the contributions from workers at any time, and any necessary top-up from taxation, pay for the pensions at that time. This is in contrast to the occupational pension schemes, which are predominantly 'funded', that is to say, assets are built up such that each pensioner contributes to a fund which accumulates sufficient assets to pay for members' pensions. The definition of sufficiency depends on the type of pension contract. Sufficient in the context of 'defined benefit' schemes would imply that the fund has sufficient to pay pensions at the rate of benefits defined in the contract for all members of that scheme. Sufficient in the context of 'defined contribution' schemes, would have to refer to sufficiency of income for the pensioners in the scheme, since as its name implies a defined contribution scheme pays out amounts based on the returns obtained by a set of contributions through time. This type of scheme has in the past led to higher pensions for any set of contributions, but it shifts the risks to the pensioner. In either case 'sufficiency' is based on the actuarial expectations and the returns to shares of the time. The assets are usually a mixture of equities and both commercial and government bonds. There is therefore now a shared responsibility for pensions, with a bare and ever-decreasing minimum relative to wages being provided by the government and most additional income being provided by the private sector following the encouragements to leave SERPS. The effect on state pensions of present government policies are clearly and briefly laid out in Hills (1993, pp. 49-55).

The support ratio provides a basis for assessing the problems posed by an ageing society. The figures produced by the OECD in 1988 for the member countries are shown in Figure 6.1 below. It can be seen that the UK faces less of a problem and much less of a change than the rest of the OECD countries.

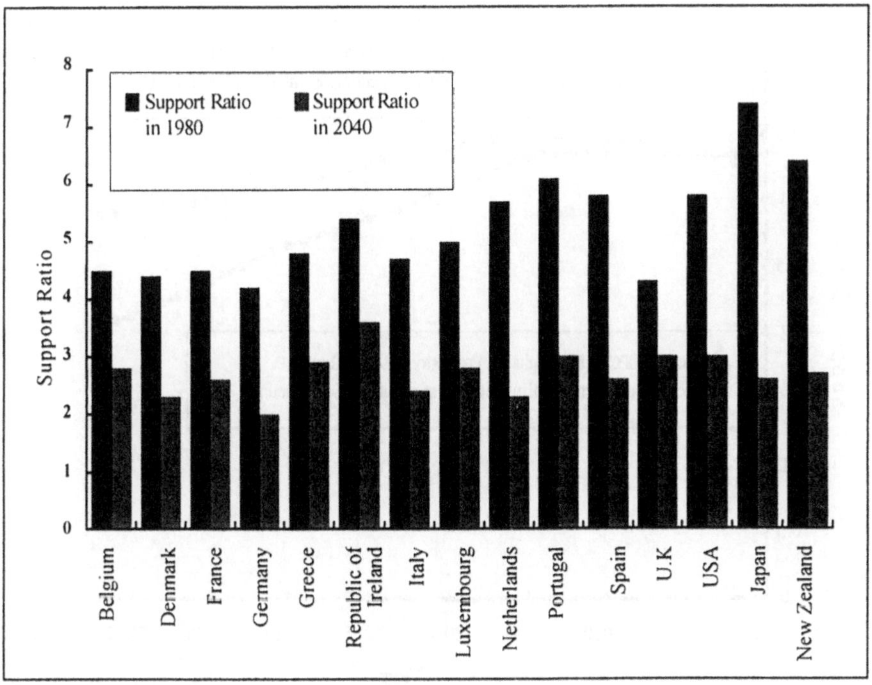

Figure 6.1: Support ratios in 1980 and 2040

Source: *Department of Social Security* (1991, pp. 34-35)

The evolution of the support ratio in the UK to the year 2032 is shown in Figure 6.2 below on two forecasting bases. The first, which shows considerably less of a problem, is derived using constant mortality rates and allows for no immigration. On this basis a support ratio of 2.9 is reached in 2032. The second, which finishes up with about 2.08 workers per retired person, follows the Government Actuary's central projection and allows for immigration at a slightly higher rate than at present of 50,000 persons per annum over the next decade (OPCS 1995, 1992-based on National Population Projections, p. 19, Table 6.3) reducing gradually to zero in 2015 and thereafter. More importantly it allows for the decline in mortality rates to continue, initially at about 2.5 percent per annum with the rate of improvement declining to 0.5 percent per annum in 2021. It can be seen that this leads to a considerably larger retired population as the result of an increase in the life expectancy from 70.5 for males and 76.6 for females in 1980 to 73.7 and 79.2 years respectively in 1993, and forecast to be 78.2 and 83.1 in 2032 (OPCS 1995, p. 12, Table 5.2). The effect of these changes is, as we will show, sensitive to the assumptions that one makes about the future.

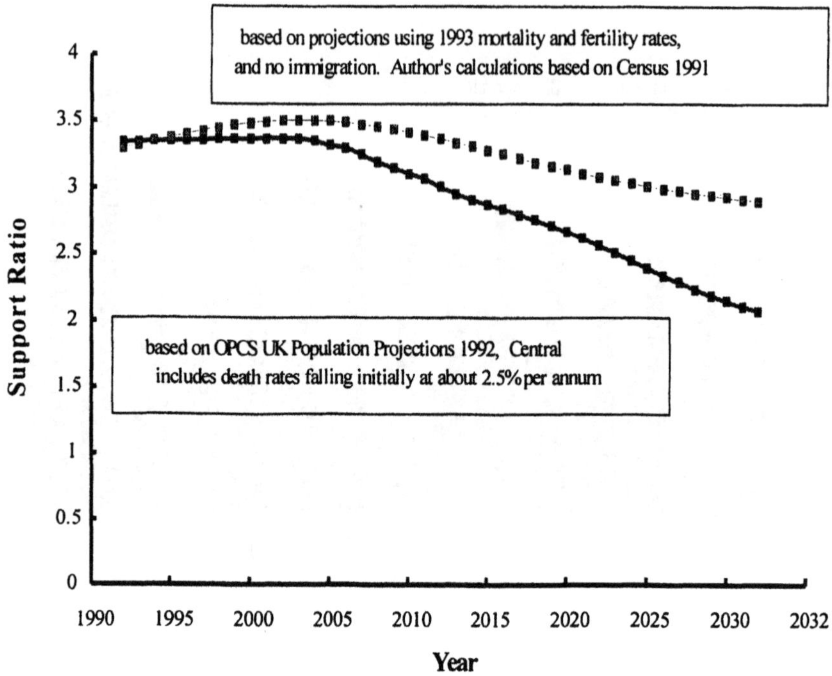

Figure 6.2: The evolution of the support ratio in the UK on two projection bases

The evolution of pension funds with an ageing population

Funding of pensions by the provision of investments, which then provide income and capital that can be used to allow consumption in old age, does little to overcome the problems raised by 'consume-as-you-go'. Funding may increase the savings rate by a small amount (Davis 1995, p. 38), particularly if tax provisions make saving for retirement attractive compared with alternative investment opportunities. However, funding may exacerbate the problems created by consumption at the time of drawing pensions, since it may provide more generous incomes than would otherwise have been possible if the capital markets perform better than expected. We will consider this issue in the next section; first, this section will examine the evolution of such pension funds in relation to their income and outgoings as the population changes structure.

A pension fund receives money in the form of pension contributions from employers and employees, and from single or regular premiums, and from the income (largely in the form of dividends) it receives on the invested funds. Its outgoings are made up of pensions and other benefits such as death benefits and widows' pensions, and its running costs. The surplus of income over outgoings can be invested in equities, bonds, property or other investments and therefore goes to increase the funds on which income is received. Conversely, a deficit decreases those funds. The situation over the years 1990-1994 is shown in Table 6.1 below. It will be noticed that there is a comfortable positive cash flow in all years.

Table 6.1 : Life assurance and pension schemes: income and expenditure of funded schemes (£ million)

	1990	1991	1992	1993	1994
Contributions of employers	9312	7974	7170	7666	7115
Contributions of employees	6633	7275	7646	8278	6599
Regular individual premiums	13654	17736	18867	2112	2034
Single individual premiums	7614	11035	13407	1497	1442
Rents dividends and interest receipts	31180	31157	33319	3426	3650
Less pensions and other benefits paid	-30734	-35265	-41273	4518	4630
Less administrative costs	-9984	-10895	-10850	1190	1142
Surplus (net increase in amount available for investment)	27799	29214	28556	2954	2754

Source: *CSO (1995) United Kingdom National Accounts,* London, HMSO, p. 53, Table 4.10

The table above includes life assurance business as it has been impossible to get data on the pension funds alone. This means that along with true pension business there are such long term life insurance schemes as endowment mortgages both in the income and in the benefits paid. This is a severe problem if the determinants of income and outgoings of life insurance business are inversely related to those of pension fund business. As an initial hypothesis, however, it seems plausible that these are predominantly either savings against such borrowings as mortgages, and hence would reflect people's ability to pay during their earning years, or that they are substitutes for pension contributions in the form of more flexible savings than pension schemes. This flexibility is particularly important in an era when more and more people are afraid of periods of unemployment, during which they might be unable to contribute to their pensions, and indeed might need to draw down their savings to maintain their standards of living.

This positive cash flow of pension and life insurance funds is both a contribution to savings at the national level and a force for increasing the value of shares and gilts by increasing the demand for them and hence keeping down the rates of interest. One must therefore ask what would happen if these funds were regularly in deficit, as one might expect them to be in the presence of too high a dependency ratio (the reciprocal of the support ratio).

It is open to question as to whether long term life insurance business should be included in the context of this chapter.[2] Inquiries have failed to reveal the extent to which these are 'disguised' pension arrangements in the form of personal pensions made through life insurance rather than pension funds in order to allow for periods of need during working life, or in the face of premature retirement. Irrespective of the extent to which these premiums are 'disguised' pensions, it would seem likely that they are largely paid out by people in employment, and that they will largely be cashed in by people on retirement. The flow of funds would in this case be closely related to that of pension premiums. This seems an important subject for further research.

The factors which would cause the balance of income less expenditure of pension funds to become negative follow directly from the components which make up their income and outgoings.

a) Falling premiums/contributions: if the working population (not just the working-age population) falls and this is not offset by rising income for those in work, one would expect falls in the income of the pension funds. Other factors such as a decline in the rate of house sales could also cause falls in life insurance company premiums in so far as old policies are maturing and new ones are not taken out. As shown below the working population is expected to decline at a rate of about 0.08 percent between 1992 and 2032; this source of change is thus small compared to the potential changes from economic growth, or conversely from decreasing participation rates.

b) If earnings of quoted companies declined in the long run, dividends would also fall and this would have serious consequences on the income of pension funds in the UK context since about 75 percent of life insurance and pension funds' assets are in equities (CSO, 1996, p. 83, Table 5.1b) although only 56 percent are in UK equities. Furthermore, this fall in earnings would be reflected in the value of the shares and so would cause a decline in the market value of the asset base of the company. If it needed to sell assets in order to pay pensions it would have to sell a larger number of shares than previously.

c) If pension payouts increase, as seems likely if the retired population increases, this will reduce the net cash flow. With a 55 percent increase in the population above retirement age, giving an annual average growth rate of 1.1 percent, this is clearly a significant factor. We should also add that much of this predicted growth is through the increased longevity of the population, which is a key actuarial assumption in relation to the cost of pensions to the pension funds.

d) For completeness we might add that, if running costs increase, the net cash flow would also be reduced. However, this is likely to be a self-balancing mechanism as the running costs are likely to be made up substantially of the salaries of workers in the City and these are likely to decline if the stock market goes into a decline. At present, annual running costs are approximately 1.3 percent of the value of assets.

If there was a change in the number of pensioners so that outgoings increased, above the income, this would involve the sale of assets by pension funds, and unless offset by some other forces increasing demand in the stock market, a fall in the price of equities would result (i.e., the yield would rise). This could be expected to accompany a rise in the rate of interest on gilts both because of arbitrage between the two, and because gilts would also be facing excess supply for the same reasons. Unfortunately such changes never occur in isolation and it is impossible to assess the likely fall in value of stocks as the result of a fall in surplus of pension funds. It is not even sure whether such a change would be self-cancelling. It would come to a stop if the fall in value of the shares, with no fall in expected earnings, caused shares to be of sufficient attraction to induce others to buy; this might be for example from those with substantial balances in the bank. If no others entered the market, however, so that it was in effect dominated by UK pension and life insurance funds, then the falls in value could force the realisation of even more assets and with sales unmatched by demand, a further fall in value would occur. The way in which such a situation would tend to right itself is that in order to achieve the same level of pension higher contributions would be required, thereby increasing revenue, but the lengths of time required to restore order can be of considerable importance in such situations, particularly if insolvency threatens.

Fortunately however, in the UK there is no sudden increase in the numbers of pensioners. The process is relatively gradual; indeed examination of Figure 2 shows that changes are deferred for approximately a decade. With plausible estimates of contributions, and real returns on capital, the problem seems to be the opposite: the pension funds continue in ever increasing surplus right up to 2032 even on the Government Actuary's relatively pessimistic scenario of increases in the proportion of the population beyond retirement age. Figure 6.3 shows the evolution of net cash flow of pension funds if one applies a constant contribution rate as a proportion of wage income, with no increases in real income per head, a constant payout per pensioner, and a real rate of return on equities of 5.26 percent and a 3.5 percent return on gilts which Wilkie (1995, p. 271) calculates to be the long-term trend over the years 1919 to 1993.

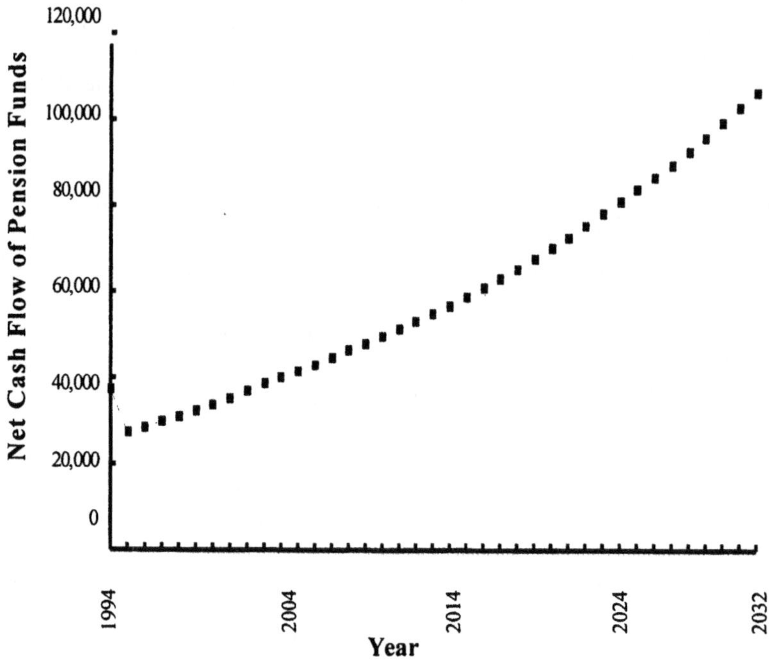

Figure 6.3: Net cash flow of pension funds with a 5.26 percent return on equities and a 3.5 percent return on government stocks

This appears to be impossible; the total assets of pension and life insurance funds stood at £882.8 bn in 1993 (CSO, 1996, p. 155), and yet with no inflation, and no economic growth, we are forecasting that they would increase by £100 billion per year by 2032! The major suspect in this calculation is the rate of return on equities. Over the same period economic growth has been calculated at between 1 percent and 3 percent, and clearly much of the value of equities is that they allow the owner to share in the growth of the economy. As our example does not include growth of incomes, which would involve growth of premiums/contributions if these are a constant proportion of income, or the consequential growth of pension payments, the interest rate should also not include anticipation of growth.

The inclusion of growth of incomes introduces several complications which would require longer to solve than was available at the time of writing. A naive view of the effect of economic growth on pension funds is given in Figure 6.4. The generally favourable effects appear manifest and robust. However, this does not allow for changes within the distribution of income or in the lifetime profile of earnings which could alter these effects. The impact of such changes is likely to be sensitive to the type of pension scheme adopted. At first sight it would appear that defined contribution schemes are proof against all disaster as far as the pensions industry is concerned, since any shortfall in contributions is matched by a shortfall in pension payments, and any failure in the growth of value of the fund is also matched by a reduction in payment. The only point at which the industry might be vulnerable is if there is a commitment to pay fixed annuities, and then the industry faces an unexpected downturn in revenues from which to pay these. In the absence of such a 'disaster', the risks are borne entirely by the pensioner, and it is therefore not surprising that the payout from such schemes is much more favourable than for defined benefit schemes in a period of increasing asset values. Such a time is a propitious one for the industry to persuade customers to switch to such schemes, particularly if there are serious risks of a downturn in fund values, whether due to an ageing population or to other factors.

Defined benefit schemes are however vulnerable to changes in the rate of growth, but again the precise definition of the terms of the scheme is essential. A scheme providing a pension based on the final year (or three years') salary and related to the number of years of pensionable service, is vulnerable to the timing of withdrawal from the labour force, and to rapidly rising final salaries; these adverse effects could be seriously compounded by a downturn in economic growth so that contributions and the value of assets was declining in the face of the commitments to pay high pensions based on high final salaries. Figure 6.3 above gives no indication of the way continued growth, increases or declines in the rate of growth, or continuations of the present trends in early withdrawal from the labour market, and increased polarisation of incomes would affect the funds. This would require a lot more modelling and considerably more disaggregated models of pension contributions and payments in relation to different employment life histories.

The effects of changing patterns of employment and potentially declining incomes if economic growth ceases (or if growth results in high incomes for a declining proportion of the population) may have an impact on the pensions industry. However, it is likely to be the population who have chequered employment records or low pay throughout their working lives who bear the brunt of these effects in terms of low pensions, and thus very possibly the Exchequer via increases in the required social security payments. Again this information would require the more disaggregated models suggested above.

The most adverse scenario is one where a falling support ratio causes decrease in the growth rate of national income. This would imply that pension incomes were fixed at the high level of income achieved as the result of previous growth, but that the incomes of the working population ceased to grow, so that contributions ceased to grow unless a larger and larger proportion of income were contributed. Insofar as tax income was being used to finance pensions and social security payments, economic growth might be reduced, if the disincentive effects of taxation are such as to affect work effort and the incentive to invest.

Decline, the complete cessation, or indeed reversal of growth, would clearly be a threat, but that growth in the UK would only have to be modest to avoid problems in the capital market is indicated by the very slow change of the population structure. The OPCS 1992 forecasts indicate a working population of 35,530,000 in 1992, which decreases to 34,374,000 in 2032, an average annual decline of just

0.08 percent. The population of pension age, however, increases by about 55 percent from 10,621,000 to 16,546,000, which sounds fairly sensational but represents only an annual rate of growth of 1.1 percent. Thus it does not need a very rapid real growth of incomes to provide for such a level of growth of what is still less than half the working population, who in this country are probably receiving something of the order of half the average income of the working population. Applying a 2 percent real rate of return to both equities and bonds in fact yields a slowly declining surplus that becomes negative in about 2030. That these are sensitive assumptions is illustrated by the case of the USA which we examine below.

Work in the USA by Schieber and Shoven (1994) on pension funds and the falling support ratio suggests that whereas pension funds now contribute to national savings about 3.5 percent of income from work, they will be contributing nothing by 2024 and will be drawing down about 1.5 percent of income from work by 2040. This implies that unlike the UK example above, they will be selling very significant levels of assets each year! As the authors point out:

> This could depress asset prices, particularly since the demographic structure of the United States does not differ that greatly from Japan and Europe, which also will have large elderly populations at that time (Schieber and Shoven, 1994, p. 25).

They go on to emphasise that all assets would probably be affected since the fall in values of equities would be matched by falls in value of government stock, and this would have similar effects on all other long-run assets such as land prices. If one wishes to anticipate a disaster, one could suggest that the world's asset markets are closely interlinked, and that therefore the much more adverse movements in population in most other OECD countries could affect our stock market in the way anticipated by Schieber and Shoven for the USA. Furthermore, the notion that capital markets are linked so that falls in the value of equities are passed around the globe from stock market to stock market, contains an apparent solution to the problem of falling asset values, namely for pension funds to buy into the emerging markets of south Asia and Latin America. As this also influences the outcome of the 'Consume as You Go' issue, which is discussed in the next section, and so the plausibility of the belief in global capital markets should be examined.

A global capital market in equities might take two forms (or hybrids of the two types). It could take the form of mobile investment capital searching for opportunities in several different markets, each market selling different and predominantly local shares, that is, firms sold only in that market. This should lead to an equalisation of expected risk adjusted returns, with the proviso that these expected returns also have to include allowance for the effects of currency fluctuations, whether by accepting the cost of currency hedging, or by allowing for the currency risk and return in the portfolio analysis. A technique for doing this is set out in Solnik (1996, ch. 4, pp. 89-129). That returns will not be fully equalised is likely since there are additional costs of currency transactions, tax asymmetries, global custody charges, and information costs of operating over a wide range of markets. Various authors have found evidence that the pricing rules and risk relationships appear to be the same such that there is no evidence of market segmentation.

> The current empirical evidence is still fragmentary, and the results are likely to evolve as the world financial markets are increasingly liberalised and transaction costs are driven down. A summary of current research tends to support the conclusion that assets are priced in an integrated international financial market. The evidence can be somewhat different for emerging and smaller markets, in which constraints are still serious (Solnik, 1996, p. 145).

He also finds that it is worth diversifying internationally to reduce the risk of equity investment, which implies relatively separate markets since the markets would otherwise be too closely correlated to make it an effective risk reduction strategy.

The alternative notion of a global market in the sense of all stocks being traded globally is not the situation. It is only a small minority of stocks that are traded in many markets and these are all such major multi-national firms as Shell, Daimler Benz, Unilever, Glaxo, and the trading of foreign stocks on the New York Stock Exchange accounted for over 10 percent of the volume of trade in 1994. Similarly there is considerable trading of foreign stocks on the London Stock Exchange (Solnik, 1996, p. 190). There is however very considerable potential for a world market to develop using modern telecommunications and computer technology.

It is however worth noting that although there may be an increasingly integrated world capital market, the market capitalisation of stocks in emerging markets is small compared to the OECD countries' markets. Europe, Japan, the USA and Canada accounted for approximately 95 percent of the world stock market values in 1994 (calculated from figures in Exhibit 6.1 in Solnik 1996, p. 168), and thus the development of a sufficient source of funds for pension payments from emerging market stocks seems likely to pose a problem.

To summarise, the transmission of falls in value from one country to another as a result of an ageing population leading to sales of assets and hence falls in value, seems plausible. The solution by the purchase of assets in emerging markets however seems implausible at present due to the difference in scales of the established markets with 95 percent of the value and the emerging markets with less than 5 percent. This in turn implies that paying pensions from the proceeds of overseas investment seems unlikely. This is unfortunate since the capital inflows from such investments would remove the balance of payments constraint on 'excess consumption' induced by pension and social security payments to a large retired population. It is to this issue of the consumption by pensioners that we now turn.

Consume as you go and savings rates

In economics it is emphasised that a nation must save in order to invest; that is to say, it must leave sufficient productive potential for investment purposes and not use all its capacity for producing consumption goods. The reality of the modern economy makes it much less transparent: does the present level of unemployment indicate that we are making excessive savings? If so does our current account deficit on the balance of payments indicate simply that we have too high a level of exchange rate? Should education be regarded as investment and thus taxation used to pay for it regarded as savings? The answer is that none of the categories is as clear cut as it seems, and indeed as Gokhale, Kotlikoff and Sabelhaus (1996, pp. 3-5) show, one of the most unreliable categories of these is personal savings. They illustrate this simply by the relabelling of national insurance contributions as savings in the form of a loan made to government, and pension payments by government as returns of that loan. We would have no problem labelling pension fund contributions as savings, and thus there is no obvious reason why the fact that this function switches from private sector to government should alter the activity from savings to taxation. Does their worry still hold up, therefore, that low savings rates, defined as the residual of production minus consumption and thus avoiding this issue, will lead to low investment levels and hence low growth rates? At one level it must do - it is simply impossible to consume more than you produce except by importing, and that can only be done for a limited period, except by selling ever more of the property rights of the country to people overseas. Even the latter process must cease when all assets are sold, though that could take so many years that the demographic processes could reverse themselves. Before trying to answer that question, the sources of this over-consumption which they analyse for the USA are worth considering and comparing to the UK situation.

In aggregate a transfer of resources has taken place such that this generation of retired people in the USA now consume relatively more per capita than they used to in 1960-61; their share of population has increased from 14.1 to 16.4 percent, but their consumption increased from 10.6 percent to 17.8 percent. ‘Based on demographics alone, the elderly’s share of consumption should have risen by 16.3 percent; instead, it rose by 67.9 percent’ (Gokhale, Kotlikoff and Sabelhaus, 1996, p. 19). One of the main sources of this increased consumption is the much higher pension income that they enjoy (ibid, pp. 20-23), which includes both public and private pension sources and veterans’ benefits. This higher level of resources goes along with a higher propensity to consume for any given level of resources and hence has a major impact on the aggregate level of consumption as a proportion of income. The savings rates of the young in contrast have slightly increased, contrary to the myth of spendthrift youth.

The large increase in consumption rates by the elderly may be the increase in the amount of income which comes in the form of annuities and in the form of Medicare and Medicaid, neither of which can be saved or passed on to the next generation. The ‘annuitisation’, or money paid for the recipient’s lifetime, whatever that is, makes it unnecessary to save as a precaution against living beyond the point at which savings run out. Thus the payment of pensions as annuities, and particularly the giving of 'income in kind' like free health treatment, fails to discourage people from consuming all their income and so decreases saving (ibid, p. 29).

The outcome of these trends when translated into forecasts is that saving in the USA will become negative at some date in the next century. This means that countries outside will have to be willing to give the Americans resources in exchange for property rights in the USA, or the trends will have to change.

We do not have comparable carefully calculated generational accounts in the UK; however, following our rough procedure for allocating expenditures in proportion to the reported sources of income in the Family Expenditure Survey of 1993 and standardising by the known totals from the National Income Accounts, we can see an evolution of pensioners' income as against income from employment as shown in Figure 4 below. The calculation assumes however that pension incomes keep pace with employment incomes; it is an estimate of the effects of demographic change alone. Thus if we have economic growth, and the government elements of pensions and social security payments are fixed in real terms (that is linked only to prices and not to average incomes) the graph represents an overestimate. Similarly with continued real income growth, pensions are mostly uprated in relation to inflation subject to a limit of 5 percent, and would reflect salaries at the time of retirement. Thus they too would lag behind the growth of contributions compared to this scenario. The worst case scenario therefore reflects a shift of pensioners' income, from being about 0.3 of income from work at present to being about 0.4 of work income in 2032. This is of course given these assumptions which ensure that both pensioners', and workers', per capita incomes remain the same, and that the shares of national income are therefore connected via the reciprocal of the support ratio.[3] This implies that we should be saving, whether in the form of taxes, national insurance contributions, pension contributions or direct personal savings, 0.3 of our income at present, and 0.4 of that income in the future. This allows neither for investment, nor the additional consumption by the retired population that might be induced through additional health expenditures, nor for the reduced expenditures on education if there is a declining young population.

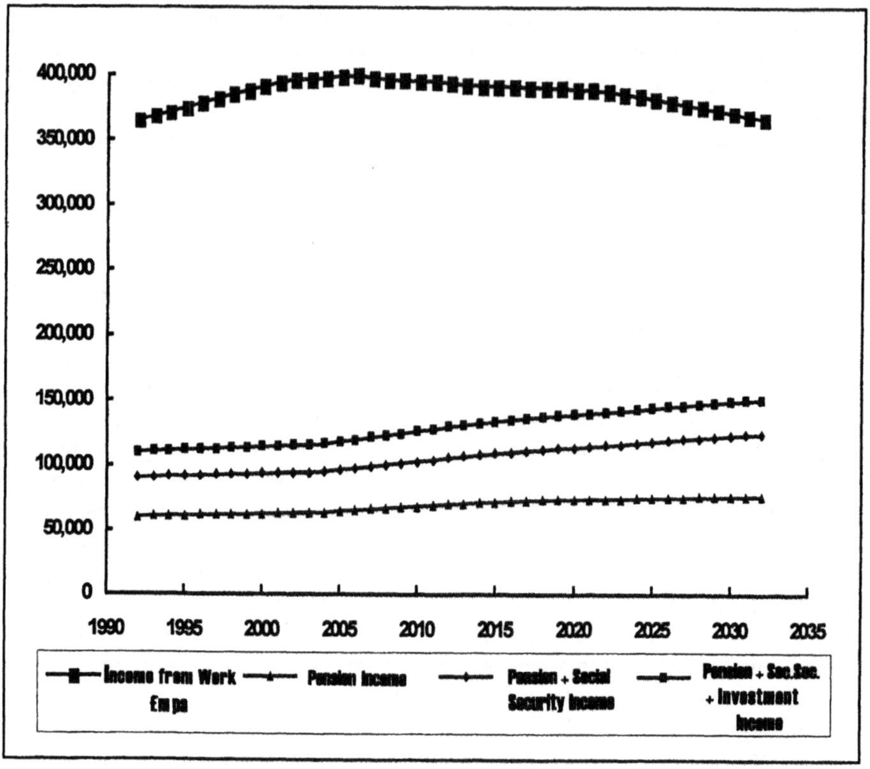

Figure 6.4: **Income from employment, compared with pensions, social security and investment incomes of the retired, 1992-2032, in real terms**

Is retirement sustainable?

Within the UK context, with present distributions of income and their continuation, demographic changes look unlikely on this methodology to create overwhelming problems. We might therefore suggest that retirement will be sustainable.

The trends do, however, clearly create pressures. The above change from retirement incomes consuming about 30 percent of income from work to consuming about 40 percent, has unpleasant implications for taxation, and these estimates do not consider health or long-term care expenditures. The way these expenditures are to be kept down is apparently to keep them indexed to prices rather than incomes. This means that in relative terms state expenditures on pensions, for example, will remain fairly static as a proportion of incomes if incomes grow at 1.5 percent (Hills, 1991, p. 52). (The 'forecast' in figure 6.4 above does not include any growth in per capita incomes, which we hope will not be the real outcome.) The effect of this freezing of state provision in relation to prices is however to make those whose lives have been relatively poor, so that they do not have substantial earnings-related pensions, relatively worse off.

The privatisation not only of provision but also payment for long-term care, is also a threat to the well being of the moderately well off who have sufficient savings to spend on care. It cannot be estimated how far this will encourage over-consumption (if patients spend in order to ensure that they benefit from state provision, given that they will lose their wealth anyway), or saving (to avoid state provision because it will be substandard).

Given the apparent security of the occupational pension, many will apparently have a well-annuitised retirement. Their housing wealth will 'cascade from generation to generation' along with any savings outside their annuities. For others, however, retirement looks as though it might be long and constrained, and one wonders whether the needs created by the increased elderly population might not be catered for by the elderly themselves. Much of the care is at present shouldered by relatives, often in poor health, and for the less well-off this is a full-time commitment. It seems like a market failure that some retired people should have the means of reducing this burden by the provision of their labour, and yet that there should be no means of getting the labour to where it is needed. The problem is that it may seem unattractive to make the commitment of extended work, very probably only part-time when newly retired, against a promise of care in the more distant future and with an uncertain need for it. Furthermore, the group who would most like increased resources, those without occupational pensions, are precisely those whose care is more or less assured by the state and who might therefore have least incentive to join in any such cooperative venture. It would appear therefore that one would have to create a new set of regulated labour markets where the elderly had privileged access to such jobs, very probably on a part-time basis. The end result might in fact be to sustain part-retirement rather than the complete retirement that dominates at present with our relatively favourable support ratio.

Acknowledgements

My thanks to many colleagues, in particular Jonathan Crook, Andy Adams, Seth Armitage, Peter Moles, and Nick Terry from the Finance and Economics group and Professor Adrian Sinfield from the Department of Social Policy for their generous assistance in helping me towards getting to grips with this large and complex subject. The errors and omissions are entirely my own.

Notes

1. The support ratio is defined as the ratio of the working-age population to the population above retirement age.
2. I am grateful to Andy Adams for raising this point.

3

$$\frac{\text{Total Pensioner Income}}{\text{Total Worker Income}} = \frac{\text{Pensioner per capita income}}{\text{worker per capita income}} \times \frac{\text{Number of pensioners}}{\text{Number of workers}}$$

$$\frac{\text{Number of pensioners}}{\text{Number of workers}} = \frac{1}{\text{Support ratio}}$$

References

Börsch-Supan, A. (1991), 'Ageing Population', *Economic Policy*, Vol. 6, April, pp. 103-39.

Central Statistical Office (CSO) (1995), *United Kingdom National Accounts*, HMSO, London.

Central Statistical Office (CSO) (1996), *Financial Statistics*, 407, March, HMSO, London.

Davis, E. P. (1995), *Pension Funds*, Clarendon Press, Oxford.

Department of Social Security (1991), *Options for Equality in State Pension Age*, Cmnd. 1723, HMSO, London.

Dilnot, A., Disney, R., Johnson, P., and Whitehouse, E. (1994), *Pensions Policy in the UK*, Institute for Fiscal Studies, London.

Gokhale, J., Kotlikoff, L. J., and Sabelhaus, J. (1996), *Understanding the Postwar Decline in U.S. Saving: A Cohort Analysis*.

Government Actuary (1994), *Occupational Pension Schemes 1991*, HMSO, London.

Hannah, L. (1986), *Inventing Retirement: the Development of Occupational Pensions in Britain*, Cambridge University Press, Cambridge.

Hills, J. (1993), *The Future of Welfare: a guide to the debate*, The Joseph Rowntree Foundation, York.

Johnson, P., Disney, R., and Stears, G. (1996), *Pensions 2000 and Beyond: Volume 2, The Retirement Income Inquiry*, London.

Myles, J. (1989), *Old Age in the Welfare State: the political economy of public pensions*, Lawrence, University Press of Kansas, Kansas.

Office of Population Census and Surveys (OPCS), (1995), *National Population Projections 1992-based*, Series PP2, No. 19, HMSO, London.

Schieber, S. J., and Shoven, J.B. (1994), *The Consequences of Population Ageing on Private Pension Fund Saving and Asset Markets*, NBER Working Paper 4665, National Bureau of Economic Research, Cambridge Mass.

Solnik, B. (1996), *International Investments*, 3rd edition, Addison Wesley, Reading, MA and Wokingham.

Wilkie, A.D. (1995), 'The Risk Premium on Ordinary Shares', *British Actuarial Journal*, 1, Part II, pp. 251-93.

7 Ageism without frontiers

Ian Glover

Introduction

In this chapter an attempt is made to develop ways of thinking about an immensely complicated relationship, that between age-related attitudes and behaviour and the characteristics and histories of nations. It has been written in an attempt to generate a few tentative ideas about how to cross a minefield with an improved probability of arriving in one piece. I have not been so optimistic or pretentious as to hope to produce reliable generalizations or laws about the subject. However the chapter may have succeeded, at least to a little effect and without too much dissimulation, in emphasizing three significant points: the need for and the difficulty of achieving relevant historical understanding; the sheer variety and unpredictability of relevant influences; and the often kaleidoscopic but also immanent character of relevant changes.

In the next section the subject of the chapter is discussed in such terms so that its complexity may be understood a little better and feared a little less. In the following one thinking and research on comparative management and related phenomena is drawn upon in an attempt to tease out some of the main economic, political and social influences on ageism in different countries. Some broad patterns and some reasonably obvious general influences are observed and on the basis of this three very general hypotheses are discussed in the next four sections, which constitute most of the second half of the chapter. One is the tradition and renewal hypothesis. This suggests that the attributes of the young, and especially those of the old, that is those of people at each end of the age scale, tend to be valued more in more traditional societies, and to be treated as inconvenient, marginal or superfluous in societies undergoing rapid change. The second hypothesis is called the external threat and response one. Here, the attributes of those at each end of the adult age range tend to be valued more in times of national crisis or emergency, as in war for example, than in times of relative stability, security, peace and prosperity. The third is called the security and affluence hypothesis. In this case high living standards and political and military complacency tend to encourage hedonistic ways of life which involve relative neglect of the upbringing of the young and the welfare and wisdom of the old. In some respects and circumstances these three hypotheses can contradict each other but since contrariness and paradox are normal features of human activity this does not concern us immediately or directly, that is at least not until later in the chapter.

The final, Discussion and Conclusion, section briefly draws a few of the main strands of the preceding pages together by emphasising the value of holistic thinking about relationships between age and economic and other phenomena, and of open handling of problems, perceived and real.

The issue

The subject of this chapter can be described in deceptively simple terms as the relationship between nationality and age-related attitudes and behaviour in the context of work and employment. Why do relationships between age and work and employment vary across frontiers? We know that they do, so there is no point in first asking whether that is the case. We also know that all international comparisons, including but not especially those that concern this chapter, tend to be facile unless informed by historical knowledge and understanding. Like individuals, human societies are the sum totals of their experiences. There is neither the space nor the inclination, nor the need, to include detailed historically based analysis of national characteristics and international differences in what follows, but some of it is historically informed and influenced, and that which is not does not pretend to be so. My historical ignorance is undoubtedly profound but I am not completely unaware of its broad outlines.

Attitudes towards age are not the same as age-related behaviour but they are subject to much the same influences. Age is multifaceted itself of course. Youth and middle and old age are the simplest categories of it and even they are defined differently in different places and at different times. The many, almost infinite, influences on relevant attitudes and behaviour can be classified as biological, economic, ideational, material, political, psychological and social, just to start with. They include, by definition, since the whole life span is involved along with all perceptions of it, virtually all aspects and patterns of human existence. Therefore they have an emergent, immanent and unpredictable quality (Sorge, 1982-83).

The limitations of historical evidence about everyday life and social attitudes in most human societies mean that it is at least as hard to generalise about past ageism as it is about its contemporary character. I am less subjective about the past, but more ignorant. However variations in attitudes, for example from reverence to contempt towards older people, seem to have been just as common in the past as they are now. Confusion about the characteristic attributes of members of different age groups appears to have always been a universal, and universally varied, phenomenon. However three tentative and very broad background generalizations do appear to have some convincing support. The first, and the least relevant to his chapter's concern with work and employment, is that both older and younger people are more happy, integrated and useful members of society when supported by strong family and community networks. The second is that industrialization and modernization create stress for older people and between generations, and that as changes slow down differences between the education and life experiences of young and old decrease and the support and valuation of the old increase (Holmes and Holmes, 1995). The third, however, is that this is certainly not always the case: rapid social change can benefit older and younger people greatly, and some features of ageing can be handled very well in any well ordered society, and others very badly (Sokolowsky, 1990; Glover and Branine, 1997).

There is a powerful immanent element in all human behaviour: just as almost every situation contains the seeds of its own destruction, so do many human beings want, at least to some genuine extent, to be the opposites of what they are. Thus, the dissolute yearn for respectability and sobriety, and the respectable and upright yearn to cut loose. And the young want to be older, and vice versa. This factor has cautioned me against efforts to 'fix', permanently or thereabouts, particular human societies as having their own unique ageist attitudes and practices regarding age, work and employment. Work done mainly in the 1970s led various writers to typify management in the United Kingdom (UK) and the United States of America (USA) as generally having much more short-term preoccupations than management in Germany and Japan (see for example Glover, 1985; Glover and Hughes, 1996; Lawrence, 1992, 1996a, 1996b), and to think that ageism against older employees would be much more prevalent in the first two of these countries. This was an over-simple and in some respects shallow view, since modified (Glover and Branine, 1997; and see below).

National patterns

In the UK there is still a strong tendency for managers to treat older employees who are close to or past the ends of their useful working lives as human commodities, which and to release them first during 'downsizings'. Human resource management tends to foster this practice, rather than, as a naïve reading of its developmental rhetoric might suggest, to oppose it (Lyon, Hallier and Glover, 1998). Younger managers and older managers and employees tend to be in opposition, ideologically, economically and socially. The former tend to be aggressively managerialist and to argue that the generally functionally specific knowledge of older employees is inadequate in downsized, delayered organizations whose management demands functional flexibility, polyvalent skills and teamworking at almost all hierarchical levels. The latter tend to be much more knowledgeable about the work and the needs of colleagues in other functions and occupations than their often younger organizational superiors would like to admit, and at times embarassingly and inconveniently knowledgeable about the failings of their organizations' managements in general. Their scepticism about fashionable management fads and management language concerning visions, missions, image and so on can be interpreted as 'lack of strategic vision' by their 'superiors'. The use of information technology has also borne more heavily on them than most, reducing their discretion and increasing the visibility of their work. Age is generally seen as a negative attribute and the relevant attitude can be summed up in the sentence 'I know s/he is good, but s/he is sixty'. However there is increasing awareness of such issues in the UK, both inside and outside the worlds of work and employment, and evidence of improving standards of age discrimination on the part of some employers.

France is traditionally far less ageist than the UK. French management, or at least its more elevated layers and segments, consists of a loose old boy network of highly educated engineers, and commercial and financial and administrative experts. Yet because it tends to be intellectually and socially elitist, and paternal, in a society which venerates age, it may be perceived as ageist towards the young. However the context is a predominantly Catholic society with a relatively high proportion of small and medium sized firms, and one of centralized political and economic power. Age is a plus factor in France in terms of credibility and authority, so that a politician of 75 will generally be more respected than one of 50. Many business leaders have had very long reigns, with the family business run by *le patron* still predominant across large swathes of the economy. The proportion of firms which are family-run is in long term decline, management has been becoming more international and commercial in outlook, and a more competitive business climate is tending to wear down the familial, hierarchical and paternal character of French employment relationships. Nonetheless France is very different from the UK in its stance towards age and employment.

Canada and the USA enjoy various links with France and the UK. Canada's origins are of course partly French, but more so partly British. Canadian management is to some extent influenced by the USA and indeed the three largest companies operating in Canada are General Motors, Ford and Chrysler. However the culture of Canadian management is relatively restrained and moderate, like that of Canada itself. Canadian managers and employment practices are in general very fair-minded, human rights-conscious and relatively un-ageist. Even so there are many subsidiaries of US multinationals in Canada and phased early retirements of people in their fifties are widely experienced and accepted in many sectors.

The USA is possibly the most obviously and superficially ageist society of those discussed here. I use the term obviously because ageism against older employees is very common and often dramatically apparent to the USA. I have added the word superficially because I would suggest that the USA is not as ageist in its underlying philosophies of employment as much of the overt behaviour indicates. Nevertheless the notion that Americans have long worshipped youth and youthfulness and that they are strongly committed to achievement, which they regard young people as being better at, is clearly supportable by all kinds of evidence on patterns of employment and on attitudes towards it (Lawrence, 1996). Americans routinely assume that younger people are less cynical, hungrier, stronger, more financially committed and more likely to be sustained by ambitious spouses than older ones. Also decisiveness is the quality of executive behaviour which Americans, with their 'right now!' approach to decision making, value most highly, and this favours the young insofar as older people are more likely to make qualified judgements. Reflectiveness is not a particularly valued trait in the USA and a tendency to believe in simple means-ends relationships also favours the young.

Other continental European countries tend to be more like France with regards to ageism than the UK and the USA, although they are different from France and each other in many relevant ways. Germany, with its very strong systems of apprenticeship and broad and vocational education and its belief in the lifetime pursuit of specialist expertise would appear to have a strongly anti-ageist culture. Both family and small and medium sized enterprises (SMEs) are strong in Germany and the backbone of its economy, is the *Mittelstand* of businesses with a few hundred employees, bigger than SMEs but smaller than UK-style public limited companies, which are often market leaders or nearly so in technical sectors and niche markets. *Mittelstand* companies tend to keep younger employees in their proper place in traditional and practical terms and to look after middle aged employees and to regulate employment and intergenerational relationships formally and bureaucratically. As a sort of 'late starter' economy, and assuming for the moment that is sensible, which in general it is not, to think of there being single and discrete manufacturing and services sectors which are somehow in opposition, Germany moved from employing more people in manufacturing to move in services only in the 1990s. To a certain extent and in the context of widespread internationalisation, the Single European Market (SEM) and unification with East Germany, Germany's economy was overloaded with manufacturing companies by the 1990s with high direct and indirect wage costs and strongly established systems of skill certification. As a consequence there was a certain amount of downsizing and offshore movement of production which weighed most heavily on older German employees. German employers, German trade unions and German people were not ageist by disposition but the economic reality was forcing them to act in ageist ways and quite often, after the 1980s.

In Switzerland the position has been very similar to Germany's, except that the process just briefly outlined has taken place more slowly. Sweden is a very un-ageist or anti-ageist society. Its systems of education and training, management, industrial relations and employment are similar to those of Germany, and core values of decency and reasonableness translate through a mixture of active public conscience and legislation into managerial actions which duly respect employees of all ages. Swedish management styles are definitely not pro-youth like those of the USA. Like Sweden and Canada, the Netherlands is also relatively un-ageist, caring and decent, with few or no management characteristics or social influences predisposing people towards ageist behaviour. Management and employment tend to be participative, regulated and socially responsible as in Germany and other North-West European and the Scandinavian countries. Moreover, economic pressures against employees in vulnerable age groups are not particularly strong in the Netherlands. Pressures favouring downsizing and offshore manufacturing have not been as strong as in Germany and Switzerland. Notwithstanding the existence of Philips and other prominent Dutch manufacturing companies, and of powerful systems of vocational education and training, the economy of the Netherlands is very strong in terms of banking and finance, the spot oil market, offshore gas extraction, transport and tourism, with manufacturing much less prominent than in France or Germany or as in several other significant medium sized EU economies. Even Philips, in which the USA has significant shareholdings, employs very few people in the Netherlands. There is a sense in which the Netherlands 'skipped' industrializaton so that Dutch employers have not experienced the same pressures to train, discard and/or retrain skilled workers on the kinds of scale experienced in economies in which manufacturing and cognate sectors have been more prominent.

We now move back south in Europe to two countries, Italy and Spain, which are closer to France, geographically and historically. Italy is a country in the Catholic mainstream with a very strong emphasis on the family and with an economy with a high population of family owned SMEs with no formal control exercised over the ages of managers. Large Italian public companies like Fiat are also often family owned and run. There is considerable respect for functional academic achievements like higher diplomas and doctorates in engineering, which as elsewhere on the Continent are more often than not obtained after the age of 25, and this tends to favour mature employees and managers. Italian management has an easy-going informal quality and tends to present itself as a milder version of Latin American clientism in which personal, familial and institutional contacts matter a great deal. So the familial and non-bureaucratic elements in Italian society and management militate against bureaucratic recourse to age as a major selection criterion for the initiation and termination of employment, and for employee deployment and development. In this sense Italian society and employers are not ageist at all, although to Anglo-Saxon eyes their paternalist tendencies are about as irrationally ageist as it is possible to be!

Spanish employers are similar in many of these respects to their Italian counterparts. There is an added element of rather anti-ageist fatalism in Spanish culture, and a preoccupation with death. Employment practices tend to be non-bureaucratic and paternal, with the influences of the Roman Catholic Church, the extended family, and the very large number and proportion of SMEs all strong.

Two societies which are of interest and outside both North America and the European Union are Israel and Columbia. Management and employment practices in Israel combine traditional and participative and Zionist values with those of Israel's version of 'modern' management. The latter is not American in style in spite of about 25 per cent of Israel's Gross Domestic Product coming from US subsidiaries based in Israel. It is a product of Israel's struggle to build a strong economy and an internationalist and of course Jewish society. Interviews conducted of Israeli managers by Lawrence yielded no evidence of ageism (Lawrence, 1990). There was no evidence of ageist assumptions, disposition or upbringing but tendencies to emphasize the importance of research and development, early promotion, and the appointment of 40 year old chief executives in the more advanced companies all embody one kind of age preference. This seemed to be reinforced by the Israeli military, which is at least superficially ageist against older people, routinely using early promotion and retirement, and with the typical colonel being thirty and the typical general 40. Most officers retire at about 45 and go into management in non-high technology sectors, except for air force officers who do often go on to work for the more sophisticated enterprises. Interestingly, many high technology companies are kibbutz based with small factories run partly by councils of elders (older males).

Finally, and like Israel, Columbia is also influenced by Europe and North America but also unique. It is less ageist than the UK and the USA and quite sympathetic to older people, employees and managers. The culture is essentially Latin so there is a strong emphasis on the family and paternalism. Young people tend not to attend universities outside their home towns, and to live at home until they marry. Columbia is fairly typical of other Latin South American countries. Clientism and network building are powerful features of management. People try to build up dependency in their relationships. No relationship is a straightforward contractual one: there is always a leader-follower element. Ageism of the 'Anglo-Saxon' type is largely conspicuous by its absence but tradition is very apparent.

There is a sub-Durkheimian, sub-Weberian tone about the above perceptions of age and employment. Protestant, northern, Anglo-Saxon countries generally commodify the employment relationship and are manifestly and at times aggressively ageist. Catholic, southern, Latin countries tend to take care of younger and older people alike and are, at least in a surface sense, institutionally (to coin a term) anti-ageist or at least non- or un-ageist. A classification of approaches to management or business styles and of national administrative heritages across the Triad economies of the USA, Japan and Europe developed by Calori (1999; Calori and de Woot, 1994) offers an interpretation which is broadly sympathetic to the preceding ones.

Competitiveness, individualism, short-term profit orientation, systemic professional management and the manager as hero are terms used by Calori to describe management in North America, albeit really the United States. By contrast Japanese management is depicted as having a long term growth orientation and as being consensual, more horizontally integrated and strongly focused on superior quality as the source of competitive advantage. American and Japanese management, so described, are easy to interpret as ageist and anti-ageist respectively, although many other factors suggest that such comparisons should not be anything like so black and white.

An old early 1990s edition of a popular and heavyweight American international business text discussed a study of attitudes to age in the Far East and the USA, and reported an apocryphal story about the same kinds of attitude in India. In the former case a large number of respondents from the USA and the Far East were asked to consider the situation of three people afloat on an ocean in a boat which could only hold two. The three people were a female child, her early middle-aged mother, and the grandmother. Whose life should be lost? The American respondents felt that it should be the grandmother's and the respondents from the Far East felt that it should be the child's. However the story from India suggested the existence of rather different values in the Far East, albeit a specific large part of it. A young family is no longer able to support the elderly father of the husband. So after urging by his wife about the need for their children to be fed the husband takes his father to the edge of a cliff with the aim of throwing him off. The father quietly begins to laugh, and his son asks him why. The father replies: 'I can remember when I came here with your grandfather'. The nature of the study's findings and of the story's message suggested that age-related attitudes and behaviour are more variable and subject to more influences than broad brush international comparisons about a cult of youth in the contemporary 'West' and persistence of traditional veneration of the elderly elsewhere.

Calori (1999) goes on to argue that it is possible to tease out elements of a European approach to management from the great diversity of western European practice. He does so in order to distinguish western Europe from North America and Japan and suggests that it is the very diversity of Europe which helps him to describe its uniqueness. In the process of doing so he argues, with particular force, that 'there is *both* unity and diversity across Europe, and the two perspectives [homogeneity or heterogeneity] complement each other' (Calori, 1999, p. 483). His list of four characteristics which distinguished Western European management from management elsewhere are managing international diversity, internal negotiation, an orientation towards people, and balance between extremes. Calori is himself European and this leads us to ask how, say, a Japanese, Arab or North American student of management might depict Western European management. However Calori's list seems quite convincing. European managers do appear to enjoy diversity and the interpersonal negotiation, within and outside their own organizations, that its sustenance demands. Herein lies their so-called people-centredness and the 'balance between extremes' of fiercely pursued efficiency and social responsiveness, American-style individualism and Japanese collectivism.

It is when Calori (1999) comes to discuss intra-European differences and to group European approaches to management and employment together that he becomes most interesting. He first depicts the UK as the major exception in Western Europe, as lying between continental European and American approaches. It seems, also, that the UK is the most important exception because of the size of its economy and the differences between its history and that of the rest of Europe, with its island location helping it to perform a semi-detached role for many centuries. It has been suggested here that age-related attitudes and behaviour in European management tend to differentiate between the Catholic South and the Protestant North. Calori puts France and Italy in his 'Latin Catholic South'. He characterises the context of management there as one of state intervention and protectionism, and argues that its character tends to be hierarchical and intuitive and at times chaotic. Management in the (more) Protestant North of Europe operated, on the other hand, in a context of less state intervention and more liberalism, and there was more employee participation in decision making and work was more organized, formally and otherwise. All of this fits with what has been written here about France, Germany, Switzerland, Sweden, the Netherlands, Italy and Spain. It accords with the view that in the South management is more familial and paternal, patriarchal and less ageist in the sense in which that word is currently used in the UK and the USA, especially about the discarding of older employees as 'dead wood', and about the cult of youth which involves disinvestment in the upbringing of the young.

More explicitly than this chapter has suggested, Calori regards France as being rather different from other Latin Catholic South countries by virtue of its more formal, more 'Northern' approach to management, employment and organization, and because of the unique relative homogeneity of its technocratic management elite. He groups Austria with Germany in the Germanic countries and he argues that the Scandinavian ones do not differ from the latter much except insofar as there is more evidence of concern with the quality of life at work there and less of with status differences in workplaces, and some evidence of American influences on approaches to management coming from experiences of being hosts to subsidiaries of US multinationals. He regards the Benelux and Scandinavian countries and Switzerland as being different from other Northern countries by virtue of their small sizes, their varied histories and their geographic locations, which make them all, in various different ways, more open to foreign influences, with companies often having quite long traditions of being international in outlook and being managed in consensual and pluralist ways.

Calori attributes relevant differences ultimately to the 'societal effect' which Maurice (1972), Sorge (1979), Maurice, Sorge and Warner (1980) and Calori, Lubatkin and Very (1994) had outlined in various ways. Employment practices and work organization were, according to this view, shaped in the first instance by such national institutions as schools and universities and financial and labour markets and at a deeper level by decisions made by politicians and other national rulers before and during industrialization about the purposes and development of such institutions. More generally, all agencies of primary and secondary socialization such as the family, religious institutions, thc mass media, schools and peer groups shaped the cognitive structures that order understanding of the external world and views about what is desirable and possible and what is not. This notion appears to be accepted widely by writers on comparative management and international business such as Bartlett and Ghoshal (1989), Whitley (1992), Smith and Meiksins (1995), Hampden-Turner and Trompenaars (1995) and Lawrence and Edwards (2000). However Lawrence and Edwards also argue that such internationalizing trends as deregulation and privatization, managerialism and an acceleration of internationalization itself, have been more influential across the world since the 1970s than before, making employment and work organization more similar than in the past. Smith and Meiksins (1995) suggested that while the societal effect approach to the study of comparative management was useful for explaining many specific features of national modes of managing and organizing it tended to ignore the way in which a kind of follow-my-leader effect operated over long periods. Thus the most ostensibly successful national economy in a given period tended to serve as a role model for others, influencing the development, not only of the day to day practice of employment and management, but also that of education and training systems, occupations and companies. Glover and Tracey (1997) concurred but also reminded their readers that societies could also both leapfrog each other economically and develop in parallel, in effect choosing to ignore each other.

Other studies and depictions of national approaches to employment and management, such as those of Ronen and Shenkar (1985) and Hofstede (1991), are broadly in accord with the patterns of difference and similarity noted above. However few writers on comparative management and related issues have concerned themselves with age, employment and management, although two books which are partial and useful exceptions with at least some relevant points to make have been those by Hampden-Turner and Trompenaars (1993) and Kennedy (1993). Hampden-Turner and Trompenaars (1993) tend at times to deal in stereotypes in their nonetheless very stimulating account of seven national ways of creating wealth. They argue that for Americans, time is sequential and a competitive 'race', whereas for Japanese it consists of synchronization and more of a harmonious and cooperative 'dance'. The USA is a this-worldly country in a hurry, competing against the clock, seeing time as a precious resource and a threat. The corporation is a machine driven by independent, analytical, brave and inner-directed individualists. Both the wider society and social ramifications of this philosophy tend to be ignored and the idea of learning from experience tends to be neglected. Cash cow corporations are there simply to be milked and are not seen as sources of innovation and wisdom. So too with mature employees. Change comes through creative destruction, demanding young people for new jobs and that 'grandad [should] move aside'. The organization is *not* a family in which status grows automatically as people gain in experience, with everyone rising as high as their qualifications, potential and achievements allow. For Americans this approach carries too many dangers of ethnic and other forms of cronyism and nepotism, of paternalism in general and of over-familiarity with subordinates. For a nation of immigrants a preference for purely achievement-based status was very understandable, and obviously fair in any context, but if linked too closely to ideas about age (older in this context) being a major barrier to achievement, a self-fulfilling prophecy could operate. In Japan and other Pacific Rim economies experience and length of service were respected so that expectations were increased, and in general fulfilled, as employees aged. Older people were expected to act as mentors for their juniors, and even if they were not particularly successful they would still have lessons, some more painful than others, to teach. However to ensure that people of all ages strove to meet their potentials, companies had to 'assume major responsibility for their development of all ... employees' (Hampden-Turner and Trompenaars, 1993, p. 91). By implication those which did not do so were actually, and in a sense actively, disinvesting in their own futures.

One particularly stimulating, and significant for present purposes, argument used by Hampden-Turner and Trompenaars concerns the relationship between organizational hierarchy and economic performance. For these authors the conventional and strongly research based Western view of this relationship was that tall or steep hierarchies were suited to simple and relatively stable technologies and products and that flat ones were suited to complexity and change. However, they go on to argue that not all relatively tall hierarchical approaches to management are the same. They could vary along a continuum, for example, from being highly centralized 'top-down bureaucratic structure[s] of subordination' to resembling 'a close family with elders caring for and developing young people'. In other words they could be 'impersonal' or 'familial' (p. 97). Relatively flat hierarchies did indeed tend to foster and sustain healthy competition of ideas and individuals, as seen in most of the main the English-speaking countries, Scandinavia and much of the rest of north-west Europe. However the 'organic ordering' societies of Southern Europe and Japan and Singapore and other Far Eastern societies were also capable of successful and sustained economic effort. More premature forms of these were the semi-feudal societies of parts of the Indian sub-continent and Latin America.

There, land and other forms of property ownership gave business proprietors both rights over and family-style obligations to employees. However in the more sophisticated versions of this approach in Japan and elsewhere in the Far East but also to varying degrees in France, Italy and Spain, relationships were more concerned with the ordering and use of relevant information, knowledge and ideas. In Japan in particular, the latter were organized hierarchically with theories being ranked above general propositions and the latter being ranked above particulars and the specific details of tasks, skills and so on. The provision of information and the initiation of change generally worked in an upwards direction, with specific information, knowledge and ideas being supplied by junior staff to senior ones, whose task was to 'weave this ... into coherent [and harmonious] visions and configurations' (p. 98). Conceptually and emotionally, relationships between hierarchical levels were intimate and close because of the need for efficient and harmonious working.

By contrast, traditional Western, meaning predominantly US, hierarchies operated in top-down ways, with precise orders being used to initiate actions rather than more vague and holistic discussion and guidance. Such orders were specific, analytic, impersonal, rational, cold, utilitarian and so on. This approach was increasingly regarded, everywhere, as rather rigid and slow but also as containing potentially rampant and destructive individualism. The authors (p. 98) called it 'propositional' because ideas, changes and order came from the top to be implemented downwards. The organic ordering philosophy was 'appositional', meaning suitable, pertinent and well adapted. Feedback from customers was highly valued and combined with ideas and related information from junior employees who were close to customers, and fed upwards into middle management and hence to senior management while all the time being processed, developed and synthesized with other relevant data and ideas. This philosophy valued junior employees as sources of vital information and as initiators of creative and harmonious change: they were not merely employed to carry out orders.

Throughout their book, Hampden-Turner and Trompenaars (1993) offer all kinds of age-related insight, sometimes we think unintentionally, but always in ways which are benign in intent and in accord with our general view that harmonious cooperation between generations is superior to all of the alternatives. They discuss 'Pure Competitiveness [American] vs. Cooperative Competing [Japanese]' (pp. 128-31). They argue that Japanese people and companies simultaneously, and sometimes at different levels, help and oppose each other. They literally love their enemies, or hate their friends, in ways intended to harmonize all the complex and of course often opposed features of economic and social life. The view that all human life consists of a struggle is one that Japanese people regarded as naïve and distasteful. Those who lose should not be crushed or left to die: they should be left with their honour, and with time to learn, to recover and to prosper again. In education, the aim of competition is not to divide people into sheep and goats. Instead its purpose is to prepare people for later cooperation by helping them to discover and develop their talents. In employment, everyone, however superficially or in reality unsuccessful, has something to teach others.

Hampden-Turner and Trompenaars (1993; see also Landes. 1998) often refer to the deep, pervasive and long term influences of topography, climate and religion when they make their comparisons. On Japanese approaches to time and age in management they focus on much of Japan having long been covered by forests and on how this has helped Japanese people to think of life as being a continual process of renewal with many hidden depths and meanings, and to understand the unity and interdependence of all forms and stages of life. It clearly is important to appreciate Japanese history, religion and society for understanding intergenerational relationships in work and employment in Japan. At the same time one may also wonder for how long early twenty-first century Japan, as a very advanced industrial society operating on a world stage, one which now has little or nothing left to prove since its traumatic defeat nearly sixty years ago, can continue to maintain and draw upon its old underlying moral strengths and social fabric.

Nonetheless there are many strong lessons to be drawn from relevant features of the Japanese approach to time, age employment, management and work. One is that it is more rational in every sense, and more robust, to focus, Japan-style, on the pull of the future in management than to be dictated to by the push of the present. In the latter case, if things go wrong, as they inevitably do, you lose your way. Another concerns the Japanese approach to innovation which is more craft-like and *ad hoc* than the more structured, linear and overtly rational Anglo-Saxon one. US and British research and development laboratories have traditionally been found in country houses in leafy country surroundings, thought to favour basic, original, blue-sky research, which if relevant is to be put to use later following appropriate financial and marketing activity and necessary process and product development. However in Japan (and Germany) technical development is equally influenced, when necessary, by inputs from natural science, but it has a far more untidy appearance and character, consisting as it does of many acts of pulling activities and innovations together in order to achieve such desired end states as improved processes, products or both (cf. Sorge and Hartmann, 1980). All effective technical change is like this in fact and Japan and Germany are by no means its only exemplars (Glover and Kelly, 1987; Leadbetter, 1997).

The Japanese large company philosophy as regards hierarchy and seniority is also very relevant. How long one works without oversight and supervision is what tends to justify seniority and promotion in Japan. This is what Jacques (1982) called the 'time span of discretion'. Its length, or duration, tends to grow with experience and age. The more a person draws on the past and considers the future in their work, the greater their status, seniority and power in many larger Japanese enterprises. This philosophy can just as sensibly be applied to specialists as well as to generalists. A suitable example might be an architect steeped in knowledge of designing and building in different historical periods and parts of the world, compared with one who was not, or with a typical building site agent or manager. This type of seniority only *tends* to be based on years of experience because depth and breadth of understanding and vision are to be found in people of all ages.

However the value placed on bureaucratic leadership, indulgent love and 'fingertip control' in Japanese management, with there being no boundary between *Gemeinschaft* and *Gesellschaft* and with work relationships having an affectionate and familial quality does generally value age and wisdom in practice. Relationships at work and those with family and friends are regarded as being little different. Promotion is generally used as an opportunity to care for less distinguished persons, not as one to get away from them. There is a powerful belief, regarding the development of both people and technology in cross-fertilisation and synergy and in 'cycles of eternal return to the living economy'.

The authors see strong elements of similar and related phenomena in German, Swedish and Dutch management. The depict German management as having orderly, 'deep', and 'romantic' elements insofar as it bases itself on the most valued lessons of Germany's history. Thus it puts premia on craft expertise and the maintenance of high technical standards, employment and management practices which are socially inclusive and relatively democratic, and the long-term development of individuals and their specialist skills and their specialist and general knowledge. The system of education and training is organised to give most people useful occupations or vocations, useful niches in the economy and self-respect. The term *beruf* is very widely used: it means skilled and useful calling, occupation and/or vocation, it has no English counterpart, and it does not distinguish between people at different levels of the system of social stratification like the English terms profession and occupation (Glover, 1978; Child et al, 1983). The German system defines most people as successful on both their terms and those of society: a qualified electrician living in and working from a suburban house has, for example, a prominent brass plate on the front of it, advertising their qualifications and business, in the manner of an Anglo-Saxon doctor or lawyer (Fores and Glover, 1978; Glover, 1978; Lawrence, 1980). Universalist notions of management being an enabling generalism consisting of a body of universally applicable knowledge and skills are rejected both tacitly and explicitly, often with a certain amount of derision (Sorge, 1978; Sorge and Warner, 1986; Locke, 1996a, 1996b, 2000). The German system and philosophy is more rational, bureaucratic and formal, and structured than the Japanese one but it also draws on close to primeval notions of dark spaces (private ones in the German case) and of continual self renewal drawing on knowledge of the past and sustained by mutual understanding and support.

Please see the Appendix for details and a discussion of further relevant elements of Swedish and Dutch and also French and British management as discussed by Hampden-Turner and Trompenaars.

Another writer interested in relevant aspects of employment and management across the world was Kennedy (1993), whose main concerns were the prospects for humanity in the present, new, century. Over and above influences specific to nations and regions of the world, he was particularly concerned with 'forces for global changes like population growth, the impact of technology, environmental danger and migration, which were *trans*national in nature and threatened the lives of us all' (p. ix). Some of his points and arguments are directly relevant to this chapter. One is that while the populations of developed regions of the world were becoming much older than in the past, those of the developing ones were growing much faster than in the former regions and becoming, on average, much younger. World population was likely to stabilise in the middle or late twenty-first century with estimates of the resultant global population varying from under eight to nearly 15 billion people, compared with the present figure of nearly 6.5 billion. In today's developing world, so-called megacities like Sao Paulo, Mexico City, Calcutta, Bombay and Shanghai had grown up, each with mainly young populations over or approaching twenty million, and with most being increasingly centers of poverty and social collapse' (p. 27). Billions of impoverished young people would come to demand education, jobs and health care but it was hard to see how they would get them. Very large scale social unrest might follow, although there were many uncertainties about population growth and its effects, including the potentially dramatic influences on population growth rates of AIDS, contraception, industrialization, and improvements in sanitation and medical care in particular and in medical capability and public health in general.

In the developed regions of the world, with their high standards of health care and living, population growth was often non-existent or negative. So whereas developing countries had to look after many millions of people under 15, developed ones would increasingly have to look after growing numbers of people aged over 65. In both types of region and country, dependency ratios would become smaller with relatively fewer productive people between 15 and 64 available to look after burgeoning numbers of under-15s in one case and over-65s in the other. There would be some variations from these patterns. In a few of the richer countries birth rates are not falling, and in the USA continued immigration combined with this would mean that the population would both continue to grow and to include a high proportion of younger people. However the general trend in the richer countries was one of prolongation of life for older people, which was very costly as regards health care, pensions and social services, and which consequently reduced investment in productive activities. On the other hand greater capital-intensiveness in industry might follow, along with higher savings to spending ratios. Yet on the other hand, older people tended to use up their savings eventually.

Kennedy (1993) discusses these issues in such particular contexts as that of Japan at some length. He admits at one point that part of the solution to Japan's 'ageing' workforce may be 'rethinking retirement regulations' (p. 155). He also continually associates the word 'ageing' with others such as 'stagnant' (see p. 158 for example). He discusses China's much larger and also 'ageing' population in similar terms. He is equally pessimistic about India's very rapidly growing population although in this case it is excessive numbers of dependent young people that cause him most concern, at least in the short and medium terms. In the longer term India may, he suggests, experience the 'ageing population' problem more, as life expectancy has long been rising there, from about 32 at independence in 1947 to about 60 in the early 1990s. Kennedy's pessimism about 'ageing' populations was near-universal in fact. Thus he bemoans the 'graying of Europe' caused partly by declining fertility rates, and suggests that in early 1989 West Germany was starting to 'commit [demographic] suicide' accordingly (p. 273).

At various junctures throughout his book Kennedy refers to automation, to the use of guest workers and to upward adjustments to retirement ages as possible parts of national and regional solutions to his ageing population problem. His views sometimes seem both ageist and unduly pessimistic. This is not only because technical change and ongoing industrialization have very often, if not invariably, produced solutions to the economic, social and political problems that they have appeared to create. It is also because Kennedy appears to assume that all people over about 65 are 'elderly' and incapable of being productive members of society. He ignores the strong possibility that longer and healthier lives tend to contain more active years, that populations are really 'juvenating', rather than 'ageing'. Thus his position is out of date, or at least obsolescent, as populations of the richer countries confront the challenge-cum-opportunity of finding useful and satisfying things for physically and mentally lively older people to do. (Here this chapter is being ageist itself in some respects because such people are probably better equipped than anyone else to use their time constructively, if not prevented from doing so by archaic attitudes and rules enforced by their conservative juniors). The same argument can also be used against his perceptions of the dependent status of ever larger numbers of young people in many of the world's developing regions. However it may have less force in that context because both the resources needed to mobilise the resource and the quality of the resource itself – much of it simply too young and incapable of productive activity of any but very elementary kinds – may be inadequate or non-existent.

In general Kennedy's views about the role of population changes in humanity's future appear slightly dated less than a decade after he expressed them. There is now more awareness than when he wrote his book that the human life span has increased considerably, and not only in the industrial or developed countries, in the twentieth century, and that the historically very capital intensive nature of much contemporary work and employment mean that the range of possibilities for the early and the later decades of life is much greater than it was a century ago, when universal schooling and universal state pension provision were recent social innovations.

The three hypotheses

As noted at the outset three tentative hypotheses about the subject of this chapter are offered in it. I called them the tradition and renewal, the external threat and response, and the security and affluence hypotheses. They have emerged rather intuitively from reading, thinking and experience. A lot of evidence has been examined and there ensued strong gut feelings and a number of logically but incompletely worked out reasons for choosing them. The hypotheses may well be mistaken but they are big and bold enough to attract comment, criticism and debate and thus they will hopefully serve their purpose. Each is discussed in relation to some relevant literature and data.

The tradition and renewal hypothesis

In this case it is suggested that members of societies in which awareness of the past is strong, and in which continuity is highly regarded, will tend to think and act quite consciously, discriminatingly and constructively towards people at different stages of the life cycle and work and employment. Above in the discussion of national patterns, the countries in which institutions and behaviour appeared to exemplify this pattern included France, Italy, Japan and Spain, and in less clear ways or to smaller degrees, Canada, Columbia, Germany, the Netherlands and Sweden. The UK and the USA appeared not to, and Israel's position was rather idiosyncratic. French management tended to be centralized, elitist and paternal and strongly influenced by the Roman Catholic religion and other traditional influences. In Italy, also a Catholic country, with many companies family owned and run, management was also paternal and familiar. Spanish management was similar in most such respects. These Latin Catholic countries exemplify the people orientation of European management discussed by Calori (1999), while also having more pronounced than average tendencies towards hierarchy, intuition, state intervention, tradition, religious influence, family ownership, paternalism and patriarchy. Age tended to be treated as an opportunity and as a resource, not as a problem and a liability. The same appeared to hold true for Japanese management. In that case the use of time was not thought of as a linear 'race', especially as in the Anglo-Saxon-West, but as a cooperative and harmonious 'dance'. Respect for age and experience became a profitable self-fulfilling prophecy. Lessons were there to be learnt from the mistakes as well as from the successes of older people. Organizational hierarchies were more like close families, with elders caring for and developing younger employees, rather than top down instruments of subordination. Thus and as noted earlier Hampden-Turner and Trompenaars (1993) wrote of the 'organic ordering' of such Southern-European societies as France, Italy and Spain, and of Japan and Singapore in the Far East. Such societies had some semi-feudal elements which caused ideas and knowledge to be fostered from above and drawn upwards from below in employing organizations, for appropriate further development, adaptation and use. Thus the abilities of junior people were integrated and developed creatively and in ways designed to ensure the continual renewal of companies. The past offered many lessons, ones to which the present continually added and enhanced. Germany appears to be much closer to the Latin Catholic and Far Eastern tradition and renewal approach or set of circumstances than US or US-influenced writers like Kennedy (1993) or Hampden-Turner and Trompenaars (1993) admit. Germany's emphasis on craft and *Technik*, its rejection of the English-language linear Science leads to Technology leads to Hardware model of technical change (Sorge and Hartmann, 1980), the strengths and the longevity of its SMEs, the very strong regional and local foci and traditions of its systems of education and training, and its emphasis on the integration of employees and management which is often greatly underrated (see especially Locke, 2000) all help to put it at least very close to, if not very firmly in, the tradition and renewal camp. Mainly because Germany and France have been the two most influential countries in Western Europe and Scandinavia as regards education, training, occupation formation, organization and management, virtually all of the European countries next or near to them, except those separated from them by the North Sea and the English Channel, can be similarly located. The Western individualism which is more pronounced in the UK and North America, for example, than in Western Europe, is of course itself both traditional and also very much about the ongoing renewal of society.

Gerontologists and sociologists have theorized relationships between age and society in various ways, with theories usually being produced by people 'in mid-life ... [who] have largely viewed old age negatively' (Wilson, 2000, p. 11). They have also tended to highlight the attitudes of elderly people who claim not to 'feel old' and who strongly prefer the company of people younger than themselves, rather than those of the majority who accept their ages and who are not ageist towards their contemporaries. Wilson (p. 11) reports that the disengagement theory of ageing of Cumming and Henry (1961) had been attacked by advocates of the theory of active ageing like Atcherly (1987). The former theory regarded disengagement of older people from society as good for older people and for society. Old age was a period of well-earned rest for such theorists, but the active ageing theorists advocated keeping the body and mind active. The theories only conflict superficially and logically, of course: it is reasonable for an older or elder person to be less involved with some activities of mid-life but also to be as active (or not) as their health permits.

The most universally popular theory of ageing has been the 'golden age' or modernization one. Once, and in traditional, stable, societies, it is thought, elders were looked up to and cared for by their families. Long experience and nearness to death gave older people wisdom and spirituality. Industrialization, Westernisation, materialism and so on had led to the such wisdom being devalued along with religious authority and family solidarity. However critics of this theory had attacked it for being too simple. The old were neither always supported in the past nor neglected in the present. Indeed they were widely supported in modern societies. In traditional societies poor people, childless people, the weak and the widowed often suffered greatly when they grew old, and in contemporary traditional societies they very often still do so.

More recent and rigorous theorizing has produced structured dependency theory (for example, Estes, 1979; Walker, 1980, 1981; Townsend, 1981; and Phillipson, 1982). Here, society was organized so as to make older people dependent. State pensions and ageist employers forced them out of labour markets. Their lack of employment reduced respect for them. If they fell ill or simply grew frail they lost control over their lives by having to live in hospitals, nursing or residential homes. They were constantly patronized and stereotyped by public agencies and in media portrayals of various kinds. Wilson (2000, p. 12) felt that while this theory contained many truths, because older people lacked citizenship rights and respect and were often denied opportunities to participate in society. However the theory depicted 'older people as victims and many do not see themselves as such'. The same could be said, for and against the theory's relevance, in respect of all people, younger and middle aged, as well as older, who find themselves to be chronological misfits in some way or in some circumstances.

Wilson (2000, pp. 12-13) herself favours an approach which focuses on identity and the life course. The notion of identity was useful for exploring and asserting the diversity of individual age-related experience, and for avoiding the trap of clumsily imposing some commonensical or academic theory on very varied realities. The notion of the life course encouraged theorizing and research to consider the pasts and the futures of those under investigation. Wilson compared the relatively constricted lives of British men who grew up in the 1930s with those of the so-called 'baby boomers', born between 1945 and 1959, who felt that they have 'inaugurated new lifestyles at each stage of their lives'. The former were far more passive, having been 'lucky to have work at all', whereas the latter were much more assertive about their needs, including, in the USA, their pensions.

Wilson then goes on to make a point which strongly reinforces the traditional and renewal notion. In the more prosperous countries of the West and elsewhere it was relatively easy for individuals to construct their own life courses. However it had always been more usual across the world for older people 'to construct their identities in relational rather than individual terms' (p. 13). Rather than seeing themselves as separate individuals they saw themselves more as family members or as community members, as fathers or daughters on one hand for example, and as performing certain roles on the other. Industrialization and globalization threatened the social cohesion which supported and gave established and clear identities to older people. Again, the same points apply to people of all ages. The 'depth' of this difference was indicated by Fry (1995) who described how in many primitive societies age was and is the basis of most or much social differentiation, which was predominantly patriarchal. Fry also discusses the modernization theory referred to earlier. She usefully focuses on state formation, whereby 'political and economic bases of power expand at the expense of those of kinship' (p. 122). Family wealth had long underpinned support given to older people. In early and feudal states families competed for wealth and power. In modern times, under capitalism, however, kinship ties were weakened by the sale of labour in free markets. Young and old competed for employment and wealth and the old were excluded from competition by a recent invention called retirement. Responsibility for elder care was shared by the state and by families. In urban industrial or otherwise highly developed societies younger people no longer needed to wait to inherit land and animals, as in stable agrarian societies.

Phillipson (1998) contextualised much of the debate about age and employment in the UK and by implication many other developed countries. He argued that 'we have ... reached a historic turning point in the debate about the character and significance of ageing populations' (p. 3). By the 1950s older people had acquired a reasonably clear identity associated with retirement and the welfare state's provision of pensions and other forms of care. By the 1990s however, and after two decades of uncertainty about economic stability, employment, retirement and state welfare provision, the contract between generations had begun to be questioned, with considerable doubt ensuing about the willingness of taxpayers to finance state pensions. Population ageing underpinned such doubts, encouraging tendencies for people to scapegoat the old and to see them as a cost and a burden to society. The decline in the proportion of jobs which were full-time and permanent and the persistence of youth unemployment also helped to generate a climate of questioning conventional thinking about all relationships between age, work and employment. This interpretation supports the view that if an existing state of equilibrium between age and employment is disturbed there will be a search for 'new' solutions, to develop new traditions of renewing labour. The work of Tout (1989) on the lives of older people in developing countries is informative about how disturbed they can be by economic and political changes. The great variety of experiences described by him shows that, as far as power and status are concerned, older people have experienced extremes of both since time immemorial, and that 'modernization' has had virtually all possible kinds of effect on their welfare. A powerful example of the ways in which age and ageing can be regarded and treated very positively was provided by Wada (1995). He describes the 'dominant filial pietism and paternalism' of the Japanese, and how they underpin the active respect and affection showed towards older people in Japan. However several contributors to the volume edited by Bengston and Achenbaum (1993) explained why pre-industrial societies should not be idealised for their treatment of older people. Nomadic societies have often treated them far more harshly than settled ones for example. In general, in poor societies most older people are poor along with everyone else, and, of course, often more so.

As far as younger people and work and employment are concerned the popular notion of modernization producing greater opportunities is subject to severe modification in the volume edited by Levi and Schmitt (1997). Several contributors discuss the manipulation and abuse of young people by political and military interests in Europe from the French Revolution to the Second World War. Important aspects of the ways in which the general economic and political changes of the last generation, especially the internationalization of economic life, have affected both younger and older employees, are discussed by Pilcher (1996). She is more sanguine about the prospects for younger people in the UK than for older ones, because relevant policy changes, in education for example, are more likely to favour the former, given the desire of ageist policy makers to show most concern for the 'long-term' future, as defined in terms of the individual life span, rather than in terms of the future of society.

Finally on the tradition and renewal hypothesis there is some further support in the work of Whitley (1999) whose classification of national and regional business systems is broadly similar to that of Calori (1999), discussed above, and to the main themes of this chapter and that of most of the other authors concerned with comparative management whose work has been considered here. Hancock's (1997) pessimism about 'neo-feudal', 'anti-modern' elements of contemporary managerial and organizational developments in the UK is also of some relevance to this chapter's concerns, irrespective of whether or not events justify his outlook. This is because his kind of thinking inplies that the pace of change in advanced societies may be decelerating in an era of unprecedented affluence and longevity (also see Ackroyd, Glover, Currie and Bull, 2000) and that as a result there is a need to re-think relationships between age, work, employment and all of the parties involved, including policy makers and educators as well as employees and employers.

The external threat and response hypothesis

There are many examples of human societies and other collectivities, including in the former case countries threatened by invasion and in the latter small groups studied in some famous social psychological experiments, closing ranks when faced by serious threats from outside. Organization and management studies are replete with evidence and arguments about how rapid technical change and fierce competitive processes generate needs for organization and management to be less formal, less mechanically bureaucratic, more 'organic' and more flexible and to involve all those who can contribute irrespective of considerations of seniority and status. The modernization theory concerning age and society is, in many respects, a societal-level version of this argument. Tout (1989) made the suggestion, superficially vague yet interesting in the immediate present context, and crucial to the concerns of this book, that older people, and by implication all those vulnerable to ageism, should strive to be part of the solution to population ageing and shortages of 'core' forms of employment (meaning those vital economic functioning and social order), rather than part of the problem. However the 'old-old' and the very young, in any society, are incapable of being productive and in extreme situations may have their needs ignored, or they may even be discarded.

The most obvious long term 'threat' to the employment of all people and to younger and older ones especially is the combination of the greater capital intensiveness of production and the much increased life span in advanced societies. For all people of all ages, since among other things all grow older, this constitutes a major long term external threat, of a kind. According to Beck (1992, 1994) and Lash (1994) there is a need in advanced societies for people to develop new kinds of identity free of the collective structures of 'simple modernity', those of trade unions, large scale bureaucracies, class and class-based political parties, mass production, retirement at or around 65, and so on. More fragmented, flexible and dispersed patterns of working and living combined with longer and more varied lives are tending to generate a 'post-traditional' society (Phillipson, 1998). This involves people developing new living patterns and styles in atmospheres of uncertainty and openness. Featherstone and Hepworth (1989), according to Phillipson, had depicted a 'modernization of ageing' in terms of an elaboration of middle life, challenges to conventional models of ageing, the development of new and more active and youthful ideas of retirement, and the extension of mid-life through very diverse stages of personal growth and development. This thesis is similar to the 'greening' one regarding the positive development of the life course spelt out by Branine and Glover (1997).

The security and affluence hypothesis

Here I assert my view that successful affluent human societies which are resting on their laurels will tend to celebrate youthfulness hedonistically at the expense of the upbringing of the young and the wisdom and welfare of elders. Ewen (1976), in a study of US advertising between the World Wars, showed how the cult of youth was developed by it as part of its wider project of valorizing new phenomena. In the new age of mass production US industrialists wanted consumer attitudes and habits to be 'modernized'. Politicians and entertainment and other mass media moguls also helped to orchestrate the relevant changes. Older people were faced with a consumer culture with images of beauty, fitness and youth which was combined with compulsory retirement to make them feel more excluded than before. The growth of state provision and care for younger and older and for infirm people of all ages in the developed and many other countries has reduced tendencies for individuals to feel a personal and familial sense of responsibility for them. However hostile attitudes to old age have, as noted earlier, always existed and co-existed with situations in which generational reciprocity, in which older people teach and find work for the young and in which the young help their elders especially if they are old and unemployed (Achenbaum, 1996). As regards pension provision, international differences of a type noted earlier in this chapter were recorded by Conrad (1991, p. 180), who wrote that 'pension funds, as part of paternalistic policies, have a longer history in German-speaking countries and France than in the Anglo-Saxon ones'.

The 'Anglo-Saxon' societies just referred to, meaning the UK, the USA, and also Canada and Australia and New Zealand, are ones which have been prime candidates, at least since 1945 but arguably for over a century, as relatively secure, affluent, successful ones with laurels to rest upon, ones which seem to exemplify the present hypothesis. The first to qualify is the richest, namely the USA after the First World War, where mass production, consumption, marketing, entertainment and affluence were experienced first. All of these societies tend to be individualist ones, meaning that institutionalised resistance to American culture in general and to the cult of youth in particular, exported from the USA from the 1930s onwards, but especially during and after the Second World War, would be weaker than in Continental European countries with stronger traditions of paternalism in employment.

There are many other arguments and plenty of evidence to support the view that in the developed world, and to a greater extent in its more Anglo-Saxon individualist parts, and to a smaller extent in the developing world, a 'global' or 'American' cult of youth has been having the kinds of effect hypothesized above. For example Hearn (1995) noted how older men were often presented as amusing objects, comical, eccentric, angry or mellow, easy-going or touchy, and active yet with their concerns usually ignored or stigmatised. Older men were usually differentiated from younger men. They were either still power figures or, and far more often, they were undermined by their relative lack of power and by their age. Both 'despite and because of their contradictory social power [older men] may subvert dominant contractions of men and masculinities' (p. 113). Hearn (1995) used Erving Goffman's term 'spoiled identity' to describe how 'the gradual ousting of people from the labour force at age 65, since the beginning of the twentieth century' had led to such characterisations of older people as 'useless', 'inefficient', 'unattractive', 'temperamental' and 'senile'. To Hearn's term characterisations, self-fulfilling prophecies might usefully be added. On the cult of youth and the treatment of older people by marketing professionals in the USA, Sawchuk (1995) noted how since the mid-1980s older consumers had become a focus of marketing and advertising interest. Increasingly marketing discussions of ageing were 'devoted to dispelling myths' (p. 185) about older people who were now seen as forming a lucrative market, whereas they had been regarded as too poor, inactive, reclusive and insignificant to bother with. For Sawchuk, what seemed to be a new attitude to a new market of older citizens was actually the same one towards the same people, the so-called baby boomers. The same people were being promised what they were already used to, but what their parents, as elders, had not had. What had 'changed is that this awareness of their market potential has catalyzed a more aggressive pursuit of seniors' (p. 185). Advertising and modelling were now on the offensive against prejudices that they had instilled in the 1960s through into the 1980s. They had depicted 'youth as the ultimate virtue, and ageing as a horrible problem'. There had of course been older consumers in the past but they had had a 'Depression mentality' and 'the wrong attitude towards getting and spending'.

The amoral hedonism associated by Sawchuk with one functional segment of US management has been applied at length to US management in general by Jackall (1988). Jackall obtained his data in the late 1970s and early 1980s, and improvements in US economic performance suggest renewed seriousness and commitment in US management since then. However his arguments are wide-ranging and persuasive enough to lend credence to our present hypothesis. Jackall concerns himself with shallow image-obsessed amoral careerism on the part of people who have little or no genuine loyalty to their work, professions or occupations or employing organizations. The lives of such people celebrated the apparent death of the Protestant Ethic and cult of youth-inspired ageism was at the centre of most of their actions.

There are some parallels with Jackall's argument and those of Phillipson (1998) on the 'destabilization' of old age in the 1980s and 1990s. Retirement, according to Phillipson, had developed as a major stage in the life course from the 1950s into the 1980s but its rapid expansion in the latter decade led to concern about its cost and to the development of policies, in North America and in most European countries, designed to delay it. But retirement and the welfare state were being undermined by the 1990s with older people increasingly scapegoated as 'burdens' to society. More and more 'third agers', the 'young old' were being supported by fewer and fewer employed second agers. First in the USA, in the 1960s and later elsewhere, 'senior citizens' enjoying active leisure in retirement began to exert a stronger political and social presence. Yet at the same time economic changes increased the numbers of those facing long term unemployment and facing or seeking premature retirement, and involved growing tendencies to question the social cost of retirement. Further, the experience of growing older was becoming more diverse than hitherto. More flexible ways of organizing employment, the internationalization of the mass media of communication and of social interaction, and a weakening of collectivist institutions of social class and the nation state were all individualizing personal identities, making them both more private and more plural, and more fluid and shifting. Under the so-called disorganized (Lash and Urry, 1987), but really more elaborately and cleverly organized (Ackroy, Glover, Currie and Bull, 2000) capitalism, individuals need to become capable of understanding, influencing and controlling their own increasingly diverse identities and destinies in ways which transcend both tradition and innovation (Beck, 1992). Those who are more able to do this will tend to be more confident and/or more wealthy people: others may continue to suffer the stigma of appearing old and useless.

Phillipson (1998) also argues that older people in the early twenty-first century are likely to face four types of exclusion (p. 138). First, ideological exclusion was being generated by the 'alarmism and scapegoating associated with population ageing' which in employment terms suggests that older employees have a duty to 'make way' for younger ones. Second, economic exclusion was generated by 'the construction of regular crises, and threats to the funding of state pensions and other types of support'. For the employment of older people this would mean ongoing neglect of their development and threats of job loss or reduced opportunities to find work if already unemployed. Third, there were dangers of civil rights being curtailed. And fourth, affective exclusion meant 'the failure to recognise emotional needs associated with the various changes running through the life course'. In employment, this could mean suffering from simple lack of respect for accumulated experience and wisdom, or lack of consideration for reduced physical capacities. Phillipson (1998) suggests that the structured dependency model was useful for explaining the situations of older people for much of the twentieth century until the 1980s but that since then older people have become more 'marginal to work and welfare' (p. 138). He suggests that the relevant difficulties are likely to increase in the twenty-first century but there are some reasons to doubt this.

One point that recurs in many discussions of the attitudes of older people is their tendency, in the UK and to varying degrees in other developed countries, is their tendency to be in denial about their age, to see other older people as constituting 'the other'. They define themselves as 'young old' at most: to be 'old old', in the 'fourth (and final) age', with all its losses of identity and meaningful citizenship, is too terrible to contemplate. At the age of 75 observation, investigation and regulation under the 'medical gaze' 'becomes almost statutory' (Higgs, 1995). Once the person's aged body is in an acute ward all their fears about the fourth age and its loss of active citizenship and consumer rights start to be realised. Denial of one's age is often literally the most healthy strategy at this time of life. However,

Higgs argues, this denial is alienating rather than liberating, and it limits the possibilities for the development of a politics for older people.

Wilson (2000) is more optimistic than both Phillipson and Higgs. She accepts that in advanced societies wisdom and experience are often seen as disqualifying people for leadership positions, rather than as qualifying them, because they are seen as signs of obsolescence. Ageism had combined with globalization to produce a negative view of older people, stigmatising them as being backward looking, bigoted and rigid. However older people's tendency to favour continuity was not the same as a tendency to favour knee-jerk conservatism. Older people tended to have relatively objective, disinterested and at times very altruistic attitudes. Once their own needs were satisfied they were often keen to invest some of their surplus in their offspring and grandchildren and great grandchildren. Similarly they understood the nature and causes of many economic, social and cultural problems and would support improved policies for ameliorating them. Their own growing numbers would help their political power to grow. In some districts or regions they would be present in much higher than average numbers, influencing local policies and elections, sometimes dramatically. The media and politicians were increasingly aware of older people as a political force 'and [of] the ageism involved in ignoring them' (p. 57). For these reasons older people were likely to be increasingly prominent as voters, customers and service users. I would add 'as employees or as other economically or potentially economically active units' to this list. In the long term it is the assertion and pursuit of their own enlightened and not quite so enlightened self-interests, by older people, in all areas of life, which will turn them into part of the solution for other problems and away from being defined as problematic by self-interested other parties like insurance companies and short-sighted politicans, employers, health and welfare professionals, civil servants and educators.

Wilson (2000, p. 162) differentiated between cultures in which the dominant ideology defines the individual as the basic unit of society and those in which the family is. In the former type of culture it is easier to see some people as burdens on others and to see the generations as competing. In the latter the opposite is the case. Wilson noted how in general, and even in societies like the USA where the individual is in theory valued more than the family, it is politicians and academics who stand to gain most from whipping up unnecessary controversy about intergenerational equity or the supposed lack of it. Most ordinary people in all societies valued the family greatly and the costs of 'ageing' populations were 'likely to be entirely sustainable in Western countries' (also see Mullan, 1999). These points all have relevance for those who argue that there is a 'need' for older employees to make way for younger ones, or that they 'should' do so, or for young people to accept short term palliative and patronizing pseudo-employment 'schemes' rather than the genuine training and other forms of encouragement, information and help needed for them to create their own productive work.

In 1996, and in a review article, Pilcher noted how in the UK and western Europe academics and policy makers were more concerned with young people engaged in the transitions from childhood to adulthood than in older people and in their transitions from work to retirement. She felt that this apparent imbalance of concern was regrettable given the ways in which many old as well as younger people were treated as commodities by employers. It is hard to be sure about what the balance should be, not only because the relevant moral judgements are complicated in theory and highly situation-dependent in practice, but especially because ageism is usually best though of as one issue, not as two or more competing ones. Pilcher (1996) felt that strong economic forces and changing demographic patterns were tending, especially in the advanced countries, to make national workforces smaller in size and older and more educated and skilled, marginalizing many less educated and skilled young people and pushing them into an 'underclass'. It is not a big step from this analysis to point to the Anglo-Saxon cult of youth and possessive individualism as predisposing factors, or to note how apprenticeship training in the UK and Germany was in decline in the former, Modern Apprenticeships notwithstanding, and being consolidated and strengthened in the latter from a much higher base (Bash and Green, 1995). Pilcher also records and discusses a three-model characterisation of the forms which the education to work transition takes in Europe (Cavalli and Galland, 1995). In all countries economic forces had been prolonging the transition, but national peculiarities were surviving nonetheless. The Northern European model was one of prolonging youth, with an extension of the period of living neither with the person's original family nor with their family of destination. The Mediterranean model was one in which the young person lived with his or her family of origin for an extended period. Britain, the third provider of a model, was different. There, young people were felt to 'mature early'. They gave up education, entered the labour market, left home, and lived as couples earlier than their counterparts on the Continent. Young Italians were generally content to take their time to assume adult responsibilities. However many young working class Britons felt blocked from forming adult identities in the absence of 'political will to fund a system [of education and training] that would encompass all socio-economic and ability levels' (Pilcher, 1996, p. 167).

There is a tendency of management researchers and sociologists interested in management to reinvent various wheels themselves while regularly castigating prescriptive management writers, including contemporary management gurus, for doing the same. For example there have been vogues amongst sociologists for regularly discovering 'the new' middle or working class or professions, and management and organization theorists regularly re-hash the important but now hardly novel thesis of Burns and Stalker (1961), that organizations affected by rapid market and technical changes need to be much more flexibly managed than those which enjoy more stable conditions, so that 'giants [must] learn to dance' and to 'thrive on chaos', and so on. However it does seem that understanding, academic, lay and political alike, of relationships between age and work and employment is on something of a cusp, that it is about to undergo something of a sea change, one which will affect understanding of work and the employment relationship in a very general sense. I mean, by the latter, that understanding of economic and social change, of the life course, of relationships between production and consumption, and of the development of aspirations and identities, is likely to become more unified and whole, partly because of the growing and broadening interest in age, work and employment of the last fifteen to twenty years. This broadening of interest comes partly from the growth of studies of comparative management, also very much a recent product, albeit one about a decade older than the one just described (see for example, Granick, 1962; Dore, 1973; Lawrence, 1980).

To illustrate this point, let us note the sightings of a small number of straws in the wind indicative of growing thoughtfulness about and understanding of what some, albeit not I, might call our present predicament or crisis regarding age and employment.

First, in the 1980s universities in the UK advertised and filled significant numbers of 'New Blood' posts, designed to rejuvenate academic labour (the ultimate oxymoron?) by injecting people aged under 35 into the system (Dolton and Makepeace, 1983). I strongly suspect that, if universities tried to advertise academic posts in this way in 2000, there would be an outcry about crudely and insensitively ageist employment policies and practices. The typical academic of 2000 is not young, but that would be widely regarded as irrelevant. To select staff judiciously on the basis of relevant forms of expertise and motivation, to aim to strike a balance between energy and novelty on the one hand and expertise and eminence on the other is very acceptable, but to broadcast the specific desires of an institution would be regarded as being in bad taste. Young and dynamic are no longer always thought of as near-synonymous and neither are old and burnt out.

Second, and for all the pretentiousness, intellectual dishonesty and use as an occupational strategy by certain provincial academics, of much postmodernist thinking, the realisation that the affluence, sophistication and complexity of much contemporary life is creatively transcending simpler modern social institutions, and that there are both regressive and progressive tendencies in contemporary forms of organization, employment and management, is very helpful for understanding *both* the always diverse character of age-employment relationships *and* the newer aspects of it engendered by greater longevity and greater affluence (cf. Hancock, 1997).

Third, the contradictions and the necessary and other hypocrisies of the management of employment – line, personnel or human resource – have been spelt out in great detail in recent years by Legge (1995), Storey (1995) and others. The gaps between the putatively developmental nature of human resource management and an often crudely ageist reality have been highlighted by Lyon, Hallier and Glover (1998).

Finally, and in relation to the policies needed to diversify employment in terms of the ages of employees, Wilson (2000, p. 167) pointed to the existence of Silver Centres in Japan. These give lowly paid work to retired people, to supplement their incomes, and are indicators for policies designed to reverse present trends, so as to keep older people employed for longer. If they were to begin to be introduced in the UK they might well be called ageist, with the word workhouse being revived, although probably not to the extent of leading to their closure.

In this section, covering the third hypothesis, it has been suggested that rampant ageism against people of all ages has tended to flourish in conspicuously good times. It has also been suggested, in this chapter's somewhat extended discussion of this phenomenon, that ageism is situationally as well as historically contingent. It is not a simple phenomenon and it never was and is never likely to be. However its often non-rational and at times absurd character, as was suggested earlier, is currently being exposed by a combination of greater longevity and higher living standards. It appears to be both increasingly evident and increasingly irrelevant. To illustrate this last point it has been suggested, through the use of four 'straw in the wind' examples, that there is much greater awareness of it than existed even half a generation ago, that such awareness was part of growing and much wider evidence of the historic variety of and the future possibilities for employment relationships, that the contradictory nature of much 'advanced' and relevant thinking and practice about human resource management was increasingly well understood, and finally that innovative and effective policies designed to combat ageism head-on were beginning to be apparent.

Discussion and conclusion

Both production and consumption are increasingly diverse and sophisticated, and the complexities of high affluence have helped to generate overly intellectual, over-complicated and often misleading accounts of contemporary developments. Further confusion about contemporary employment, management and organization has been generated by the novelty of relatively recent increases in longevity, and by the facts of a developed world with an ageing population and a developing one with a young one. The meaning of the term ageing as just used here is also contestable, of course. When individuals aged 60 look like people used to in their early 40s, is that ageing, or would a neologism like 'juvenation' be more appropriate?

Ageism, the inevitably and the dread of death, immaturity, and the specific and usually quiet changes of 'middle' age are all universal phenomena, but all are experienced in diverse contexts. Societies or cultures which appear to cope most adequately with them appear to be those which confront them more or less openly, by not only living in the present, but also by respecting the past and its lessons. Such societies tend to have holistic attitudes towards personal and public relationships, understanding and creatively using the interdependence of family members and of diverse economic and social institutions for mutual learning and benefit. They understand that there are five factors which mean that human beings are not all equal, except in the eyes of the law and of the supreme intelligence, God, the Force, whoever or whatever. Some people have more ability than others, some are more experienced and wiser than others, some are braver and more optimistic (and cheerful!) than others, and above all some are more benevolent than others. The fifth reason is citizenship: in a democratic society, one of rational and benevolent adults, the citizen is the master of those employed to provide him or her with publicly-funded services. These principles revolve around the notion of interdependence, which operates both across human collectivities and in their journeys through time. All five factors, including a sense of democratic citizenship, can be inculcated early in life and developed through it. This certainly does not, however, mean that older people are automatically superior to younger ones and that age has a right to demand automatic respect. It does however suggest that people are in general likely to be more able, wise, courageous, benevolent and so on as they gain experience, that without a certain amount of automatic respect being given across all generations, everyday life will become pointlessly abrasive, and that the notion of seniority, based on relevant experience in specific situations, and not on mere chronological age, has at least some practical relevance.

Acknowledgements

The author thanks Professor Peter Lawrence of Loughborough University for his copious, excellent, generous and indispensable, and often amusing, advice on many of the international variations discussed in this chapter. He also thanks Dr. Mohamed Branine for many valuable individual pieces of advice. Faults and flaws in the chapter are of course entirely the responsibility of the author.

References

Achenbaum, W.A. (1996), 'Historical Perspectives on Ageing', in R.H. Binstock and L.K. George (eds), *Handbook of Ageing and the Social Sciences*, Academic Press, San Diego, pp. 137-52.

Ackroyd, S.J., Glover, I.A., Currie, W.L. and Bull, S. (2000), 'The Triumph of Hierarchies over Markets', in I. Glover and M. Hughes (eds), *Professions at Bay: Control and Encouragement of Ingenuity in British Management*, Ashgate, Aldershot.

Albert, M. (1993), *Capitalism versus Capitalism*, Whurr, London.

Atcherly, R.C. (1987), *Aging: Continuity and Change*, Wadsworth, Belmont, CA.

Bartlett, C.A. and Ghoshal, S. (1989), *Managing Across Borders: the Transnational Solution*, Harvard Business School Press, Boston, Mass.

Bash, L. and Green, A. (eds) (1995), *World Yearbook of Education: Youth, Education and Work*, Kogan Page, London.

Beck, U. (1992), *Risk Society*, Sage, London.

Beck, U. (1994), 'The reinvention of politics', in U. Beck, A. Giddens and S. Lash (eds), *Reflexive Modernisation*, Polity, Cambridge.

Bengston, V.L. and Achenbaum, W.A. (eds) (1993), *The Changing Contract Across the Generations*, Aldine De Gruyter, New York.

Branine, M. and Glover, I.A. (1997), 'Ageism in work and employment: thinking about connections', *Personnel Review*, Vol. 26, No. 4, pp. 233-44.

Burns, T. and Stalker, G.M. (1961), *The Management of Innovation*, Tavistock, London.

Calori, R. (1999), 'National Administrative Heritages in Borderless Organizations', Reading 15 in R.H. Rosenfeld and D.C. Wilson, *Managing Organizations*, McGraw-Hill, London, pp. 481-90.

Calori, R. and De Woot, P. (1994), *A European Management Model: Beyond Diversity*, Prentice-Hall, Hemel Hempstead.

Calori, R., Lubatkin, M. and Very, P. (1994), 'Control Mechanisms in Cross-Border Acquisitions: An International Comparison', *Organization Studies*, Vol. 15, 3, pp. 361-79.

Cavalli, A. and Galland, O. (eds), (1995), *Youth in Europe*, Frances Pinter, London.

Child, J., Fores, M., Glover, I. and Lawrence, P. (1983), 'A Price to Pay? Professionalism and Work Organization in Britain and West Germany', *Sociology*, Vol. 17. 1, pp. 63-78.

Churchill, W.S. (1951), *The Hinge of Fate*, Cassell, London.

Conrad, C. (1991), 'The emergence of modern retirement: Germany in international comparison (1950-1960)', *Population*, Vol. 3, pp. 171-200.

Cumming, E. and Henry, W.E. (1961), *Growing Old: The Process of Disengagement*, Basic Books, New York.

Dolton, P.J. and Makepeace, G.H. (1983), 'New blood or bad blood? The allocation of new blood posts in British universtities', *Higher Education Review*, Vol. 16, No. 1, pp. 49-57.

Dore, R. (1973), *British Factory, Japanese Factory*, Allen and Unwin, London.

Estes, C. (1979), *The Aging Enterprise*, Jossey Bass, San Fransicso, CA.

Ewen, S.I. (1976), *Captains of Consciousness*, McGraw-Hill, New York.

Featherstone, M. and Hepworth, M. (1989), 'Ageing and old age: reflections on the postmodern life course', in B. Bytheway, T. Keil, P. Allat and A. Bryman (eds), *Becoming and Being Old*, Sage, London.

Featherstone, M. and Wernick, A. (eds) (1995), *Images of Ageing*, Routledge, London.

Fores, M. and Glover, I. (1978), 'Professionalism: the British Disease', *The Times Higher Education Supplement*, 24 February 1978, p. 16.

Fores, M., Glover, I. and Rey, L. (1976), 'Management versus *Technik*: A Note on the Work of Executives', Department of Industry, London.

Fry, C.L. (1995), 'Age, Aging and Culture', chapter 7 in R.H. Binstock and L.K. George (eds), *Handbook of Aging and the Social Sciences*, Academic Press, San Diego.

Glover, I. (1978), 'Professionalism and Manufacturing Industry', in M. Fores and I. Glover (eds), *Manufacturing and Management*, HMSO Books, London.

Glover, I. (1985), 'How the West was Lost? Decline of Engineering and Manufacturing in Britain and the United States', *Higher Education Review*, Vol. 17, No. 3, pp. 3-34.

Glover, I.A. (1999), 'British Management and British History: Assessing the Responsibility of Individuals for Economic Difficulties', *Contemporary British History*, Vol. 13, No. 3, pp. 121-47.

Glover, I.A. and Branine, M. (1997), 'Ageism and the Labour Process: Towards a Research Agenda', *Personnel Review*, Vol. 26, No. 4, pp. 274-92.

Glover, I.A. and Hughes, M.D. (1996), 'British Management in the Pursuer Mode', in I.A. Glover and M.D. Hughes (eds), *The Professional-Managerial Class: Contemporary British Management in the Pursuer Mode*, Avebury, Aldershot, pp. 3-33.

Glover, I.A. and Kelly, M.P. (1987), *Engineers in Britain: A Sociological Study of the Engineering Dimension*, Unwin Hyman, London.

Glover, I.A. and Tracey, P.J. (1997), 'In Search of *Technik*: Will Engineering Outgrow Management?', *Work, Employment and Society*, Vol. 11, No. 4, pp. 759-96.

Glover, I.A., Tracey, P.J. and Currie, W.L. (1998), 'Engineering Our Future Again: Towards a Long Term Strategy for Manufacturing and Management in the United Kingdom', in R. Delbridge and J. Lowe (eds), *Manufacturing in Transition*, Routledge, London, pp. 199-223.

Granick, D. (1962), *The European Executive*, Weidenfield and Nicholson, London.

Hampden-Turner, C. and Trompenaars, A. (1993), *The Seven Cultures of Capitalism*, Doubleday, New York.

Hancock, P.G. (1997), 'Citizenship or Vassalage? Organizational Membership in the Age Unreason', *Organization*, Vol. 4, No. 1, pp. 93-111.

Hareven, T.K. (1995), 'Changing Images and the Social Construction of the Life Course', in M. Featherstone and A. Wernick (eds), op. cit., pp. 119-34.

Hearn, J. (1995), 'Imaging the Image of Men', in M. Featherstone and A. Wernick (eds), op. cit., pp. 97-115.

Higgs, P. (1995), 'Citizenship and Old Age: The End of the Road?', *Ageing and Society*, Vol. 15, pp. 535-50.

Hofstede, G. (1991), *Cultures and Organizations - Software of the Mind*, McGraw-Hill, London.

Holmes, E.R. and Holmes, L.D. (1995), *Other Cultures, Elder Years,* Sage, Thousand Oaks, CA.

Jackall, R. (1988), *Moral Mazes: Inside the World of Corporate Managers*, Oxford, Oxford University Press.

Jacques, E. (1982), *Free Enterprise, Fair Employment*, Grase Russak, New York

Kennedy, P. (1993), *Preparing for the Twenty-First Century*, HarperCollins, London.

Landes, D.S. (1998), *The Wealth and Poverty of Nations*, Norton, New York.

Lash, S. (1994), 'Reflexivity and its doubles: structure, aesthetics, community', in U. Beck, A. Giddens and S. Lash (eds), *Reflexive Modernization*, Polity, Cambridge.

Lash, S. and Urry, J. (1987), *The End of Organised Capitalism*, Polity, Cambridge.

Lawrence, P.A. (1980), *Managers and Management in West Germany*, Croom Helm, London.

Lawrence, P.A. (1990), *Management in the Land of Israel*, Stanley Thornes, Cheltenham.

Lawrence, P.A. (1992), 'West Germany: A Study in Consistency', in G. Lee and C. Smith (eds), *Engineers in Management: International Comparisons*, Routledge,

London.
Lawrence, P.A. (1996a), *Management in the USA*, OUP, Oxford.
Lawrence, P.A. (1996b), 'Through a glass darkly: towards a characterization of British management', in I. Glover and M. Hughes (eds), *The Professional-Managerial Class*, op. cit., pp. 37-48.
Lawrence, P.A. and Edwards, V. (2000), *Management in Western Europe*, Macmillan, Basingstoke.
Leadbetter, C. (1997), *Britain, the California of Europe: What the UK can learn from the West Coast*, Demos, London.
Legge, K. (1995), *Human Resource Management – Rhetorics and Realities*, Macmillan, Basingstoke.
Levi, G. and Schmitt, J-C. (eds) (1997), *A History of Young People in the West, Vol. 2, Stormy Evolution to Modern Times*, Harvard University Press, Cambridge, Mass.
Locke, R.R. (1989), *The End of the Practical Man: Entrepreneurship in Higher Education in Germany, France and Great Britain, 1880-1940*, Jai Press, Greenwich, Conn.
Locke, R.R. (1996a), 'The limits of America's *Pax Oeconomica*: Germany and Japan after World War II', in I.A. Glover and M.D. Hughes (eds.) *The Professional-Managerial Class: Contemporary British Management in the Pursuer Mode*, Avebury, Aldershot, pp. 49-88.
Locke, R.R. (1996b), *The Collapse of the American Management Mystique*, OUP, Oxford.
Locke, R.R. (2000), 'A Contrast in Military Traditions and Outcomes: the French and German Armies in 1940', mimeo, University of Hawaii.
Lyon, H.P., Hallier, J.R. and Glover, I.A. (1998), 'Divestment or Investment? The Contradictions of HRM in Relation to Older Employees', *Human Resource Management Journal*, Vol. 8, 1, pp. 55-66.
Maurice, M. (1972), 'Propos sur la sociologie des professions', *Sociologie du Travail*, Vol. 13, pp. 213-25.
Maurice, M., Sorge, A. and Warner, M. (1980), 'Societal Differences in Organizing Manufacturing Units: a comparison of France, West Germany and Great Britain', *Organization Studies*, Vol.1, pp. 59-86.
Mullan, P. (1999), *The Imaginary Time Bomb: Why an Ageing Population is Not a Social Problem*, Tauris, London.
Phillipson, C. (1982), *Capitalism and the Construction of Old Age*, Macmillan, London.
Phillipson, C. (1998), *Reconstructing Old Age: New Agendas in Social Theory and Practice*, Sage, London.
Pilcher, J. (1996), 'Transitions to and from the Labour Maket: Younger and Older People and Employment', *Work, Employment and Society*, Vol. 10, No. 1, pp. 161-73.
Ronen, S. and Shenkar, O. (1985), 'Clustering countries on attitudinal dimensions: A review and synthesis', *Academy of Management Review*, Vol. 10, No. 3, pp. 435-54.

Sawchuk, K.A. (1995), 'From Gloom to Boom: Age, identity and target marketing', chapter 11 in M. Featherstone and A. Wernick (eds), *Images of Ageing*, op. cit., pp. 173-87.

Smith, C.S. and Meiksins, P. (1995), 'Ageism, Society and Dominance Effects in Cross-National Organizational Analysis', *Work, Employment and Society*, Vol. 9, No. 2, pp. 241-67.

Sokolowsky, J. (ed.) (1990), *The Cultural Context of Ageing: Worldwide Perspectives*, Bergin and Garvey, New York, NY.

Sorge, A. (1978), 'The management tradition: A continental view', in M. Fores and I. Glover (eds), *Manufacturing and Management*, HMSO Books, London.

Sorge, A. (1979), 'Engineers in Management: a study of the British, German and French Traditions', *The Journal of General Management*, Vol. 5, pp. 46-57.

Sorge, A. (1982-83), 'Cultured Organization', *International Studies of Management and Organization*, Vol. 12, pp. 106-38.

Sorge, A. and Hartmann, G. (1980), 'Technology and Labour Markets', Discussion Paper 80-39, International Institute of Management, Berlin.

Sorge, A. and Warner, M. (1986), *Comparative Factory Management: An Anglo-German Comparison of Manufacturing, Management and Manpower*, Gower, Aldershot.

Storey, J. (ed.) (1995), *Human Resource Management – A Critical Text*, Routledge, London and New York.

Tout, K. (1989), *Ageing in Developing Countries*, OUP, Oxford.

Townsend, P. (1981), 'The Structured Dependency of the Elderly: the creation of social policy in the twentieth century', *Ageing and Society*, Vol. 1, No. 1, pp. 5-28.

Veblen, T. (1921), *The Engineers and the Price System*, Viking, New York, NY.

Wada, S. (1995), 'The Status and Image of the Elderly in Japan: Understanding the Paternalistic Ideology', in M. Featherstone and A. Wernick (eds), op. cit., *Images of Ageing*, pp. 48-60.

Walker, A. (1980), 'The social creation of poverty and dependency in old age', *Journal of Social Policy*, Vol. 9, No. 1, pp. 45-75.

Walker, A. (1981), 'Towards a political economy of old age', *Ageing and Society*, Vol. 1, No. 1, pp. 73-94.

Whitley, R.D. (ed.) (1992), *European Business Systems: Firms and Markets in their National Contexts*, Sage, London.

Whitley, R.D. (1999), 'Competing Logics and Units of Analysis in the Comparative Study of Economic Organization', *International Studies of Management and Organization*, Vol. 29, No, 2, pp. 113-26.

Wilson, G. (2000), *Understanding Old Age: Critical and Global Perspectives*, Sage, London.

Wouk, H. (1951), *The 'Caine' Mutiny*, Cape, London.

Appendix

Relevant aspects of management, age and employment in Sweden the Netherlands, France and the UK

These points follow on from the discussion of Hampden-Turner's and Trompenaars' thinking which ends on page 127 above.

Hampden-Turner and Trompenaars depict Sweden as being quite unique, by virtue of its geography, specifically its large land (and forest and lake) area and its small population, and its often ruggedly independent history. They list rationality, a strong but not overweening individualism social concern and responsibility, internationalism and egalitarianism as among its more notable features. There is also a strong engineering orientation, less influential than that of a generation ago, but deep-rooted and persistent and strongly concerned for product quality and safety and environmental fit. In Swedish management moral or social and economic concerns are thought of as co-equal. There is a strong belief that everyone should be employed usefully, including the disabled and handicapped people, for example. Unemployment rates tend to be very low and a 'workfare' philosophy has long been practised. Employers tend to adapt work to people, rather than vice-versa, more than in almost any other country. Management, apart from having a well-entrenched international quality, tends to be egalitarian and inclusive and to rely on harmony between the generations. Such characteristics involve and are sustained by high standards of formal education and training, health and life expectancy, and by high proportions of women in particular and of the population in general being in employment.

Like Germany and Sweden the Netherlands has an approach to education and training which has long-term origins in French experience and which therefore has a strong, but not exclusive, of course, emphasis on technical education. Holland is a small country, with much of its land reclaimed and protected from the sea, one which has had to suffer for its independence, and one which as considerable experience of overseas expansion and trade. Its approach to management tends to be very egalitarian and opposed to hierarchical structures and actions. Its tone tends to be downbeat, humble, even homely and feminine, and socially responsible. There is a powerful element of restrained emotion channelled very effectively. Authority is based on relevant knowledge and individuals are often outspoken but in ways which assert a mixture of egalitarianism, friendship and independence.

The paradoxical character of authority relationships in general and of employment relationships in particular is well apparent in Hampden-Turner's and Trompenaars' discussion of French 'difference', idiosyncrasy, exceptionalism and contradiction. Although a major part of what Calori (1999) called Europe's Latin Catholic South with a clear majority of its population Roman Catholic, France had a strongly 'republican, secular and frequently anticlerical state' (p. 337). It was a 'very hierarchical, often inegalitarian state' (p. 337). It was a very hierarchical, often inegalitarian Western democracy with a powerful tradition of 'successful uprisings from below, unleashed in the name of equality and fraternity' (p. 337). French society was highly regulated from the centre but one in which 'pulling strings' and otherwise using influence to bend the rules are widely used and admired. Flexible principles were preferred to universal laws. They were often abused by insiders against outsiders but this often meant, too, that the rules were being bent in line with 'the human purposes those rules were designed to serve' (p. 338). Managerial authority was highly personalized. Organizations could not be reduced readily to functions, tasks and profits: the whole was greater than the sum of the part. Vision, drawing on the best of culture and historical experience, and power used as a means for projecting it, were powerful elements of a broadly holistic and intuitive, yet also often highly intellectual approach to management. This approach could be distinguished by its group orientation which subordinates individual achievements and interests to general ones. At work, status tended to be ascribed on the basis of achievements at school, college or university rather than ones achieved in employment. Companies were ordered on the basis of educational qualifications and their attainment, yet leadership was strong and hierarchical, partly in order to resolve rivalries between departments and groups in companies and other organizations, and also because of important attitudes towards France's history.

One of these attitudes was that many periods of the past were more remarkable and praiseworthy than the present or the likely future. Absolutist monarchy had survived longer in France than in much of Europe and the English-speaking world. France had been a rich country and a 'byword for splendor and the grandeur' (p. 347) until violent revolution came in 1789. Strong elements of an aristocratic, exclusive, mysterious and royal culture based on appreciation of the finer things of life had persisted to the present. A history of upheaval, insurrection and of revolution in the full sense of the world, in which 'everything changes but remains the same', except for the underlying rationale of social arrangements, helped to highlight the achievements and glories or such specific periods as the Enlightenment, *la belle epoque* and *la trente glorieuse*, and of such great leaders as Charlemagne, Henry VI, Louis XIV, Napoleon Bonaparte and Charles de Gaulle. The Revolution of 1789 had been a bourgeois and not a proletarian one. It had given permanent power and status to the senior bourgeois occupations of civil administration, education, engineering, medicine, military service and law and to the educational institutions and processes constructed to produce and reproduce them. It had done so in the name of reason and it had made the status of intellectuals, especially of writers aiming to influence events, at least as high in France as anywhere else in the world. French intellectuals confronted rather than shied away from contentious moral and political issues. Similarly French managers took a strongly cerebral approach to their problems, and coveted such intellectual jobs as those in planning, research and development and strategy.

At the same time the national experience of discontinuous change had thrown up great leaders while its traditions of drawing on its past, of hierarchy, religion family and group orientation meant that organizations were far more than systems of rational authority and rational decision making. They were plural and diverse political entities best governed by managers who combined negotiation, flair, personal leadership, intelligence, and concern for the well-being of all. Business relationships were personal and familial: this helped to justify and to oil the wheels of qualification-based hierarchies. Authority, unlike in the USA, was not task-specific. French bosses were deferred to widely while feeling personally responsible to subordinates and their dependants. French management was not authoritarian. Managers tended to be reluctant to distance themselves from subordinates, whom they thought of as their 'children'. They could feel and show a parental kind of concern without undermining their own positions, partly because their own status had an attributed character, earned before they entered their current employment and not achieved competitively during it. The authors (p. 363) draw on work by Amado, Faucheux and Laurent to contrast American and French views of organizational development. For Americans, French suspicion of it was 'cynical, adversarial and theoretical'. To the French it was unworkable because it was 'naïve, idealistic and psychological' (and also) 'a-historical, superficial and (amounting) to "false consciousness"'. It neglected fundamental and genuine differences in interest, and used notions of 'truth, love and trust' to manipulate subordinates. Both views are right and wrong, depending on context. This paradox is at the heart of understanding the role of age in employment and management. There are eternal truths and hard facts, such as experience and maturity and the lack of them, and the inevitability of physical decay. The appropriateness of approaches which assume that glasses are half-full or half-empty is always historically and socially contingent, although never entirely so.

On the UK, Hampden-Turner and Trompenaars were writing in the early 1990s, just after the economic and political turmoil of the 1980s and during a relatively short but for some a traumatic period of recession. As a consequence their account of the UK's economic and managerial culture appears to be one-sidedly and overly pessimistic. Even so they discuss, to some considerable effect, the reactive shallowness of 1980s' British management, which tended to define productive 'industry' as a thing of the past and to valorize sometimes parasitical 'business' and 'pure' money-making (cf. Veblen, 1921). They are interestingly scathing about the obsession with image and the premium put on commanding social presence in management in and after the 1980s, and on the 1980s' cult of youth in managerial recruitment and selection. They are also scathing about the socially divisive arms' length and heavily financial character of the management of UK-style conglomerates, and of overly analytical and abstract management using economic theory, of both the economy in general and of individual businesses in particular. There is much that is relevant in their account of the UK and its tendencies to disinvest in and to commodify 'human resources' in the pursuit of certain kinds of efficiency, but it is also partly a product of a period, the last twenty years of the last century, in which the UK was coming to painful terms with the detritus of past overachievement and taking serious action, some of it unduly dramatic, to put harmful trends into reverse (cf. Glover, Tracey and Currie, 1998; Lawrence and Edwards, 2000). During the twenty years in question, for example, the output of higher education in the UK has more than trebled and its character is much more vocational and economically and socially responsive in 2000 than it was in 1980, and far more so than in 1960 (Glover, 1999). The criticisms of UK management quality of Hampden-Turner and Trompenaars do not acknowledge this sea change. However most of their criticisms of the experience and confused shallowness of many recent British approaches to the recruitment, selection, deployment, use and development of people and to their termination of their employment ring true (see for example the chapter by Peter Herriot in this book).

Part III
The experience and practice of age discrimination in employment

8 Ageism in retailing: myth or reality?

Adelina Broadbridge

Introduction

The way in which the structure of society is changing has placed ageism firmly on the public policy agenda (Employment Department, 1992). Concerns over an ageing population and fewer young people entering the labour market have resulted in some companies modifying their employment policies and practices. The population changes taking place will have considerable impact on the retail industry which has traditionally relied on young people as an important labour source. There have been few academic studies of age discrimination (Laczko and Phillipson, 1991) and relatively few studies specifically examining age in retailing. Those that have addressed this issue (NIESR, 1986; Hogarth and Barth, 1991) have concentrated on shop floor, non-managerial positions. Research into issues regarding age and retail managers is lacking. Using empirical evidence from a survey examining career development within the retail sector, the aim of this chapter is to begin to redress this imbalance.

The first part of the chapter sets a context for the empirical research by considering briefly some of the difficulties in defining older workers and when age discrimination occurs. It outlines some attitudes related to older workers and the subsequent effects these can have on career development. It then considers the population changes happening at a macro level which affect individual company decisions regarding the employment of older persons. The characteristics of the retail industry with regard to age are then described, and examples are provided to show how some companies have responded to the macro level changes. Many of the changes, however, have occurred specifically at shop floor level and little evidence of actively employing older workers has been provided at managerial levels. The second part of the article uses empirical evidence from a survey of retail companies to investigate the career development of retail managers. Any differences in attitudes and experience of older managers (defined as 40 and over) will be highlighted. This will enable retail companies to adapt, if necessary, their managerial employment policies for an ageing society.

Background

The term ageism is usually connected with discrimination towards older persons (Comfort, 1977; Butler, 1987; Norman, 1987), although its definition is more complex and may affect a person at any age or at any time (Lucas 1995). At work, some employees in their twenties may feel that the term applies to them, as they perceive their age as preventing their ascent to senior management positions; childless women in their thirties may experience it from the perspective that employers are passing them over for promotion in the expectation they will soon exit the labour market to 'settle down and start a family'. Those in their forties may believe that their career has plateaued, demonstrating the notion that they are regarded as being in their twilight years of employment. Although it may be more appropriate to think of ageism as being any unwarranted response to any age (Bytheway and Johnson, 1990), in practice, many companies discriminate against older workers and this tends to be the main form of 'ageism' commonly referred to.

Defining the age at which employees are considered to be old or when age discrimination may occur is difficult as is demonstrated by various researchers' definitions of 'older workers'. For example, some use the term to describe workers over the age of 50 (Britton and Thomas, 1973, Laczko, 1990; Hassell and Perrewe, 1995), others at 45 (International Labour Office, 1979; Parker, 1980; Schuller, 1990). In another study, Metcalf and Thompson (1990) found employers' definitions of older workers to range between 40 to 50 years. Furthermore Lucas (1995) found age was used to exclude people from the age of 30 from entering hotel and catering work, while 55 percent of her respondents defined mature workers as those above the age of 40.

Deciding the age at which to compare managers' career development in retailing for the purposes of the current investigation therefore proved difficult. Lucas' (1995) work, however, demonstrated that many of the employment characteristics of the hotel industry mirror those of the retail industry. Like the hotel industry, the retail industry is characterised by the employment of young people (NIESR, 1986) and women, many of whom work part-time (Broadbridge, 1995). Moreover, retail managers, both at store level and at head office, can progress their careers relatively quickly at an early stage. Thus, it is not unusual for large retail stores to be managed by people in their late twenties and thirties. How their careers thereafter progress is uncertain. For the purpose of the present investigation, therefore, it was proposed to compare those managers' attitudes towards their current jobs and future prospects below and above the age of 40. This seemingly low definition of older workers was further justified by Metcalf and Thompson's (1990) findings from a personnel director of a retail company who stated that 'it depends very much on the median age of the organisation or the occupation in question. In a young company older tends to be younger' (Metcalf and Thompson, 1990, p. 11). This statement was further supported by the work of Perrewe et al (1991) and Skills and Enterprise Briefing (1991). In addition, more recent research suggests that 40 year olds are beginning to suffer the effects of negative stereotyping (IDS, 1996) and that career prospects become limited around the age of

42 (Banel, 1996). Therefore there was enough evidence to justify using 40 as the age at which comparisons should be made.

Attitudes towards older workers

There exist many positive and negative attitudes towards older workers. It is the negative beliefs about older workers that prevail, however, which inevitably result in discrimination (Hassel and Perrewe, 1995). Several studies have described the stereotypical beliefs about older workers (distinguishing older workers as young as 40). Among the negative beliefs about older workers are that they are perceived as less efficient (Victor, 1994), lower in performance capacity (Rosen and Jerdee, 1976a, 1976b, 1977); less creative and more resistant to change (Rosen and Jerdee, 1976a; 1976b; 1977; Metcalf and Thompson, 1990), less adaptable (International Labour Organisation, 1979) and less able to grasp new ideas or accept the introduction of new technology (IDS, 1996). They are assumed to be less career minded (Metcalf and Thompson, 1990), less motivated to remain up-to-date in their professions (Rosen and Jerdee, 19876a; 1976b; 1977), and be less interested in training (IDS, 1996) or more difficult to train (Britton and Thomas, 1973; Metcalf and Thompson, 1990) or retrain (Victor, 1994).

On the positive side, older workers have been described as having greater overall job satisfaction (Doering et al, 1983), with older senior managers being most enthusiastic about their work (Benbour, 1995). They have more experience (Victor, 1994), can still contribute much in career terms (IDS, 1996), and can be used as mentors for younger employees (IDS, 1996). They have been found to be more reliable (NIESR, 1986; Metcalf and Thompson, 1990; Trinder et al, 199), more responsible (Metcalf and Thompson, 1990), more conscientious and hard-working and may be more efficient (International Labour Office, 1979) and effective in their jobs (IDS, 1996). They have better managerial skills (Trinder et al, 1992) and interpersonal skills (Rosen and Jerdee, 1976, 1976b, 1977) which improves standards of customer service (IDS, 1996). They work better in teams (IDS, 1996), have greater organisational commitment (Doering et al, 1983; Metcalf and Thompson, 1990; Trinder et al, 1992) and lower turnover rates (Hogarth and Barth, 1991; IDS, 1996).

There appears, therefore, to be some contradiction regarding the attributes of older workers. Whether organisations adopt a positive or negative attitude towards older workers can naturally affect an older person's career development. As well as being a status organising concept, work provides a sense of identity for the individual (Victor, 1994). Hence the thwarting of a career or the onset of retirement can result in a crisis of identity for the manager. Middle aged managers may find that their career has reached a plateau and that there are fewer promotion opportunities open to them (Marshall and Cooper, 1978), or that the chance of being head hunted is lessened (Banel, 1996).

Macro issues

One of the macro level developments which brought age related issues onto the workforce agenda was the demographic changes in the structure of the country. This was first noticed with any concern during the 1980s when it became evident that the population was ageing and that fewer youths would be available to work in the labour market. Some organisations reacted to these changes by adapting their employment policies, realising the potential benefits of employing older staff, although these were mainly aimed at non-managerial levels (e.g. Metcalf and Thompson, 1990; Hogarth and Barth, 1991). In general, however, few employers have developed distinctive policies on older workers, their approach being limited to raising awareness to unintentional discrimination by age (IDS, 1996). Perhaps one of the reasons for this, was the effects of the recession at this time, which halted any immediate effects of the demographic time bomb. Recession can lead to two outcomes: redundancy and early retirement, both of which have increased in the UK over the last decade. The service sector suffered the most redundancies during 1995, with the distribution, hotels and restaurant sector having higher than average redundancy rates (Potter, 1995). Over the past 20 years the age at which people actually retire has fallen, with opportunities for early retirement being greatest amongst those working in professional and non-manual occupations (Victor, 1994).

Early retirement has two uses: it can help reduce the number of people employed or it can change the composition of the workforce. With many companies down sizing and de-layering their management levels, many employers offer enhanced early retirement packages as an alternative to compulsory redundancy (IDS, 1996). This also has the advantage of maintaining a company's good PR image. In addition, early retirement helps to ease out employees who are perceived to be less efficient as well as helping to remove promotion blockages (IDS, 1996). Changing the composition of the workforce by early retirement policies provides opportunities for younger people to be hired, thus reducing the scale of unemployment. Hence in times of high unemployment older workers are most vulnerable to be expelled from the labour market (Britton and Thomas, 1973; Victor, 1994).

The number of people working beyond the normal retirement age is small. However, Beck (1995) notes that with people generally living longer, and an ageing population, there will soon come the time when the official retirement age will have to rise as the state pension becomes too expensive. This argument may prove too simple however as the introduction of new technologies is changing the nature of work. Capital is replacing labour in many areas and it is likely these developments will witness new forms of employment emerging. These may provide more flexibility, enabling older workers to take on more part-time employment. This presents certain benefits: companies retain the skill levels of older workers, retirement ages may be more flexible and unemployment rates are kept low. Instead of the official retirement age rising, it is more likely that people will be encouraged to make their own provisions for pensions in the knowledge they may no longer be able to rely on the state for benefits.

Age and the retail industry

The age profile of employees in many retail companies is typically young (Hogarth and Barth, 1991), with over a quarter of the workforce being under the age of 25 (NIESR, 1986). While the Labour Force Survey suggests that 21.5 percent of all employees are aged 50 or over, this figure is about 12 percent for retail companies (IDS, 1996). Furthermore, retail managers are younger than the general retail workforce. At B & Q the proportion of warehouse managers over the age of 50 is 8.5 percent while at supercentres it is just 5 percent (IDS, 1996). Store managers are most likely to be in their late 20s to late 30s. The average age of a Tesco store manager in 1991 was 37, with senior store managers generally being younger than some junior and middle store managers (company statistics). Older personnel have traditionally been found at head office and in certain non-managerial functions such as security and cleaning.

Since the late 1980s this situation has altered as some retail companies have realised the consequences of the changing population and the genuine need to re-evaluate recruitment strategies as well as the business advantages of employing older workers. Metcalf and Thompson (1990) found that the main reasons provided by the retail companies who were targeting older workers (all for non-managerial branch positions) were the decline in numbers of school leavers, high turnover and tight labour markets in the South East. Those retailers not targeting older workers responded to the labour shortages by recruiting women returners and competing for youths.

One of the first attempts to redress the balance of employing older workers was the B & Q experiment at its Macclesfield store where the entire store (with the exception of the store manager who was 28) was staffed by employees over the age of 50 (Hogarth and Barth, 1991). The decision to hire older workers was in response to a need to ease recruitment difficulties; to lower labour turnover which stood at 48.5 percent in 1990; to improve product knowledge among sales staff (by encouraging the employment of retired tradesmen) and to improve customer care standards generally. Older workers in the DIY industry were regarded as possessing certain qualities: they are home owners with ready-made product knowledge and a lifetime of experience in carrying out repairs around their homes.

Dispelling any of the negative beliefs about older workers, the B & Q Macclesfield experiment found older workers to be no more apprehensive about using technology than other groups; they did not require additional training nor were they reluctant to undergo training; they were not more expensive to employ and they took less time off over a year than did younger workers. They were found to be more knowledgeable about products than younger workers, providing friendly and cooperative service. They were less prone to labour turnover and willing to work extra hours when required. Pilferage in the store was lower than the company average while profitability levels were higher, and in commercial terms the store surpassed its trading targets. The results of the experiment were so successful that the company has encouraged the employment of older workers throughout their stores.

Regarding other specific policies on employing older people, W H Smith has an equal opportunities statement which states that it will not discriminate against people on the grounds of age. Consequently, age bars are not used in advertisements, and age is not used in recruitment and selection criteria (Employment Department Group, 1994) and application forms have been redesigned so that age details are provided on a separate sheet to the main application form (IDS, 1996). These strategies are clearly related to seeking a business opportunity. Their Chief Executive states 'we believe it is good commercial sense to have a strategy to recruit and retain older workers. By the year 2000, 35 percent of the labour force will be over 45' (Employment Department Group, 1994). Therefore the company is aiming to maximise competitive advantage by recognising the current and future trends in the age distribution of the population, by developing a workforce profile that reflects the age structure of the community they serve.

Again Sainsbury's acknowledges the commercial sense in employing older people at shop floor level: 'Serving the customer is paramount now' and 'we value older workers particularly with the customer interface - on tills and behind counter service departments' (Employment Department Group, 1994; 32). Furthermore, Sainsbury's older workers are regarded by their managers for their reliability, dependability, attitude, enthusiasm and ability to mix well with people (Employment Department Group, 1994). Similarly, W H Smith claims that older workers are more knowledgeable about products, which results in increased customer satisfaction. Like other retailers W H Smith found that its staff turnover rates have reduced, which is attributed to older workers' higher levels of job satisfaction (IDS, 1996).

Certainly the opportunity to work beyond the normal retirement age (usually on a fixed-term contract basis) is available in some retail companies, which means that it is possible to phase in an employee's eventual retirement (IDS, 1996). With flexible working arrangements available at non-managerial positions in retailing, the older person may work part time, perhaps even having taken early retirement from another occupation. A good example of this flexibility is Boots. It has introduced term-time working to help those staff with families. Cover for their absence can be provided by retired staff (Employment Department Group, 1991). Both the company and the older employee benefit from these arrangements: the company retains cooperative and dedicated workers, while the older person is able to begin to adapt to the process of retiring while keeping a commercial interest.

Although there are considerable business advantages in employing older workers in retailing, a recent IDS survey found that a third of Sainsbury's staff had retired before the age of 55 (IDS, 1996). It was not specified in which occupations these retirements had occurred, but given the preceding evidence on Sainsbury's commitment to older workers at the shop floor level, it is speculated these early retirals were in management positions. The perceived benefits of employing older persons in retailing appear to apply mainly in those occupations where staff shortages are most acute - non-managerial positions. Retailing remains a youthful sector and managers, particularly at store level, are expected to be 'young and dynamic'. There are no reasons why the qualities older workers bring to non-managerial positions in retailing may not equally be applied to managerial occupations. More detailed research into where, and in what occupations, older workers in retailing are located is necessary to gauge whether the majority of opportunities lie within non-managerial positions. If discrimination on the grounds of age is discouraged throughout all occupations in retailing, so it would be expected that there would be no appreciable differences in attitudes between managers over and under the age of 40 toward their career development opportunities.

Methodology

The present investigation considered age differences in the career development among managers in the retail environment. It involved the development of quantitative measures in the form of a self completed survey questionnaire. The aims of the research were to consider for managers below and above the age of 40 any differences in:

- their levels of satisfaction with current job positions;
- the factors helping and barriers hindering their career development;
- their future career aspirations, including the actions necessary to and barriers preventing them from attaining these positions; and,
- the extent to which retail managers believe that their goals can be achieved.

Questionnaires were mailed in May 1995 to a sample of retail managers who had completed, or are in the process of completing, the MBA in Retailing and Wholesaling by distance learning at the University of Stirling. Although it is recognised these managers could be criticised for being untypical of the retail management population generally, the research was regarded as preliminary and some attempt was taken to counteract this imbalance. All respondents were asked in a covering letter to distribute copies of the questionnaire to other managers to complete. A total of 132 questionnaires were returned (55 percent from MBA students; 45 percent from other respondents). This represents an overall response rate of 52 percent. Data analysis was conducted using SPSS. First descriptive statistics are presented. Second, in order to compare the statistical differences between managers over and under the age of 40, t-tests and chi-square tests are applied to the data.

Findings

Demographic profile

Demographic data were collected for age, gender, marital status, employment status of respondents' partners, whether they had children, educational and professional qualifications. Descriptive statistics for these variables are presented in Table 8.1. The ages of the respondents ranged from 23 to 60, with the mean age being 35. For analysis purposes, managers under 40 (77 percent) are compared with those over 40 (23 percent). As Table 8.1 shows, retail managers over the age of 40 were more likely to be male (Chi=3.34, df=1, p=0.068), married and have children (Chi = 11.21, df=1, p=0.001). Their partners (if applicable) were less likely to be in paid employment than the partners of respondents under 40 (chi=7.60, df=2, p=0.022), which probably relates to the fact that more of the managers over 40 were male and have children. Fewer older managers have been educated beyond A level standard (45 percent) than their younger counterparts (58 percent), although they were more likely to possess additional professional qualifications.

Table 8.1 : Job demographics of retail managers

	Under 40		Over 40	
	Mean	Range (Min - Max)	Mean	Range (Min - Max)
Years of total work experience	13.26	(2-22)	26.75	(9-44)
Years at managerial level	7.71	(1-20)	17.22	(5-40)
Years with present employer	8.27	(1-20)	16.84	(1-34)
	2.2	(.80-11)	6.6	(0.42-20)
Years in present post				
	4.57	(1-8)	4.19	(1-8)
Number of jobs	1.99	(1-6)	2.13	(1-6)
Number of companies worked for	50	(36-86)	50	(32-70)
Total hours worked				
Management Level	<40 (%)		>40 (%)	
Junior Management	31		16	
Middle Management	32		32	
Senior Management	35		53	
Location of Job				
Store/Branch	26		19	
Head Office	66		59	
Area Manager	8		22	
Function Specialist or Generalist				
Functional Specialist	47		57	
Generalist	53		43	
Full-time				
Full-time				
Part-time	99		97	
	1		3	

Table 8.2 shows the job demographic details of the respondents. Obviously, the managers over 40 have more working experience than those under 40, and have, on average, 10 years more managerial experience. This is reflected in the managerial positions held, with managers over 40 being concentrated in the highest levels of management. However, the relationship between the respondents' age and their level of managerial responsibility, the location and nature of their jobs was not found to be statistically significant.

Table 8.2 : Level of satisfaction with current job

	Managers Under 40		Managers Over 40	
	Mean		Mean	
The degree of responsibility you have	1.88		1.75	
The use made of your skills and abilities	2.22		2.13	
The calibre of work allocated to you	2.02		1.84	
Your credibility with line managers	1.93		1.69	
Your credibility with staff	1.79		1.48	
Your working relationships with superiors	1.96		1.91	
Your working relationship with colleagues	1.66		1.66	
Your working relationships with subordinates	1.94		1.62	
The level of training you've had	2.25		1.84	
Recognition for work achievement	2.50		2.31	
Support from immediate seniors	2.44		2.13	
Level of authority delegated to you	1.99		1.91	
Opportunities for involvement in challenging work situations	1.97		1.93	
Opportunities for self development	2.21		2.16	
Opportunities for promotion	2.67		2.74	
Opportunities to influence organisational Policies	2.62		2.10	
Opportunities to achieve career aims	2.47		2.35	
Opportunities for travel	2.87		2.45	
Your hours of work	2.43		2.31	
Your working conditions	2.19		2.13	
Your salary	2.48		2.34	
Your status/prestige	2.27		2.00	
Your level of autonomy/independence	2.02		1.68	
The degree of job security you have	2.17		2.13	
The location of your job	2.04		1.56	
Overall satisfaction with current job	**2.20**		**2.01**	

Key
1= Very Satisfied
2= Fairly Satisfied
3= Neither Satisfied nor Dissatisfied
4= Fairly Dissatisfied
5 = Very Dissatisfied

Managers over 40 were more likely to work in head office positions as functional specialists, a finding which fits the general trends in retailing. The younger managers were also more likely to be located at head offices, although they were slightly more likely to be generalists. This may be significant for career development as managers in specialist functions can experience difficulty in gaining higher positions (Wilson, 1991), finding that their job related training is too narrow for a broader appointment (Rothwell, 1984).

The findings tend to suggest that older managers are more stable in their employment patterns. Given the differences in their age, it is interesting to note that all respondents, on average, have worked for the same number of companies and had the same number of jobs. On average, however, managers over 40 have been with their present employer twice as long than those under 40, and in their present post for six and a half years against just over two years for younger managers. This may support findings by Hayes (1981) that older managers spend longer in each job, either because they are regarded as lacking the potential required for advancement, and/or because suitable openings in the narrowing pyramid are not available.

Satisfaction levels with current positions

Given that previous research suggests that older people enjoy more job satisfaction than younger people (Doering et al, 1983; IDS, 1996), respondents were asked a series of questions to rate their levels of satisfaction with various aspects of their current work. First, respondents were asked in an open ended question to state the most satisfying and dissatisfying aspects of their current job. Second, based on previous research (Brief and Oliver, 1976; Rosen et al, 1981; Long, 1984), they were provided with a series of statements, and asked to indicate their level of satisfaction with each, using a 5-point Likert scale from very satisfied (1) to very dissatisfied (5). Analysis of the responses showed little variance between aspects of the job younger and older managers found most satisfying and dissatisfying. From the open ended questions, the most satisfying aspects of the job provided by approximately a quarter of all managers, irrespective of age, was achieving sales and developing people. In addition, about a sixth of the younger and older managers alike considered that having strategic responsibilities, working autonomously, the diversity of the job and customer contact were job satisfiers. There were no specific dissatisfying aspects of the job that respondents mentioned with any regularity. Each factor was reported by fewer than 10 percent of the sample. Dealings with other people, work overload, stress, lack of resources and administration work were mentioned by both older and younger managers. Older managers were slightly more likely than younger managers to be dissatisfied with the management culture while younger managers were more concerned with office politics, the two of which may, of course, be interrelated.

Table 8.3 shows the mean scores for each listed statement together with their standard deviations. Both the managers below and above the age of 40 were satisfied with the various aspects of their current job. On the whole, however, managers over 40 were more satisfied than the managers under 40 which supports the findings of

Doering et al (1983), Benbour (1995) and Victor (1994). The older managers' overall average score was 2.01 against an average score of 2.20 for younger managers. For every statement, with the exception of one (opportunities for promotion), the mean scores indicate that managers over 40 were more satisfied with the various aspects of their jobs than managers under 40.

Table 8.3 : Job satisfaction: Significant differences between managers under and above the age of 40

	Mean	SD	t	P
Location of the Job				
Managers under 40	2.04	1.22	2.63	.010
Managers over 40	1.56	0.76		
Credibility with Staff				
Managers under 40	1.79	0.84	2.27	.026
Managers over 40	1.48	0.57		
Level of Training Received				
Manages under 40	2.25	1.12	2.24	.028
Managers over 40	1.84	0.81		
Opportunity to Influence Organisational Policies				
Managers under 40	2.62	1.21	2.19	.030
Managers over 40	2.10	0.98		
Level of Autonomy/Independence				
Managers under 40	2.02	0.99	2.14	.036
Managers over 40	1.68	0.70		
Opportunities for Travel				
Managers under 40	2.87	1.13	1.80	.074
Managers over 40	2.45	1.15		

Key
1 = Very Satisfied
2 = Fairly Satisfied
3 = Neither Satisfied nor Dissatisfied
4 = Fairly Dissatisfied
5 = Very Satisfied

The aspects of the job which most satisfied managers over 40 were their credibility with staff (1.48), the location of their job (1.56) and their working relationships with colleagues (1.66). They were least satisfied with their opportunities for promotion

(2.74) and to travel (2.45). Managers under 40 also mentioned their working relationships with colleagues (1.66) and their credibility with staff (1.79) and line managers (1.93) as the most satisfying aspects, together with their working relationships with subordinates (1.94). They were least satisfied with their opportunities for travel (2.87) and promotion (2.67), and also their opportunities to influence organisational policies (2.62).

To compare whether there were any statistical differences between younger and older managers and their level of job satisfaction, t-tests were performed on all the statements. The results are shown in Table 8.4. Significant differences between the mean scores for managers under and over the age of 40 were found for six of the 25 variables. Older managers were found to be significantly more likely to be satisfied than younger managers with the location of their jobs (t=2.63, p=0.01), their credibility with staff (t=2.27, p=0.026), the levels of training they received (t=2.24, p=0.028), their opportunities to influence organisational policies (t=2.19, p=0.030), their level of autonomy/independence (t=2.14, p=0.036), and their opportunities for travel (t=1.80, p=0.074). Overall, the findings regarding retail managers' satisfaction with their current jobs suggests that all managers are satisfied, although older managers appear to be slightly more satisfied with their current jobs than younger managers.

Factors helping and barriers hindering career development and problems encountered

Based on previous research (Alban-Metcalfe and Nicholson, 1984; Gold and Pringle, 1988), respondents were provided with a list of factors and asked to indicate to what extent they had helped or hindered their career development, using a 5-point Likert scale where 1= a great deal and 5=not at all. Respondents were able to indicate if a factor was not applicable to them, in which case no score was assigned to them. Table 8.5 shows the mean scores and standard deviations for each factor. Overall, managers over 40 were slightly more likely to believe the combined factors had helped their career development (2.35) than managers under 40 (2.42). There was general consensus between younger and older managers over the factors which have assisted their career development the most (their attitude to work, their experience, personal skills and past and present performance). Only three factors showed significant differences in the replies between younger and older managers. Older managers were significantly more likely than younger managers to believe that their attitude to work (t=1.92, p=0.059) and the level of training they have received (t=1.67, p=0.098) have helped in their career development. Younger managers, however, were significantly more likely to believe that their educational credentials have helped in their career development (t=-2.09, p=0.038). Respondents were less likely to state that a given factor had hindered their career development. Most factors have had only moderately hindered respondents' career development such as lack of political 'savvy' or not hindered them at all. Furthermore, no statistical differences between younger and older managers were found in their responses to factors that had hindered their careers.

Table 8.4 : Factors helping and hindering career development

	Managers Under 40		Managers Over 40	
	Mean		Mean	
Assistance or coaching by others	2.29		2.45	
Training	2.32		1.97	
Experience	1.66		1.48	
Personal skills	1.76		1.61	
Attitude to work (conscientious, hard working)	1.48		1.26	
Luck-being in the right place at the right time	2.71		2.40	
Networks	3.40		3.46	
Past and present performance	1.77		1.72	
Willingness to be mobile	2.62		2.57	
Support from home or partner	2.12		1.86	
Having a career plan	2.99		3.15	
Educational credentials	2.66		3.14	
Willingness to take risks	2.44		2.41	
Knowing and influencing the right people	3.01		2.81	
Impersonal decisions made at higher levels	3.13		2.92	
Bosses withholding guidance or encouragement?	3.26		3.65	
Lack of political savvy	3.24		3.38	
Lack of own career strategies	3.56		3.91	
Low personal expectations	3.89		4.09	
Lack of mobility	4.08		4.28	
Requirements of family life	4.09		4.00	
Life events (e.g. divorce, poor health)	4.28		4.17	
Personal factors (e.g. too blunt, outspoken)	3.52		3.33	
Organisational attitudes to women	4.08		3.71	
Sex discrimination	4.46		4.00	

Key

1 = Great deal
2 = Quite a lot
3 = Moderate
4 = Little
5 = Not at all

Table 8.5 : Percentage of managers encountering various problems

	Managers Under 40	Managers Over 40
Absence of mentors	30	9
Lack of challenging, high profile assignments	22	9
Exclusion from high profile training programmes	15	9
Lack of support from male colleagues	13	9
Lack of support from female colleagues	7	3
Lack of support from male bosses	22	13
Lack of support from female bosses	7	7
Lack of feedback on performance	34	22
Compensation inequities	14	16
Double standards for evaluating performance	22	19
Lack of female role models	15	6
Exclusion from informal networks	29	9
Hitting the glass ceiling (blocked career progress)	20	16
Dual career family conflicts	15	6
Difficulty with child care arrangements	5	-
Sexual harassment	4	3

Problems encountered by managers

Respondents were also provided with a list of problems encountered by managers (based on research by Rosen et al, 1989) and asked to indicate any from which they had suffered. Table 8.6 shows the percentage of managers reporting having encountered these problems. With the exception of compensation inequities, managers under 40 reported encountering each problem with more frequency than those over 40. The problems most likely to have been encountered by managers under 40 were lack of feedback on performance, absence of mentors and exclusion from informal networks. Although mentioned with less frequency, managers over 40 were more likely to have encountered problems of lack of feedback on performance and double standards for evaluating performance. Chi-square tests were performed on all these variables, and significant differences between younger and older managers were found for only two variables. Younger managers were significantly more likely to have encountered problems of being excluded from informal networks (chi=5.19, df=1, p=0.023) and absence of mentors (chi=5.62, df=1, p=0.018), even though they were more likely to have had a mentor (50 percent) than older managers (43 percent).

Table 8.6 : Likelihood of changing jobs in the next 12 months

	Managers Under 40		Managers Over 40		t-Value	2 Tail-Probability
	Mean	SD	Mean	SD		
Stay in same job (but Changes in duties/ activities)	2.41	1.55	2.81	1.66	-1.25	0.22
Be promoted	3.08	1.22	3.93	1.16	-3.32	0.001
Move within company	3.11	1.36	3.63	1.27	-1.86	0.066
Move to a different Employer	3.85	1.26	4.37	1.10	-2.04	0.044
Be made redundant	4.21	0.90	4.10	1.21	0.50	0.62

Key
1 = Very Likely
2 = Likely
3 = Unsure
4 = Unlikely
5 = Very Unlikely

Career advancement

In order to gauge managers' perceptions of their short-term career progression, they were asked to indicate on a 5 point Likert scale the likelihood that they would change jobs in the next twelve months. Table 8.7 shows the results. Generally, there was some degree of uncertainty as to whether they were likely to change jobs within the next twelve months. Both the managers above and below the age of 40 were more likely to consider they would remain in their existing jobs, but that the activities within these jobs would change, which may reflect the programme of management restructuring then occurring within the retail sector. Significant differences between younger and older managers were found for three of the five statements. Younger managers were significantly more likely than older managers to believe that they will be promoted within the next twelve months or to move either within the company or to a different company. Another interesting finding from Table 8.7 is that all managers felt it was unlikely they would be made redundant within the next twelve months. Although there has been some evidence of economic recovery since 1991 (Cockerham, 1995; Potter, 1996) this is still quite a surprising finding given the amount of management restructuring occurring in retailing, and the number of redundancies in services during 1995 (Potter, 1995). Clearly the respondents in this sample do not consider that any company changes, nor their ages will affect their jobs adversely.

Table 8.7 : Ultimate position desired (percentages)

	Managers Under 40	Managers Over 40
Director	44	38
Senior Manager	27	24
Middle Manager	4	-
Other	11	10
Already Achieved	15	28

Before ascertaining their ultimate career objectives, respondents were asked whether they had set themselves a careers life plan. Most replied they had only done so as their career developed (52 percent of younger managers against 66 percent of older managers). Few had planned their careers right from the beginning (15 percent of younger managers; 14 percent of older managers), while a large minority (33 percent of young managers and 21 percent of older manager) had not planned their careers at all.

Future career aspirations

The next series of questions were open ended, and asked respondents to indicate the highest position they ultimately desired to achieve, together with the actions necessary and barriers hindering them attaining this desired position. Table 8.8 shows the ultimate positions desired. Over a quarter of the managers over 40 (28 percent) against 15 percent of the managers under 40 had already achieved their career ambitions. This is to be expected as more of the older managers already held senior and director level posts. Of the managers still to realise their career ambitions, the majority are aiming high. Most desire director level positions while approximately a quarter desire a position in senior management. Their age does not appear to restrain their ambitions; no significant differences were found between the ages of managers and their ultimate position desired. Only a few differences were found between the responses of managers below and above the age of 40. A few of the younger managers stated they would ultimately like to run their own retail companies. By contrast, none of the older managers desired to set up their own businesses. Included in the 'other' category were younger managers who stated they wanted to progress up the career ladder but did not as yet know the ultimate post they desired. This reflects the higher proportion of younger managers not having set themselves a career life plan. A few older managers stated they were not looking for status, while a minority stated they wanted a career out of retailing, which may reflect a perception that they have reached their career ceilings in the retail sector.

Table 8.8 : Extent to which ultimate career goals are realistic (percentages)

	Managers Under 40	Managers Over 40
Very realistic	37	31
Somewhat realistic	42	41
Unsure	15	9
Somewhat unrealistic	4	9
Very unrealistic	3	9

In terms of the actions needed for reaching their ultimate career ambitions, just over a third of the managers over 40 believed it was a matter of time and they just needed to continue as present, working hard and applying for promotion as the opportunity arose. About a quarter felt they needed to broaden their experience and to further their education or change companies because of the lack of positions available with their present employer. Another quarter, however, felt it was all an element of luck, out of their control or did not know what actions they needed to take.

Gaining broader working experience was the single most important action managers under 40 felt they required to achieve their career aims, with a quarter regarding this as a necessary action. A similar proportion of younger to older managers mentioned continuing as present, furthering their education, and changing company as necessary actions. Fewer managers under 40, however, perceived it as out of their control, due to luck or not knowing what actions were needed.

More barriers hindering, rather than actions necessary, were provided by managers from attaining their desired career position. A quarter of the managers over 40 regarded the lack of available positions as a barrier, although recession and management restructuring were not attributed to this lack of available positions. Clearly, they see the narrowing occupational pyramid as the major problem, which supports the findings of Hayes (1981). Their concentration in functional specialist areas may also be attributable to the lack of available positions open to them, supporting the findings of Rothwell (1984) and Wilson (1991). Age was mentioned by a fifth of the older managers as a perceived barrier in attaining their ultimate career aims. These managers were in their forties or early fifties, and already occupied senior management posts, but had aspirations for board level positions. Although other factors (such as ability to relocate and lack of training) were provided as potential barriers to older managers, these were only mentioned in individual cases.

A similar proportion of managers under 40 foresaw the lack of available positions as a barrier to them attaining their desired ones. Several, however, mentioned the effect of the recession and the management restructuring and delayering taking place within the retail industry as potential barriers. A few younger managers also mentioned their lack of self confidence and the subjectivity of senior managers as potential problems in them achieving their career aims, while a few women regarded their gender as a major barrier. Age was only mentioned as a barrier by a minority of younger managers. For example, one senior manager who was 34 thought his age would be held against him in attaining a director level position.

Table 8.8 shows the extent to which managers believed their career goals to be realistic. Those who had already achieved their career goals or did not state a desired position were excluded from the analysis. Overall, respondents are optimistic that they can achieve their career goals. The results between managers below and above the age of 40 were not found to be statistically significant, and so there appears to be no association between a manager's age and their perceived ability to attain their career goals. Even analysing those who had specifically commented that their age was a barrier to their career progression, showed no particular patterns. While a few believed their goals to be very unrealistic, an equal proportion were unsure and a few more were optimistic that their goals could somewhat realistically be achieved.

Conclusions

One of the major employment characteristics of retailing has been its young age profile. Not only does it employ a high proportion of young people on the shop floor, but managerial positions are also occupied by young managers often in their late twenties or thirties. In response to the population changes, some retail companies have adopted distinctive policies for older workers, but these have been aimed at non-managerial staff where shortages have been most acute - namely at checkouts and areas of customer contact. Little is known about any policies regarding the employment of older managerial employees in retailing or whether they are discriminated against because of their age. This chapter has attempted to begin to address some of these issues by analysing whether managers over the age of 40 perceive any more difficulties in their career progression than those in their twenties and thirties. The overall conclusion drawn, for this sample, is that there are no appreciable differences between younger and older retail managers' perceived ability to progress their careers.

It was encouraging to find that all the respondents in this sample were satisfied with the various aspects of their current jobs. Overall, however, older managers were found to be slightly more satisfied with the various aspects of their jobs than younger managers (Table 8.3) which supports the findings of Doering et al (1983), Victor (1994) and Benbour (1995). Furthermore, they were significantly more likely than younger managers to report feelings of satisfaction with six aspects of their current jobs (Table 8.4). These findings suggest that, based on current job satisfaction levels, there are no negative associations regarding the employment of older managers within the retail environment. Nor do they indicate any reasons why their future developmental opportunities should be curtailed.

The only factor which older managers reported themselves as being less satisfied with than their younger counterparts were opportunities for promotion. However, only a fifth (20 percent) reported actual dissatisfaction with this factor, and over half of the older managers (52 percent) reported to be fairly satisfied with their opportunities for promotion. On average, the older managers had been in their present positions three times as long as the younger managers, which may explain why older managers reported this factor as being the least satisfying aspect of their current jobs. Given that the older managers in this study were more likely to occupy senior management positions, and that most of them were fairly satisfied with their opportunities for promotion, the lack of available positions to advance to (as found by Hayes, 1981) is likely to be a contributing factor in their perceived lack of opportunities for promotion, as opposed to discriminatory practices by their employers.

Respondents were in general agreement over the factors which have assisted their career development to date (Table 8.5). Both younger and older managers alike believe that their attitude to work has been the most important factor in assisting their career development. Although younger managers were significantly more likely than older managers to believe their educational credentials have helped their career development, older managers were more likely to believe that their experience and training they have received has been helpful in developing their careers.

No significant differences were found between the two samples and the factors hindering their career development. In fact, none of the factors were regarded by either the older or younger managers as hindering their career development to any great extent. Furthermore, older managers reported encountering various problems with less frequency than younger managers. The fact that very few significant differences were found between the older and younger managers in the factors helping and hindering their career development, and the problems they have encountered, suggests that age has not been perceived by the retail managers in this sample as an obstacle in their career development to date.

Regarding their short-term employment prospects, some interesting findings emerged (Table 8.7). Although the retail industry is currently undergoing considerable management restructuring exercises, resulting in down-sizing and de-layering exercises, neither older nor younger retail managers foresaw any adverse changes in their employment prospects over the short-term. Age was not perceived to be a threat in terms of them being made redundant, with 55 percent of the managers over 40 (against 49 percent of those under 40) believing it was very unlikely they would be made redundant over the next 12 months. However the managers over 40 were significantly less likely than those under 40 to believe they will be promoted, move to a different employer or move within the company over the next 12 months. While this demonstrates the older managers' greater organisational commitment, supporting the findings of Doering et al (1983), Metcalf and Thompson (1990) and Trinder et al (1992), these findings do appear to indicate that the younger managers believe they have more potential to change their jobs in the short-term. The extent to which these findings are attributable to management restructuring changes is unknown, and is worthy of further research.

While Metcalf and Thompson (1990) found that the quest for promotion and career development was perceived to decline with age, the results of this study do not support this view (Table 8.8). Almost two thirds (62 percent) of the managers over 40 aspire to senior management or board level positions, with no significant differences being found between a manager's age and their ultimate career ambitions. Moreover, almost three quarters (72 percent) of the managers over 40 believed that they could realise their ultimate career goals, which although slightly lower than the managers under 40 (79 percent) was not found to be significant. Rather surprising, however, was that the younger managers appeared to have more definite ideas about the actions needed to gain their ultimate positions. They were more likely to state that gaining broader experience was the major action needed to achieve their career aims. The older managers, on average however, have 10 years more managerial experience than the younger managers, and they were more likely than their younger counterparts to state they did not know what actions were necessary to achieve their ultimate positions, or else state that they were out of their control or due to luck. Their age and experience may have demonstrated to them the very real difficulties in achieving career ambitions in a narrowing occupational pyramid.

Age was mentioned as a perceived barrier by some older managers in achieving their career ambitions, all of whom already occupied senior management positions and desired board level positions. If their ages match those of the present board level incumbents, it is understandable they may perceive their age as a barrier to progression. So whether it was a manager's age or the availability of the ultimate career position which was regarded as a barrier is uncertain. Most respondents did not mention their age as a perceived barrier, however, nor did they regard themselves as lacking the potential for advancement. In conclusion therefore age is not regarded as an overriding issue in retail managers achieving their long-term career ambitions.

More work is needed to explore and test the generalities of the present findings. Another study comparing the career development of a representative sample of retail managers at all levels and areas of the managerial structure would facilitate rigorous analysis of the issues regarding age and the retail manager. Little is known about the employment structure of managerial retail occupations by age, although older personnel tend to be employed in head offices. A detailed analysis of the age structure of retail managers by occupational position held would contribute greatly to existing knowledge. In particular, this research area would benefit from qualitative research methods, exploring in more depth the issues of age and career development for employees at various management levels in retailing. It may also benefit from longitudinal analysis, examining the career development of a group of middle managers of various ages but with similar career ambitions, to see if age can be isolated as a significant factor in their achieving their ultimate career goals.

References

Alban-Metcalfe, B. and Nicholson, N. (1984), *The Career Development of British Managers*, British Institute of Management Foundation: BIM Management Survey Report.

Banel, R. (1996), 'It's Good to be Grey', *The Scotsman*, 19 January, p. 37.

Beck, B. (1995), 'The World's Most Intractable Problem', *The Economist*, November, pp. 38-39.

Benbour, N. (1995), *Survival of the Fittest: A Survey of Managers' Experience of, and Attitudes to, Work in the Post Recession Economy*, Institute of Management, London.

Britton, J. and Thomas, K. (1973), 'Age and Sex as Employment Variables: Views of Employment Service Interviewers', *Journal of Employment Counselling*, Vol. 10, pp. 180-86.

Brief, A.P. and Oliver, R.L. (1976), 'Male-Female Differences in Work, Attitudes Among Retail Sales Managers', *Journal of Applied Psychology*, Vol. 61, No. 4, pp. 526-28.

Broadbridge, A. (1995), 'Female and Male Earnings Differentials in Retailing', *The Service Industries Journal*, Vol. 15, No. 1, pp. 14-34.

Butler, R.N. (1987), 'Ageism', *The Encyclopedia of Aging*, Springer Publishing Company, New York.

Bytheway, B. and Johnson, J. (1990), 'On Defining Ageism', *Critical Social Policy*, Vol. 27, pp. 27-39.

Cockerham, J. (1995), 'Redundancies in Great Britain: Results from the Spring 1994 Labour Force Survey', *Employment Gazette*, Vol. 103, No. 1, pp. 21-27.

Comfort, A. (1977), *A Good Age*, Mitchell Beazley, London.

Doering, M., Rhodes, S. and Schuster, M. (1983), *The Aging Worker*, Sage Publications, Beverly Hills, C.A.

Employment Department (1992), 'Ageism Attacked - 'Absurd, Wasteful and Shortsighted", *Employment Gazette*, Vol. 100, No. 6, p. 263, HMSO, London.

Employment Department Group (1991), *The Best of Both Worlds: The Benefits of a Flexible Approach to Working Arrangements*, Employment Department Group, London.

Employment Department Group (1994), *Getting On: The Benefits of an Older Workforce*, Employment Department Group, London.

Gold, U.O.C. and Pringle, J.K. (1988), 'Gender-Specific Actors in Manangement Promotion', *Journal of Managerial Psychology*, Vol. 3, No. 4, pp. 17-22.

Hassell, B.L. and Perrewe, P.L. (1995), 'An Examination of Benefits about Older Workers: Do Stereotypes Still Exist?', *Journal of Organizational Behaviour*, Vol. 16, No. 5, pp. 457-68.

Hayes, J. (1981), 'Over Forties in Professional, Managerial, and Administrative Work', in C.L. Cooper, and D.P. Torrington (eds), *After Forty*, John Wiley and Sons Ltd, Chichester.

Hogarth, T. and Barth, M.C. (1991), *Age Works: A Case Study of B & Q's Use of Older Workers*, Institute of Employment Research, University of Warwick.

IDS (1996), *Older Workers*, IDS Study 595, February.

International Labour Office (1979), *Older Workers: Work and Retirement - Sixth Item on the Agenda*, International Labour Office, Geneva.

Laczko, F. (1990), 'Between Work and Retirement: Becoming 'Old' in the 1980s', in B. Bytheway, T. Keil, P. Allant and A. Bryman (eds), *Becoming and Being Old: Sociological Approaches to Later Life*, Sage, London.

Laczko, F. and Phillipson, C. (1991), *Changing Work and Retirement*, Open University Press, Milton Keynes.

Long, P. (1984), *The Personnel Professionals: A Comparative Study of Male and Female Careers*, Institute of Personnel Management, London.

Lucas, R. (1995), 'Some Age Related Issues in Hotel and Catering Employment', *The Service Industries Journal*, Vol. 15, No. 2, pp. 234-50.

Marshall, J. and Cooper, C.L. (1978), *Understanding Executive Stress*, Macmillan Press, London.

Metcalf, H. and Thompson. M. (1990), *Older Workers: Employers' Attitudes and Practices*, IMS Report No, 194, Institute of Manpower Studies, Sussex.

NIESR (1986), *Young People's Employment in Retailing*, NEDO, London.

Norman, A. (1987), *Aspects of Ageism*, Centre for Policy and Aging, London.

Parker, S.R. (1980), 'Settling for Roses Round the Door: The Experience of Early Retirement', *Employment Gazette*, December.

Perrewe, P.L., Bryner, R.A. and Stepina, L.A. (1991), 'A Casual Model Examining the Effects of Age Discrimination on Employee Psychological Reactions and Subsequent Turnover Intentions', *International Journal of Hospitality Management*, Vol. 10, pp. 245-60.

Potter, J. (1996), 'Redundancies in Great Britain: Results from the Labour Force Survey', *Labour Market Trends*, Vol. 104, No. 2, pp. 41-48.

Rosen, B. and Jerdee, T. (1976a), 'The Influence of Age Stereotypes on Managerial Decisions', *Journal of Applied Psychology*, Vol. 61, pp. 428-32.

Rosen, B. and Jerdee, T. (1976b), 'The Nature of Job-Related Age Stereotypes', *Journal of Applied Psychology*, Vol. 61, pp. 180-83.

Rosen, B. and Jerdee, T. (1977), 'Too Old or Not Too Old?', *Harvard Business Review*, Vol. 55, pp. 97-106.

Rosen, B., Templeton, M.E. and Kichline, K. (1981), 'The First Few Years on the Job: Women in Manangement', *Business Horizons*, Vol. 24, No. 6, pp. 26-29.

Rosen, B., Miguel, M. and Peirce, E. (1989), 'Stemming the Exodus of Women Managers', *Human Resource Management*, Vol. 28, No. 4, pp. 475-91.

Schuller, T. (199) 'Work-Ending: Employment and Ambiguity in Later Life' in B. Bytheway, T. Keil, P. Allant and A. Bryman (eds), *Becoming and Being Old: Sociological Approaches to Later Life*, Sage, London.

Skills and Enterprise Briefing (1991), '*The Old Worker: A Force to Be Reckoned With*', SEN 42, October, Employment Department Group.

Taylor, P. and Walker, A. (1994), 'The Ageing Workforce: Employers' Attitudes Towards Older Workers', *Work, Employment and Society*, Vol. 8, No. 4, pp. 569-91.

Trinder, C., Hulme, G. and McCarthy, U. (1992), *Employment: The Role of Work in the Third Age*, The Carnegie United Kingdom Trust.

Victor, C.R. (1994), *Old Age in Modern Society: A Textbook of Social Gerontology*, Chapman and Hall, London.

Wilson, P. (1991), 'Women Employees and Senior Management', *Personnel Review*, Vol. 20, No. 1, pp. 32-6.

9 Ageism, young academics and the buffalo stance

Karen Rodham (née Gadd)

Introduction

> Ageism, discrimination on the basis of chronological age, is a deep seated social phenomenon in British culture and specifically, of the workplace (Lyon and Pollard, 1997, p. 245).

The origins of this chapter can be found in a conference paper which focused upon ageism as experienced by young female academics (Gadd, 1996). Since then, the paper has been expanded to include the experiences of young male academics. The data included are anecdotal, and have been collected via informal conversations with 20 young academics (seven males and 13 females) aged between 27 and 36 years. 'Young' is how the respondents were defined by their colleagues in their respective departments. Respondents were based in different geographical locations and came from a number of different academic disciplines (psychology, nursing, business/management, sociology and economics). It is recognised that the small sample who agreed to share their experiences of ageism are by no means representative of academia or other work environments, and that the data drawn upon are subjective. Indeed, collecting any objective data about discrimination on the grounds of age has been described as being 'hard to come by' (Walker and Maltby, 1997). Nevertheless, this does not negate the validity of the issues that are raised; instead it can be suggested that the need for systematic research into this area of ageism is highlighted. Indeed, many of those who offered their experiences of ageism for the purposes of this chapter mentioned that they were startled to discover the negative attitudes directed towards them because of their age.

Perhaps at the outset, in the same way that Bill Bytheway (1995, p. 2) declared his background at the start of his book entitled '*Ageism*', I should declare mine. As I write this, I am aged 28, I am white, female, able-bodied, heterosexual and I am employed by a British university. Like Bytheway, I too recognise that this gives me a particular perspective on life, and I also like to think that I do not underestimate the significance of this perspective. Nevertheless, I feel that this perspective gives me the ability and sensitivity to write about ageism as experienced at the younger end of the age scale. This is not to deny that ageism is experienced by 'older' people. Indeed, it is not the intention of this chapter to criticise the valuable work which has already demonstrated that older workers are sometimes at a disadvantage because of ageism. For example Taylor and Walker (1995) point out that 'age discrimination towards older workers is widely practised by employers', furthermore, 'despite evidence of age discrimination, older workers receive no protection or rights under the law' (Laczko and Phillipson, 1991). However, what this chapter does aim to do, is to address the imbalance in the literature, and demonstrate that younger workers can also be on the receiving end of age discrimination, or ageism.

Thus this chapter has three objectives. Firstly, the literature which focuses on ageism at work will be shown to be ageist. Secondly, drawing from anecdotal evidence collected from colleagues and acquaintances, the problems experienced by young academics as a result of ageism will be highlighted and explored. Thirdly, and finally, some coping strategies that have been used by the young academics who contributed to this chapter are described.

Ageist ageism literature

Awareness of the potentially unfair and inefficient nature of discrimination in employment has begun to increase in recent years (McGoldrick and Arrowsmith, 1996). However, 'the discussion has always been about older workers and their exclusion from the labour market' (Labour Research, 1995, p. 15). Indeed, the use of the word ageism in much of the published literature conjures up images of the problems and discrimination faced by people at the older end of the spectrum (my emphasis added):

> Ageism is a negative attitude that reflects and subsequently influences the attitudes communicated towards *ageing* and *elderly* people (Whitbourne and Hulicka, 1990).
>
> Ageism is often linked to sexism and racism. In one respect, however, it is different, for while people are born a certain sex or race, they are not born *old* (Darwin, 1989).
>
> Ageism - the differential association of negative traits with the *aged* (Perdue and Gurtman, 1990).
>
> Ageism - discrimination on the grounds of being *old* (Comfort, 1977).

In defining ageism in such a way, the authors expose themselves to the charge of being ageist, because they do not acknowledge the experience of ageism at the younger end of the spectrum. Emphasis tends to have been given either to beliefs concerning the ability of older workers, or to discrimination as experienced by older workers (see for example: Copley, 1990; Taylor and Walker, 1994, 1995;

Herriot et al, 1993; Bytheway and Johnson, 1990; Lyon and Pollard, 1996; Broadridge, 1996; Jones, 1996; Butler and Lewis, 1973 and Itzin and Phillipson, 1993). It is not surprising then, that the term ageism tends to be associated with the experiences of older people. For example, Bytheway (1995, p. 3) suggests that ageism is about age and prejudice, and also points out that it occurs in all sorts of situation while affecting people of all ages. However, later in the same book, he explains that although ageism experienced by young people is essentially the same phenomenon as that experienced by older people; the experience of the phenomenon itself is radically different. For that reason, the remainder of his book focuses primarily on ageism in later life. Thus, Bytheway (1995) merely pays lip service to the fact that ageism is experienced at all ages before proceeding to concentrate on the experiences of older people. This chapter therefore aims to demonstrate that just as older people are blocked or excluded on the basis of their age, so too are younger people. Therefore, whatever a person's age, the experience is of discrimination.

Kimmel (1988), Westman (1991) and Branine and Glover (1997) are among the few exceptions in the literature who do acknowledge that ageism can be experienced at the younger end of the spectrum. For example, Branine and Glover (1997) note that 'ageism is inadequately defined if it is focused solely on old people'. In keeping with this more enlightened approach to ageism, the remainder of this chapter attempts to highlight the different types of ageist comments which have been directed at young academics. Finally the ageist attitudes are categorised and strategies for coping are outlined.

Young academics' experiences of ageism

Comments from colleagues

Many of the comments that were relayed by the respondents seemed to be aimed at overtly denigrating the younger academics achievements:

> I don't know - these twenty five year olds coming in with PhDs what do they know about anything? I don't know what all the fuss is all about - I have at least two half written PhDs lying around at home I could submit - Tell me how it has changed your life - I am sure it is not worth the time.

The implication of this type of comment is that the achievements of the young academic are regarded as negligible. The emphasis in these comments is placed upon age ('these twenty five year olds'). In this particular case, the academic concerned was in her early thirties and had six years' university teaching under her belt.

Other older academics chose to attribute younger academics' achievements to luck and fate, while ignoring the hard work that had gone into the achievement. For example, a common remark was:

> You landed on your feet. You were lucky to do that so young.

Clearly, such comments, although apparently positive, can also be seen from a different perspective - whereby the older academic is denying the younger person's ability. The net result of both the above types of comment can be frustration and an erosion of the younger academics' confidence.

In addition, young academics often found that administrative support was distinctly lacking (fifteen out of twenty respondents mentioned this issue). Administrative staff concentrated on the older, more senior members of staff, preferring not to work for someone who was younger and therefore was considered as being less important. It was also assumed that because they were younger, they would be IT literate and therefore would not need such help. As a result, many of the younger academics admitted that they did their own photocopying and letter writing in order to avoid a dispute with the administrative staff.

Other tactics indulged in included 'gossiping' about younger members of staff. In one case, the older members of staff were overheard suggesting that one particular individual had not really got a PhD because of being too young.

With increasing emphasis being placed upon research output in the world of academia, those lecturers who entered the profession straight from their first degrees and spent the next twenty or thirty years focusing on teaching, rather than research are beginning to feel threatened. One senior lecturer was surprised to find that a young academic in her first year of teaching (but who had a strong publishing track record and a PhD) could theoretically both apply for a more senior post, and was also likely to be shortlisted if she did. This older academic was heard to remark - 'God! Even these youngsters with PhDs can apply!' He, alongside the other older academics in the department believed that promotion was something that you were entitled to if you worked in one place for enough years - actual ability was not something which they placed a great deal of emphasis upon. For example, the following comment that was made pays no attention to the young academics' qualifications and previous experience, the only issue is length of service:

> If they get the post then I give up - they have hardly been here any length of time - who do they think they are?

Similarly, during an appraisal, a young academic asked about the prospects of promotion, and was told in no uncertain terms that a senior lectureship would be possible when they reached their mid to late thirties; that it was very unusual for someone younger than that to attain such a position. Although other criteria were mentioned in passing, the emphasis was heavily placed on the issue of age. This notion of serving your time, which is ingrained in the thinking of the ageist (and often older academics), is also demonstrated in the comments made about a member of staff who was leaving to go and work in a different university in a more senior position. A number of the older academics decided that they were not going to contribute to her leaving present because she had hardly been at the university any length of time. In fact she had been working there for four years!

Comments from students

Of course it is not just fellow academics who display ageist attitudes, many young academics have also received ageist comments from their students:

> You don't look like a lecturer, you don't look old enough to be one.

Such a remark begs the questions 'How should lecturers look?' and 'Where do students get their ideas from about this issue?' (surely not the now infamous appearance of many lecturers in 1970s programmes of the Open University!). Other comments particularly from mature students, revolved around the difficulty they clearly experienced on being taught by lecturers close in age to, or younger than themselves.

> If my children spoke to me the way you do, they would get a slap.

This was a response to a young lecturer who had asked a mature student a question in class. This type of response has strong parallels with the ageism bound up in the relationship between children and their parents. Bytheway (1995, p. 77) notes that conflicts between children and their parents are often articulated in terms of each others' age: 'Don't talk to me like that! When I was your age ...' he continues; '... and so it goes on, moving rapidly into wilder assertions about each others' generation. In this way, a powerful generation specific and mutually reinforcing form of ageism develops. This downward spiral is not constructive and only serves to aggravate the situation'.

Other students are less patronising, but still obviously uncertain about someone younger than, or close in age to them, standing in front of their class as their teacher. In fact many students were very eager to discover exactly what younger academics' qualifications actually were before they would accept them as their 'teachers'. For example, one respondent remarked with relief at the beginning of this year:

> I can start my introductory lectures by saying that this is my fourth year teaching.

The respondent felt the need to do this in order to demonstrate to the doubting students before her, that she did in fact have prior experience of teaching and was a perfectly competent teacher. Indeed, seventeen out of twenty respondents mentioned that students had often challenged them to justify their academic credibility before they would accept them as their lecturer.

Strategies employed to combat ageism

All of the above types of ageist comments and attitudes towards younger members of academic staff can be described in terms of strategies employed by older individuals who are trying to assert their power. Morgan (1986) suggests that 'power is the medium through which conflicts of interest are ultimately resolved. Power influences who gets what, when and how'. This is in line with Dahl's (1957) suggestion that 'power involves an ability to get another person to do something that he or she would not otherwise have done'. Similarly, Hunt (1992) defines power as the capacity to affect other people's behaviour with or without their consent and allows for the deployment of resources to achieve ends'.

A framework which can be employed to clarify the power relationships amongst the older and younger individuals discussed in this chapter is the three dimensional view of power, which are described by Lukes (1974) as

> for consideration of the many ways in which potential issues are kept out of politics whether through the operation of social forces and institutional practices, or through individuals' decisions. This, moreover, can occur in the absence of actual observable conflict which may have been successfully averted, though there remains here an implicit reference to potential conflict. This potential may never in fact be actualised. What one may have here is a *latent conflict* which consists in a contradiction between the interests of those exerting power and the *real interests* of those they exclude. This conflict is latent in the sense that it is assumed there *would be* a conflict of wants or preferences between those exercising power and those subject to it, were the latter to become aware of their interests (Lukes, 1977, pp. 24-25).

Thus, although younger academic staff may be less powerful in terms of their present hierarchical position or in terms of length of service, they may be able to exert power over the older staff by means of 'fabrication' (to use Goffman's 1974 term). In other words, younger members of staff may choose to comply with, and not make an issue of the ageist comments, whilst retaliating; perhaps through increasing their academic output and thereby consolidating their positions. As a result, observable conflict will be absent, nevertheless the potential for conflict is ever present. An example of this type of strategy is illustrated by a young member of staff who appeared to be conforming to the ageist comments. Having worked in a department for two years, he was heard to say:

'I'm sorry, I am only new, you had better ask 'x''. There are two ways of viewing this tactic. On the one hand, it could seem that this person had begun to lose confidence in his ability and had 'fallen-in' with the view that it was length of service which counted over and above everything else. On the other hand, this behaviour can be explained in terms of fabrication, whereby the younger staff member feigns an inability to cope. In doing so, he in effect delegates responsibility to older academics, thereby freeing up his time considerably to focus on his research, whilst at the same time appearing to comply with the ageist viewpoint, thereby avoiding conflict. This younger member of staff therefore managed to exert power over the older staff in the absence of observable conflict, for the older staff were given the impression that he was in fact conforming to their expectations. This strategy can be called the 'Fox Syndrome', whereby the younger member of staff appears to comply with the ageist comments, but subtly (and slyly?) retaliates.

An alternative method of exerting power and authority is by means of rules. Functionalists for example, view rules as the formal requirements of an organisation which seem to determine and shape the actions of individuals and groups within that organisation. Alternatively, Interactionists view rules as being the way in which individuals interpret their own actions and those of others. Thus, instead of the rules being 'a set of statements intended to determine the appropriateness of an action; the interactionist views rules as the explanations an individual provides for themselves and others' (Mills and Murgatroyd 1991, p. 31). Whatever the theoretical perspective adopted, the fact remains that all organisations have rules (both formal and informal) to which individuals are expected to conform. One example of informal rules was provided by a respondent who mentioned that in his department the older members of staff had an informal rule that to have your title on your office door was in conflict with the equal opportunities policy. The few younger individuals in the department who had titles faced the dilemma - to conform and be accepted by their colleagues in the department; or to put up their title and risk conflict. Most decided to plump for the former, in spite of the fact that all other departments in the university encouraged staff to put titles on their doors. This tactic can be called the 'Ostrich Syndrome', whereby the young academics ignore the ageist comments; bury their heads in the sand; and get on with their job in the best way they can, whilst avoiding conflict at all costs.

The final strategy which has been employed by those who offered their experiences for this paper, conforms to the view that 'ageism is the type of prejudice and discrimination which consists of the unjustifiable use of social notions associated with chronological or biological age against individuals, groups or other classes of people' (Branine and Glover, 1997, p. 228). This viewpoint equates ageism with other 'isms' such as racism and sexism, suggesting that it too, is based on 'fear and folklore' (Comfort, 1977). As Neugarten (1982, quoted in Vincent, 1995, p. 21) notes, chronological age simply does not correlate reliably with many socially important characteristics. It does not determine and hence does not predict attitudes, health, interests, education, family relationships, work capacity or intellect'.

> Like racism, it [ageism] needs to be met by information, contradiction and when necessary, confrontation. And the people who are being victimised have to stand up for themselves in order for it to be put down' (Comfort, 1977, p. 35).

In short, this strategy is named 'The Buffalo Stance'. Buffalos are known in Africa as 'Brave Fighters'. They are famous for their 'keen sense of smell and are said to know the presence of intruders at a distance of 500 metres' (Safari Guide, 1991). Thus, this option involves the younger staff being prepared to meet 'head-on' those making ageist comments and confront the prejudices consciously or unconsciously expressed.

Conclusion

> We do not typically treat our attitude as just a matter of opinion - we regard our attitude as 'the truth' at least until someone can introduce new facts or arguments to change our mind (Mills and Murgatroyd, 1991, p. 31).

It appears that ageism directed towards 'younger' members of staff needs to be brought on to the agenda in order for it to be recognised and challenged. Although a number of authors have acknowledged that ageism is experienced by younger people, it is not something that is explored in depth. It is reasonable to conclude from the anecdotal evidence presented above, that the experiences described by the respondents are likely to continue unless the ageist attitudes discussed in this chapter are brought to people's attention, perhaps in the same manner that notions of sexist, racist and politically incorrect language were brought to our attention. For example, Westman (1991) points out that before racism was generally accepted as being a social problem, many people believed benevolently that slaves were actually content; and before sexism was openly revealed, it was often thought that women were actually satisfied with subservient occupations. Clearly all three ideologies (sexism, racism and ageism) depend on prejudice which serves to justify forms of inequality (Gearing 1995, p. *x*). They are three philosophies which are 'offensive and which we would expect ordinary, liberal, tolerant, intelligent people to be against' (Bytheway, 1995, p. 9). Such an assumption appears to be behind the UK Government's attempts to persuade employers to abandon ageist attitudes and appoint or promote on merit, irrespective of applicant age. In turning its back on the legislative route, the then Conservative Government and the Institute of Personnel Development put considerable faith in the prospect of attitude and behavioural change on the part of employers and their agents (Lyon and Pollard, 1996). There has been no change with the New Labour Government who are walking the same route with the announcement of a code of practice on ageism which is currently being drawn up

> 'Employers should not impose arbitrary age limits when recruiting. They should consider a wide range of candidates and choose on the basis of ability to do the job regardless of age (Smith, 1998).

Thus, faith is still being placed in voluntary support and not legislation. The problem with this approach as Westman (1991, p. 237) notes is that 'individuals and groups have difficulty in recognising their own prejudices, even when they obviously exploit others'. This is because human beings hold preconceived ideas that guide their attitudes and choices. As a result, everyone's perceptions and judgements are prejudiced to some degree by their past experiences and their current emotional states, and contradictions of these preconceptions tend on the whole to be rejected. Nevertheless, in the same way that racism and sexism are being addressed, ageism with regard to younger people *as well* as older people needs to be brought firmly onto the agenda. Researchers need to widen their view and focus on ageism as a whole, not solely upon ageism as experienced by older people. In order to achieve this, it seems that we need to directly challenge these preconceived ideas, attitudes and choices identified above. Perhaps then, the 'Buffalo Stance' is the logical way forward?

Acknowledgement

My thanks are offered to Dr Gore and Dr Myers for their helpful suggestions and to all those who shared their experiences of ageism.

References

Braithwaite, V., Lynd-Stevenson, R. and Pigram, D. (1993), 'An Empirical Study of Ageism: From Polemics to Scientific Utility', *Australian Psychologist,* Vol. 28, No. 1, pp. 9-15.

Branine, M. and Glover, I. (1997), 'Ageism and the Labour Process: Towards a Research Agenda', *Personnel Review,* Vol. 26, No. 4, pp. 233-44.

Broadbridge, A. (2000), *Ageism in Retailing: Myth or Reality?,* Chapter 8 of this book.

Butler, R.N. and Lewis, M.I. (1973), *Ageing and Mental Health*, CV Mosby: St Louis MD [quoted in Bytheway , B. (1995) - see below].

Bytheway, B. (1995), *Ageism*, Open University Press, Buckingham.

Bytheway, B. and Johnson, J. (1990), 'On Defining Ageism', *Critical Social Policy,* 27, pp. 27-39.

Capowski, G. (1994), 'Ageism: The New Diversity Issue', *Management Review,* Vol. 83, No. 10, pp. 10-15.

Comfort, A. (1977), *A Good Age,* Mitchell Beazley.

Copley, J. (1990), 'Workers Face Ageism at 30, Surveys Show', *The Scotsman*, 26 October, [cited in Branine and Glover, 1997].

Dahl, R.A. (1957), 'The Concept of Power', *Behavioural Science*, 2, pp. 201-5.

Darwin, J. (ed.) (1989), *Against Ageism*, Search Project, Newcastle-Upon-Tyne.

Gadd, K. (1996), 'Young Female Academics - Their Story!', paper presented at the Ageism, Work and Employment Conference, University of Stirling, July.

Gearing, B. (1995), Series Editors' preface in B. Bytheway (1995) *Ageism*, Open University Press, Buckingham.

Goffman, E. (1974), *Frame Analysis: An Essay on the Organisation of Experience*; Penguin, Harmondsworth.

Hassel, B. and Perreive, P.L. (1995), An Examination of the Beliefs About Older Workers - Do Stereotypes Still Exist?, *Journal of Organisational Behaviour*, Vol. 16, No. 5, pp. 457-68.

Herriot, P., Gibson, G., Pemberton, C. and Pinder, R. (1993), 'Dashed Hopes: Organisational Determinants and Personal Perceptions of Managerial Careers', *The Journal of Occupational and Organisational Psychology*, 66, pp. 115-23.

Hunt, J.W. (1992), *Managing People at Work: A Managers Guide to Behaviour in Organisations*, McGraw-Hill Book Company, London.

Itzin, C. and Phillipson, C. (1993), *Age Barriers at Work: Maximising the Potential of Mature and Older People*, Metropolitan Authorities Recruitment Agency, Solihull.

Jones, P. (1996), 'Age Old Problems', *Scottish Business Insider*, December 4-6 [cited in Branine and Glover, 1997].

Kimmel, D.C. (1988), 'Ageism, Psychology and Public Policy', *American Psychologist*, Vol. 43, No. 3, pp. 175-78.

Labour Research (1995), 'Jobs Bias Against Young and Old', *Labour Research*, Vol. 84, No. 1, pp. 15-16.

Laczko, F. and Phillipson, C. (1991), 'Great Britain: The Contradictions of early Exit' in M. Kohli, M. Rein, A.M. Guillemard and H. Van Gunsteren (eds), *Time for Retirement*, Cambridge University Press, Cambridge.

Lukes, S. (1974), *Power: A Radical View,* Macmillan, London.

Lyon, P. and Pollard, D. (1997), 'Perceptions of the Older Employee: Is Anything Really Changing?', *Personnel Review*, Vol. 26, No. 4, pp. 245-57.

McGoldrick, A. and Arrowsmith, J. (1996), *Age Discrimination in Employment: Managerial Views and Organisational Practice*, paper presented at the Ageism, Work and Employment Conference, University of Stirling, July.

Mills, A.J. and Murgatroyd, S.J. (1991), *Organisational Rules: A framework for Understanding Organisational Action*, Open University Press, Milton Keynes.

Morgan, G. (1986), *Images of Organisation*, Sage Publications, London.

Perdue, C.W. and Gurtman, M.B. (1990), 'Evidence for the Automaticity of Ageism', *Journal of Experimental Social Psychology*, 26, pp. 199-216.

Safari Guide (1991), *On Safari*, Kashmircraft, Nairobi.

Smith, A. (1998), Speech made by the Employment Minister at the Employers Forum on Age in London 30 June.

Taylor, P. and Walker, A. (1994), 'The Ageing Workforce: Employers Attitudes Towards Older People', *Work Employment and Society*, Vol. 8, 4, pp. 569-91.

Taylor, P. and Walker, A. (1995), 'Combating Age Barriers in Job Recruitment and Training', *Policy Studies*, Vol. 16, No. 1, pp. 4-13.

Vincent, J.A. (1995), *Inequality and Old Age,* UCL Press, London.

Walker, B. and Maltby, T. (1997), *Ageing Europe*, OUP, Buckingham.

Westman, J.V. (1991), 'Juvenile Ageism: Unrecognised Prejudice and Discrimination Against the Young', *Child Psychiatry and Human Development,* Vol. 21, No. 4, pp. 237-56.

Whitbourne, S.K. and Hulicka, I.M. (1990), 'Ageism in Undergraduate Psychology Texts', *American Psychologist*, 45, pp. 1127-36.

10 Ageism and arm's length management: the voice of experience

David Jenkins, interviewed by Ian Glover

Introduction

David Jenkins has degrees in history from Oxford University and in law, and by evening study, from the London School of Economics. He is in his mid-seventies and for the last eighteen years he has worked full-time in his own management consultancy, TEK Associates. Before that he worked for twelve years for the Engineering Industry Training Board (EITB) as a Training Adviser. Before that he worked for the British Printing Corporation (BPC) for three years, where he was in charge of training and also involved in industrial relations, with the job title of Deputy Personnel Controller. Before that he was with BTR for twelve years. He had various responsibilities there, as a Training Manager, Production Manager and Marketing Manager for different periods. After leaving Oxford and before going to BTR he was employed for three years by Short Brothers in Belfast, initially as a Project Engineer and then as a Training Manager.

He has also held other posts for shorter periods. The longest of these was one of two years as a head of a department of management studies in a further education college. In his mid-twenties he worked for a short while with the former General Bruce Ismay who had been Churchill's close confidante in Whitehall throughout most of the Second World War.

David is the author of two books and a number of articles about management. His second book, *Managing Empowerment*, published in 1996, explained why re-engineering a business can only work properly if staff are given the power to do the jobs for which they are employed and if the resultant organization is flexible, transparent and carries no passengers. It also explained the radical effects of empowerment on traditional career paths. The book has attracted substantial academic and media attention.

David is a friend of Michael Fores whose team of economists at the Department of Industry and various academic associates, including Ian Glover and Peter Herriot who have chapters in this volume, helped to develop the study of comparative management in the 1970s to help publicise weaknesses of UK manufacturing, management and of related aspects of higher, further and secondary education

(Glover and Kelly, 1993; Sorge, 1994). David was involved in their discussions and has been in contact with several of them since that time. His interview with Ian Glover began in Oxford in early 2000 and was completed by telephone a little over a month later. The aim was to explore some of David's considerable experience of management, consultancy and employment in order to draw out his thoughts on age, work and employment along with some of his general views about management and employment in the UK. Some of the facts and views revealed here draw on another interview of David conducted by Ian Glover, also in early 2000, on management in the UK. However almost all draw on the present interview and David's statements and views are recorded here as fully as possible.

The interview

Ian Glover: Why did you spend as much time as you did in the management of training?

David Jenkins: It happened several times, yes. I got moved into training. Companies decided it was important and thought I was the best to do it. I should have stuck with marketing really, though. [In the other interview David was asked for his views on difficult functional specialisms and he described marketing staff as 'more infantile ... the level of emotional maturity is below zero! They are obsessed with material status, for example company cars. Ninety percent are lousy salesmen ... I trained them ... they are self-defeating ... good salesmen listen, but you get people with the gift of the gab who only listen to themselves']. If you're an adult you stand out in marketing. This the most important function. It defines all the rest of the work. Most are so bad at it, that you only have to be normal to stand out.

Ian Glover: Current ideas about Quality Function Deployment suggest this. There's a very comprehensive approach to quality which begins with the customer.

David Jenkins: Toyota is just about the only company where quality works. It's all theory apart from Toyota and a few others.

Ian Glover: What does your consultancy do?

David Jenkins: We do anything a customer wants. Me and a couple of guys .... Subcontractors ... all about my age ... all geriatric! We've had one or two younger guys. They were unreliable, not because of their age. It was just the sort of people they were. They wouldn't learn, but others would of course. One of these, I asked him to put a proposal together for a company. I glanced over it and was absolutely aghast. It was so slapdash. I told him and he said 'it's only for Bob, the Chief Engineer'. I said that Bob's boss would be shown it and he is very sceptical about us! The bloke had no common-sense, no experience in business. He was just a fresh graduate in technology who had done a non-job for a Training Board and then he came to us, but he was no good. But age itself has nothing to do with this. I just use people who I've known for ages and who do the job. We have no employees, we only have subcontractors. We do various things. For example we help companies to reduce change-over times on machinery between production runs and we help them with customisation, process optimisation, developing self-managing teams and supervisor or team leader training. I went into consultancy because it is simpler and more civilised to work for clients than as an employed manager for company bosses.

Ian Glover: Why do you still work at your age?

David Jenkins: Because I enjoy it. It gives me stimulation, that's it! I'd feel a bit lost without it. Do I enjoy it? Yes!

Ian Glover: We define ageism in terms of people using a person's age, whatever their age is, against them, unfairly, unreasonably. Have you experienced it?

David Jenkins: It has never actually applied to me. Yet I know that after forty-five I wouldn't have got a job. At sixty a chap told me that he'd put me up for a job. He didn't know my age. So nothing happened. But I accept that. Once I fell into the trap myself. At one large company I looked at the cv of a forty-eight year old. I rejected him in my mind but he did get a job, and turned into an absolute reptile. He was a mason who by-passed the personnel system. The masons are diabolical. People get jobs regardless of merit. I've had proof of it in other situations. One man was a company secretary and a mason. He asked for all Engineering Industry Training Board (EITB) advisers all over the UK to have their cars serviced in North London. I mean people from Penzance, Hull, Glasgow and so on! It made no sense. It was to do with the masons. It nearly went up to the chairman who wasn't a mason, and they backed down. Once I was asked to eliminate all staff who were three years over an age limit. I fell into the trap. Later I realised how stupid it was. Attitudes to age are a bit amorphous. There was a chap who ran a pension fund who said 'the average age in this company is 28 ...'. I could have worked for them. People don't really think it through. They have impressions like 'he is old and fuddy-duddy', all very vague. Some industries are populated by young people, as with Silicon Valley, but this is quite rare. Young people's culture may be right in Silicon Valley company. The skills and knowledge needed may only be held by young people.

Ian Glover: About 25 years ago, in a university I once saw a 26 year old academic researcher, the equivalent of a lecturer, turn down an application for a research fellow job from a very well qualified experienced man in his mid-fifties without batting an eyelid. He picked up the application form, saw the person's age, and instantly dismissed it on the totally irrelevant or rather mistaken ground that the person was too old. I was quietly shocked. It just seemed such an irrational response on the part of a well educated and self-styled left of centre industrial relations researcher. It was part of what started off my interest in ageism. Have you seen this sort of thing happen yourself, so brazenly and thoughtlessly?

David Jenkins: Not directly and not so obviously, no, but I know it happens. I've heard personnel/HRM people – they're the worst – they do instant dismissals of older applicants – 'X is too old', My current client in industry is about 54. The Human Resources woman reports to him but she would *never* have appointed him. He got his job through the managing director because of the relevance of his experience.

Ian Glover: We've developed the idea of the 'chronological misfit' to refer to people of all ages, but particularly those in their middle working years, who don't fit in their organizations' career time frames because of their ages. In 1959 and the early 1960s I worked in the tax office after I left school. One chap, a friend, had been in a Catholic seminary for four years and then did two years National Service before he joined us. Others had been in the war: one had been in the Merchant Navy and torpedoed. He was a very good jazz musician. Another had fought against Rommel in North Africa. Another had been a repertory actor. He was forty-five and needed a regular income. He reminded me of Frankie Howerd. He ran the Inland Revenue Dramatic Society in Sheffield. All of these were sort of 'passing through'. There were lots of people like them, although there were others who had joined the Inland Revenue straight after school or university and it was these who had prospects, careers, not just jobs, in the tax office. It was unfair, really. It seemed so small-minded and unimaginative because the people in the first category had far more experience of life and were usually far more fun.

David Jenkins: Yes, companies don't handle such people well. Once, around 1980, I had to interview some people at the head office of a major aircraft manufacturer. Most were over forty-five. All of these, the ones over forty-five, had written themselves off. They had all been doing some job for a very long time. All were senior people also had been employed by the company for ages. One was the Patents Officer. They had very little job interest. One of them was a younger guy, a 'high-flier' (ugh!), on the 'inside track'. They used young guys like him as Personal Assistants to senior managers, as he was. He might have been alright, but he was so nervous about his Ps and Qs, terrified of losing his senior position. He had a sort of non-job in a privileged position. Why was he in this situation and all the others written off? It was so silly! This was the first time I was really aware of ageism.

After forty-five you change from a bright rising star to someone who never made it irrespective of what you are doing. Unless that is you are at main board level at or by forty-five. At that level age doesn't matter so much.

Ian Glover: What about ageism against younger people? Often they can't cope with rejection, whatever, as well as older ones.

David Jenkins: Managers have a certain unspoken assumption about the age suited to certain jobs. They relate ages to jobs at certain levels. This applies to most jobs. For example they'll say or think that thirty-eight to forty-two is the age band for a certain job level. Usually it is very implicit. They use words like *gravitas* or energy. But explicit discrimination against individuals just because of their youth? Not really. Once young people have got jobs they are criticised for lack of experience. And I have heard the very familiar thing about young people seeking jobs *en masse*: 'we'll be interested when you have the experience'. It's a Catch 22 trap. I've heard it many, many times. Similarly I've hear people saying a person is too young to be promoted, or too inexperienced. No-one asks for experience or inexperience to be defined. It is pure prejudice. Senior managers do carry about a lot of assumptions about ages for particular types and levels of job. Another client, in his early forties, was felt 'to be about the right age' when he got his job a couple of years back. Someone of about 30 wouldn't have got his job. Assumptions work in all directions. It is totally, 150 percent, prejudice. There is no rationality at all.

Management is essentially irrational, full of committee sorts of thinking, even when people could behave like individuals, there is still the conformity and mediocrity.

Ian Glover: About 15 years ago I used to think a lot about such prejudice, when I knew of a manager, five years younger than someone else, a friend of my sister, who had far more flair than him and who he seemed jealous of and threatened by, push forward people who were about five years younger than he was, very much at the expense and in the face of his older subordinate. This older colleague, my sister's friend, had left home young and worked for nearly ten years in all sorts of job before he had graduated and qualified, and although the person who was most obviously used against him, and promoted over his head, was only ten years younger than he was, he was behind him by almost twenty in terms of (relevant and other) experience of life and the world of work. The boss was out of his depth in dealing with him and indeed seemed frightened of him at one stage. The older colleague got *very* grumpy about all this. It wasn't fair, what was done to him: it was hardly as if as if he was actually old for promotion and he was better qualified and in fact more successful than everyone involved. He even invented a word, 'sawldate', meaning 'start of working life date', for making relevant comparisons. He used to say that line managers and HRM people never seemed to think about such things. They had very short term and even more so very narrow ideas about experience and abilities. Do you think that they ever think more broadly and creatively?

David Jenkins: Those involved, but especially the relevant supervisor or line manager involved in a replacement or promotion, will not think about anything much apart from experience of relevant technology, relevant skills or expected level of education. They would *never* consider whether someone had been a patrol leader in the scouts, whatever, unless they were selecting young graduates for their first jobs, and even then it wouldn't count for much, especially after someone had been appointed, when it soon becomes all about fitting in. In graduate recruitment managers do ask about sports at university, about rugger blues and so on. When they have so little to go on they grasp at any straw. Actually it isn't relevant at all.

Ian Glover: I agree. They're so young and there is so little indication at that stage of someone's ability, and especially of their motivation, to do a job. There are a few exceptions at each extreme, the outstanding and the very weak, but in general it is true.

David Jenkins: The best example was the (expletive deleted) wallies who ran one of my own main big industrial company employers, when they got several applicants in response to an advert for their head of planning post. One interviewee was ex-GEC and and had passed out of Sandhurst with the Sword of Honour, as the top cadet in his year. They were so impressed by this that they told him that 'We can't appoint you to this planning job, but we'd like to bear you in mind for other senior posts'. They were simply so impressed by his background. They gave him a job a bit later on as managing director of one of their subsidiaries. He was a total disaster. He did the ex-GEC thing, slashing the payroll by 20 percent in his first year. He did this wherever he went. He kept moving on before the shit hit the fan. His reputation failed to precede him unfortunately! Yet he had eventually been sacked by our company for incompetence, after seven years of total havoc. It all went back to the total irrationality of the people who first appointed him, and to the Sword of Honour. What the heck had that got to do with running a big industrial company? He went north and caused havoc in a big health authority. I read about it in the papers six or seven years ago. But managers are never actually expected, even in graduate recruitment, to take past relevant but nonetheless non-managerial experience into account. They don't look at the whole person.

Ian Glover: When I was 18 I was in charge, not to very great effect, of the tax affairs of 2,500 people in a tax office in Sheffield. In those days all kinds of thing made you exempt from paying some tax and so the job taught you about people's family and financial commitments as well as about their occupations and professions, qualifications, careers, incomes, patterns of residence and so on, sort of real economics and sociology, minus the theory. Looking back a few years ago I realised that I learnt a huge amount about society, hugely relevant to my research in later years, from that job. I'm also a so-called GPO-trained telephonist, of 30-odd years ago, a job which also had some very interesting moments, and I worked for nearly six months in a cold store for Walls Ices in North London, which was great fun with some very interesting colleagues from all kinds of background from medical student to ex-prisoner to the Labour Party agent for Margaret Thatcher's constituency. I worked in about ten tax offices and five telephone exchanges in two cities in Yorkshire and in and around London between the ages of 16 and 25. From 21 to 30 I was a full-time student too, from A levels to doctoral research, at a technical college, three universities and the best place, the old Regent Street Polytechnic. Moving around and meeting and working and living and being friends with different kinds of people in different sectors and places was so marvellous at that age. It was having so many comparisons to make that taught me so much, for better than being a sandwich degree student for example, getting 'managerial' experience on a placement, I think!

David Jenkins: No-one takes that sort of varied experience into account, whether relevant or not. Employers and HRM people haven't got the time or the experience or the imagination. Academics who teach future managers about employing people ought to teach them to understand people in terms of such things, as whole people, but they have even less experience. They'd never see the relevance of what you're talking about. They'd probably make some pathetic jibe like 'Well, it isn't relevant!', which would say an awful lot about them. The operations director of a biotechnology company that I know has just appointed a process manager: the technology involved is a process one. I put up a guy with a lot of relevant technical experience in the food industry. But he wasn't a graduate. The operations director said 'no, I have to appoint a graduate to manage graduates and we also need pharmaceutical experience'. Actually he is right in this case. The technology is so specialised and complex.

Ian Glover: What about when people are turned down for a job or a promotion because of ageism? Isn't there a sort of self-fulfilling prophecy of reduced motivation, disenchanted and resentful behaviour and so on?

David Jenkins: If you are rejected you may only be told that you had the right experience and left to guess about your other kinds of deficiency (if any). This will not affect most people, those who are well adjusted, but if X has several or many rejections and is feeling defeated and *then* they get a job of the type they want they may then work extremely, maybe too, hard proving themselves. This happened to me once.

Ian Glover: And people rejected for internal promotions?

David Jenkins: The people at the aircraft company that I was telling you about turned into automatons. They couldn't afford to leave. They had 15 to 20 years to go. They just came in brain dead. They couldn't wait to go home. They were just waiting for retirement. They didn't fight or protest. Lots of people are like this. If they consider that a promoted person is inferior to them and that they have been promoted because of something irrelevant like being in the in-crowd, playing golf with the managing director, then they *do* get upset. If they think it's unfair of course they get upset.

This can have dire effects on them. Ages ago I knew someone, the mildest guy imaginable, about 30, a solicitor with the Metropolitan Water Board. He was passed over and his rival who was promoted was someone who he thought was much inferior to himself. His heart went out of his job for years. He only got over it after he left and got a new job in industry. People are really hurt when this happens: it is a personal affront. The key is perceived unfairness.

Ian Glover: Yes quite a long time ago I knew a man, a friend of my father's and then mine, who was really hurt like that. He died at 58 of a heart attack while jogging about ten years after he had been sent, in effect, to his organization's corporate Siberia. He was a very able and pleasant man, a polytechnic head of department whose principal had apparently appointed him about 15 years earlier on the understanding that he would become vice-principal in due course. I suspect that the principal didn't find him abrasive enough for the sort of management that he exemplified himself, certainly not as abrasive as the people who became his vice-principals. By his mid to late forties our man was trapped in this very abrasively managed institution with a very heavy administrative workload and in a subject area for which student demand was slowly changing and in some respects declining, not fast enough to threaten his job but nonetheless fast enough to make aspects of his job difficult. He was not disliked, not even I think by the principal, and indeed he was reasonably popular for a senior manager and certainly trusted for his competence and integrity. But he knew that he had few obvious options apart from resigning himself to what he with at least some justification felt was a treadmill to obscurity. I think that it got to him in the end, the rejection and humiliation. I know that his widow hated the principal because of it. He was a sensitive, humble, good man. The management style was often one of cruelly hanging people out to dry. The last thing that they would do would be to be creatively kind, including trying to counsel the pain of perceived unfair rejection out, to say for example we appreciate the good job you are doing but we think you are too nice a guy for the one you aspire to, but we are going to try and change your job and spread your workload to give your more time to do more creative stuff and to develop some of your subordinates as teachers, managers, and researchers. That way we can accelerate the change of direction your department needs and by the way we will make you a professor. Maybe he was programmed to have a coronary at 58 anyway but at least he might have died a lot happier and more useful and fulfilled. They wanted him to be unhappy, unfulfilled and useful, and they won. They used younger promotions to keep potential threats and rivals down, in quite an explicit way (cf. Lyon, Hallier and Glover, 1998). The principal had made a speech to the staff about many of them being 'deadwood' years before the term got into common usage.

What do you think about older people, say those over 50, looking for jobs?

David Jenkins: Most, at that age, see no point in looking for jobs of the kind that they've lost. Some try to set up as consultants. What they do depends on the income they have at that age. Some will concentrate on leisure and some will look for jobs. Many would just laugh if you ask them if they are looking for work. A chap in his early fifties keeps asking me for work as a consultant. He's an experienced one but I can't help at present. I know other people who have been made redundant, one is another ex-consultant, a former holder of supervisory jobs, a former holder of a good Training Board job, who is now looking for a job like a hospital porter. Does he feel humiliated? No, he's quite philosophical about it.

Ian Glover: What about appearance? Of people of all ages I mean. Have attitudes towards it changed over time?

David Jenkins: I remember someone being amazed when he was rejected by BTR in the 1960s when he wore winkle picker shoes to an interview! This sort of rejection still happens in some cases. You have to wear a suit at an interview. Beards are seen as boffinish. It is OK for you as an academic. But if I was a sales manager I'd ask a person to shave their beard off. Beards really matter. At Shorts I was ill and grew a beard because I was too weak to shave. But I shaved it off on the day when I went back to work. This was about 50 years ago. But working for a biotechnology company is different ... no-one would give a damn.

Ian Glover: (Teasing) There's a razor in my bag. I'll shave my beard off if you like! What about looking old and looking young?

David Jenkins: You can suffer from looking younger than your age. One chap who worked for me looked like a young boffin and acted a bit like it. It was an embarrassment to me, in this business, where appearances counting is simply a fact of life.

Ian Glover: What about subordinates? I mean about differences in age between managers and managed?

David Jenkins: I've had to sack a few. It has nothing to do with age. It has far more to do with unwillingness to learn and change. Age itself is completely irrelevant. I've had older and younger subordinates. Age makes no difference. I totally ignore age in that context. It is all about competence and development and being fair.

Ian Glover: Have you seen people being derogatory to bright young people?

David Jenkins: Yes, for example just now. A guy, an ex-apprentice in a company near Oxford went to university to for a degree in Engineering. He has become

Assistant to a Production Manager. He is 25-ish. He's been doing, I can't focus … doing, how can I describe him … he flits across the top of everything. He's aware of it … he gets his leg pulled … he feels that he should get a line job as a Section Leader. He wants real responsibility. He wants the harsh realities. He's the object of a lot of barbed wit, because he's young, and because he is without a real job.

I used to recruit graduates for a factory 30 years ago, in the late 1960s. It could have happened yesterday. Three guys were put on a job as part of their training. Their job was to observe how to run a new high technology department better. Its cost would have been about £30 million at 2000 prices. One of the guys was a graduate equivalent with an HNC in Rubber Technology. The other two were university graduates. Their report criticised the department's management. The Factory Director, a little man, very able, who chewed cigars in a big chair, he gave them the Department to run! This was because of their critical report. They did it. They had quite a good stab at it for six months. It was a very hard job to do well. Their report was a bit arrogant. In six months of having to run it like blue-arsed flies they lost all their arrogance. It was a brilliant decision on his part. It really developed them and they did a decent job.

The supervisors in the factory were taken off their jobs while the young blokes did them. They were sent on a course by another young bloke, on an IPM personnel management course. He taught them crap by Etzioni, Herzberg, McGregor and so on. It bored the backsides off them. It was too academic.

Ian Glover: What about foreign companies and the ages of their employees and their management?

David Jenkins: I have limited experience. I did some research on Volvo in Sweden for an article but that's all. My thoughts would be too speculative for your needs.

Ian Glover: What about expectations associated with age in a general sense? People are pressurised to 'act their age', whatever. It is often called 'social ageing'.

David Jenkins: Yes. Attitudes have changed quite noticeably over a long period. When I was younger age got respect from younger people. Not as much as in Germany, nothing like as much. I knew a company that made diesel engines and it exchanged salesmen between Staines and a German diesel engine company. An apprentice of about twenty-one came back from a secondment to Germany. He said that when the German foreman said 'jump', the apprentices asked 'how high?'. But in the UK there is no respect for age like this. Is this bad? No. Why? We shouldn't respect people simply on the grounds that they are older. Competence is what matters. This is immediately respected. If I visit a company and I mention a name, people tend either to express respect or derision. Such people who tend to be held in the esteem of shop floor people are rarely those high in the esteem of managers. This is because managers are absolutely out of touch! On the shop floor or equivalent age doesn't matter. Nobody cares! X is the best welder and their age is never considered. There is a total lack of concern for it. This is good. Yet managers lazily employ age and other stereotypes. They form impressions. For example a general manager in one company told me that the key person, 'a good chap, good lad', on the shop floor was an Indian call Jaz. But the shop floor people saw him as a servile self-seeking (expletive deleted). He was both bad at his job and self-seeking: I witnessed it. This was not at all racist, nor ageist, or anything else, just to do with a lack of competence and honesty in his particular case. Most ordinary people, on the shop floor, are not ageist, or at least less so than managers. But managers need stereotypes. It saves them from thinking.

Ian Glover: What about apprenticeship, as a regulator of relationships between people of different levels of experience among other things?

David Jenkins: There's no place for it now. It should have declined. It is not relevant as it was. It was relevant, when, as in printing, engineering, many jobs had lots of skill. Technology has take the skill out of things. Printing, for example, is all done by computers and information technology. All the old respected apprenticeship routes have gone.

Ian Glover: Someone I know, from Northern Ireland, has been arguing that we need to rediscover apprenticeship somehow though (Dingley, 1996). He argues that in the past apprentices were taught to be good citizens, not just good workers.

David Jenkins: I understand and sympathise but we won't get what you want in the old way. The Modern Apprenticeships and the National Vocational Qualifications in engineering for example and so on, are crap! The 'competencies' are all spelt out in very vague ways, like 'communication', 'handling tools', and so on, not very specific to tasks as in the old days. There are no skills left to learn. It is all very skin-deep now. All workshops have computer numerically controlled (CNC) machines now. They do need programming. This is the only skill. It takes three to six months to learn and then the machines do the jobs. The minder just services the machine and makes sure that it has enough material to work with. That's all. Of course some old type skills do exist, such as those of motor mechanics, and in engineering when some kind of diagnostics is needed, or the equivalent in companies with machines that can break down. There is still some need for apprenticeships. But in construction for example lots of things come ready-made like windows and doors. That's the trend. Though you still have brickies and plasterers. There are a few skilled trades left. In ships and aircraft you also need skills of the old type, in maintenance, largely.

Ian Glover: What of the role of personnel and human resource management in all this? I mean with regard to ageism?

David Jenkins: They are particularly, as much if not more than anyone, likely to use age to stereotype and select. It saves them time. They never question the prejudices of managers. They go into personnel because they have a vague thing about working with people. They are just twits, weak and wimpish. The ageist prejudices of line management are a major source of their power! They just 'give the bullets for the manager to fire'. People don't go to personnel with problems. They know the personnel department leaks everything to managers.

Ian Glover; What do you think about age and careers? How have careers been changing?

David Jenkins: This is interesting, because although it is widely recognized that career ladders are shorter, people still think in terms of careers. For example in a biotechnology company that I work with, some jobs could be done by people with no qualifications at all, just basic literacy and numeracy perhaps. Yet they employ twenty-one to twenty-four year old graduates, in biochemistry and so on. They leave to start careers with other companies, but the same will happen there. Lots of jobs in high-tech companies don't need graduates at all. They are very boring, laboratory jobs. So where do they end up? There aren't enough careers for highly qualified people. In the biotechnology company I have a group of people who the company needed for identifying proteins. It was a unique and very advanced process. I asked them to design a career structure for their department. They designed a very convoluted hierarchical structure. But all the jobs were semi-skilled! I told them – laughingly - 'you've reinvented the Mexican Army – all generalissimos!'. They took it very well, but it shattered their aspirations. They were vastly out of touch with reality.

Ian Glover: I read something in a book about the race for the South Pole by Amundsen and Scott. In the interwar period a ski instructor on Spitzbergen was asked if any of the students from different European countries whom he taught were any different from the others. He said 'Yes, the English all want to be heroes'. Is that relevant?

David Jenkins: Maybe. There is an old joke still with some truth in it. A ship went down and an American, a German and an Englishman were marooned on an island in the South Seas. The natives thought they were gods and let them rule them. The island was divided into three accordingly. The American built a factory for canning pineapples, with an assembly line. The German put 'his' natives into an army and got them all saluting him at a podium. The Englishman did nothing. He just walked around waiting to be introduced …

Ian Glover: The more you think about it the less dated and more subtle it is, about the Englishman! Maybe the ski instructor in my story was an advocate of mediocrity or maybe the English students were really arrogant. What about selection for redundancy? What about that and age?

David Jenkins: Last in, first out (LIFO) is simple, and easy to use, again. This isn't really ageist. But it is more complicated in practice: managers get rid of people whom they don't like or whom they feel are incompetent. Their judgements often seem wrong!

Ian Glover: Do you think that there is a general tendency for managers to gang up on clever people, towards mediocrity? Northcote Parkinson used to write about 'injelitance', as a deadly combination of incompetence and jealousy. Is this linked to age in any way?

David Jenkins: Not sure, but intolerance, mediocrity and so on are universal. 'Genius' is a threat and they all close ranks. You see this in politics, everywhere.

Ian Glover: Is there a stigma concerning decrepitude, senility, and so on?

David Jenkins: Appearance matters, age as such much less. I once had a boss of about 60 or a bit older. He was senile, very stupid, asinine. It had little to do with his age. He genuinely had dementia.

Ian Glover; Do you ever think about the idea of managerialism?

David Jenkins: There's no such thing! It is pure theory.

Ian Glover: I mean the abuse of managerial power and people rationalising it, that's all.

David Jenkins: Oh yes, of course that exists, as with personnel managers being ageist.

Ian Glover: What do you think of business process engineering (BPR)? In the 1980s and 1990s I used to think it was just a predictable fad. We produced the wrong sorts of people in Britain, who predictably fought each other, so along came the consultants to (expensively) re-engineer the process. It wouldn't be needed in Germany and Japan and so on. Their people were more relevantly educated and far more focused to start with. In the 1970s we had got the Department of Industry to see this sort of thing and later published articles in *Sociology* (Child et al, 1983, 1985; Fores, Glover and Lawrence, 1991). But now I see that BPR was, in part, about solving the problems that we'd exposed. I'm a bit more sensible now that I'm older!

David Jenkins: The quality movement and human resource management are sort of similar. Sometimes they have uses. But BPR usually hasn't worked, for lots of reasons, especially resistance to change! Yet while they are all fads, they all have some point. Take that company which was the first that I told Paul Tracey, your former research student, to contact. Their US parent company leaned on them to apply BPR. The company realised that it needed to demote all the senior managers who weren't contributing to the process. Most of them had great expertise, all very relevant to the company, but not as managers! The managing director backed off when it was realised that we'd have to make changes on that scale.

Ian Glover: So is rampant ageism the underlying problem in all of this, or is it just bad management, whatever?

David Jenkins: It is definitely more than just bad management. Ageism does exist. A lot of over forty-fives are simply assumed to be going downhill.

Ian Glover: Yes it was recently suggested to me that it has taken me so long to edit another book recently, compared with the great speed that I performed a similar task with four years ago, because I must have aged! I'm a lot fitter than I was four years ago. Actually it was my boss who is also over fifty and he was teasing me and, by his deeds, being very supportive. On the other hand you do get the odd well meant comments from younger friends about how 'amazing' it is that you produce so many publications 'at your age'. This is respectful and friendly and yet part of you thinks that it is a bit like someone telling a black person how 'amazing it is that they are so intelligent ...'. What about older bosses in industry?

David Jenkins: There are very outstanding older guys running companies. Hanson, for example, from his late fifties to his late seventies, was one. He was very ruthless but very successful. Age should never lead to people being shunted. There are lots of very able and also very moral older people who are perfectly capable of filling top posts, though Hanson couldn't even spell the word integrity!

Ian Glover: What about specialists? There was a well established research tradition in management studies and the sociology of science and technology in the UK and North America concerned with 'obsolescent engineers'. They are assumed to have started becoming out of date about ten years after leaving university, and to be increasingly incapable of learning new knowledge. I think that the ideas in use here are fundamentally misconceived because virtually all serious evidence on the work of engineers shows that it is a useful art, unpredictable ingenuity, not the application of new scientific knowledge (Fores, 1994). If this is the case, engineering is a craft writ large, so that the personal skills and the knowledge of engineers should grow as they get older. It is hardly as if it demanded youthful physical energy, like competitive swimming or rugby! It is like writing or playing bridge. Maybe, although I doubt it, the sharp penetrating insights of youth are fewer, but the ability to see links between things seems to multiply with age and this must be crucial in engineering. To be an old engineer could be very easy! Maybe they are simply bored, rather than obsolescent.

David Jenkins: I don't know really ... but I'd have thought that anyone could be competent as long as they kept working. British Aerospace stress engineers work competently until they are sixty five. They never deteriorate. It is an art.

Ian Glover: Some people suggest that ageism is to do with contemporary moral chaos. There is so much change, they argue, that people worship youth and neglect the moral development of their children. They reject traditional values and the wisdom of age.

David Jenkins: I am a very focused, practical, empirical sort of person. This whole sort ... this way of thinking has no meaning to me, it is a non-question. I have no views.

Ian Glover: I bet you do, really! For instance we have these ideas about commodification and greening. They are two opposed scenarios about the ways in which employment and work and peoples' lives are changing. Commodification envisages employees regarding people as commodities to be used up. Until about twenty-five or thirty they are assumed to have no skills or knowledge or sense of responsibility. Then they marry and get mortgages and for about fifteen to twenty - five years until some time in their forties or early fifties or so they are employable. Then they become too expensive, increasingly decrepit as you suggest, and maybe they know too much about the management. So they get redundancy, or early retirement if they are lucky. Greening, however, is a much more optimistic idea. Here everyone lives until they are about ninety. (This is of course happening, now). For the first third of their lives, until they are about thirty, they are engaged in self-discovery, learning. They have all sorts of jobs, holidays and relationships, and they study. From around thirty, for the next thirty or so years, they do. They have interesting work and careers, they bring their children up, and they pay into pension schemes and pay off their mortgages. Then, from around sixty and for the next thirty years or so, they enjoy the fruits of their labour, and pass their knowledge on to the next generation. They teach. They are engaged in civic, leisure and social pursuits. Unlike most of those who experience commodification, they generally have marketable qualifications from further and higher education and professions, and occupational pensions.

David Jenkins: If I'm right about the sort of thing that you are implying by this, I'd go further. I'd chuck out about a third of university students. It is crazy that forty or fifty per cent of young people go to university. I'd replace the third with people over sixty. They could help the teaching staff deal with the inexperienced striplings!

Ian Glover: Thank you very much.

References

Child, J., Fores, M., Glover, I. and Lawrence, P. (1983), 'A Price to Pay? Professionalism and Work Organization in Britain and West Germany', *Sociology*, Vol. 17, No. 1, pp. 63-78.

Child, J., Fores, M., Glover, I and Lawrence, P. (1985), 'Professionalism and Work Organization: Reply to McCormick', *Sociology*, Vol. 20, No. 4, pp. 607-11.

Dingley, J. (1996), 'Durkheim, professionals and moral integration', in I. Glover and M. Hughes (eds), *The Professional-Managerial Class: Comtemporary British Management in the Pursuer Mode*, Avebury, Aldershot.

Fores, M. (1994), 'Hamelet without the prince: the strange death of technical skills in history', *History of Technology*, Vol. 16, No. 1, pp. 160-83.

Fores, M., Glover, I and Lawrence, P. (1991), 'Professionalism and Rationality: a study in misapprehension', *Sociology*, Vol. 25, No. 1, pp. 79-100.

Glover, I. and Kelly, M. (1993), 'Engineering better management', in G. Payne and M. Cross (eds), *Sociology in Action: Applications and opportunities for the 1990s*, Macmillan, Basingstoke.

Glover, I. and Hughes, M.D. (1996), *The Professional-Managerial Class: Comtemporary British Management in the Pursuer Mode*, Avebury, Aldershot.

Glover, I.A and Hughes, M.D (2000), 'Fragmentation, Cooperation and Continuity: towards a flexible technocratic synthesis', in I. Glover and M. Hughes (eds), *Professions at Bay*, Ashgate, Aldershot.

Jenkins, D. (1996), *Managing Empowerment*, Century, London.

Sorge, A. (1994), 'The Reform of Technical Education and Training in Great Britain: a comparison of institutional learning in Europe', *European Journal of Vocational Training*, No. 3, pp. 58-68.

Sorge, A. and Warner, M. (1986) *Comparative Factory Management*, Gower, Aldershot.

11 Anti-ageist legislation: the Australian experience

Jenny Hamilton

Introduction

Discrimination on grounds of age can be defined generally as the practice of making judgements or decisions about a person based upon irrational prejudice or stereotyping rather than on a proper consideration of objective factors such as that person's skills abilities and experiences (see Buck, 1992).

Such discrimination can be seen unacceptable on (at least) two levels. At one level it operates so as to deny an individual the opportunity to obtain personal fulfilment or to reach their full potential. At the second level, such discrimination can have adverse consequences for society in general. At this level the focus of attention has been the potential economic effect of age discrimination on industry and on the public purse in the face of an ageing population generally. Research such as that carried out by the European Commission's First Action Programme demonstrated that by 2000, one third of the British workforce would be over 40 (Employment Observatory, 1993). This will have implications for the potential labour pool from which employers can draw, but it will also have implications for the funding of pensions and benefits for a growing number of pensionable persons from the taxes and contributions of a static or reducing number of younger workers (see Carnegie, 1993). The biggest single contribution to reducing that potential burden, it has been argued, is to encourage and enable 'third agers' (those roughly between the ages of 50 and 74) to work, but for this to happen, age discrimination must be challenged (Carnegie, 1993).

However if we accept that discrimination on the basis of age is unacceptable, the next question is whether legislation is the best means of tackling the problem. Three previous attempts to introduce legislation by way of Private Members' Bills have taken place in 1989, 1992 and 1996 and all have failed. In part at least, their failure could be said to be the result of the then Conservative government's preference for voluntary self-regulatory action by employers on the basis that self-regulatory codes are more likely to be successful because of the sense of 'ownership' of them by industry. Within British industry there is the view that there is already too much employment legislation and regulation by government. Such a multitude of rules, it is argued, impose an excessive burden on business (see *New Law Journal*, 1996).

More recently, however, the English Law Society, whilst acknowledging the value of measures taken by some companies to tackle age discrimination, has recommended that legislation be introduced as a 'matter of urgency' (Law Society Report, 1997). As Richard Worsley, Director of the Carnegie Third Age Programme pointed out, because legislation combating disability discrimination has now been introduced, there is a 'danger that if age is left as the only major cause of discrimination not regulated by law, people will think that it doesn't matter' (Worsley, 1995).

While it is true that the introduction of anti-sex and race discrimination legislation has not changed discriminatory behaviour, still less discriminatory attitudes, overnight, it is important to recognise that the law has a powerful symbolic function within our society. It signals, at the highest level, that certain types of behaviour are unacceptable within society, and it provides a formal structure which enables individuals affected by that behaviour to challenge them. In doing so, it validates the feelings of those individuals. It also has the effect of creating a space within which the discourse of formal equality is privileged and legitimated (witness the extent to which concerns of sex and race equality have achieved a currency of acceptance).

If we accept that such legislation is necessary, other issues then arise - namely, how should that legislation be structured? In other words, how will we define age discrimination; should the prohibition be limited just to the employment sphere; what defences and exceptions (if any) should be permitted, and, what enforcement mechanisms should be put in place? The practical 'bite' of the legislation will depend on the answers to these questions.

The UK would not be breaking new ground in introducing anti-age discrimination legislation. A number of other countries, such as the USA, Canada and Australia already have some form of legislation in place. In Australia, for example, anti discrimination legislation is in place at Federal ('Commonwealth') and State level prohibiting a number of grounds of discrimination, including age.

It is the purpose of this chapter to outline the approach taken in the South Australian anti-discrimination legislation (which bears structural similarities to existing UK sex and race legislation, and from which comparisons will be drawn, where appropriate) and to identify any issues arising from it which may help inform the debate in the UK about the structure of any proposed legislation. This chapter will focus on the following: the background to the legislation; the scope of the anti-age discrimination provisions; the enforcement mechanism; and, the approach of the courts to the legislation.

The Australian experience

One of the reasons why the Australian legislation in this area is of particular interest is the fact that the background debate surrounding the eventual enactment of anti-age discrimination provisions in Australia was very similar to the debate taking place in the UK today. There too, the business community resisted the imposition of legislative change on the basis that it would place further restrictions and requirements on already overburdened businesses, who it was argued, were being asked to bear the brunt of social change through legislative compulsion. The business community also considered that legislation would do little to change existing social attitudes. Against this, it was argued that previous experience with anti-discrimination provisions, such as those relating to sex, had demonstrated that legislation has an important part to play in setting standards and may well act as a vehicle to facilitate a change in public attitudes for the better.

Other similarities in experiences are also apparent. The same challenges, such as a declining birth rate and increasingly ageing population have been and continue to be experienced by both countries. The problem of supporting such an ageing population is, therefore, one that has also had to be addressed in Australia. However, it is not only the profile of employees making up the workforce that is changing, but also the types of jobs available for this new workforce.

The introduction of technology into many parts of industry has led to the diminishment of semi-skilled and skilled positions. Business re-organisations such as those which have recently taken place in banking have led to the disappearance of a whole strata of middle management positions in both countries.

Hence in Australia, and increasingly in the UK and Europe where anti-age discrimination legislation is also being considered, there has been an increasing recognition of the need for society in general, and employers in particular, to develop strategies to effectively and efficiently manage a rapidly changing labour pool. One of these strategies in Australia has been to introduce anti-age discrimination legislation.

South Australia led the field in this respect when it made age discrimination unlawful in 1991 by means of an amendment to the South Australian Equal Opportunity Act of 1984. South Australia was the first State to introduce any form of anti-discrimination legislation with the 1975 Sex Discrimination Act, which has now been replaced by the Equal Opportunities Act 1984 and which remains in force today.

The Equal Opportunities Act, 1984, is an umbrella piece of legislation expressly prohibiting discrimination on a variety of grounds. These include sex, marital status, race, physical disability, intellectual impairment, sexuality, pregnancy, sexual harassment and, since July 1991, age.

Other States quickly followed the South Australian example and, in 1993 at Federal level, age discrimination was included as a ground of complaint within the terms of the Commonwealth Industrial Relations Act 1988, as a result of an amendment thereto by the Industrial Relations Reform Act 1993. The provisions of that Act have now been repealed but have subsequently been substantially re-enacted in the terms of the Workplace Relations Act 1996. This Act makes unlawful the dismissal of an employee on grounds of (amongst others) age.

The introduction of this Commonwealth legislation has served to further implement Australia's obligations under various international conventions, including the International Covenant on Civil and Political Rights. That Covenant provides that all individuals should enjoy the rights recognised in the Covenant 'without distinction of any kind', such as race, colour, sex, language, religion, political or other opinion, national or social origin, property, birth or 'other status' – a phrase that has been interpreted to imply an obligation to avoid discrimination generally, including discrimination on the ground of age (Australian and New Zealand Equal Opportunity Law and Practice, 1994).

The 'age' amendment to the South Australian legislation arose as a result of a government task force established to examine the impact of age discrimination in the community and the appropriateness of amending the Equal Opportunities Act 1984. The task force determined that assumptions were being made about people's skills, abilities and personal qualities on the basis of their age, and that the incidence of such discrimination was high enough to justify amending the Act.

Support for this view was to be found in the annual reports of the Commissioner for Equal Opportunity, whose role is to monitor and consider complaints of discrimination in South Australia. The Reports for 1987-88 and 1988-89 showed the Commission receiving hundreds of complaints from South Australians relating to age discrimination. The majority related to discrimination in employment, but others included complaints regarding access to goods and service, education, accommodation and clubs.

It is indicative of the responsiveness of the South Australian legislature that it took only 13 months from the date upon which the task force Report (SA Government, 1989) was presented to the government to the date upon which the amendment was passed in April 1990 with bi-partisan support.

The introduction of the new law was not without controversy, however, and the provisions were, despite a fairly broad consensus on the need to eliminate age discrimination, frequently attacked by a range of groups including, predictably, employers. This reaction came as no surprise to those who had previous experience of anti-discrimination legislation being introduced. In 1994 Josephine Tiddy, the then South Australian Commissioner for Equal Opportunity, remarked that 'Equal Opportunity Laws are almost always controversial because they encode and bring to a head social change.'

Tiddy drew an analogy between the law passed to combat age discrimination and the Sex Discrimination Act passed in South Australia in 1975. Despite widespread consensus surrounding the need for sex discrimination laws, the fact that the Act had a direct affect on the lives of many South Australians meant that its introduction was accompanied by controversy and heated debate. The debate surrounding the introduction of anti-age discrimination legislation was predictable because 'unlike other grounds of discrimination, age discrimination has the potential to directly affect all of us (and) is one of the biggest issues facing Australia in the nineties' (Tiddy, 1994).

The Australian legislation: an overview

The South Australian Equal Opportunities Act 1984 now prohibits discrimination on the grounds of age in most areas of public life (see Part 5A of the Act generally). In New South Wales, the Anti-Discrimination Act 1977 (as amended) goes even further and prohibits discrimination on the ground of the age of the person concerned, or on the basis of the age of any of the person's relatives - thus to discriminate on the basis that the person has young children is unlawful in that State (s 49ZYA).

A key focus of the South Australian Act is to prevent discrimination in the field of employment. This was perhaps because, as the Hon. Diane Laidlaw pointed out in the debate preceding the enactment of these provisions: 'employment usually determines a person's position in relation to the poverty line and their access to accommodation and other services, including credit'. Perhaps as a result of this, the Act has a wide scope. Its provisions will apply not just to ordinary contracts of employment between 'employer' and 'employee', whether full or part time, but also to situations where services are procured on a more informal 'casual' basis, including where the person is unpaid (s5). Also covered are persons engaged on unpaid work, agents, partners and contract employees (see ss 85C-E generally).

The provisions apply to all stages of employment, from advertising a vacancy to redundancy and dismissal. Although initially the provisions did not affect the age of retirement, it was recognised that to force a perfectly healthy individual to retire on the basis that they had reached a certain age was also discriminatory and, in 1993, the imposition of a standard retiring age by employers became unlawful.

Although employment was undoubtedly a key focus of the legislative provisions, the Act also applies to other areas of public life, such as the provision of goods and services, accommodation, membership of clubs and associations, access to education, the sale of land, and the conferral of qualifications. There is no general upper or lower age limit applied under the Act above or below which a person is not permitted to bring a complaint. Thus the legislation appears to be wide ranging, but a number of general exceptions are provided based upon considerations of social policy. For example, the legislation does not affect the legal capacity of children, nor the age of consent, nor the ability to obtain a driving licence, drink alcohol or vote.

Charities and projects established for the benefit of persons belonging to a particular age group are also excluded from the effect of the new provisions. In this respect age discrimination is permissible as it is presumably based upon a rational assessment of the particular needs of a certain age group. However, it would be interesting to consider whether the exemption for charities for the benefit of certain age groups may in fact perpetuate the very stereotypes which the legislation seeks to break down.

Where discrimination in the employment context is concerned, additional exceptions apply. Here, discrimination on the basis of age may be permissible under the South Australian Act on a variety of grounds. The Act was amended in 1992 to allow for employers to specifically advertise, recruit and employ a young person where the rate of pay for that employment is fixed by an award or industrial agreement made or approved under the Industrial Relations Act 1972, even if the rate applicable to the younger person is at a rate less than that applicable to an adult. Thus discrimination sanctioned by other legislation is permissible.

In addition, the legislation states that the provisions do not apply where there is a genuine occupational requirement that a person be of a particular age (s85F(2)). Hence, as was noted by the Hon. L.H. Davis in the debate preceding the enactment of this provision: 'that would rule out the 90 year old actor who wants to play the part of a child in a professional theatre company'.

Also excluded is the situation where it can be established that the person would not be able to perform the work adequately which is genuinely and reasonably required in that position (s85F(3)(a)). In this latter regard, the test is objective and will depend on the ability of the employee to so perform without endangering himself/herself or other persons while doing so. The legislation also provides that the employee must have the ability to respond adequately to emergency situations; a proviso that was presumably intended to deal primarily with employees operating in safety critical fields, such as medicine and aviation (see ss 85F(3)(b)). These two exceptions reveal an interesting implicit assumption by the legislature - that the ability to perform or respond is dependent upon age. While there is some evidence for this assumption (see Grimley Evans, 1992), it may equally be that such diminished ability is the result of, for example, inadequate or outdated training by the employer.

The definition of discrimination

As with UK sex and race discrimination legislation, the South Australian legislation prohibits direct and indirect discrimination. Unlike that UK legislation however, the South Australian legislation also prohibits 'characterisation'.

Direct discrimination

It is clear that there are similarities to be drawn between the structure of the South Australian Equal Opportunity Act 1984 and the United Kingdom legislation combating sex and race discrimination (the Sex Discrimination Act 1975, the Race Relations Act 1976). In the UK, that legislation makes unlawful treatment towards the protected group which is '*less favourable*' than that which would be afforded to the other group (s1 of both Acts). This is an objective test and will be satisfied thus - would the complainant have received the same treatment *but for* his or her sex or race? (See the decision of the House of Lords in *James v Eastleigh Borough Council* [1990] IRLR 288 HL.) An employer will not therefore necessarily be protected simply because he/she acted with no discriminatory intent, or with a superior motive (e.g. for health and safety reasons).

The Equal Opportunity Act provides that direct discrimination will occur where a person:

treats another unfavourably because of the other's age (s85A(a));

To treat another unfavourably is to:

treat that person less favourably than in identical or similar circumstances he treats, or would treat, a person who does not have that attribute or is affected by that circumstance (s6(3)).

Is intention to discriminate required under this legislation? This matter have proved contentious in Australian jurisdictions generally and has not been fully resolved, although the weight would appear to be in favour of a requirement of subjective intention before unlawful discrimination is made out – see e.g. *Arumugam v Health Commission of Victoria* (1986) EOC 92-115; Lockhart CJ in *HREOC v Mt Isa Mines* (1993) 118 ALR 80; but also Mason CJ and Gaudron J in *Waters v Public Transport Cop. (Vic)* 173 CLR 349. An employer who imposes a policy which has the effect of discriminating against a particular group may escape liability if they can establish that they did not in fact intend to so discriminate.

Indirect discrimination

Both the UK and the South Australian anti-discrimination legislation also seek to control indirect as well as direct discrimination. Indirect discrimination occurs where there is a requirement imposed which, at first glance, seems fair, but which in practice is results in one group being treated less favourably than another.

Under the South Australian legislation indirect age discrimination occurs where:

(i) he or she has been treated unfavourably because (ii) he or she does not comply, or is not able to comply, with a particular requirement, and ... (iii) a substantially higher proportions of persons of a different age or age group complies or is able to comply, and ... (iv) that requirement is unreasonable ... (See ss 85A(b))

Thus to impose a requirement, for example, that an applicant must possess a particular 'modern' qualification may amount to indirect discrimination if the effect of that requirement is that fewer older persons will be able to comply, compared with those in a different age group. Similarly the practice of selecting workers for redundancy on the basis of 'last in - first out' may also amount to indirect discrimination if it disproportionately affects younger workers.

While the definition of indirect discrimination is structurally very similar to that provided under UK sex and race legislation, the South Australian legislation appears to operate more favourably for the complainant in at least one respect. In the UK the judiciary have in the past interpreted the phrase 'applies a requirement of condition' as meaning a 'must' - something which the complainant must have had to comply within the sense that lack of compliance would be an absolute bar to employment, for example (*Perera v Civil Service Commission* [1983] IRLR 166 CA, but see also the more recent UK decision of *Falkirk Council v White* [1997] IRLR 560). Thus if the employer simply stipulated 'English as a first language 'preferred'', rather than 'required', this may not amount to the imposition of a 'requirement or condition' and thus may not constitute indirect discrimination under the UK Race Relations Act, 1976.

In Australia, at Federal level at least, a broader view of these terms has been adopted. In *Re The Secretary of the Department of Foreign Affairs and Trade and Styles* (1988) 23 FCR 251, the Federal Court of Australia expressly stated that the meaning of 'requirement or condition' contained in the then Commonwealth Sex Discrimination Act, 1984, was altogether different to that adopted by the English Court of Appeal in *Perera*. There, the court stated that these words should not be given a narrow construction, but rather should be interpreted liberally to give effect to the intent of the legislature. Hence, they should be held to include all stipulations which, while not an absolute bar, in practice operate against the complainant (see also the recent decision of the Commonwealth Human Rights and Equal Opportunity Commission in *Finance Sector Union v Commonwealth Bank of Australia* 1997 No. H94/63).

So, employer stipulations or practices which might not be caught under the *Perera* type interpretation of indirect discrimination might fare better in Australian jurisdictions (State legislation containing similar provisions to Federal legislation is likely to be interpreted in the same way), thus giving the Australian legislation a potentially wider scope than that of UK law.

The South Australian legislation provides employers and service providers with a specific 'defence' to a claim of indirect discrimination, a 'defence' which is not available in the case of direct discrimination. The legislation provides that no indirect discrimination occurs where the requirement imposed is *reasonable* (section 85A(b)(ii). In the UK, there will be no indirect discrimination where the imposition of the condition or requirement can be *justified* irrespective of sex/race (sections 1(1)(b)).

In the case of the Australian legislation it would seem likely that reasonable means reasonable in all the circumstances and therefore a tribunal/court is not limited to considering only the circumstances of the complainant ('is it reasonable in the circumstances of the complainant to impose the requirement or condition?'), but is entitled to consider the general financial and organisational needs of the employer. (See *Waters v Public Transport Corp.* (1992) 173 CLR 349, a case involving alleged discrimination upon the grounds of disability in which the High Court of Australia (the highest appellate court for both Federal and State cases) ruled on the proper interpretation the (now repealed) Equal Opportunity Act, 1984, of Victoria, which contained a similar provision to the current section 85A(b) of the South Australian Act).

It is a contested issue whether it should be possible to justify indirect discrimination on broad grounds such as efficiency and so on particularly when no such broad justification is available in the case of direct discrimination - indirect discrimination is no less harmful than direct. The presence of such a broad defence has the potential to severely limit the protection given by the Act if, for example, an employer is allowed to argue that cost factors justify the imposition of a requirement which has the effect of discriminating against persons of a particular age group. This is particularly so when certain costs associated with employment inevitably rise with the age of the employee.

Characterisation

The South Australian Act also prohibits discrimination based upon the presumed characteristics of the group to which the complainant belongs. Section 85A(c) provides that persons are specifically prohibited from treating:

> another person unfavourably on the basis of a characteristic that appertains generally to persons of the other group or age group, on the basis of a presumed characteristic that is generally imputed to persons of that age or age group.

Thus, under the South Australian legislation, a refusal to employ an older person because of the assumptions that 'an old dog can't learn new tricks' or to refuse to employ a young person on the assumption that young people lack the maturity to cope with the job, would be unlawful direct discrimination on the basis of age.

A provision that was proposed at draft stage but did not survive debate was one providing that it would not be unlawful 'to pursue genuine schemes to promote the employment of persons of any particular age group that have been disadvantaged in that area or disadvantaged because of lack of experience in a particular field of employment'. Thus, positive discrimination schemes to favour those previously discriminated against in the employment sphere are unlawful because their implementation runs against the idea of formal equality of opportunity between persons.

The introduction of positive discrimination provisions has been problematic in the field of anti-discrimination law generally. In the UK there is little scope under the sex and race legislation for such schemes. Similarly, at European level, schemes which would give preferential employment to women over equally qualified men have been made unlawful in the context of sex discrimination for similar reasons (see the decision of the European Court in *Kalanke v Freie Hansestadt Bremen* [1995] IRLR 660, but see also *Marschall v Land Nordrhein-Westfalen* [1998] IRLR 39 where the court appears to give some recognition to positive discrimination measures). The problem it seems with such 'reverse discrimination' schemes is that although they have the benefit of tackling the effects of historical discrimination, thus accelerating the progress of the 'protected' group into a position of equality, their de facto effect on the date of implementation is to discriminate against the unprotected group. In short, it is impossible to give extra to one group without taking away from the another (see Sheik, 1996) and this argument is no less relevant in the case of anti-age discrimination measures.

The legislation in action

Complaints and conciliation

The differences that are apparent in the structure of the anti-discrimination provisions of Australia and the UK sex and race legislation are indicative of slight variances of approach towards tackling the mischief that is discrimination. These differences are not merely theoretical, however, but continue to be apparent in the day to day practical experiences of those who allege they have been discriminated against. Primarily, these are differences in the system set up to deal with complaints. In the UK, the progress of a case will depend on the type of complaint. If the matter concerns alleged discrimination against an employee by his or her employer, the matter will go to an Employment Tribunal, whose proceedings are, almost without exception, open to the public and whose decisions are regularly reported, both in the press and in legal volumes. If a Tribunal finds for the complainant, it can (i) make an order declaring the rights of the complainant (such as, the entitlement to certain training etc.); (ii) order compensation; (iii) recommend the respondent take certain action to remove the discrimination. Appeals against such decisions are taken by the Employment Appeal Tribunal, and thereafter, via the civil appeal courts.

Complaints of discrimination concerning access to goods and services travel immediately through the civil court system and once again, all hearings are generally open to the public and may be reported.

The situation in South Australia is entirely different. There, if someone believes that they have been the subject of unlawful discrimination, the procedure under the South Australian Equality of Opportunity Act, which is similar to that which is in place in the other Australian States, is that the person should lodge a complaint with the Equal Opportunity Commission. The Commission can hear a complaint about any matter covered by the Equal Opportunity Act.

A Commission member will investigate the complaint and attempt to settle the matter informally between the parties. If this is unsuccessful, then a compulsory confidential conciliation conference will be called. At such conferences, a settlement may be reached and may involve:

- apologies (public and/or private)
- agreement to provide what was denied
- compensation
- re-instatement
- changes to policies and/or procedure

If the complaint cannot be settled at this stage, the Commissioner may refer the matter to the Equal Opportunity Tribunal for judicial determination. At this stage complaints are no longer confidential and can be reported in the media. The Tribunal has the power to award unlimited compensation and/or order any changes it thinks necessary to avoid further complaints. In practice, however only between one and five percent of cases reach the Tribunal. The majority are resolved in conciliation, whilst others are withdrawn by the complainant or declined by the Commission, perhaps because they lack substance.

One advantage of the conciliation system over the UK system is that the complainant avoids the stress (and perhaps embarrassment) of imposed by a system based upon a more formal, and public, hearing. However, it has certain disadvantages in that conciliated outcomes carry no precedential value, and it is difficult for the general community to be informed and influenced by cases which are resolved on a confidential basis.

One general criticism which can be levelled at the Equal Opportunity Act (and also at the UK sex and race legislation) is that it focuses upon the experience of the individual. This means that the legislation fails to recognise the group nature of discrimination. Both the South Australian and UK anti-discrimination legislation rely upon individuals to bring complaints about specific instances of discrimination which affect him or her. The assumption is therefore that such instances of discriminatory behaviour are 'not the norm', and can therefore be left to be tackled on an individual basis. The hope presumably is that these complaints will then have a knock on effect of discouraging others from engaging in similar discriminatory behaviour. While the Equal Opportunity Act does allow a complaint to be brought by an aggrieved person on their own behalf or on behalf of him/herself and any other aggrieved person, it does not allow representative actions to be brought by others on behalf of aggrieved persons. Giving a right to a trade union, for example, to bring an action to challenge structural discrimination across a sector of industry where that industry routinely imposes upper age limits would arguably provide a more effective and timely mechanism for challenging such discrimination.

The fact that the Australian anti-age discrimination legislation is relatively new, combined with the system of confidential conciliation means that assessing its impact is difficult to achieve by normal case study method. However, some light may be shed on the matter by the Annual Reports and publications of the various State Equal Opportunity Commissions. These reports may be instructive in determining the level of complaints submitted to the EOC since the passage of the legislation, together with clarifying what constitutes the most common type of complainant.

In South Australia, where the legislation has been in place for the longest period of time, the picture being painted is one which appears to reinforce the arguments of those who argued in favour of anti-age discrimination legislation. In the year spanning 1992-3, the Commissioner for Equal Opportunity received a total of just over 300 complaints (19.5 percent of complaints in total) relating to age discrimination. By 1994-5, however, this figure had fallen to approximately 100 (approximately nine percent of total complaints), figures that would appear to show that the problem being experienced is gradually diminishing in frequency. One possible interpretation of this reduction is that discrimination on age grounds is decreasing since the introduction of the Act, however, without further information about the profiles of those making complaints, and about how statistics are process and compiled and so on, it is not possible to do more than speculate.

In both periods in South Australia, the majority of complaints relating to age discrimination concerned employment, and of those complaints, the majority concerned selection for promotion and training opportunities, and losing employment to younger persons. The majority of complaints were made by men, particularly in the upper age groups, so that in the 45-54 age group, there were twice as many complaints originating from men as women. In the 55-64 age group, this had increased to four times that experienced by women of the same age. It may be that these statistics indicate that more older men than women experience age discrimination, or it may also be that men have higher expectations of the availability of training and promotion opportunities and therefore are more likely to find themselves in a position where they can be discriminated against, than do women. (See also Rutherglen, G, 1995), for a similar discussion in relation to the US Age Discrimination in Employment Act, 1977).

At the other end of the spectrum, females within the 15-24 age group were more likely to lodge a complaint than their male counterparts. Many of these complaints concerned women working in retailing, most commonly supermarkets, whose practice was to reduce the number of hours available to staff for working when they reached 'adult' rates of pay.

These statistics must be considered in the context of the numbers of men and women in employment in these categories in order to determine the extent to which the statistics truly represent male and female patterns of employment across the age strata before any firm conclusions can be drawn about their significance.

Judicial intervention

Some cases fail to reach settlement at the conciliation stage and will need to go to the South Australian Equal Opportunity Tribunal for the issues to be decided. Appeals against the decisions of the Tribunal go to the South Australian Supreme Court. Only one case has been reported from South Australia since the passing of the legislation, the remainder having been dealt with primarily on a confidential basis. This case, *Wright v City of Brighton* (1991 EOC 92-389), concerned discrimination in the provision of accommodation. Here, the City of Brighton Council had granted planning consent to a developer to build houses on a site, on the condition that the houses built there would be occupied only by persons over 55 years of age. The developer and the Council had entered into an agreement to this effect, but at a later date the developer requested that the council withdraw the restriction contained in the agreement - a request which the Council refused.

The complainant, who was a potential purchaser of two of the cottages, argued that the clause restricting tenancy and ownership of the properties to persons over the age of 55 was discriminatory against persons under 55, contrary to s85J of the 1984 Act (which prohibits discrimination in the provision of accommodation on the ground of age). The issue before the court was whether the housing arrangement constituted an excepted 'scheme or undertaking for the benefit of persons of a particular age group', within the meaning of s85P of the same Act. The court held that the housing agreement did fall within the exception because the cottages within the plan were specifically designed and built to provide relatively low cost housing to meet the identified needs of a particular group of retired and elderly people in South Australia. One can speculate whether the developer sought to use the legislation simply in order to increase the size of the potential market for the development, rather than because of any principled objection to age restrictions in housing provision.

In other Australian jurisdictions too, the matter has come under judicial scrutiny albeit that the different States will be guided not by the South Australian Equality of Opportunity Act but by legislative provisions applicable to their own jurisdiction. Hence, the terms under consideration may differ in form, causing the courts to be forced to determine different questions of interpretation. That having been said, the mischief which the legislation seeks to avoid is clearly the same in all States, hence some guidance may be sought from an examination of such decisions, many of which relate to the application of the legislation in the employment field.

One such decision is the ruling handed down by the Supreme Court of New South Wales Court of Appeal in *Lorang v Mater Misericordiae Hospital and Another* (1994 CA 40098). Here, the court was considering the effect of the New South Wales Anti-Discrimination Act 1977, as amended in 1993 to take account of the problem of age discrimination. That Act specifically provides that it is unlawful for an employer to retire an employee on the ground of that employee's age, or to engage in conduct which causes that employee to retire from employment. A specialist anaesthetist was appointed as Visiting Medical Officer to the Mater hospital. That accreditation enabled him to use the hospital facilities for the treatment of his patients, whom he billed separately from the hospital, once the surgery was completed. The hospital's by-laws required him to retire at the age of 65. On being informed that his accreditation was to be terminated for this reason, the anaesthetist argued that the hospital's conduct was unlawful, under s49ZV of the 1977 Act (the anti-age discrimination provision).

At first instance, while it was conceded that the anaesthetist was not an employee of the hospital, it was argued that he was nevertheless an employee of the patients for whom he acted as anaesthetist ('employee' under the NSW Act includes a person who provides a service as well as a person acting under a contract of employment). By removing his accreditation to the hospital, the complainant insisted that the hospital had effectively forced him to retire from this employment, contrary to the amendment to that Act.

While the New South Wales Equal Opportunity tribunal initially found in Lorang's favour, the Court of Appeal disagreed. It pointed out that Mr Lorang was still able to continue to carry out the work required of an anaesthetist - albeit not at the Mater Misericordiae Hospital. All that had been done was that an accreditation to carry out work on an appointment basis had been terminated, no contract of employment between the hospital and Mr Lorang had come to an end, nor was Mr Lorang unable to continue providing his services elsewhere. Accordingly, there had been no conduct which could satisfy the requirement that it had caused Mr Lorang to 'retire' within the meaning of the Act.

In addition, the court held that to 'retire' meant to retire from (an) existing contract or contracts of employment. The effect of the removal of accreditation was to prevent Lorang entering into new contracts with patients, using the Mater hospital facilities. The removal did not affect his existing contracts, therefore Lorang could not be said to have been forced to 'retire' in any event.

Mandatory retirement at the traditional age is obviously something which the legislators have sought to avoid. Yet, as is demonstrated by *Lorang*, problems may be experienced by individuals in seeking to enforce these provisions in practice. Clearly, the *de facto* effect of the hospital by-laws was to deny Mr Lorang of work when he reached the age of 65, but the New South Wales legislation could not assist in that regard for the accreditation arrangement between the hospital and the consultant did not fall into a category anticipated by the employment provisions of the Act.

Although this decision was arguably based on a correct interpretation of the Act's provisions, (but see the decision of the dissenting judge who adopted a more 'purposive' interpretation of those provisions), this case does illustrate the importance of careful drafting of legislation. That Mr Lorang was excluded from the protection of the Act perhaps stemmed from poor foresight on the legislator's behalf, rather than from any active intention of parliament to exclude such persons from the ambit of the provisions (a provision has subsequently been inserted into the Act to prevent a body from refusing to renew an authorisation which facilitates the practice of a profession, on the grounds of age - s49ZYG).

Even where it can safely be said that the complainant falls into a category of persons within the ambit of the provisions, other difficulties may be experienced. All Australian anti-discrimination legislation provides for exceptions by which discrimination on the grounds of age may be permitted. For example, the Equal Opportunity Act provides for an exception where age is a 'genuine occupation requirement' of that employment. Under the Commonwealth Industrial Relations Act 1988, section 170DF(2) (now sections 170CK of the Workplace Relations Act 1996) (which made a dismissal unlawful where the decision to dismiss was based on certain grounds, including age), direct discrimination on the grounds of age was permissible where age was an 'inherent requirement' of the particular position. This exception has recently been the subject of a high profile High Court of Australia appeal.

Qantas Airways, the Australian national airline (and subject to Federal law), has continued to force its pilots to retire at the age of 60 pursuant to the International Civil Aviation Convention (which permits contracting states to exclude from their airspace any aircraft flown by a pilot aged 60 or over). One such pilot, Mr John Baillie Christie, a pilot of Boeing 747 aircraft, argued before the Federal Industrial Relations Court of Australia that such conduct was contrary to the provisions of the Industrial Relations Act.

At first instance, the court held that because Qantas was bound to follow the rules laid down by the Convention, and because Mr Christie would not be able to undertake many of the international flights required of a pilot in his position as a number of countries operated the exclusion it could fairly be said that age was an ‘inherent requirement’ of the particular position in question within the terms of the legislation (*John Baillie Christie v Qantas Airlines* (1995) 60 I.R. 17).

On appeal however (Case no. 960257 IRC 1996), the Full Court of the Industrial Relations Court of Australia held that the fact that Christie’s contract of employment required him to fly anywhere in the world did not make age an inherent requirement of his position. Section 170DF(2), said the court, focused on the position of the employee rather than the business of the employer. As a first step the court must characterise the nature of the job which the employee is employed to do. Then, for the exception to apply, there must be a definite relationship between that job and the supposed ‘inherent requirement’, without which the employee would not be able to perform the characteristic tasks or skills required of that job. In this particular case, Mr Christie was not disqualified from being able to perform the characteristic tasks or skills required of a Boeing 474 pilot by being over 60. Rather, said the court, he was simply inhibited geographically as to where he could perform those tasks.

In addition, the court held that any difficulty which Qantas may have in rostering Mr Christie to fly only to those destinations where he was not prohibited from landing did not mean that the defence was made out. This was simply an ‘operational issue’ and as such was not necessarily a matter that bore upon the inherent requirements of the particular job. Hence, Qantas could no more terminate a contract of employment on the basis of age to accommodate their operational requirements than they could on the basis of, for example, pregnancy or race. The Full Court has chosen to interpret the defence very narrowly, to exclude ‘administrative’ considerations, even though these administrative considerations resulted from the obligations imposed under an international convention.

On further appeal to the High Court, that court took a different approach. It held that the inherent requirements of a particular position are those requirements which are ‘essential’ to that position (in this case, a B747 pilot employed to fly international routes). Some members of the bench were prepared to hold that this involved not just asking whether the employee possessed the necessary aeronautical skills and licenses to fly B747s on international routes, but also whether the employee could comply with the operational or administrative requirements imposed by the employer – in this case the Qantas rostering system. Because he could no longer comply once he turned 60, age was an inherent requirement of that position.

Compare the majority approach with that of the minority judge, Kirby, J. He argued that to allow administrative or operational requirements to justify discriminatory termination would significantly erode the protection of the legislation. For him, a requirement was only inherent if it was a permanent and integral requirement of the position. As there was evidence the upper age limit had varied over time, it could not be said to be permanent. Similarly, the fact that Qantas was complying with an international convention did not make age an inherent requirement: ‘Only be upholding the application of the Act is it likely that the employer would be persuaded to lend its support to the international review of the arbitrary and discriminatory standards of the International Civil Aviation

Organisation ...' (par. 165). He also noted that if operational requirements could be cited in the case of age they could be cited in relation to other grounds and this might result, for example, in a return to the days when lack of toilet facilities was put forward as an excuse for sex discrimination (par. 164).

The introduction of any broad defence, like an inherent requirements or genuine occupational requirement defence, into any UK anti-age discrimination legislation would need careful consideration. As the Qantas case shows, such a defence has the potential to permit employers to organise their businesses in such a way as to exclude certain groups, and then to justify that exclusion on the basis of organisational or administrative reasons.

Of course it is not only those at the upper age ranges who can suffer a detriment because of age, however, but also younger employees. In Queensland, the Anti-Discrimination Act 1991 prohibits discrimination on the basis of age and, as is the case with all Australian State and Federal anti-age discrimination legislation, can be employed to combat discriminatory practices affecting people of all ages, not merely that which affects people of middle or older age. This is illustrated in the case *Brooks v Flight West Airlines Pty Ltd.,* (1994 IRC (Hall CIC) B478), where the Act was employed to challenge an employer's policy of selecting employees for redundancy on the basis of 'last on, first off'. The effect of this policy was the dismissal of the youngest workers, and so the policy was held by the Queensland Industrial Relations Commission to be contrary to the terms of the 1991 Act. This decision was subsequently upheld on the basis that the employer's practice had the effect of discriminating indirectly against younger persons and so was unlawful.

Conclusion

The amendment to the South Australian Equal Opportunity Act adding age to the list of grounds on which discrimination is to be prohibited occurred against a background of pressures similar to those apparent in the UK today. Such discrimination was deemed unacceptable both at a personal level, because it resulted in decisions being made about individuals on the basis of stereotypical assumptions rather than individual aptitudes and capabilities, and at a public level, because of the industrial and economic implications of an increasingly ageing population.

It is worth considering whether such an integrated approach to anti-discrimination legislation as exists in South Australia may have advantages over the piecemeal framework of the UK anti-discrimination legislation.

The SA Equal Opportunity Act is a piece of 'umbrella' legislation which identifies all the grounds of discrimination made unlawful in that State, and under which the structure of the legislative provision is fundamentally the same for each ground. One effect of this structure is to facilitate the development of a body of case law and practice which is equally applicable to all grounds of discrimination.

This is to be compared with the approach in the UK where there is separate legislation for sex, race and disability (and equal pay), and where, for example, the court has declined to interpret the meaning of 'indirect discrimination' under the Sex Discrimination Act in the same way as it has been interpreted under identical provisions in the Race Relations Act (see the decision in *Perera* compared with that in *Falkirk* above). The fact that the structure of the new disability legislation is different again may reflect recognition of the different needs of the disabled (e.g. the Act imposes a duty on employers to make 'reasonable accommodation' for disabled employees), but equally it also raises the suspicion that some grounds of discrimination are less objectionable than others and therefore suitable for 'different' control.

Also, where there is one piece of legislation applicable to all groups there is an argument that this should allow for greater opportunity for these groups to collectively focus on particular aspects of that legislation which, for example, are perceived by those groups not to be working well.

Similarly, the existence of one monitoring body in South Australia, the Equal Opportunity Commission, arguably provides for a more co-ordinated approach to discrimination issues generally, and gives that body a more powerful voice for reform than do the existence of separate Commissions in the UK (on the 'failures' of the UK Equal Opportunities Commission see Honeyball, 1991).

The fact that the SA Equal Opportunity Commission also carries out the compulsory conciliation function under the Act is a feature perhaps worthy of further consideration, particularly at a time when the cost of Employment Tribunals are escalating, and procedures are becoming more formal and 'court like'. However, one disadvantage of a confidential conciliation service is that it may veil the impact of the legislation from public scrutiny.

There are other issues raised by the South Australian anti-discrimination legislation which are worthy of consideration. These include first, the issue of compulsory retirement. In South Australia the provisions making compulsory retirement unlawful were introduced in 1993, and only after debate about what effect allowing workers to work longer might have on the job and promotional opportunities of younger workers. There was a fear that removing the compulsory retirement age might cause a 'bottleneck' in organisations, limiting the opportunities for new recruitment and promotion. However, research into similar legislation in other countries showed that the removal of a compulsory retirement age would have little impact on the numbers of older workers choosing to stay on; relatively few employees chose to postpone retirement. What the removal has done in South Australia is to force employers to reassess their retirement policies so that those with the desire and ability to continue are not prevented from doing so simply by arbitrary age limits imposed by employers.

Second, and at the risk of stating the obvious, there is a need for any legislation to be carefully drafted, as the *Lorang* case illustrates: the nature of some professions may make it difficult to enforce legislation based predominantly around the concept of the 'employee'.

Third, there needs to be careful discussion of the provision of any defences and exceptions to discrimination. Exceptions from the provisions of the Act for charities for the aged, for example, may in fact perpetuate stereotypical views about the characteristics of all recipients of that charity.

To what extent should rational decisions based on, for example, economic or administrative factors ever be a justification for indirect discrimination? If they are a valid justification for indirect discrimination, then why not also for direct discrimination? Should an employer be entitled to deny employment to an older person because that person is, under a collective agreement perhaps, entitled to a higher rate of pay calculated according to a formula which contains an age component? Should 'new blood' recruitment schemes be permissible?

There are no doubt other issues in relation to the proposed UK legislation which could be usefully informed by a closer study of the operation of the South Australian Act, but it will be disappointing if the Labour government does not act to introduce legislation initially promised when it took office – particularly given the poor response to its Code of Practice published in 1999 (Equal Opportunity Review, 1999). The introduction of such legislation would represent an opportunity for the law to give formal recognition to the rights of citizens to participate in society irrespective simply of their age, and will make a welcome addition to the existing sex, race and disability legislation.

Of course behaviour and (especially) attitudes may not change overnight. Nevertheless, if we believe age discrimination is unacceptable then there are good arguments for the introduction of legislation. The legal environment is a part of our cultural heritage and as such it is one of the teaching systems from which we learn about socially (and commercially) acceptable behaviour. The law embodies the rules of the game. If enlightened societies live by the rule of law then logically that requires the formal acceptance on behalf of society that certain practices are unfair and unjust and must not be applied despite personal or arbitrary beliefs.

In this case it could be argued that it is the duty of the law to actively influence cultural change (rather than passively reflecting it) and to embody within the legal framework a set of principles which promote the behaviour and attitudes that we believe society should value.

Acknowledgements

I would like to thank Marianne Morrison for her invaluable assistance in preparing the draft of this chapter, and the Carnegie Trust for the Universities of Scotland for its research funding.

References

Anti-Discrimination Board (1995), *Annual Report 1994-5*, New South Wales.

Australian and New Zealand Equal Opportunity Law and Practice (1994), CCH Australia.

Buck, T. (1992), 'Ageism and Legal Control', in Hepple, B. and Szyszczak, E. (eds), *Discrimination: The Limits of the Law*, Mansell, London.

Carnegie Inquiry into the Third Age (1993), *Life, Work and Livelihood in the Third Age*, Bailey Management Services. London.

Commission for Racial Equality (1992), *Second Review of the Race Relations Act.*

Commissioner for Equal Opportunity (1987-1995), *Annual Reports*, Equal Opportunity Commission, South Australia.

Editorial (1996), 'The Age of Discrimination', *The New Law Journal*, March 15.

Eurolink Age (1993), 'Age Discrimination Against Older Workers in the European Community', *IDS European Report,* October, No. 382.

Grimley Evans, J., Goodacre, M.J., Hodkinson, M., Lamb, S. and Savory, M. (1992), *Health: Abilities and Well-Being in the Third Age,* Research Paper 9, Carnegie Trust, Dunfirmline.

Hepple, B. and Szyszczak, E. (1992), *Discrimination: The Limits of the Law*, Mansell, London.

Hervey, T. (1993), *Justifications for Sex Discrimination in Employment*, Butterworths, London.

Honeyball, S. (1991), *Sex, Employment and the Law*, Blackwell, London.

Labour Party (1997), 'Equal Rights', *Policy Information.*

Law Society (1997), *Age Discrimination and Employment Law Report.*

News (1999), 'Age Code Making Little Impact', *Equal Opportunity Review*, No.88, p. 14.

Rutherglen, G. (1995), 'From Race to Age: The Expanding Scope of Employment Discrimination Law', *Journal of Legal Studies* Vol. 24, p. 491.

Sheik, D. (1996), 'Positive Action in Community Law', *Industrial Law Journal* Vol. 25, No. 3, p. 239.

Tiddy, J. (1994), 'Age - An Overview', *Address - South Australia National Conference on Equal Opportunity Law and Practice.*

Worsley, R. (1993), 'Carnegie Third Age Programme', *Equal Opportunities Review,* March/April, No. 60.

12 Old enough to know better: age stereotypes in New Zealand

Darren J. Smith

Introduction

Throughout the developed world the average age of populations is increasing. The New Zealand Department of Statistics' population projection for 1991-2031 predicts that compared with a median age of 30 years in 1988, by 2031 half of the population of New Zealand will be older than 41, and there will be an increase of 62 percent in the number of people in the 40-59 age group (an increase of 425,000 people), reflecting the passage into middle age of the large number of children born during the 'baby-boom' period of 1945-65 and shortly thereafter. This increase in the population's median age is consistent with the experiences and projections of a number of other more developed countries.

Table 12.1 : Age projections for selected countries

Projected Year	*Median Age (Years)*						
	NZ	Australia	Canada	France	Japan	UK	US
2005	35.2	36.0	38.9	42.0	40.4	39.3	37.7
2025	39.6	39.5	42.4	42.0	45.2	42.3	40.6

Source: *Department of Statistics, Population, Labour Force and Household Projections 1991-2031*, p. 6

Recognising the ageing population, New Zealand's government outlawed discrimination on the basis of an individual's age with the passing of the Human Rights Commission Amendment Act (HRCA Act) 1992.[1] This legislation recognises that age discrimination is bipolar. People may be discriminated against because they are considered to be too old, or alternatively they may be deemed to be too young. New Zealand's legislation also includes exemptions citing circumstances under which an otherwise discriminatory action is to be permitted.[2] But how are older employees viewed by managers? Studies suggest an underlying cause of discriminatory practices: the influence of stereotypes held about older employees. Brigham (1971) accepts a definition of stereotypes as factually incorrect, rigid and produced through illogical reasoning. They are usually seen as generalisations which, in some cases, are undesirable because they may serve as justifications for prejudicial or discriminatory social practices.

This chapter looks at the types of stereotypes held by people in positions where these 'preconceived notions' may affect the treatment of older people in either the allocation of work or in the selection of new employees. The 'reasonableness' of such discriminatory practices will now be discussed.

Preconceived notions

A number of studies have been carried out in other countries which indicate the prevalence of age discrimination and some of the ways in which it manifests itself (for example Avolio and Barrett, 1987; Rosen and Jerdee, 1976). Past research into age discrimination has usually focused on one of two areas: the effect of age discrimination on performance evaluations, or the effect of applicant age on employment decisions.

Generally, existing gerontology literature (for example Barkin, 1970; Giniger, Dispenzieri and Eisenberg, 1983; Odell, 1970) indicates that chronological age is not a valid predictor of performance for a specific individual in a particular job (Rendell, 1992). Given this, age discrimination may not be a valid practice in employment relations.

Older employees and performance evaluations

Research on age discrimination and performance evaluation predominantly focuses on one of the work-related dimensions tested by Rosen and Jerdee (1976). The majority of these studies find that old employees may receive lower performance ratings than their younger counterparts (for example Schwab and Heneman III, 1978; Tuckman & Lorge, 1952; Waldman & Avolio, 1986), even though the older employee may in fact have experience allowing for greater performance (suggested by Giniger, Dispenzieri, and Eisenberg (1983)). There is no evidence of the research participants perceiving this enhanced performance, drawing attention to the possible existence of negative attitudes held about older persons.

Stereotypes held by performance raters about older employees may negate any increased (or equivalent) performance actually exhibited by these employees. Nevertheless, further research has indicated that older employees may be viewed more positively than younger employees when there is evidence of positive performance information for both younger and older employees (Lee and Clemons, 1985). There is also evidence suggesting that the age of the person conducting the evaluation may affect the rating of the older employees, with older raters perceiving older employees more negatively than younger raters (Schwab and Heneman, 1978); and that positions have age stereotypes associated with them (Cleveland and Landy, 1983; Singer, 1986). While Ferris and King (1992) have posited an explanation for negative performance stereotypes based on the lack of 'political activity' adopted by older employees in their organisations this needs further study for any confidence to be established.

Older employees and employment selection decisions

Research focusing on applicant age and employment decisions has found a tendency to favour younger applicants for lower status jobs (Haefner, 1977; Singer and Sewell, 1989; Triandis, 1963). This suggests that jobs have related stereotypes with regards to the age of the incumbent perceived to be suitable for the position, perceptions which may be based on a factor as arbitrary as the age of a number of applicants for a position (Cleveland, Festa and Montgomery, 1988). These studies have also introduced a variable in the form of the sex of the interviewer, males rating older applicants higher on intelligence and subsequent hiring recommendations, with females rating older applicants lower on attractiveness (Raza and Carpenter, 1987). Also of significance is the attribution of failure to employees who have been evaluated as equals to the subject's age (Locke-Conner and Walsh, 1980). Research has indicated that older persons are perceived to be significantly less capable of effective performance with respect to creative, motivational, and productive job demands, depicting older people as less interested in change and less capable of coping with future challenges.

Studies have shown that stereotypes held about older employees can be altered with the provision of age-related information to managers involved in employment decisions, but the relevant researchers have not been able to establish the extent of the information focus necessary to mitigate against discriminatory stereotypes without encouraging a new age-related bias through an over-emphasis on positive or negative attributes (Singer and Sewell, 1988).

While the above studies tended to find that negative discriminatory practices towards older employees or applicants occurred, not everyone has come to this same conclusion. Rosen and Jerdee (1976) found in their study that older people were rated higher on certain characteristics of behaviour. These authors found that older people were rated higher on stability (Arvey, Miller, Gould and Burch, 1987); concluding that for jobs which emphasise quality, reliability and integrity, the older employee may be viewed more favourably compared to a younger person (Warr, 1992).

Lee and Clemons (1985) noted that in their study, younger employees were rated significantly lower than were older employees when a choice had to be made, and moderately positive information was provided for both employees. These authors note that their findings are consistent with those of Crockett, Press and Osterkamp (1979) though inconsistent with (Haefner (1977).

Arvey, Miller, Gould and Burch (1987) found that females and older applicants received higher average interview evaluations for seasonal sales clerks' positions, but that regression lines did not differ significantly among the age and gender subgroups.

Studies which have been reported recently include two which suggest that the age of the subjects does not play a significant role in selection interview outcomes. Lin, Dobbins and Farh (1992) looked at the effects of interviewer and interviewee race similarity on interview outcomes under two different interview formats: a conventional structured panel interview, and a situational panel interview. These authors found no age similarity effects in either interview format and went on to suggest that raters in the real world would have more job-related information available to them, minimising the need to use age as a primary factor in selection recommendations.

Ugbah and Majors' (1992) study suggested that communication factors exhibited by applicants in employment interviews may affect the ratings given. 'An applicant's support for arguments and social attributes appeared to be more important to younger recruiters than to older recruiters, but neither gender nor gender by age interaction significantly affected factor importance' (Ugbah and Majors, 1992: 145).

Generally, while existing gerontology literature (e.g. Barkin, 1970; Giniger, Dispenzieri and Eisenberg, 1983; Odell, 1970) indicates that chronological age is not a valid predictor of performance, the problems that older employees encounter in the work setting suggest that age is being used as an indicator of performance, and, consequently, negatively influencing performance decisions concerning the older person. It appears that the belief that performance declines substantially with increasing age is largely unsupported. Such beliefs, inaccurate as they may be, about individual members of a particular group can be classified as stereotypes. It is possible that a negative age stereotype exists about older employees and that these widely shared beliefs influence decisions that we make at work.

The New Zealand situation

Recognising the ageing nature of the New Zealand population, with employees over the age of 40 years comprising an increasing proportion of the labour force, it was considered important to clarify what stereotypes are held about these older employees, and the implications they hold. Previous research into age discrimination in New Zealand has focused upon whether stereotypes exist, their effect upon employment decisions, and possible means for eliminating such bias (Singer, 1986; Singer and Sewell, 1988; Singer and Sewell, 1989). These studies however, do not identify the specific make-up of these stereotypes. Earlier research into the effect of age stereotypes in performance evaluation has also focused predominantly on the evaluation of managerial or professional employees, and it is the void in knowledge about stereotypes affecting the evaluation of older non-managerial employee performance that this paper addresses.

Without research identifying the stereotypes held by managers in New Zealand about older non-managerial employees, it is difficult to know what measures to adopt to correct stereotypes which may lead to discriminatory practices. The study was conducted in an effort to clarify the required focus for information which may mitigate against the discriminatory effect of these notions, or may result in a change in managerial attitudes towards older non-managerial employees.

The study

A questionnaire adapted from Warr's (1992) study was sent to 300 randomly selected members of the New Zealand Institute for Personnel Management (IPMNZ). The number of completed and usable questionnaires was 106, providing a response rate of 35.5 percent. The age of the respondents ranged between 26 and 65 years with 67 percent being between 36 and 50 years of age. Of those respondents who indicated their gender (97 out of the 106 usable responses) 64 percent were male, and 36 percent female.

A factor analysis was conducted in order to determine what Warr's questionnaire had indeed measured. Factors which were tested were based upon Rosen and Jerdee's (1976) four work related characteristics of Work Effectiveness, Interpersonal Skills, Stability, and Adaptability. The questionnaire provided results which focused on two of these factors, Work Effectiveness and Adaptability.

Following the Factor Analysis of the attitude scale used for this study, it was found that it was not possible to identify and aggregate individual questions into factors measuring respondent attitudes towards Interpersonal Skills or Stability when comparing older and younger non-managerial employees. The results for the individual items suggest however, that older IPM members relative to younger members, perceive older non-managerial employees to be more interpersonally skilled than younger employees, and that IPM members as a whole perceive older non-managerial employees as more loyal to their employing organisation than younger employees.

The Work Effectiveness and Adaptability factors consisted of the following items:

Work effectiveness
- reliability
- hard working
- conscientious
- effective in job
- useful experience

Adaptability
- accept new technology
- adapt to change
- can grasp new ideas
- learn quickly

The composition of the identified factors was then analysed for reliability. The Cronbach Coefficient Alpha for Factor One (Work Effectiveness) is 0.7931 (4 decimal places) surpassing the 0.7 reliability minimum imposed by the researcher. When adding most other items the reliability of the factor is reduced. While Factor One's reliability can be increased with the inclusion of the 'interpersonal skills' and 'loyal to one's organisation' items (to 0.8338: 4 decimal places), these items are deemed to be sufficiently dissimilar to the 'Work Effectiveness' construct to warrant their exclusion.

The Cronbach Coefficient Alpha for Factor Two (Adaptability) is 0.7750 (4 decimal places). The inclusion of other items serves only to reduce the reliability figure which results. This indicates that other items in the scale do not possess enough similarity to the identified factor to justify their inclusion in the factor's composition. As such the second factor is defined as comprising the items identified above.

Having found reliable factors, questionnaire responses were analysed to determine whether a respondent's age or sex affected responses received to the factors identified, or to any other items. Focusing on respondent sex, t-tests were conducted to ascertain whether there were any significant differences existing in how respondents answered items individually, and the two identified factors as a whole (Table 12.2). No significant difference is found to exist in how male and female respondents answered the items when they were amalgamated into factors. Significant differences were found for individual items however. At the 0.05 level of significance, a difference was identified in how male and female respondents rated older non-managerial employees (when compared with younger non-managerial employees) on their effectiveness in the job. Male respondents rated older employees as more effective in their jobs than younger non-managerial employees. Significant differences were also found for the 'useful experience' and 'learn quickly' items (Table 12.2), with male respondents viewing older employees as possessing more useful experience than younger employees, and with females viewing older employees as being more able to learn quickly than younger ones.

Other items to which there appears a significant difference between female and male respondents include 'length of time in position' (prob>□T□ = 0.0362), and 'first hand experience of ageism' (prob>□T□ = 0.0168). Male respondents are likely to have been in their current positions longer than the female respondents in the study; while, female respondents have experienced ageism first-hand more often than male (Table 12.2).

Table 12.2 : Comparison of respondent answers by sex

Characteristic	*Mean* Female	Male	*Prob>|T|*	*t-value*
Factor One:				
WORK EFFECTIVENESS	17.1765	19.9016	0.1144	-1.5937
- reliability	3.5882	3.7903	0.1525	-1.4425
- hard working	3.3235	3.2419	0.4915	0.6906
- conscientious	3.4118	3.3770	0.7908	0.2661
- effective in job	3.1176	3.3387	0.0181	-2.4066
- useful experience	3.7353	4.1290	0.0027	-3.0867
Factor Two:				
ADAPTABILITY	10.5294	9.8852	0.0909	1.7084
- accept new technology	2.4412	2.2787	0.2167	1.2439
- adapt to change	2.5000	2.3710	0.2789	1.0892
- can grasp new ideas	2.7647	2.6452	0.3264	0.9865
- learns quickly	2.8235	2.5806	0.0469	2.0134
Other Characteristics:				
- length of time in position	3.2353	4.7419	0.0362	-2.1246
- first hand experience of ageism	1.4412	1.2097	0.0168	2.4350
- ageism problem exists	1.2121	1.5000	0.0060	-2.8105

Figures rounded to 4 decimal places; n= 106

T-tests conducted to test whether a respondent's age affected the way in which they responded to the questionnaire indicated that there is a significant difference at the 0.5 level in the way that younger and older respondents rated older employees on the Work Effectiveness factor (prob>|T| = 0.0114), and the individual 'hard working' item (prob>|T| = 0.0307) (Table 12.3). These results indicate that older IPM members consider older non-managerial employees to exhibit greater work effectiveness in their positions, than considered to be the case by younger IPM members. Other items indicating significant differences in the way that respondents (younger versus older) answered are the 'take things easy' (prob>|T| = 0.0452) items (Table 12.3).

Table 12.3 : Comparison of respondent answers by age

Characteristic	*Mean* Younger	Older	*Prob>|T|*	*t-value*
Factor One:				
WORK EFFECTIVENESS	16.9714	18.0882	0.0144	-2.5766
- reliability	3.5429	3.8000	0.0598	-1.9029
- hard working	3.1429	3.4000	0.0307	-2.1916
- conscientious	3.2571	3.5072	0.0508	-1.9763
- effective in job	3.1714	3.3188	0.1114	-1.6059
- useful experience	3.8571	4.1000	0.0581	-1.9167
Factor Two:				
ADAPTABILITY	10.0286	9.9855	0.9075	1.7084
-accept new technology	2.2857	2.3333	0.7020	-0.3837
- adapt to change	2.3714	2.4143	0.7074	-0.3764
- can grasp new ideas	2.6286	2.6571	0.8105	-0.2404
- learns quickly	2.7429	2.5714	0.1515	1.4449
Other Characteristics:				
- takes things easy	3.0571	2.6714	0.0060	2.8086
- interpersonally skilled	3.4571	3.7353	0.0452	-2.0276

Figures rounded to 4 decimal places; n= 106

Older IPM members consider older non-managerial employees as 'taking things easy' much less than younger employees, while younger IPM members consider it likely that older employees 'take it easy' more than younger employees. Older IPM members also consider older non-managerial employees to more interpersonally skilled than younger employees. Again, it may be posited with 95 percent confidence that the observed differences in responses from IPM members have occurred due to differences in the perceptions held by the respondents, and not due to chance.

Table 12.4 : Respondents' attitudes to existence on ageism problem

Is there a problem with Age Discrimination?	*Number*	*Percent*
Yes	61	59.2
No	42	40.8
Total	103	100

Number of respondents missing = 3

Over 59 percent of respondents consider ageism to be a problem in New Zealand (Table 12.4). Analysing whether the age or sex of the respondent makes a significant impact on the respondent's attitude to whether ageism is a problem in New Zealand in personnel practice or business it is found that the age of the respondent (younger versus older) does not account for any difference in the way the sample responds (prob>|T| = 0.4848), yet the sex of the respondent does suggest a difference (prob>|T| = 0.0060) at the 0.05 level of significance. Male IPM members consider age discrimination to be more of a problem than female members.

Comparing responses gained from New Zealand and United Kingdom Institute members, the items identified by the United Kingdom researchers to form the Work Effectiveness factor are adopted. These items are identified in Table 12.5. Points of note include the difference between the attitudes held with regards to the 'thinking before they act' and 'effective in their job' items. A larger proportion of the New Zealand respondents think that there does not exist any difference between whether older and younger non-managerial employees think before they act (50.5 percent vs. 40 percent). New Zealand respondents agree however, that older non-managerial employees are more effective in their jobs than younger employees (26.9 percent vs. 19 percent).

Table 12.5 : NZ and UK comparison of responses to items in factor one: worker effectiveness

IPM Members see older employees as more:	*Agree (%)*		*Disagree (%)*		*No Difference (%)*	
	NZ	UK	NZ	UK	NZ	UK
- reliable	60.0	60	0.0	1	40.0	39
- thinking before they act	46.7	59	2.9	1	50.5	40
- interpersonally skilled	59.3	56	2.9	3	37.9	41
- conscientious	39.4	43	1.9	2	58.7	55
- effective in their job	26.9	19	0.0	2	73.1	79

When comparing the New Zealand and United Kingdom Institute members' attitudes towards the second identified factor (comprised of identical items for both the NZ and UK samples), Adaptability, New Zealand respondents are less inclined to consider older non-managerial employees to be less 'able to grasp new ideas' (40.0 percent vs. 47 percent) and less inclined to view older employees as having less ability to 'learn quickly' (41.9 percent vs. 48 percent) (Table 12.6).

Table 12.6 : NZ and UK comparison of responses to items in factor two: adaptability

IPM Members see older employees as less:	*Agree (%)*		*Disagree (%)*		*No Difference (%)*	
	NZ	UK	NZ	UK	NZ	UK
- accepting of new technology	63.5	66	1.0	1	35.6	33
- adaptable to change	59.0	63	1.0	2	40.0	35
- quick learners	41.9	48	4.8	1	53.3	51
- able to grasp new ideas	40.0	47	4.8	2	55.2	51

Discussion

When considering the results of this study on stereotypes, the writer is all too aware of the dangers which exist with the temptation to generalise the current findings across the sample (and by implication, the population) of New Zealand Institute of Personnel Management members. As such, readers of this study should remind themselves of the limitations of using stereotypes arising from this study's results as a 'basis of truth' from which to view individual IPM members.

Having stated this, I will follow with a discussion of the findings of this study with regards to the attitudes held by IPMNZ members about older non-managerial employees, and attitudes towards age discrimination legislation.

This study finds that New Zealand IPM members hold differing notions about older and younger non-managerial employees at their work sites. The results show some similarities to those found by previous researchers (for example, Rosen and Jerdee, 1976 and Warr, 1992), with respect to particular items responded to. A point to note is that when respondents indicate a difference between the older and younger employee at their sites, not all of these differences indicate a negative attitude towards older employees. For example the present study suggests that New Zealand IPM members judge older employees to be significantly more reliable than their younger counterparts, to possess greater interpersonal skills than younger employees, to have useful experience, and to be more loyal to their employing organisation than younger employees. These results may have implications for the allocation of responsibility among non-managerial employees, such as favouring older employees as team leaders, for example, based on a stereotype held about a group which may or may not be accurate for the individual in question, and effectively discriminating against younger employees for these positions.

While the attitudes towards older employees in this study are similar to those found by researchers both in the United States (Rosen and Jerdee, 1976) and the United Kingdom (Warr, 1992), the stereotypes do not always represent accurate descriptions of older non-managerial employees. Logically, differences will be able to be discerned in every situation, due to the variable nature of people in various situations - not all older employees will be more reliable than their younger workmates, and not all older employees have experience which is more useful than that of employees under 40 years of age.

The present study finds however, that younger employees are perceived to be significantly more accepting of new technology, to be more adaptive to change, better suited to learning quickly, and more interested in training. While these findings concur with the results of previous researchers (Rosen and Jerdee, 1976; Warr, 1992), they too cannot claim to be accurate assessments of all situations in which both younger and older employees may be present. Employee adaptability may vary individual by individual, and indeed may also depend upon other factors such as the nature of the individual's job, the organisational climate in which they work, or other environmental or external influences. It is suggested that the sorts of attitudes held by managers towards the ability to train older non-managerial employees represent a narrow focus towards the issue of training in general

(Barkin, 1970). Barkin (1970) argues that the challenge facing managers is to develop special training techniques for older employees, instead of resigning themselves to the proposition that older employees cannot learn. Instead, it is argued that the problems which have been experienced in the past have arisen because the *teachers* did not adapt. As Barkin (1970) states:

> The traditional methods of teaching based on exposition and presentation of theory followed by later application may work well with younger people ... but it appears that these methods which are refined slowly through school life do not survive as natural and easy ways of learning once the individual has long left behind [their] school room experience (p. 18).

Put simply, older employees learn in a manner different to younger employees. Research demonstrates that many older employees do not exhibit decline in performance as they age (Avolio and Waldman, 1989), and that using age as a predictor for performance may lead to negative performance decisions about older employees which are unfounded. However, in situations which necessitate the re/training of older employees, the present study suggests that some managers who are responsible for the provision of opportunities for re/training are unlikely to appreciate the potential which older employees hold, and as such may implicitly or explicitly discriminate against older employees based on ill-founded preconceived notions about an older employee's capacity for re/training.

The present study also finds significant differences in the way that male and female respondents rate older non-managerial employees on their effectiveness in their jobs and the useful nature of their experience. These results suggest that male respondents are more likely to perceive older employees as having more useful experience than is perceived by female respondents. They also indicate that male IPM members when compared with female members, perceive older non-managerial employees as being more effective in their jobs than younger non-managerial employees. This may arise from a difference in importance weighting by female and male IPM members to the requirement for experience held by job incumbents for the particular task(s) the respondent considered when considering this question.

With a larger proportion of New Zealand IPM respondents viewing older and younger non-managerial employees differently on the experience item (the majority viewing these older employees as having more useful experience than younger employees), and the majority of members considering there to be less of a difference between each age group's effectiveness in the job, the current researcher may speculate that male IPM members weigh the importance of job experience more heavily than female IPM members. If, for example, male respondents attach more importance to useful experience when rating non-managerial employees, then this may account for the finding that male respondents also consider older non-managerial employees to be more effective in their positions. While previous research has indicated that a rater's age may influence their rating of job incumbents (for example, Avolio and Waldman, 1989; Cleveland and Landy, 1981;

Kirchner and Dunnette, 1954), the present study suggests that the sex of the rater may also play a role in the determination of non-managerial job incumbent ratings. This parallels Raza and Carpenter's (1987) findings, these researchers noting significant effects of interviewer sex on skill ratings of job applicants.

When considering the Work Effectiveness factor as a whole, the age of the respondents, when divided into two groups (those over 40 years of age, and those under 40) produces a significant difference suggesting that older IPM members consider older non-managerial employees to be more effective in their jobs than younger members do. As noted above, this perception may be based on the skill characteristics which each of the respondents considers important for the task being considered, and as Avolio and Waldman (1989) suggest, the age of the respondent (i.e. the IPM member) may actually account for the important ratings for different skills more than the age of the job incumbent. Analysing the Work Effectiveness factor's individual items, a significant difference is also indicated suggesting that IPM members over the age of 40 years perceive older non-managerial employees to work harder than younger employees. This corresponds to the rating given on the 'takes things easy' item, younger IPM members viewing older employees as more likely to take things easy when compared with younger employees.

No explanation for this perceived effectiveness of older employees by older IPM members is offered by the results of the study. Again a possible explanation may lie in the importance weighting attached to the 'hard work' item by older IPM members when comparing older and younger non-managerial employees, as suggested by Avolio and Waldman (1989). It may also suggest that, as Ferris and King (1992) posit, older employees (and older IPM members as employees also) do not consider ingratiating behaviour which may be adopted by younger employees to be necessary. Such behaviour only serves to distract younger employees from focusing on the task at hand. These suggestions however, are only speculative and would require further research to ascertain their true representativeness.

Considering the Adaptability factor as a whole, no significant age or sex effects are found in the responses from IPM respondents in New Zealand. The research did find however, that the sex of the IPMNZ member affects their perception with regards to an older employee's ability to learn quickly. The study finds that female IPM members, more than male members, consider older employees quicker at learning than younger non-managerial employees. The present research does not however, provide a reason for this finding, and the current author finds it difficult to speculate on a reason for such an occurrence.

The sex of the IPM member has been found to affect whether they consider age discrimination to be a problem in personnel practice and business. The results indicate that male respondents perceive ageism to be more of a problem than female respondents. It may be speculated that this indicates that female managers require an increased awareness of the potential problems and pitfalls with assuming their perceptions of employees are correct, when they may be based on incorrect foundations. Alternatively, male managers may be over-concerned with the issue, arising from more experience of age discrimination, either as victims, or as parties to grievances. While also conjecture, it may be suggested that the exhibited differences between male and female respondents have arisen due to the socialisation of individuals into traditionally stereotyped roles. For example, it could be postulated that traditionally women have been socialised into viewing any paid work undertaken as a 'job' rather than a 'career,' and that males have been socialised into aspiring to positions as the traditional household breadwinners. In these stereotyped roles, it may be likely that males consider age discrimination as more of a problem, due to its 'greater' effect on their position in society if personally experienced; potentially reducing their status as the main provider for the family.

While flaws may exist in the logic of these arguments in today's society of closer equality between males and females (although Hofstede (1984) suggests that the fact that women have jobs rather than stay at home in itself means no reversal of a traditional sex role distribution pattern and may even reinforce it), and the shift from the traditional nuclear family unit (2 adults and 2.4 children) to other family structures, the present author would suggest that further study into the reasons why female and male IPMNZ members perceive the age discrimination problem differently may be warranted.

In determining the comparability of the New Zealand and United Kingdom results, reference must be made to the cultural identities held by each society. It may be suggested that similarities exist between New Zealand and the United Kingdom, recognising New Zealand's cultural heritage as a former dominion of Great Britain. Based on his cross-cultural research, Hofstede (1984) suggests that similarities do exist between the cultures of each country. While Hofstede (1984) did not specifically address a New Zealand/United Kingdom comparison, both countries were surveyed as part of his research into international differences in work-related values. Both New Zealand and the United Kingdom scored similarly on dimensions tested by Hofstede (1984): Power Distance, Uncertainty Avoidance, and Masculinity.

As a whole, above average Masculine work-related values were found to be held by both New Zealand and United Kingdom respondents. This means that advancement, earnings, training, and up-to-datedness were found to be values held highly in work places. The results of the present study indicate that both New Zealand and United Kingdom IPM members rate older employees more negatively for the Adaptability factor identified previously. With the United Kingdom society valuing these adaptability characteristics in the workplace more than New Zealand respondents (Hofstede, 1984), and the present study finding that United Kingdom IPM members perceive older non-managerial employees more negatively than younger employees than New Zealand IPM members, it may be suggested that older employees are more appreciated in New Zealand.

While speculative, possible reasons for the above finding include the value placed upon equality in New Zealand society, considered later, and/or an increased appreciation of older employee capabilities following the publication of information on the subject following the relatively recent introduction of the Human Rights Commission Amendment Act 1992 into New Zealand law. Finding that older employees are appreciated by New Zealand IPM members in a relatively more positive manner than United Kingdom members does not justify however, the inaccurate stereotypes which may be held about the adaptability of older non-managerial employees in New Zealand. Members of the New Zealand IPM still perceive older non-managerial employees negatively (relative to younger employees) on the Adaptability factor - a dimension of work which is valued by New Zealand employees (Hofstede, 1984).

With regards to the Power Distance and Uncertainty Avoidance dimensions studied by Hofstede (1984), both countries were found to score below the average of the 39 nations studied. While New Zealand was ranked lower than Great Britain on the Power Distance Index, the results indicate that both New Zealand and Great Britain respondents value cooperativeness between employees, and are concerned with the maintenance of equality between individuals. It could be speculated that the relative difference in the rankings between the two countries offers a reason for the New Zealand IPM member preference for legislation discouraging age discrimination more than United Kingdom members. With a greater concern for these issues, New Zealand members may logically prefer legislation over a voluntary code in an effort to preserve their cultural value for equality, for example. This orientation may also account for a larger number of New Zealand IPM members viewing no difference between older and younger workers in their propensity to think before they act.

For the Uncertainty Avoidance dimension tested by Hofstede (1984), while both countries again ranked below the study's international average, United Kingdom respondents were found to hold a more extreme view. Hofstede (1984) suggests that neither New Zealand nor United Kingdom respondents value hard work per se. He also notes that respondents from these countries do not view loyalty to an employer as a virtue, and have a more positive view of younger people. The present study's findings concur with those of Hofstede's - older workers are perceived to be more loyal than younger workers - an attribute which may not benefit older workers significantly.

Variables other than an IPMNZ member's age and sex, affecting the types of stereotypes held towards older workers, which were not examined in the present study include the ethnicity of the study's participants, the legislative position of the country at the time of the study, the types of position which IPM members used as the basis of their comparison of older and younger employees, and the educational background of IPM members. It is beyond the scope of this paper to discuss these factors.

Conclusion

The present study finds that stereotypes are held by members of the IPMNZ about older non-managerial employees. Many of these stereotypes portray older non-managerial employees in a negative manner relative to younger non-managerial employees. In particular, negative stereotypes are found to exist about an older employee's ability to adapt to change and to learn new skills and/or ideas.

When the IPMNZ members' responses are analysed to determine if their age affects their attitudes towards older non-managerial employees, it is found that older IPM members view older non-managerial employees to be more effective in their work than younger employees. Specifically, they perceive older non-managerial employees to be harder working than younger employees, and to possess greater interpersonal skills. While these items offer some hope for older employees, when compared with the dimensions and qualities which Hofstede (1984) identified as valuable in the country's workplaces these same items do not appear to be considered important.

Analysing IPM member responses to gauge the effect of their sex, the present study finds that male IPM members perceive older non-managerial employees to be more effective in their jobs, and as having useful experience relative to younger non-managerial employees. Again, it is not clear whether these characteristics are considered important in New Zealand workplaces, and attributing these stereotypes to older non-managerial employees may not provide for any significant advantage in employment.

Implications arising from the present study for New Zealand and the treatment of older non-managerial employees, include the need for either the re-education of managers who are responsible for (e.g.) employment and performance decisions or for a programme designed to increase these same managers' awareness of biases which may exist in an effort to encourage them to question their practices and attitudes, potentially leading to a re-assessment of older employees and their abilities. With an ageing population base in New Zealand, these employees are likely to make up a larger proportion of the labour force, and action instituted on stereotypes held about their real and potential performance capabilities may influence the success or survival of businesses.

Having found that stereotypes are held about older non-managerial employees by New Zealand managers, the present researcher recommends a more detailed study in an attempt to gauge more accurately the nature of these stereotypes, expanding the focus of the study to include information allowing for generalisations to be made about all four work-related dimensions identified by Rosen and Jerdee (1976), namely Work Effectiveness, Adaptability, Stability, and Interpersonal Skills.

The present study's results also suggest that some similarities exist between the attitudes held by IPM members from both the United Kingdom and New Zealand towards older non-managerial employees. These similarities have been suggested to be founded in the similar cultures and work-related values held by each society. While the attitudes found to exist towards older workers are not identical, suggested to be due to differences in influencing variables such as the ethnic diversity of each country, there may be some leeway for generalising the stereotypes between these two countries, and even further to other Anglicised nations such as Australia, Canada, and the United States of America.

Notes

1. This legislation has since been superseded by the Human Rights Act (1993).
2. For example when the position is one of domestic employment in a private household; and when the duties to be performed are done so wholly or mainly outside New Zealand and are such that, because of the law of the country in which those duties are to be performed, they can be carried out effectively only by a person of a particular age (HRCA Act, 1992).

References

Arvey, R.D., Miller, H.E., Gould, R., and Burch, P. (1987), 'Interview Validity for Selecting Sales Clerks', *Personnel Psychology*, Vol. 40, pp. 1-12.

Avolio, B.J., and Barrett, G.V. (1987), 'Effects of Age Stereotyping in a Simulated Interview', *Psychology and Aging*, Vol. 2, No. 1, pp. 56-63.

Avolio, B.J., and Waldman, D.A. (1989), 'Ratings of Managerial Skill Requirements: comparison of age- and job-related factors', *Psychology and Aging*, Vol. 4, No. 4, pp. 464-70.

Barkin, S. (1970), 'Retraining and Job Redesign: Positive approaches to the continued employment of older persons', in H.L. Sheppard (ed.), *Toward an Industrial Gerontology* (pp. 17-30), National Council on the Aging, New York.

Brigham, J.C. (1971), 'Ethnic Stereotypes', *Psychological Bulletin*, 87(1), pp. 15-38.

Cleveland, J.N., Festa, R.M., and Montgomery, L. (1988), 'Applicant Pool Composition and Job Perceptions: Impact on Decisions Regarding an Older Applicant' *Journal of Vocational Behaviour*, Vol. 32, pp. 112-25.

Cleveland, J.N., and Landy, F.J. (1981), 'The Influence of Rater and Ratee Age on Two Performance Judgements', *Personnel Psychology*, Vol. 34, pp. 19-29.

Cleveland, J.N., and Landy, F.J. (1983), 'The Effects of Person and Job Stereotypes on Two Personnel Decisions', *Journal of Applied Psychology*, Vol. 68, No. 4, pp. 609-19.

Crockett, W.H., Press, A.N., and Osterkamp, M. (1979), The Effects of Deviations from Stereotyped Expectations upon Attitudes towards Older Persons', *Journal of Gerontology*, Vol. 34, pp. 368-74.

Department of Statistics (1992), *New Zealand Official 1992 Year Book*, 95th Edition.

Ferris, G.R., and King, T.R. (1992), 'The Politics of Age Discrimination in Organisations', *Journal of Business Ethics*, Vol. 11, pp. 341-50.

Giniger, S., Dispenzieri, A., and Eisenberg, J. (1983), 'Age, Experience, and Performance on Speed and Skill Jobs in an Applied Setting', *Journal of Applied Psychology*, Vol. 68, No. 3, pp. 469-75.

Haefner, J.E. (1977), Race, Age, Sex, and Competence as Factors in Employer Selection of the Disadvantaged', *Journal of Applied Psychology*, Vol. 62, No. 2, pp. 199-202.

Hofstede, G. (1984), *Culture's Consequences: International Differences in Work-Related Values*, Abridged Edition, Sage, California.

Kirchner, W.K., and Dunnette, M.D. (1954), 'Attitudes Towards Older Workers', *Personnel Psychology*, Vol. 7, pp. 257-65.

Lee, J.A., and Clemons, T. (1985), 'Factors Affecting Employment Decisions About Older Workers', *Journal of Applied Psychology*, 70(4), pp. 785-88.

Lin, T.R., Dobbins, G.H., and Farh, J.L. (1992), 'A Field Study of Race and Age Similarity Effects on Interview Ratings in Conventional and Situational Interviews', *Journal of Applied Psychology*, Vol. 77, No. 3, pp. 363-71.

Locke-Conner, C., and Walsh, R.P. (1980), 'Attitudes Towards the Older Job Applicant: Just as Competent, But More Likely to Fail', *Journal of Gerontology*, Vol. 35, No. 6, pp. 920-27.

Odell, C.E. (1970), 'Industrial Gerontology in the Employment Service', in H.L. Sheppard (ed.), *Toward an Industrial Gerontology* (pp. 12-16), The National Council on Aging, New York.

Raza, S.M., and Carpenter, B.N. (1987), 'A Model of Hiring Decisions in Real Employment Interviews', *Journal of Applied Psychology*, Vol. 72, No. 4, pp. 596-603.

Rendell, H. with the EEO Section, State Services Commission (1992), *Age Discrimination and Equal Employment Opportunities: a review of the literature and bibliography*, State Services Commission, March.

Rosen, B., and Jerdee, T.H. (1976), 'The Nature of Job-Related Age Stereotypes', *Journal of Applied Psychology*, Vol. 63, No. 2, pp. 573-78.

Schwab, D.P., and Heneman III, H.G. (1978), 'Age Stereotyping in Performance Appraisal', *Journal of Applied Psychology*, Vol. 63, No. 2, pp. 573-578.

Singer, M.S. (1986), 'Age Stereotypes as a Function of Profession', *Journal of Social Psychology*, Vol. 126, No. 5, pp. 691-92.

Singer, M.S., and Sewell, C. (1988), 'Age Stereotyping and the Age Bias Effect in Selection Interviews', *New Zealand Journal of Business*, Vol. 10, pp. 37-47.

Singer, M.S., and Sewell, C. (1989), 'Applicant Age and Selection Interview Decisions: Effect of Information Exposure on Age Discrimination in Personnel Selection', *Personnel Psychology*, Vol. 42 (Spring), pp. 135-54.

Triandis, H.C. (1963), 'Factors Affecting Employee Selection in Two Cultures', *Journal of Applied Psychology*, Vol. 47, pp. 89-96.

Tuckman, J., and Lorge, I. (1952), 'The Attitudes of the Aged toward the Older Worker for Institutionalised and Non-Institutionalised Adults', *Journal of Gerontology*, Vol. 7, pp. 559-64.

Ugbah, S.D., and Majors, R.E. (1992), 'Influential Communication Factors in Employment Interviews', *Journal of Business Communication*, Vol. 29, No. 2, pp. 145-59.

Waldman, D.A., and Avolio, B.J. (1986), 'A Meta-Analysis of Age Differences in Job Performance', *Journal of Applied Psychology*, Vol. 71, No. 1, pp. 33-38.

Warr, P. (1992), *Views about Older Workers*, IPM Harrogate Conference, United Kingdom, October.

13 Ageism and work in the EU: a comparative review of corporate innovation and practice

David Parsons and Lesley Mayne

Introduction

The consequences for work organisation and industrial competitiveness of the widespread ageing of the workforce in Europe has emerged since the late 1980s as an important public policy issue in many of the EU member states. The European Commission's First Action Programme and the Observatory on Older Workers collated a variety of evidence on the emerging trends, and the economic and demographic backcloth. Research was also conducted on retirement practices and age-based employment discrimination.

Outside this, a variety of national studies have been conducted on these issues although with patchy and incompatible coverage in different member states. The focus for much of this work has been on the demographic backcloth and age discrimination (Parsons, 1994; Whitting, Moore & Tilson, 1995). The practical scope for social partners to address this at workplace level has received very little attention. Where it has been assessed the focus is often theoretical or conjectural with little or no analysis of practical business circumstances and initiatives. What research has been conducted is heavily dependent on organisational experiences in the USA.

Recognising the importance of this issue to European labour markets and social policy, this chapter will attempt to address the lack of evidence from which to identify innovation by European employers. The evidence used in this chapter is drawn from a research project based upon an annual survey of organisational policies and practices in human resource management of organisations in Europe employing over 200 people. It is the largest survey of its kind ever conducted, with organisations participating from the European Union (EU) and the European Free Trade Area (EFTA). In 1995 the survey covered 15 countries: Belgium (B), Denmark (DK), Finland (FIN), France (F), Germany-East (D(w)), Germany-West (D(e)), Ireland (IRE), Italy (I), the Netherlands (NL), Norway (N), Spain (E),

Sweden (S), Switzerland (CH), Turkey (T) and the United Kingdom of Great Britain and Northern Ireland (UK).

The questions discussed here were part of the larger survey. Like all of that survey they were developed in multinational teams of academics concerned with HRM: translated and re-translated and any variations resolved by discussion (see Brislin 1970; Brislin, Lounder and Thorndike 1973). The resultant questions were piloted with panels of practitioners prior to distribution.

The demographic backcloth

Europe led the world into the population explosion of the nineteenth century. Today the picture is very different and member states of the European Union are on the edge of leading the developed world into 'zero growth' and then to population decline. In one member state - Germany - the population has been falling for some time and four other states are following this pattern. Demographic projection is an impenetrable science but over the last 30 years it has become much more accurate. The slowing population growth rates in Europe were anticipated long before the former Iron Curtain was raised. We have every reason to put great faith in the picture that today's demographers supply of tomorrow - certainly up to 2015 and a little less reliably up to 2025. Beyond that it is conjecture.

The most recent analysis for the European Commission make sober if sterile reading. They show that by 2015, seven of the current member states will have joined Germany to go beyond 'zero growth' to population decline (Table 13.1). The UK will be one of these, albeit a later addition, unlikely to start population decline until nearly the second decade of the twenty first century. Only Ireland will be increasing its population significantly - although at 0.4 per cent a year by low global rates.

Table 13.1 : The population in the European Union 1990-2015

Member State	*Projected Populations (x 1000)*	
	1990	*2015*
Belgium	9866	9147
Denmark	5085	4722
France	56117	56997
Germany	61672	53556
Greece	10027	9529
Ireland	3537	4037
Italy	57276	53473
Luxembourg	366	326
Netherlands	14716	14789
Portugal	10287	9961
Spain	38993	39368
United Kingdom	56938	56689
EU-12	324884	312593

Source: *European Commission,* 1993 (Projected Fertility)

The other member states of France, the Netherlands and Spain will have roughly stable populations with Germany and Italy topping the list in the rate of decline. The population of the current member states overall will have fallen by over 12 million people to 313 million by 2015.

Much more could be made of this data but this is not the place to tackle the detail of the projections or demographic *caveats*. The fall in European fertility rates and changing patterns of morbidity are part of a longstanding trend as explored in the European Commission's (EC) European Observatory Report (Walker et al, 1993). One consequence of these progressive trends is that the population of Europe is not so much falling but ageing. About one in six of the EU's population are over 60 years of age and by 2015 this will be one in four. Looking more broadly, a third of the population is currently over 50. This proportion will top 40 per cent by 2015.

Even more dramatic is the projected trend among those of 70 years of age or more. This group may seem to have little relevance to the human resource strategies of employers yet the eldercare burden on employees in their forties and fifties is already starting to be recognised as an employment policy issue. It is set to intensify. In 1990 one person in 13 in the EU came within this age group. By 2015 it will be one in nine.

Table 13.2 : Female and male life expectancy in the European Union at age 60

Member State	*Life Expectancy at age 60*	
	Females	*Males*
Belgium	82.7	77.8
Denmark	81.6	77.4
France	84.2	79.0
Germany	82.2	77.8
Greece	82.3	79.2
Ireland	80.6	76.6
Italy	82.7	78.2
Luxembourg	82.4	77.8
Netherlands	83.1	78.1
Portugal	81.2	77.2
Spain	83.2	79.0
United Kingdom	81.7	77.6

Source: Employment Observatory Trends: Statistical Supplement No. 15 (1993)

A consequence of these shifts is rising life expectancy for older people. Men reaching 60 years of age can now expect to live, on average, to nearly 78 years of age, and women to over 82. Unlike earlier in the post-war period, growing consistency across Europe in standards if health care and health education have seen if expectancy differences between EU countries shrink. A man or woman taking early retirement in their mid-fifties is now on average expected to live for another 25 years. For many it will be much longer. In Britain alone, for example, there will be over 1.1 million 85 year olds by the early twenty first century, double the 1981 level.

Set against this backcloth both the trend - and people's expectations - of retirement have been changing. Patterns of retirement vary substantially across Europe but important common themes have been identified in the EC's *Observatory Report* (Walker, Alber and Guillemard, 1993).

Table 13.3 : State retirement ages in the European Union, 1992

Member State	*Men*	*Women*	Comments
Austria	60	65	From 2019 a gradual reduction in age difference planned
Belgium	60-65	60-65	Pre-1990, 65 for men and 60 for women
Denmark	67	67	
Finland	65	65	63 for public sector employees
France	60	60	Lowered in 1983 from 63
Germany	65	60	In practice, most men retire at 63
Greece	65	60	
Ireland	65	65	
Italy	60	55	Current debate on a common age of 60 or 65. Women can work until 60
Luxembourg	65	65	
Netherlands	65	65	
Norway	67	67	
Portugal	65	62	Government decision on equalisation at 65 by 1999
Spain	65	60	
Sweden	65	65	Is variable between 60 - 70 with full benefits
Switzerland	65	62	
United Kingdom	65	60	Government decision on equalisation at 65 by 2020

Source: Abstracted from Moore, Tilson and Whitting (1994)

State retirement ages (Table 13.3) and rules are currently being reshaped across much of Europe (Parsons, 1994). As in the UK the predominant trend is for government and social partners to endorse an upward revisions usually to 65 or 67. This is sometimes accompanied with provisions for flexibility, but in Europe only Sweden maintains a fully flexible process putting into practice the 'decade of flexible retirement' long supported by the UK government and employers bodies but yet to develop within public policy. This trend in public policy has been led by the need in some member states, such as the UK, to equalise state rules for men's and women's retirement. The upward revisions however, have been led by the predominant concern in public pension and retirement policy of cost containment.

This upward trend conflicts with what is happening in the labour market itself. Throughout the last century Europe has seen a progressive trend toward earlier exit from the labour force. Until recently this was conditioned mainly by the development of pension systems. Until the early 1970s, age 65 - the most common age for entitlement to full pension rights - progressively became the 'normal' threshold of transition to economic inactivity.

Since the early 1970s this has started to change. The threshold of transition has progressively moved downward with a gap opening up between age of access to full pension rights and common retirement behaviour. The first age group affected was white collar 60 to 65 year olds. By the early 1980s a cross-occupational effect was observed with the falling age of transition substantially affecting male activity rates at 55-59 years. The causes are complex and vary between Member States but recent analysis suggests a combination of:

- public policy effects with active labour market programmes encouraging early exits through subsidy schemes, such as in the UK, Netherlands, Denmark, France and Germany in the early to mid 1980s.
- broadening and maturing pension systems, with the extended development and take-up of private and occupational pensions schemes in particular.
- the effects of age discrimination and de-selection, focusing on older employees in employers' recruitment and workforce management practices.

The balance between these and other issues is the subject of great public policy controversy and especially on the pattern of 'voluntary' and 'involuntary' earlier exits.

This is not the place to review these underlying themes in detail. What is clear is that over the last 15 years much of Europe has witnessed an escalation in early retirement led largely by employer's responses to falling labour demand. Although similar trends can be observed in most other developed economies they are nowhere as acute as within the EU. Today much of the older workforce in the EU have sharply reduced opportunity for extending their working lives to the age at which full pension rights are likely to be obtained. This is compounded by employment policy in organisations and by the expectations and attitudes of many older employees themselves. The trend has had short-term value for employers and some employees alike, but public policy shapers in Europe are now struggling with the longer term implications.

Employment policy context

The greying of the workforce received surprisingly little attention in the labour skill supply debate of the mid and late 1980s. More recently the growing concerns about 'third age' issues offers little practical information to guide European personnel strategists and practitioners on the issues and options for organisations.[1] What practical research that does exist has focused on pre-retirement provision and practice. With the equalisation issue now well advanced, much of this is now dated. Early evidence on targeted recruitment and retention of older people has been provided by a HOST consultancy survey for NEDO (Berry-Lound, 1991) and by the Institute of Manpower Studies (Thompson, 1991). The report of the Carnegie Inquiry and its earlier study reports (Trinder, 1992) provided a valuable overview of the employment policy content but beyond research for the Institute of Personnel and Development by PSI, HOST and others (IPM, 1993) there has been little recent attention in the UK paid to the wider internal labour market issues and the human resource policy implications. This is despite growing evidence that organisations' ability to adapt to, and profit from the greying workforce is hampered by often ill-informed or short-sighted management practices and attitudes which underpin 'ageist' attitudes in recruitment and selection, performance review and training or career development and investment. This has been clearly evidenced in the UK through survey research, mapping employers practices relating to older workers by the HOST Consultancy in 1992 for IPM and the Re-action Trust (Berry-Lound, 1992) and more recently through an Economic and Social Research Council project (Taylor and Walker, 1993). Practitioner information in the UK to guide and shape more enlightened management practices on these issues, is limited. In other member states it is rare and the Eurolink Age Report (Drury, 1993) has called for EC initiatives to identify and promote best practice.

Since the late 1970s, most of the energy and innovations of human resource practitioners in respect of the third age workforce has consequently focused on 'de-selection'. In much of Europe early retirement and voluntary redundancy packages favouring older employees have come to be seen as the acceptable face of the organisations' downsizing and restructuring strategies in the 1980s. Even in a period of strong employment growth in the UK in the second half of the 1980s, nearly one firm in five continued to regard early retirement as an important element of personnel strategies.

Table 13.4 : Male activity rates for the 55-64 age groups, in percentages

Selected Countries	*1971*	*1990*
USA	77.3	64.5
Sweden	82.8	74.5
France	73.0	43.0
Germany	77.1	51.7
Netherlands	79.3	43.9
United Kingdom	82.9	63.4
Ireland	82.4	59.1
Portugal	82.1	65.4
Spain	82.7	57.2

Source: *OECD*, 1992

These polices and structural changes in labour markets have brought about dramatic changes in the activity rates of older people. The reduction in the UK in the 1980s has been particularly marked but rates have recently been accelerating in most EU member states. An important European exception is Sweden, which maintains policies supporting a flexible decade of retirement and has seen activity rates for men in their fifties eroding much less. Although falling sharply in the 1980s, the UK activity rates for 55 to 64 year old men in the population of working age are among the highest in the EU (Table 13.4) although less clearly for the over 65s (Table 5).

Table 13.5 : Employment rates for men aged 65 and over, in percentages

Selected Countries	*1971*	*1990*
France	18.2	3.7
Germany	16.0	4.4
United Kingdom	19.2	8.6
Spain	25.7	3.7
Portugal	41.0	20.0
Italy	8.6	5.0
Ireland	41.1	15.3
Belgium	6.8	1.9
Denmark	47.0	23.0

Source: *OECD*, 1992

Even against this background of falling activity rates for men the more buoyant rates for older women in many member states and the 'cohort' effect mean that the overall share of 'older' people in the labour force will rise. The latest EC projections show that by 2015, a quarter of the labour force will be 50 or over (Table 13.6).

Table 13.6 : Ageing of the labour force 1990-2015 (% in age group)

Member state	*% in 50 + age group*	
	1990	*2015*
Belgium	14.1	19.2
Denmark	19.1	27.5
France	17.4	22.3
Germany	21.8	30.0
Greece	25.5	26.4
Ireland	18.3	20.3
Italy	19.6	24.2
Luxembourg	17.1	24.3
Netherlands	14.2	22.6
Portugal	21.0	25.2
Spain	18.7	21.7
United Kingdom	20.2	25.9
EU – 12	19.5	24.9

Source: *European Commission Projections*, 1993

Against this demographic backcloth it seems likely early retirement will remain a feature of employers' labour adjustment strategies across most member states. In some countries, notably Germany, pressures for rapid labour cost reduction and overcapacity in many sectors may make this a particularly attractive option. Across Europe, however, this is set to take place in a different business and social climate to that of the 1980s.

- Pension fund surpluses in occupational or private schemes, where they exist, that underpinned the ability if many of the larger employers to afford extensive and generous early retirement programmes in the 1980s, are set to be under rather greater pressure and discipline in the future.
- There is a vocal and increasingly well informed lobby on age discrimination in employment, which may have an adverse effect on mature employees' willingness to go. Certainly research is now confirming that early retirees seeking to re-enter part-or full-time work find it very difficult to do so even in tight labour market circumstances.
- US concepts of 'productive' ageing, if gaining ground this side of the Atlantic may have a similar affect on employees' attitudes and even on public policy.
- Employers will need to respond more effectively to growing exhortation by government and its agencies to tackle ageism in the workplace. Failure to do so may yet give rise to some form of voluntary campaign to combat ageism in the workplace. The EU and Parliament are likely to be considering sterner measures.
- Employers' responses to the equalisation issue on pensions and retirement age are set to make early retirement in the pattern of the 1980s a costly option.
- Any re-emergence of the skill pressures discussed earlier is set to see more organisations giving greater emphasis to the selective development and retention of mature employees.

The role and relationship of early retirement practices to wider HR policies must now be questioned. This must go deeper than the tactics of downsizing. It will need to question the apparent devaluing of age and experience in European labour markets. For this, the starting point is understanding the practices of organisations in the EU. Until the 1995 European Cranfield (CRANET-E) study, such data were not available.

The Cranfield Survey

In 1995 the survey yielded over 6,340 returns from the headquarters or corporate level of organisations, over 4,875 of which employed 200 or more people, an average of 19 percent response rate across all 15 countries. The survey provides a statistically powerful database, with the numbers of returns from each country broadly representative of population size. The survey covers all sectors of employment; and is most likely to be over-representative of larger organisations (for full methodological details see Brewster and Hegewisch, 1994).

The comparative dimension in context

Practice in the UK

Six out of every ten organisations in the UK collect data on the age structure of their own organisation, with the largest percentage (i.e. 36 percent) of these organisations reporting their average as between 41 and 50 years of age. The smallest number of organisations were in the under 30 age group and the over 50s with 8 percent and 0 percent respectively.

More than nine out of every ten organisations in the UK reported having equal opportunity/diversity policies, 79 percent of which were written. Fewer than one organisation out of every ten reported having no equal opportunity policies at all. However, when asked if older people were targeted in their recruitment process only one in every ten said yes.

The question was then asked as to whether there had been a change in the number of older recruits (over 50 years of age)? One out of every ten organisations said that they had increased the number of older recruits while over half of all organisations reported having stayed the same, and more than one in ten organisations reported having decreased their numbers of older recruits.

When asked if organisations recruited past state retirement age only one in every ten organisations in the UK said yes. Not one single organisation had any intention of doing so in the future. Of the 10 percent who said that they did recruit past state retirement age, the person recruited in the UK was most likely to be recruited into a manual position (Table 13.7).

Table 13.7: Percentage of organisations recruiting persons past state retirement age into different occupational categories (valid percentage)

Senior management post	7
Other management post	8
Prof./technical post	31
Clerical post	43
Manual post	59

Source: *CRANET-E,* 1995

It became increasingly apparent from the data that organisations were not specifically aiding the recruitment or retention of older workers when looking at the next set of data; data which reported any different methods specifically introduced to aid the recruitment or retention of older workers over the last three years. Fewer than one in every ten organisations reported introducing any of the following to aid the recruitment or retention of older workers: flexible working time; the removal of age criteria for training; re-training programmes for older workers; or phased retirement; the introduction of re-entry programmes went down to less than one in every twenty organisations. The only criterion that had more than a one in ten ratio was the removal of age criteria from recruitment advertising and then only 14 percent of all organisations reported doing so.

If the data are broken down by size and sector there are limited questions we are able to report on with any reliability due to the response rate for certain questions being very low.

However, from the data we can address the organisations most likely to collect data on age structure in the UK are those in manufacturing followed by the public sector and then private sector services. The average age across sectors also varies, with the older on average tending to be in manufacturing and the younger more likely to be in services. The public sector falls between both on the continuum. If this question is broken down by size we see no significant differences between organisations with more than 1,000 employees and those with less. However, the average age of employees differs between these groups with organisations of less than 1,000 employees most likely to have their highest averages in the 40 to 50 years of age group and the more than 1,000 employees group having their highest average in the under 30 years of age group. As one would expect organisations most likely to have written equal opportunity/diversity policies are in the public sector and such organisations are also most likely to have more than 1,000 employees, also representative of the public sector.

In the UK, the private services sector is most likely to target people over 50 in recruitment. These figures however are from a very low base of only 15 percent of organisations surveyed. There is no difference in the targeting of older workers between organisations of different sizes.

The only other reliable data broken down by size and sector concern the issue of whether there has been a change in the proportions of older recruits over the last three years. Most organisations reported, in sum, that the numbers had remained the same across all sectors and sizes of organisation in the UK. Broadly speaking there has been a small decrease in the population of older recruits across the economy.

The wider EU dimension

In June 1995 the Employment and Social Affairs Council of the European Commission adopted a resolution on the employment of older people. It called for measures to avoid their exclusion from labour markets and to make the most of their experience. However the situation of older people is barely touched on in the Commission's employment progress and strategy report of October 1995 and part of the follow-up to the European Council declaration issued at Essen in December 1994. The meeting of EU Social Affairs Ministers in December 1995 failed to agree about a programme of follow up actions and a final report was not developed until December 1996 for the European Council meeting in Ireland.

Research compiled for the Employment Department (Moore, Tilson and Whitting) in 1994 looked at employment practices in 22 countries and found little evidence to show that legislation against ageism is successful. In the following section we consider the policy and practices already in place in organisations across Europe since 1994 and compare them to those of the UK.

More than half of all organisations across Europe collect data on the age structures of their workforces. In Belgium, western Germany, France and the Netherlands this increases to more than eight out of every ten organisations. The range of the average age of the workforce across Europe however, is extremely varied. For instance, in Ireland and Italy the greatest number of organisations are reported in the 30 years or less category, in Belgium, western Germany, the Netherlands and Switzerland it is the 36 to 40 year age group and alongside the UK with a 41 to 50 years average age are Denmark, Finland, France, eastern Germany, Norway and Sweden.

When broken down by sector and size of organisation we can see that there is very little difference in the average age of organisations and that of the national averages. In the manufacturing breakdown a point worth noting is that in three countries, Ireland, Norway and Sweden, a minority of organisations actually have an average age of over 50; and in Finland, Sweden and in the UK the services sectors have a slightly lower age average than thc national average; smaller organisations with slightly lower than the national average age of employees were recorded in Spain and the UK; larger organisations only differed in averages in Ireland, the Netherlands and Switzerland, where the average ages of employees were slightly higher.

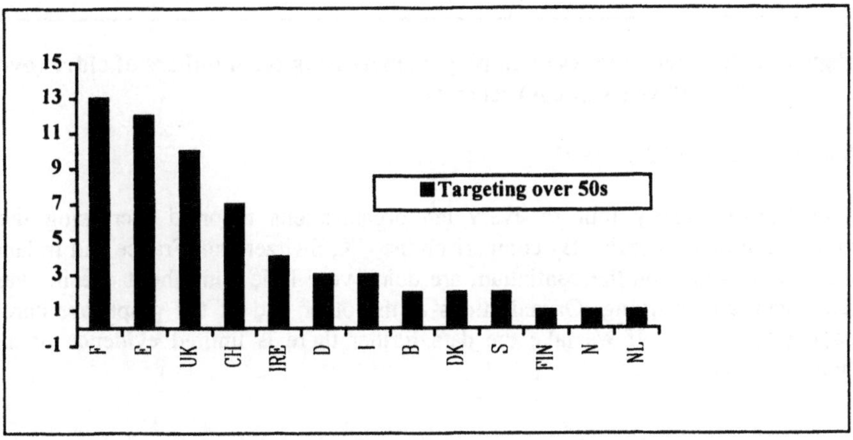

Figure 13.1: Percentages of organisations targeting older people in their recruitment processes

Source: *CRANET-E,* 1995

There were relatively few organisations across Europe who targeted over 50s as part of their recruitment processes, which left reduced numbers to break the data down further. However, in general organisations in services were more likely to target people over 50 than those in manufacturing, with this result being similarly reported for public sector organisations, where the sample size was large enough to compare. The interesting exception from these results was for that of the UK public sector organizations, which were less likely to target older people than those in manufacturing, remembering that over 90 per cent of UK public sector employers have written equal opportunities policies.

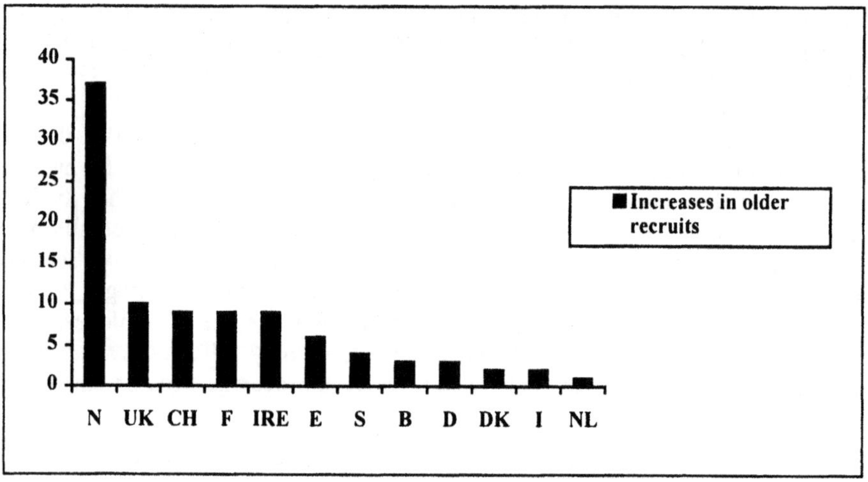

Figure 13.2: Percentages of employers increasing the numbers of older (over 50 years of age) recruits

Source: *CRANET-E,* 1995

In Norway nearly four in every ten organisations reported increasing their numbers of older recruits. By comparison the UK, Switzerland, France and Ireland, the countries next on the continuum are doing very little with about one in every ten organisations trying. Organisations at the other end of the graph are barely paying lip service. If we take the data further there is limited evidence of any significant activity.

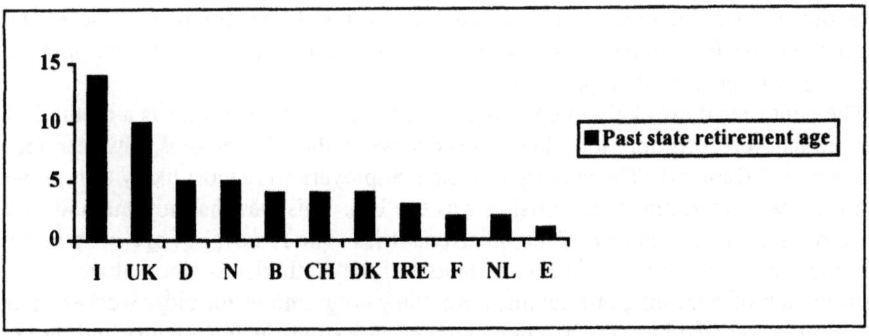

Figure 13.3: Percentages of employers recruiting people past state retirement age

Source: *CRANET-E*, 1995

With the exceptions of Italy and Turkey very few organisations recruit persons past state retirement age. Following these two countries UK employers are nearly twice as likely to be so as those in the remaining countries and even then only one in every ten UK employers reported this practice. No UK employers intended to adopt this practice in the future.

In general, where the practice of recruiting past state retirement is reported, the following table (13.8) highlights the occupational categories into which they are appointed. Only those countries with sufficient numbers to make worthwhile analysis have been used.

Table 13.8 : Percentages of employers recruiting past state retirement to different occupational categories

Country	B	CH	D	DK	N	T	UK
Senior Managers	31	29	0	6	11	41	7
Other managers	15	0	6	11	0	55	8
Prof./Technical	39	29	12	33	63	50	31
Clerical	0	0	12	11	16	17	43
Manual	31	43	71	72	21	12	59

Source: *CRANET-E*, 1995

We can see from this table that the practice of recruiting past state retirement to different occupational categories is quite varied across Europe, with the Turks recruiting most into the other management category; the Belgians and Norwegians recruiting into professional and technical posts; but in general most people recruited past state retirement age are recruited into manual positions.

We saw from the previous section that UK employers did not fare very well when it came to introducing different methods specifically to aid the recruitment or retention of older workers over the last three years. If we compare these to the results to those from other countries we get a very varied picture. However, in some countries we see a much improved one.

The countries most likely to be introducing flexible working time as a method of recruitment or retention for older workers were the Netherlands, Switzerland, Norway and Denmark. The country in which employers were most likely to remove age criteria in recruitment advertising was the UK. This was the only method that the UK used more than any of the other countries. The removal of age criteria for training was only dominant in Switzerland and the Netherlands stood alone in the introduction of retraining programmes. Re-entry programmes for older workers had not been introduced in more than one in ten organisations in any country and by far the most commonly introduced method was from phased retirement.

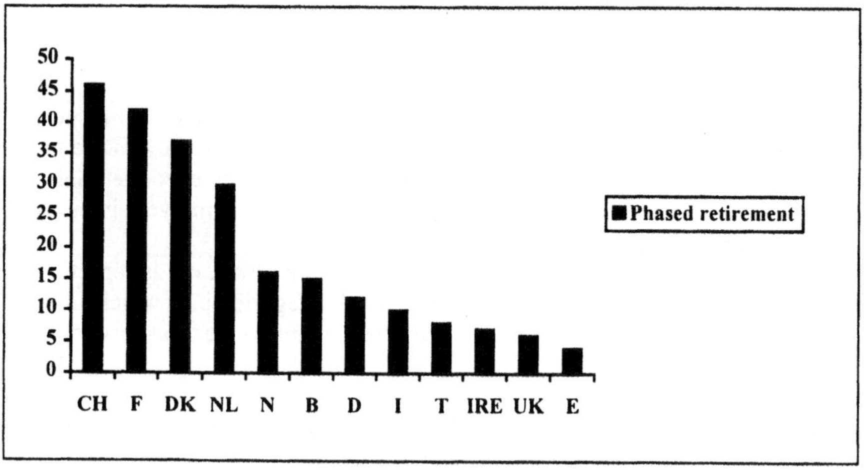

Figure 13.4: Percentages of employers introducing phased retirement to aid the recruitment and retention of workers over 50 in the past three years

Source: CRANET-E, 1995

Switzerland was the country most likely to use a combination of different methods such as the introduction of flexible working time, raising or removing age criteria for training, retraining programmes and phased retirement designed to aid recruitment or retention. Most countries, similarly to the UK, concentrated on one method as an aid, but to a greater degree than the UK. The Netherlands concentrated on re-training programmes with more than four out of every ten organisations introducing it. In France, and Denmark the impetus was in the use of phased retirement with 42 percent and 37 percent of employers using it respectively. Norway preferred the introduction of flexible working time with a quarter of all organisations introducing it as a method. Spain, eastern Germany, Italy, Ireland and Turkey had relatively low levels of all methods.

Issues and implications

The workforce in the UK and continental Europe is greying. This is not a surprise to corporate strategists or HR practitioners. The publication in Britain in 1988 of *Young People and the Labour Market* by the National Economic Development Office (Parsons, 1988) and the surrounding media 'hype' saw the demographic issue rise high on the agenda of many human resource (HR) strategists. Similar concerns were being reported in Germany, France and the Netherlands. In the late 1980s it seemed that no European discussion on so-called education and training and recruitment was complete without drawing on the demographic imperative. As late as Spring 1990, demographic changes in the UK were being cited by seven out of ten HR managers as a key factor determining their employment strategies for the 1990s.

The comparative data reported here together with other national research suggests that this interest has not been translated into action at organisational level. However after 1990 the business environment changed radically. Personnel priorities were once again focused on survival. Research by the Institute of Personnel Management (IPM) showed that, by early Spring 1992, only two in ten HR managers in Britain continued to think about demographic changes for personnel strategies for the 1990s. More broadly-based research by the Swiss based Institute for Management Development (IMD) showed an even lower profile for age-related employer initiatives elsewhere in continental Europe. This shift to reduced concern in the early to mid 1990s owe much to cost cutting and downsizing and unemployment. But it also suggests managerial short-sightedness and misunderstanding of the enduring nature of changes taking place in the shape and structure of the UK workforce (Parsons 1989).

The longest UK recession for half a century diverted management attention until the late 1990s from the need for employers to start to adapt their employment practices to the changing composition of the workforce. The demographic imperative of an ageing workforce has continued to be strong into the twenty first century.

The difficulties may not be dramatic but the need to understand their effects on employment practices must be anticipated. As in the late 1980s those who 'wait and see' are finding themselves again beset by skill and even labour shortages in many parts of the country with little option but to buy their way out of trouble (Parsons, 1990). Some have been finding the 'cure' more crippling than the disease.

In the UK the speed and extent to which skill problems are acting as constraints on organisational performance are not easy to anticipate. Much depends on various, capital or labour intensive, ways in which post-recessionary investment and development is being translated into external recruitment.

The jury is still out on the issue of what has been happening in the UK with the 'experts' divided in their forecasts. Personnel strategists should find little ground for complacency in recent years' uncertainties about the changing nature of labour demand.

UK personnel strategists should recognise that skill constraints have re-emerged as barriers to the performance and competitiveness of many organisations. Such problems have been happening in more varied ways and more quickly than in the recovery from and in the aftermath of other recessions. This is not the place, however, to explore the reasons, but in large measure it will be because HR professionals have taken their eye off the skill and labour supply ball. Too many have failed to recognise the deep seated nature of the changes taking place in the workforce composition, and in particular the ageing working population. As these pressures become more acute it may be that the casualties of corporate downsizing in the 1980s and 1990s, the over 40s will be seen as a key labour source in flexible labour markets.

Note

[1] Extensive statistical information and commentary (not considered here) on wider labour force trends and prospects relating to the greying workforce and on some of the external labour market issues (e.g. trainability of older people) is available from independent organisations such as IMS, PSI, HOST, IER and others. In the US the internal labour market issues have been given greater attention and have done much to keep the ageing of the workforce high on corporate agendas against a similar economic backcloth.

References

Berry-Lound, D.J. (1991), 'Targeting mature workers', *Employment Gazette,* Vol. 99, No. 1, pp. 27-43.

Berry-Lound, D.J. (1992), *Older Workers and Current Employment Practice,* The HOST Consultancy, Horsham.

Brislin, R.W. (1970), 'Back translation for cross-cultural research', *Journal of Cross-cultural Psychology*, Vol. 1, pp. 185-216.

Brislin, R.W., Lounder, W.J. and Thorndike, R.M. (1973), *Cross-cultural Research Methods*, Wiley-interscience, London.

Brewster, C., Hegewisch, A., Mayne, L. and Tregaskis, O. 'Methodology of the Price Waterhouse Cranfield Project', in C. Brewster and A. Hegewisch (eds), *Policy and Practice in European Human Resource Management: The Price Waterhouse Cranfield Survey*, Routledge, London.

Carnegie Inquiry (1993), *Life, Work and Livelihood in the Third Age,* Final Report, Carnegie Inquiry into the Third Age, London.

Derr, B. and Woods, J. (1992), *HR2000, Practitioners' Perspective*, Institute of Personnel Management, Wimbledon.

Drury, E. (ed.) (1993), *Age Discrimination against Older Workers in the EC: a Comparative Analysis,* Eurolink Age, London.

Employment Observatory (1993), *Employment in Europe*, No. 15. EC, Brussels.

Eurostat (1993), *Older People in the European Community - Population and Employment*, Rapid Reports: Population and Social Conditions 1993:1, Eurostat, Luxembourg, EN, FR, DE.

IPM (1993), *Age and Employment Practices: Policies, Attitudes and Practices,* Institute of Personnel Management, London.

KPMG (1990), *Europe 1992, Trends and Development in Human Resource Management,* KPMG Peat Marwick Management Consultants, London.

OECD (1992), *Employment Outlook*, July 1992.

Parsons, D.J. (1988), *Young People and the Labour Market,* National Economic and Development Office and Training Commission, London.

Parsons, D.J. (ed.) (1989), *Defusing the Demographic Time Bomb,* National Economic Development Office and Training Agency, London.

Parsons D.J. (1990), 'Winning the workers: rising to the demographic challenge' *Employment Gazette,* Vol. 98, No. 2, February.

Parsons D. (1994), *The Labour Market Patterns of Ageing in the European Community*, paper presented at The European Conference on Investing in Older People at Work, HEA. London.

Taylor, P. and Walker, A. (1993), 'Employers and Older Workers', *Employment Gazette*, Vol. 101, No. 4, pp. 371-78.

Thompson, M. (1991), *Last in the Queue: Corporate Employment Policies and the Older Worker,* Institute of Manpower Studies, Brighton.

Trinder, C., Hulme, G. and McCarthy, U. (1992), *Employment: the Role of Work in the Third Age,* Research paper No. 1. Carnegie Inquiry into the Third Age, London.

Walker, A., Alber, J. and Guillemard, A. M. (1993), *Older People in Europe: Social and Economic Policies*, Commission of the European Communities, Brussels.

Whitting G., Moore J. and Tilson B. (1995), 'Employment Policies and Practices Towards Older Workers: an International Overview', in *Employment Gazette*, April, pp. 147-52.

14 Ageism in the 'Quarter Acre, Pavlova Paradise'- will she be right?*

Graham Elkin

Introduction

New Zealand has an ageing workforce and a growing economy. These two factors have come together to bring about some shortage of skills (*Otago Daily Times, February, 15, 1995)* and virtually full employment. This chapter chronicles the growing age dependency of the population together with the creation of new jobs that is likely to bring this about. A series of alternatives to the likely competition for labour are considered. In particular, strategies designed to free women from the eldercare burden so as to remain in and return to the workforce are discussed in the context of the burden of eldercare generally. More enlightened attitudes to older people and their possible contribution to solving the labour shortage are explored. This involves a move from Static Flexibility in attitudes to employees through Transitional Flexibility to a Radical Flexibility in employment.

The greying of New Zealand

In common with most of the 'western' world, New Zealand is experiencing its own demographic transition. Low rates of fertility have led to a reducing number of young people in the population. At the same time declining mortality has led to the increasing size of older age groups in the population structure. In 1951, nine percent of New Zealand's population was aged 65 and over. This was higher than the 1950 levels in countries such as Australia, Canada and the United States, but less than the levels in France, Sweden and the United Kingdom. By 2020 New Zealand's elderly are expected to make up around 16 percent of the total population. This is similar to Australia. But countries such as Denmark, Finland,

* New Zealand is often described in this fashion – referring to all New Zealanders owning their own quarter acre with a house on it, serving Pavlova at every function and adopting a casual 'she'll be right' approach to life.

Sweden and Japan will have more than one in five dependent people in particular. The growth in Japan's elderly population is expected to be spectacular, with the elderly projected to increase from 5 percent to almost 25 percent of Japan's total population.

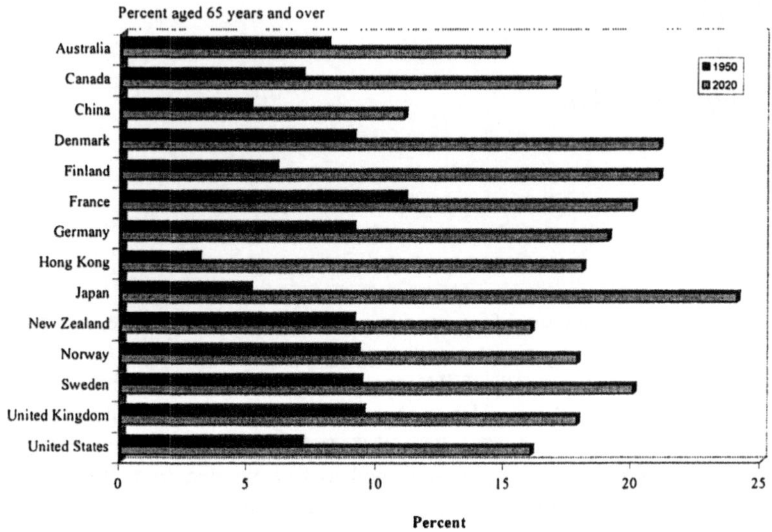

Figure 14.1: Elderly population, selected countries 1950 and 2020

Source: *65 Plus New Zealand Now,* Statistics New Zealand, May, 1995

The population of New Zealand is expected to continue to become more aged. By 2031 about 19 percent of the population will be elderly (defined in this paper as 65 years or more in age). This is up from 9.2 percent in 1951 to 11.4 percent in 1991. It represents a major shift in the balance of the nation in terms of age. The dependency ratio, calculated as those under 16 and over 65, was 52 per 100 in the population in 1952. The ratio is expected to rise to 63 per 100 by 2031. There is also a declining youth dependency ratio, which hides the real rise in the elderly dependent. Changes in the labour force dependency, rate calculated as the proportion of those over 65 compared to the working age population, are far more dramatic (Figure 14.2). There were seven working-age people to each elderly person in 1951. By 1991 it had fallen to six and by the year 2031 there will be just three people of working age to each elderly person.

If we consider the ratio of people actually working to the elderly we see a workforce moving from 1.6 million (with 2.2 million aged between 15 and 65 from a population of 3.4 million in 1991) to a workforce of 2.0 million (with 2.8 million aged between 15 and 65 years from a total population of 4.6 in 2031). The net result is for there to be a rise from 24 elderly for every 100 workers in the workforce to 45 per 100 workers in 2031.

This rise has large scale implications for the sustainability of the national guaranteed retirement income (superannuation), the provision of residential care facilities and the need for working aged people to forego some part of their work to care for elderly people.

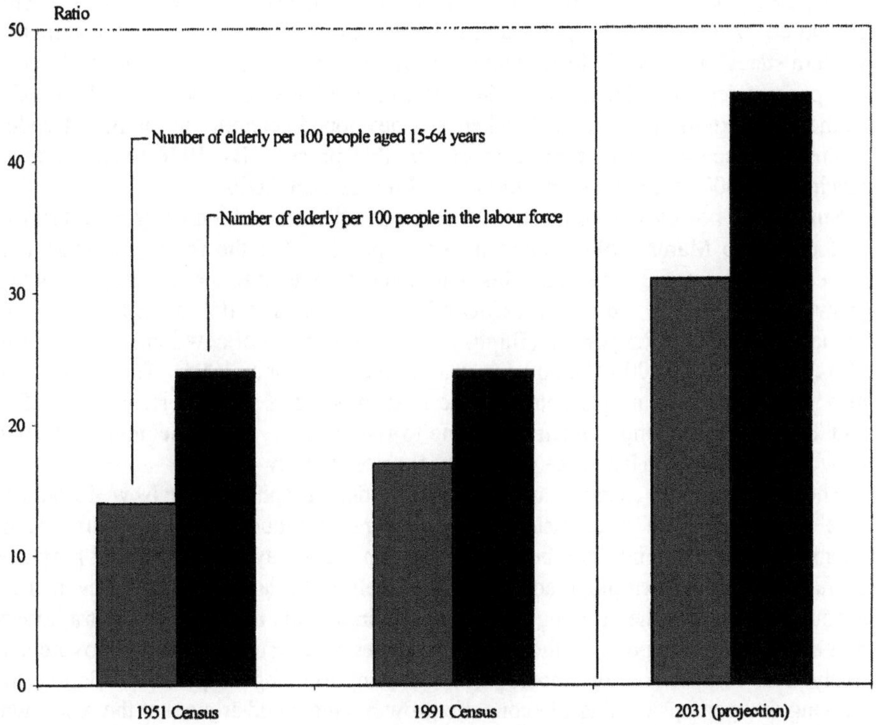

Figure 14.2: Elderly dependency ratios 1951, 1991 and 2031

Source: 65 *Plus: New Zealand Now,* Statistics New Zealand, May, 1995, p. 21

The growing economy

In the 1950s New Zealand had one of the highest standards of living in the world. During the 1950s and 1960s a decline in that standard set in. The 1970s and 1980s saw economic growth settled at around 1.5 percent per annum. Countries which were comparable with New Zealand in 1950 now achieve two and three times as much

Gross Domestic Product per head of population each year. The reasons for this decline are open to dispute but it is clear that the increasing reliance on government intervention, the growth of protectionism and statutory regulation of industrial relations are part of the reason for the decline. Until the early 1990s the rate of growth of the New Zealand economy was among the lowest in the developed world. The economy stagnated and local industry survived with protection from imports and from new working practices.

In 1984 the fourth Labour Government was elected. The subsequent events amounted to 'changing the political culture of one of the world's most entrenched welfare states'. Campbell-Hunt, Harper and Hamilton (1995) asserted that 'the scope and pace of economic liberalisation in New Zealand have been judged by the OECD as the most extensive of any undertaken in a developed economy in the past decade'. There were some initial negative results of this process. By 1988 unemployment reached 100,000 for the first time and in 1992 it rose to 200,000.

Since 1992 however there has been increased and sustained higher growth. Growth in the year to March 1994 amounted to five percent. For the following years it is projected to average 3.8 percent. This is in marked contrast to the last 20 years when growth averaged only 1.6 percent. Unemployment peaked at 10.9 percent in 1991. In January 1995 it was 7.5 percent (Birch, 1995). The number of new jobs in the year to March 1994 was 57,000 (64,000 for year ended November 1994). Thirty thousand new jobs every year are predicted for the next three years. The projections for 2003 and 2004 are for unemployment to decline to five percent. By the beginning of 1996 New Zealand had also had three years of near price stability.

The result of these changes and the changing demographics is for New Zealand to face the prospect of a consistent and fairly rapid reduction in the numbers of unemployed to the point, long before 2031, when there may for all practical purposes be full or even over employment. There are likely to be labour shortages even if no account is taken for the growing dependency ratio and the reduction of the traditional non-aged workforce pool. Without new strategies one result of over employment is likely to be competition for labour, perhaps leading to rising wage rates, inflation, the slowing and perhaps ceasing of economic growth. One could argue that the result will be an economic level that is appropriate to the balance of the population that exists.

Alternative strategies in full employment

It is appropriate and perhaps prudent to consider alternative responses to the labour market pressure that full employment may bring. Many of these involve those who are commonly called 'the elderly'. A first alternative is to extend the working life. Worsley (1996) noted that the twentieth century has provided each of us with three extra decades of useful life. In New Zealand the age of retirement (or to be correct the age for entitlement to the Guaranteed Retirement Income) is gradually being raised to 65 years by 1999. If the 1991 elderly labour force ratio (24 per 100) were to be maintained then the retirement age would need to be raised to the mid seventies by the year 2031. This gradual raising can be seen in a variety of ways as imposing the burden of work on many who do not want to work or alternatively it can be seen as the end of discrimination against those who are 60 or 65 years old.

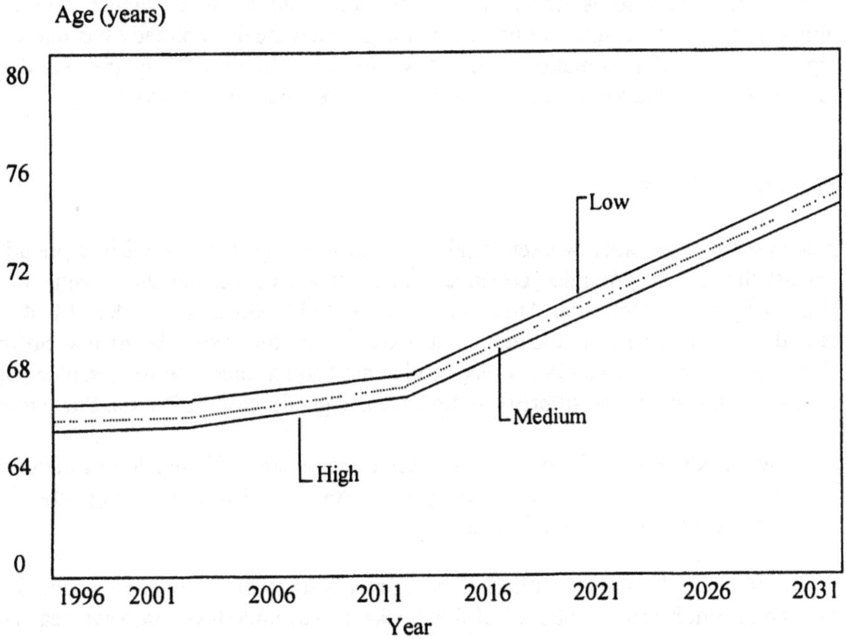

Figure 14.3: Adjusted retirement age to maintain the 1991 level of elderly dependency, by labour force projection, 1991- 2031

Source: *65 Plus: New Zealand Now*, p. 21

In 1991 more than 31 percent of women participated in the workforce. There has been a growing recognition of the need for and sporadic provision of crêche and child care facilities throughout New Zealand. Most New Zealand organisations are tiny by world standards. It is unlikely that corporate crêches have much future in this country. They are few in number and normally only in the largest organisations. Even if there was widespread provision of child care it would only ease the situation a little due to the eldercare burden that has many women, and it is largely women, caring for their own and their husbands' parents. Walker (1996) wrote: 'As a workforce issue eldercare surfaced less than ten years ago. A survey of 1050 major US employers by Hewitt Associates found 26 percent offered eldercare benefits in 1995 - more than double the number offering such benefits in 1990'. An underlying and so far relatively intractable problem is that a growing number of women who could work do not do so because of eldercare responsibility.

A study by 65 plus suggests that workforce growth may come from immigration. This issue is already emotionally charged in New Zealand - in particular with respect to Asian immigrants. It is unlikely that large scale immigration will be adopted as a policy. New Zealand is developing its services, tourism in particular. These are unlikely areas for the substitution of technology. New Zealand already has one of the highest usages of information technology products and services in the world, and further large scale growth from the substitution of technology is unlikely.

Prejudice and age

Attempts to value older workers tend to be thwarted by well established prejudices against them. Age prejudice continues largely unabated despite the passing of the Human Rights Commission Amendment Act in 1992. Anecdotal evidence that such prejudice is widespread abounds. For example at the 1993 Women's Suffrage Conference Hekia Parata (1993) reported having had an interview for a senior public sector position and being surprised to find age and gender discrimination. She wrote:

> I was asked how old I was, presumably as some sort of indication of maturity. I said 'My father's 73 and he has yet to grow up'. Biological longevity is not necessarily an indicator of maturity.

In 1993 the only study of attitudes among managers to older people was carried out by Darren Smith (see chapter 12 of this book). It was undertaken in New Zealand to address the issue of age discrimination at work. It focused upon the stereotypes held by members of the New Zealand Institute of Personnel Management (IPMNZ) about older non-managerial workers. In general, IPMNZ members view older non-managerial workers as more reliable, more interpersonally skilled and more loyal than their younger counterparts. Older non-managerial workers were also viewed to be less accepting of new technology, less adaptable to change, less suited to learning quickly and less interested in training than younger workers. The study reproduced the results of Peter Warr's British work and found similar results.

It could be argued that personnel managers are more liberally minded than the population at large. The evidence for negative stereotypes in terms of acceptance of new technology and change along with less ability to learn quickly and training are ominous.

Worsley (1996) cited six broad headings of business reasons why employers need an older element in their workforces. The first is return on investment. Older workers are more likely to have significant service with an employer. They represent a heavy investment in training and a wealth of accumulated experience, which is expensive to waste. Second, older workers are a source of skill and labour on which employers may come to depend when traditional sources are exhausted. Third, if older people are not considered in recruitment the best people may not be taken into account. Fourth, the age profile of customers is increasingly changing and employers will need to reflect that change in their workforces. Fifth, older workers are the memory of older people who have within their heads the lessons of experience, ones that are not written down. Lastly, employers increasingly wish to be seen as good employers.

The most publicised British organisation in this respect is B & Q, a national chain of DIY and building suppliers. They staffed a complete store with people over 55. The productivity of the store outstripped all the others in the group. They discovered that older people have a fund of information about home renovations, and are stable, committed and effective employees. Tesco, Sainsbury's, Marks and Spencer and numerous other employers have followed the example.

Eldercare

The revaluing of the skills of older workers comes at a time of an increasing eldercare burden. A substantial and growing proportion of the aged need care. For economic reasons, for example it costs more than most people earn to care for an institutionalised or disabled parent, women are choosing to care for their parents and their husband's parents and not to work. While the ability of women to earn the same as a man remains less the norm and more the exception there are economic reasons as well as cultural reasons for the burden to fall upon women rather than men. There are also compelling moral and cultural reasons for women to care for their parents.

The results of an early study of the Travelers company in 1985 (Worsley, 1996) showed that 28 percent of the workforce over 30 were found to be providing some form of care for an older person. On average their responsibilities took between six and ten hours each week, but eight percent of employees put in at least 35 hours per week. One third of people were helping more than one person. On average the eldercare lasted for five and a half years.

Even where there are few requests for help with eldercare problems through existing Employee Assistance Programmes, there is enormous interest from employees whenever a workshop on eldercare is arranged. Pathfinders, a case management and consulting service in Scarsdale, New York, developed eldercare workshops for Mobil Corporation and Consolidated Edison of New York. Ten times as many people enrolled in the workshops as sought help through Employee Assistance Programmes (Birch, 1995). When IBM established an eldercare help line in parallel with its child care line it took twice the number of calls already received concerning child care (Worsley, 1996).

In Britain the Carers National Association estimated that 1.5 million carers live with the person they care for and that 75 percent of the carers care for an elderly person. In the UK one in nine of all full-time workers are carers according to the Family Policies Study Centre (65 Plus, May 1995). Twenty-five percent of all 45 to 64 year old workers are carers. In 1995 Buck Consultants (Walker, 1996) surveyed 313 employers in New York and found that 37 percent offer resources and referral on eldercare.

Even with rapid growth of female participation in the workforce eldercare remains largely women's work. A study in the USA in 1982 (cited in Birch, 1995) found that 80 percent of care giving employees were women with 50 percent reporting themselves as being the chief provider. The majority of carers are women even where the person needing care is the husband's parent.

The Travelers study (Campbell-Hunt, Harper and Hamilton, 1995) found that 40 percent of the carers also cared for school age children. A national survey of carers conducted in 1989 by the Older Women's League (Walker, 1996) reported that while women can expect to spend 17 years of their life bringing up children, they can expect to spend 18 years helping an ageing parent. These carers are commonly described in the American literature as a 'sandwich generation' caught between two demands, both of which interfere with family and work life. A UK Family Policies Study Centre paper (65 Plus, May 1995) pointed out:

> The years of middle age, a period of their lives when women are most likely to be returning to full participation in the labour market, are precisely those years when they are most likely to face the responsibilities of caring for other, older dependants. This may entail, perhaps, irreconcilable demands of work, family and domestic responsibilities.

This burden is increasing quickly and is preventing the flexibility that is needed to encourage women to stay at work or to return to it. It may be time for more organisations to take the initiative and free some women and a few men from the parent care task so they can work. In a study by Transamerica Life (Parata, 1993), emotional strain was reported by 80 percent of caregiving employees and physical strain by 55 percent. In addition a range of social disruptions was reported by more than 50 percent. Other studies have found that care givers are more likely than non-care givers to experience anxiety, depression, mental and physical ill-health. A two year study at the University of Maryland School of Nursing found that carers were three times more likely to report anxiety symptoms and four times more likely to report anger than the general population.

A 1987 study (see Smith, 1993) indicates substantial proportions of working women reported that parent care had resulted in misses work (58 percent), work interruptions (47 percent), loss of pay (18 percent), regretting their choice to work (17 percent), and loss of energy to do their work well (15 percent).

Care givers are also known to miss opportunities for career advancement, to refuse job travel, to turn down promotion and to forego valuable training and overtime. Forty-two percent of the care givers in the Transamerica study (Parata, 1993) had given up holiday time to care for elderly relatives. Many women use benefits such as sick leave, personal time off and vacation time to provide for their elderly parents rather than maintaining their own mental health and wellbeing.

A Philadelphia study (see Smith, 1993) of 150 families in which married women provided most of the care for their widowed mothers, found that 28 percent of the non-working women had left their jobs to care for their mothers and that 26 percent of employed women had considered stopping work for the same reason. In Britain half of all women carers feel that they were prevented from going out to work. Thirty percent felt they were restricted in the hours they could work, while ten percent had to take time off to look after dependants (Worsley, 1996).

As the number of employees who care for elders increases, the workplace is affected directly. Carers bring their worries and concerns to work. They also bring the aftermath and consequences of their commitment. Numerous and lengthy phone calls, tardiness, excessive absenteeism, unscheduled time off and lost concentration can reduce productivity and increase costs.

In 1984 the New York Business Group on Health surveyed its member firms (cited in Walker, 1996) and found that reports of lateness and absenteeism were linked to the care of elderly relatives. Seventy-three percent of the 90 organisations responding reported unscheduled absences as a consequence, 60 percent noted excessive phone use, 60 percent cited visible signs of stress and about 50 percent reported a decrease in productivity and quality of work. Almost none had taken an action to deal with eldercare. Other studies show similar results. A common theme was the loss of some of the most valuable people at critical times in their careers.

Corporate responses

A growing number of companies in the US are responding to the eldercare problem with a range of initiatives. They point the way for New Zealand employers and for those wishing to negotiate conditions more suited to women in the workplace. New Zealand and Australia (Stone, 1995) are however slow to follow the practices overseas. The New Zealand 1995 Work and Family Directions report (Ministry of Women's Affairs and Equal Employment Opportunities Trust [MWAEEOT], 1995) contains information on the best practice in terms of family friendliness. None of the 50 pages makes a single reference to any help with eldercare.

The first need of employees under eldercare pressure is for information. Eighty percent of care givers indicate that they need more information; information about the process of ageing, about how the employer can help with the problem, and external services and support. All companies taking any initiative in the eldercare field provide information. Sometimes it is the only action taken. Some employers, such as Pepsico Inc. (cited in Walker, 1996), provide a resource guide for carers. It is usually a collection of material on the process of ageing and sources for help. Some guides list contact people paid by the employer to find the support needed.

Some organisations arrange in-house seminars and 'Care Fairs'. A Care Fair is a meeting of eldercare suppliers offering services held at the employer's premises with presentations, seminars, resources and stalls. Often held partly in worktime and partly at lunchtime and after work, they bring together those with needs and those with services. Libraries, take-home videos and resource centres have been developed at Travelers and many other companies. A small number of organisations, such as Travelers, arrange groups for the mutual support of carers. With the aid of a facilitator or on a self-organising basis, the groups provide emotional support and the practical interchange of information.

Hot lines and telephone referral services are increasingly popular. When IBM (Worsley, 1996) established an Eldercare Hotline it received 7,000 calls in the first eight months. Seventy percent were requests for immediate help. Often these services are funded by the corporation but staffed from outside the organisation. In some cases they provide one-to-one counselling. They often provide searching facilities for care all over the country to help with the problem of distant dependants. Schering-Plough Pharmaceutical, a New Jersey based company with 10,000 domestic employees, has offered an 0800 number since 1991. In 1995 about 15 percent of the workforce used the service for eldercare help.

A number of companies have developed approaches allowing individuals more flexibility for solving their own problems. Flexitime working is the most widespread way of helping individuals to cope. In 1986 Kodak established a Work and Family Task Force. As a result the company has introduced the concept of Family Leave. Employees are allowed up to 17 weeks' unpaid leave in a two year period for family purposes. They are also developing a scheme whereby individuals can renegotiate alternative work schedules to cope with eldercare and other needs. Travelers have also introduced the Family Leave concept. The idea of Family Sick Time acknowledges that employees do take time off for child and eldercare sickness. 'Cafeteria' benefit schemes would also allow individuals to opt for time off rather than more money. In one case employees may have benefits supplied for caring for an aged relative instead of income.

A handful of companies have experimented with eldercare day centres. These facilities are partly or wholly funded by companies and allow employees to leave aged dependants in a caring and stimulating environment while they work. Wang (cited in a report by Ministry of Women's Affairs and Equal Employment Opportunities Trust, [MWAEEOT] 1995) is the best known example. With money from the administration on ageing, elderservices are providing adult day care to dependants of Wang employees over 35 years old who have completed a questionnaire on the effects of eldercare. Elderservices provides transportation and care through a number of facilities. The intention is to monitor the effects of provision of eldercare on employees. Herman Miller Inc. of Michigan (cited in Smith, 1993) makes financial contributions to Evergreen Commons, a senior centre minutes from the company. The centre provides adult day care, a noon time meal and courses for seniors.

Where there are already child care facilities, these could perhaps be made cross-generational. Parkside Human Services, Des Plaines Illinois (cited in MWAEEOT 1995), has an adult day care programme that combines age groups. It claims that combining ages is not only convenient but natural. Children benefit from the extra affection, knowledge and skills of the elderly and the elderly have an increased sense of usefulness. Such an approach would be extremely compatible with the Maori notions of extended family and responsibility. It would also facilitate the passing down of cultural traditions and the respect for elders that are important parts of the Maori way of life. Co-operative adult care centres could be established by groups of organisations. Self-help groups of the retired would be another alternative, whereby the active elderly network with and help the less active - and then eventually are helped themselves as they grow older. Employers could organise the networks.

Money can often reduce the problem of stress of long-term care of the elderly. The funding of respite care and home attendance are clearly more costly than the provision of referral services and information for self help. Already both are provided for some employees.

A radical new flexibility

Figure 14.4 shows something of the change in thinking needed. At present we have a static flexibility. We employ those who are traditionally suitable candidates. We tend to employ those who are able to arrange their whole lives around a company or their organisation as a trade off for some sense of identity and 'career'. The evidence that career and stability are largely illusory grows day by day. Few people are willing to orientate themselves around an employer. Increasingly employers will have to orientate themselves to potential employees.

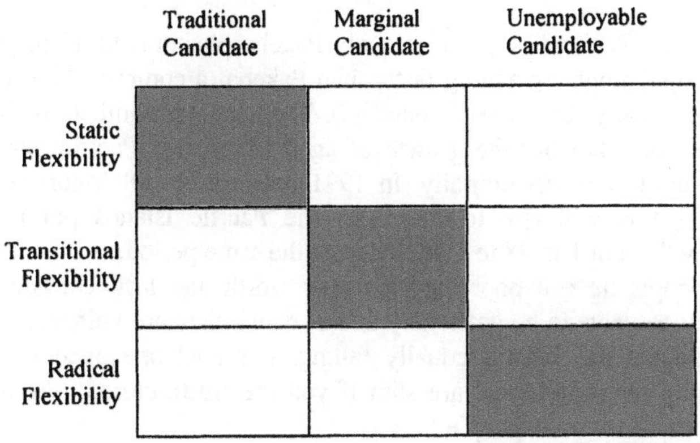

Figure 14.4: An increase in flexibility

Those who make different choices in their lives, perhaps preferring to child rear instead of working, find little flexibility in the workplace in New Zealand. They are fortunate to find family friendly workplaces and so are more generally marginalised. The gradual growth of child care facilities has generated a little flexibility and allows more women to work. It would be sensible to include eldercare in any attempts to restructure work to allow more women to participate in work and for carers to be relieved of some of the burdens that reduce their productivity.

We have been considering the need to take action concerning eldercare. Chief among the marginal candidates for employment are the able elderly themselves. A whole new attitude that rejects chronological years as the test for employment is required. We need to show some transitional flexibility to include and retain them in the workforce. Different styles of learning are required, more flexible working hours, job sharing and other arrangements may help. The elderly need the same range of alternatives that we seek for men and women with children. We also need to begin to move in our conceptions of what is meant to be old and introduce some transitional flexibility and begin to consider those who are not traditionally well suited to employment.

Those who are disabled mentally and physically, are often written off. There are also those who are mobility impaired, visually or hearing impaired. Those with only a small amount of time to offer - and then perhaps at home. It is doubtful whether the small moves to what I have called transitional flexibility will be sufficient to solve the labour shortage. We will need to move on to radical flexibility - the consideration of the disabled and the unemployable. We need to redefine what we mean by unemployable. Ken Douglas (1996) claims there are only unemployed ones. The whole education reform currently under way in New Zealand may help with this desire.

Hope from the treaty

The greying of New Zealand is not a uniquely Pakeha phenomena. Both Maori and Pacific Islands populations are ageing faster than Pakeha (a common Maori word for the largely white anglo saxon New Zealanders). The absolute numbers of Maori and Pacific Islanders are small but the growth of aged Maori and Pacific Islanders has significance culturally and bi-culturally. In 1991 only one in 40 Maori people was elderly. By 2031 this will rise to 1 in 11. The Pacific Islands population will experience a growth from 1 in 38 to 1 in 12 during the same period.

Many older people have a poor view of their worth and lack confidence in an environment they perceive to be unfriendly and in which they are vulnerable. The age for discarding people has been gradually falling. For someone aged over 40 the chances of gaining re-employment are slim if you are 'restructured'. Above 50 the chance approaches nil for most people.

It is arguable that New Zealanders live in a youth culture recently highlighted by the Olympic Games and the young role models in our advertising and mass circulation magazines. There is a pakeha tradition in New Zealand that has come from the past when young men and women settled in New Zealand. Our national icons tend to be sports people. Both the All Blacks and the Silver Ferns are young and fit. This preoccupation with youth is not shared by many Maori, Pacific Island and other cultures in New Zealand. In those cultures age has a chronological dimension. Eldership is not conferred on the young and wisdom has to do with grey hair, knowledge of the past and cultural issues!

In the past the European way of work and career has been imposed. Maori conceptions of old age differs from the European idea. For Maori and Pacific Islanders the notion of elder means just that - old age! Wisdom comes with years and older people are seen as a source of traditional and current wisdom. The ideas of old age being a burden to be borne by the children of the aged is particularly non-Maori. Respect for parents and the old is ingrained in Maori culture and may show the way ahead for the European majority in New Zealand. The Maori and/or Pacific Island view of age may become more widely accepted and age will move from being a difficulty in employment to being an advantage.

Given a change in the way we view older people and women, and a move towards more flexible working arrangements and corporate initiatives in elder care, ageism in the 'quarter acre, pavlova paradise' may turn out to be thing of the past.

References

Birch, B. [Minister of Finance], (1995), *Speech to Auckland Rotary Club*, Kingsgate Centre, 25 January 1995.

Campbell-Hunt, C., Harper, D.A. and Hamilton, R. (1995), 'National renewal and strategic change: first lessons from an early mover in deregulation', *Working Paper, Graduate School of Business and Government Management*, Victoria University of Wellington, Wellington.

Ministry of Women's Affairs and Equal Employment Opportunities Trust (MWAEEOT), (1995), *Work and Family Directions: What New Zealand Champions are Doing?*, Wellington.

Otago Daily Times 'Skills lack worries', Sealord, Tuesday, February 15, 1995.

Parata, H. (1993), 'Looking Ahead: Management, Barriers and Opportunities for Women' (Key note address), *Papers from the State Commission Women's Suffrage Conference,* State Services Commission, Wellington, 15-16 July 1993.

Smith, D. (1993), *Stereotypes about older non-managerial workers: A study of New Zealand IPM members' attitudes and comparison with UK IPM members*, Dissertation as part of B.Comm(Hons), Department of Management, University of Otago, Otago.

Stone, R. (1995), *Human Resource Management*, Wiley, Melbourne.

Walker, K. (1996), 'Eldercare Obligations', *HR Magazine,* July 1996.

Worsley, R. (1996), *Age and Employment: Why employers should think again about older workers*, Ace Books, London.

Part IV
Remedies and prospects

15 Older workers and the cult of youth: ageism in public policy

Philip Taylor

Introduction

Since the 1970s industrial decline and other economic restructuring in the UK have resulted in the premature exit of large numbers of older employees. In the face of persistently high levels of youth unemployment successive governments have joined with employers and trade unions to facilitate early exit among older workers in order to create jobs for younger people. Declining fertility and mortality rates in the UK mean that, between 1990 and 2020, the percentage of people aged over 50 in the general population will have risen from 31.2 percent to 38 percent (Walker, Guillemard and Alber, 1991). However, paradoxically, this trend appears against a background of declining numbers of older people in the labour market. The UK has experienced a substantial decline in the employment of older men since the 1950s. This accelerated in the 1970s and 1980s and resulted in three quarters of men aged 55-59, half of men aged 60-64 and less than one-tenth of men aged 65 and over being economically active in 1996 (Taylor and Walker, 1998). A similar trend has occurred among older women, although it is less steep than the male one (Guillemard, 1993).

The main factors explaining the growth of early exit from the labour market among UK workers are demand-related, particularly the recessions of the last two decades (Walker, 1985; Trinder, 1989). According to Trinder (1989), older workers have been affected in three ways. First, their share of employment has fallen most in declining industries and increased least in industries where there has been growth. Second, they are both more likely to be dismissed than younger ones and less likely to find employment if they are made redundant (see Labour Market Trends, 1998 pp. S46 and; Potter, 1996). Third, for organisations needing to shed staff quickly, it has been relatively easy to negotiate early retirement for those close to retirement age. Rather than signifying an increasing trend towards early retirement in order to enjoy a 'happier old age', research suggests that the major factor in explaining falling levels of economic activity has been a deterioration in the labour market. Thus the situation in which many older workers have found themselves might be more correctly described as form of unemployment than a form of retirement (Casey and Laczko, 1989).

What is, in effect, premature retirement for many older people is not a universally preferred option but is forced upon them as the result of job loss and a fruitless search for employment. Such people who are often, in effect, early retired although they lack the economic security which might provide them with the opportunity to classify themselves as such, are caught between the twin pressures of an inhospitable labour market and a need to be in paid employment. Young and Schuller (1991) described this as the 'age trap'. Unemployed older workers report feelings of loss and stigmatisation, that they are discouraged from seeking employment, that their prospects of finding work again are poor and that, even where jobs are available, these are often only part-time or low paid (e.g. see Taylor and Walker, 1991; Walker, 1985; Young and Schuller, 1991). Contrary to the popular image of the older worker winding down before retirement, many unemployed older people report high levels of employment commitment and poor psychological well-being as a result of being out of work (Jackson and Taylor, 1994). This chapter reviews developments in public policies towards older workers in the last 20 years. It will show that, despite supposed growing awareness among policy makers, radical policies which might have a significant effect on older workers' employment patterns have yet to emerge.

Employers' policies, practices and attitudes

A number of studies have been conducted among UK employers in order to assess their attitudes, policies and practices towards older workers. Research indicates that few have developed strategies geared to the recruitment or retention of older workers. For example, Taylor and Walker (1994) found that, among larger employers, less than a fifth were seeking to recruit more older people, and less than a tenth had in place a gradual retirement scheme or were encouraging later retirement. In addition, 15 percent specified age bars in recruitment advertisements and 43 percent stated that age was an important consideration in the recruitment of staff. According to employers, factors discouraging recruitment and employment of older workers were that they lacked the appropriate skills, the pay-back period on training, maximum recruitment ages and pension scheme rules.

A study of local authorities conducted by Itzin and Phillipson (1993) found that these were only just beginning to introduce 'positive' older worker policies. In addition, line managers' attitudes towards, and beliefs about, older workers were identified by senior management respondents as being significant obstacles to the recruitment, training and promotion of older workers. Moreover, Warr and Pennington (1993) conducted a survey of personnel managers and found that, while older workers were seen as being more effective than average in terms of experience, loyalty, reliability, conscientiousness and team working, they were also seen as being less adaptable.

Young and Schuller (1991) describe the development of segmentation of the life-cycle and argue that this is primarily the result of growth in the role of the state which began with the introduction of compulsory schooling and the state pension. They identify three 'age classes': the young, those of prime working age, and the old, and argue that each can be ranked according to its status with those people of working age first, the young second and the old third. The ages at which people enter each age class are not fixed. In the following sections the recent history of public policies towards younger and older workers is briefly discussed. It will be shown that the state has played an important role in extending the length of time many people will spend in the third age class. It will also be shown that, in terms of public policy, younger people have tended to fare much better than older workers.

Public policies towards older workers in the 1970s and 1980s

Until recently, government policy was overtly aimed at removing older people from the labour market. During the recessions of the mid 1970s and early 1980s, when the UK experienced a simultaneous contraction of full-time employment and high numbers of young people entering the labour market, older people were actively encouraged to take early retirement (Walker, 1985). Youth unemployment was given a high priority by government. This led to the introduction of the Job Release Scheme in 1977, which was intended to help alleviate unemployment among younger workers by providing allowances for men and women to retire one year prior to the state pension age if their employer replaced them with a previously unemployed person. The programme was closed in 1988 (Casey and Wood, 1994). In addition, from 1981 unemployed men in the age range 60-64 were offered additional income support if they withdrew from the unemployment register (Walker and Taylor, 1993). Moreover, older workers were discouraged from seeking work by Job Centre staff (Taylor and Walker, 1991).

Policies towards older workers between 1990 and 1997

Since the early 1990s there has been an apparent shift in policy in favour of older workers. With the expansion of the UK economy in the second half of the 1980s, coupled with the so-called 'demographic time-bomb' of falling numbers of younger labour market entrants, the government introduced a series of measures aimed at encouraging older people to remain in or to re-enter the labour market. These included the abolition, in 1989, of the earnings rule which penalised people who worked beyond the state pension age earning more than £75 per week. In 1993 the government set up a Ministerial Advisory Group on Older Workers.

Also in 1993, the age limit for access to Training for Work (TfW), the main government training programme for long-term unemployed people, was raised from 59 years to 63 years. However, as has been pointed out elsewhere (Taylor and Walker, 1997) this overlooked the fact that the 1995 operating agreement between the government and TECs to administer TfW stated that first priority on the programme should be given to people aged 18 to 24. In addition, TECs were not obliged to give training providers bonuses for taking on older workers, unlike other disadvantaged groups.

In addition, legislation against unfair dismissal (Employment Protection (Consolidation) Act 1978) does not apply where an employee has reached a organisation's 'normal' age of retirement provided that the age of retirement is the same for men and women (IRS, 1993). On the other hand, it has been established that a person's age alone is insufficient grounds for making them redundant. An industrial tribunal upheld the claim of three workers aged between 61 and 62 who were made redundant on the grounds of their age that their dismissals were unfair (Equal Opportunities Review, 1994).

An ideological belief in the need for an unfettered labour market meant that the previous Conservative government consistently expressed its opposition to legislation outlawing age discrimination in employment. Instead it favoured a voluntary approach. For example, in 1993 it launched the 'Getting-On' campaign which aimed to make employers more aware of the issue and to help them devise policies aimed at the recruitment and retention of older workers. It included the production of a booklet providing advice and best practice case studies. The government also produced a leaflet for staff in Job Centres, *What's age got to do with it?*, which provided them with information about age discrimination.

As well as a general belief in the importance of an unfettered labour market, it was the Conservative government's view that age discrimination legislation had not been shown to discourage employers from discriminating against older workers. It commissioned research (Moore, Tilson and Whitting, 1994) which, it claimed, showed 'no conclusive evidence that anti-age discrimination legislation has been successful in improving either the economic activity rates of older workers or their employment prospects' (Employment Department press release, July 1994). A critique of this study and this interpretation of its findings has already appeared elsewhere (Taylor and Walker, 1997). Others have argued that the legislation has benefited older people (O'Meara, 1989; Ventrell-Monsees, 1993; Young and Schuller, 1991).

The issue of the legislative versus the educative approach was explored in detail in a report commissioned by the then Conservative government (Hayward, Taylor, Smith and Davies, 1997). This report was based on surveys of employers' attitudes and practices, and aimed to assess the impact of the Getting-on campaign. Not surprisingly the government claimed that this research supported its approach. For example, when asked if they preferred legislation or a voluntary approach the majority of a random sample of employers, not surprisingly, stated that they would prefer the latter. Curiously, whereas other recent studies have simply asked whether respondents were in favour of legislation this government commissioned survey asked respondents to state a preference. Put that way, it is not surprising that most employers stated that they would *prefer* a voluntary approach. However, while a majority also stated that legislation would be unlikely to work in practice, an even larger majority felt that legislation might improve the employment prospects of older workers. A large majority also felt that, because there was equal opportunities legislation in other areas there should also be age discrimination legislation.

What then of the voluntary approach? There was little evidence that the Conservative government's preferred option, education and persuasion, had improved the prospects of older workers. Hayward et al's survey of employers found that the vast majority did not mention age in their equal opportunities statements. Moreover, 87 percent thought it unlikely that they would ever do so. In addition, 20 percent stated that they advertised with either an implicit or explicit age range and 32 percent stated that redundancy decisions were made on grounds of age. Moreover, a problem with this kind of approach is that asking a group of employers, the majority of whom are ignorant of the issue, about their practices towards older workers, will almost inevitably lead to an underestimate of the true extent of age discrimination. As many employment decisions will be left to individual line managers, individual respondents to surveys may find it difficult to make accurate statements about employment practices and adherence to policies.

More importantly, this study also included telephone interviews with 100 employers who had attended presentations as part of the Getting On campaign activities. A key finding was that many attending these presentations were doing so out of professional interest, rather in the capacity of an employer, suggesting, according to the report, that the presentations were not always reaching their target audience. In addition, when asked about their prior knowledge of the campaign, only three out of 10 of those attending the presentations, were aware of it and even then, not in much detail. Moreover, even among, what according the researchers acknowledge, was a self-selected and interested group less than a third had taken any action subsequently with regard to older workers. In fact, the option of education campaigns was tried and rejected over 30 years ago prior to the introduction of the Age Discrimination in Employment Act in the USA in 1967 (Ventrell-Monsees, 1993; Wirtz, 1965).

Despite these recent policy changes, it would appear that there is a firmly entrenched early exit culture in the UK. A recent study found that over 95 percent of retirees were aged under 65 and two thirds had begun to draw their pensions before the age of 60 (IDS, 1995). In many instances retirement was at the employer's request. On the other hand, retirement after normal pension age was rare. In addition, research (e.g. Taylor and Walker, 1996a) indicates that it is easier and more palatable to employers and trade unions if, in times of crisis, older labour is shed first. Hence employers will often target older people for redundancy or early retirement. As a result, early retirement is now a feature of most programmes of redundancies (IRS, 1995).

Present policies towards older workers

After the Labour government came to power in 1997 it dropped a commitment to make age discrimination in employment illegal. While not ruling out the possibility of legislation in the future, it has for now taken on the Conservative mantra of voluntary persuasion.

The government carried out a consultation exercise (Department for Education and Employment, 1998) among employers, employers' federations, the TUC and groups representing older people. According to the government this indicated that a non-statutory code of practice for employers could be beneficial. The code was launched in the Spring of 1999. It sets out principles of non-age biased employment practices. Included is guidance on the application of the principles and examples of best practice. The success of this approach will depend on whether it can overcome the basic problems facing campaigns and codes of practice: will they reach the people they will need to reach and will anyone take any notice?

As organisations move towards more decentralised management structures, with greater responsibility for personnel matters being vested in individual line managers, it will become increasingly difficult to reach those with the responsibility for making recruitment decisions. Thus for the voluntary approach to work a very high level of penetration must be achieved, something that previous campaigns have failed to do. In a survey of employers conducted by Alan Walker and myself (Taylor and Walker, 1994) we questioned personnel managers about guidelines on the employment of older workers, which had recently been issued by the former Institute of Personnel Management (now the Institute of Personnel and Development), and found that just under half (49 percent) of them had not seen or did not remember seeing a copy. Hayward et al's (1997) survey also asked about knowledge of these guidelines. They found that even fewer were aware of their existence. The Government has committed itself to evaluating the impact of this latest campaign and has now said that it will legislate if it is found not to have been successful. A preliminary evaluation of the code three months after its launch indicated that awareness amongst business was low (Employers' Forum on Age 1999). Among 430 businesses contacted by an independent research agency 30 per cent were unaware of the existence of the code, less than 10 per cent intended to make any changes in the way they recruited or trained and 60 per cent stated that a code would make no difference to the way they ran their businesses. On the other hand, given that the implementation of the code is in its infancy it would be unwise to label it a failure on the basis of these findings alone. But they can be taken as indication of the considerable amount of convincing employers will require before they begin to implement age-aware human resource management policies. Thus on the basis of the available evidence it is not possible to conclude that education campaigns alone will offer an effective solution to the problem of age discrimination in the labour market.

Additionally, the government recently announced that Job Centres will no longer take vacancies with upper age limits. This extended existing Employment Service practice whereby Job Centre staff would try to dissuade employers from specifying age limits in advertisements placed in Job Centres.

Despite considerable debate of the issue of flexibility in retirement over the last two decades new policies have been slow to emerge. For some time the Labour party has been a strong advocate of increasing flexibility in the age of retirement. Pension reform is high on the policy agenda. Advocacy groups are calling for changes in current pension regulations to enhance flexibility and allow gradual retirement. In contrast to other European countries where Government schemes have been introduced in an attempt to encourage gradual retirement, this is rare among employers in the UK. Occupational pension scheme rules and tax laws have discouraged gradual retirement. Currently, the rules which have to be observed if an occupational pension scheme is not to be taxed, require a person to be fully retired and to have ceased contributions to the scheme before they are entitled to receive their pension. The only way a person can draw a pension and carry on working is if they become a consultant or take full early retirement from one employer and move to another. The present rules are designed to prevent people from gaining tax advantages on investment schemes that are not being used for retirement pensions. The Government published a consultation document which may be the first step towards encouraging much greater flexibility in retirement (Inland Revenue 1998). However, the government is yet to set out proposals on increasing flexibility in retirement.

Additionally, the government is also implementing a new program for non-working mature-age people – New Deal 50+ - which aims to provide them with the practical assistance and support needed to compete effectively in the labour market (Department for Education and Employment 2000). It offers employment advice to older people who have been on benefits for six months or more and who wish to return to work. The programme is voluntary and is open to people inactive on benefits as well as those who are registered unemployed. A training grant is offered for accredited training. An employment credit is also offered for those entering full-time work. This is reduced for part-timers. The programme began to roll out nationally from Spring 2000.

It will be some time before it will be possible to assess the impact of these measures. However, it should be pointed out that previous schemes aimed at getting older workers back into work have had a limited effect. In France and Germany schemes which provided subsidies to employers who took on older workers have not been successful (Frerichs, 1995; Guillemard, Taylor and Walker, 1996; Weber, Whitting, Sidaway and Moore, 1997). For example, in France *Contrat de Retour à l'Emploi* (return to employment contracts) were introduced in order to encourage employers to recruit people aged 50 and over. Despite substantial financial incentives (exemption from paying social insurance contributions up to date of the employee's retirement) employers were reluctant to participate. In the UK the Job Release Scheme was followed by a pilot scheme known as 50 Plus Job Start Allowance which aimed to encourage people aged 50 or over in to part-time work with the ultimate goal of translating this into full-time employment. Under the scheme participants received a top-up of £20 on what they were paid by an employer for a period of up to six months. However, this scheme was abandoned in 1991 because of low take up (Taylor and Walker, 1991).

In addition, the UK Better Government for Older People programme was launched in June 1998 to improve the delivery of services to older people at the level of local Government. This program has established 28 pilot projects across the UK designed to pilot integrated inter-agency projects tackling a range of issues including employment and lifelong learning among mature-age workers. Recognising that age discrimination affects many areas of policy, the UK Government has also created a Ministerial Group on Older People to coordinate work across Government departments.

New public policies

This section sets out, in broad terms, ways in which public policies on age discrimination and older workers might develop and identifies areas where problems might arise. For a detailed discussion of some of the issues and potential remedies see Taylor and Walker (1997) and Young and Schuller (1991).

As we have already seen voluntary persuasion of employers appears to have been a failure. There is no doubt that age discrimination is a complex issue and would be difficult to proscribe in law and there are important questions about its scope and coverage. For example, should legislation apply to people of any age? Should it apply to all sizes of employer? How will it be enforced? Should it be comprehensive or only cover, for example, age restrictions in recruitment advertisements? Would it allow governments to provide preferential access to training schemes for younger (or older) workers? Some opponents of the legislative approach have also argued that legislation might actually harm older workers, their protected status discouraging employers from considering them for employment (Taylor and Walker, 1993). However, this seems unlikely in a situation where other equal opportunities and unfair dismissal legislation exists.

However, legislation proscribing discrimination is only likely to provide a partial solution. It is also important that government undertakes a broad review of employment legislation, policies and practices in all areas to ensure that as much as is possible is done to remove the barriers to employment and training in order to increase job opportunities for older workers. In particular, it has been argued that institutional ageism partly has its origins in the development of the state pension system and fixed pension ages, with occupational schemes tending to follow those of the state (Walker and Taylor, 1993; Young and Schuller, 1991). Thus it is essential that government takes the lead in encouraging employers to develop more flexible approaches to retirement. In addition, a few examples of employer best practice in this area have already been identified (Taylor and Walker, 1996b) and these could be usefully be disseminated to employers.

As an initial step a recent report commissioned by the Government and prepared by the Cabinet Office's Performance and Innovation Unit (2000) sets out a number of recommendations for the development of policies towards people in the third age. Key recommendations for Government are as follows:

- Develop a strategy for setting out its vision of the role and value of older people in society.
- Introduce age discrimination legislation if the code of practice on age diversity has been shown to have failed.
- Increase contact with and job-search assistance for people on sickness and disability benefits.
- Provide careers information and advice for older displaced workers.
- Raise the minimum age at which an immediate pension is payable.
- Increase the transparency of occupational pension schemes by showing the cost of early retirement in company accounts.

- Promote the advantages of diversity and flexibility in working practices through a group of 'champion' employers.
- Each Civil Service department to review the case for increasing its retirement age to 65.

The report recommends that responsibility for actioning the conclusions of the report and for championing it should rest with the Ministerial Group on Older People. It suggests that in order to achieve this the Group will require a higher profile, more resources, a clearer remit and central backing from within Government.

Without cultural change progress will be limited because, as has been pointed out by Young and Schuller (1991), the 'whole society is obsessed with age' (p. 14). Education campaigns among employers and general public will have an important role but the age debate still has a long way to go before it is elevated to the levels occupied by race or gender. For example, while it could be argued that the issue is now part of gerontological mainstream (Bytheway, 1995) and articles have been appearing in the popular personnel management literature for a number of years (e.g. Naylor, 1987) it is only now beginning to enter the academic management literature in the UK as an issue for serious consideration (e.g. Lyon, Hallier and Glover, 1998).

More generally, there appears to be some dissatisfaction among older people with Government policy on pensions and a view that Government policy is 'youth' oriented (*The Guardian* 2000a). Recently the political debate about older people has intensified with the Conservative party attempting to capitalise on this apparent dissatisfaction by announcing a number of policy initiatives targeting older people, particularly in the areas of health and pensions. Given their past hostility towards the notion of age discrimination legislation it would seem unlikely that the Conservatives will go so far as to support the implementation of such legislation. On the other hand, under considerable public pressure, the previous Conservative government did introduce legislation outlawing discrimination on grounds of disability. Labour has already committed itself to legislate on age if its education campaign fails, although it will be important to see whether this commitment actually appears in the party's manifesto for the next General Election. Thus in the battle for the 'grey' vote in the run up to the next General Election, both the main political parties may be forced to opt to include a firm commitment to introduce legislation on age discrimination in their election manifestos. However, it is likely that this will be opposed vigorously by organizations representing employers (*The Guardian* 2000b). Thus, it is likely that consideration of the rights of older people will increasingly be a feature of policy debates in the UK in coming years.

A lesson of recent government education campaigns and private members' bills must be that age discrimination is so deep-rooted that only a sustained, consistent and well co-ordinated approach will be successful. For government, the lesson is that by giving the impression that they have been emphasising 'youth' issues in the past they may have appeared to have been practising and to have been sanctioning discrimination against older people. Thus employers and older workers may have been receiving conflicting messages. For older people already debilitated by their experiences of unemployment a perceived emphasis on 'youth' in pronouncements by government ministers may have added to feelings of worthlessness, alienation and despair.

Future prospects

In this chapter we have seen that, despite signs that it was going to be radical while in opposition, much of the present Labour government's approach to older workers has shown a familiar pattern. While the present government is promoting initiatives which may benefit older workers and it is certainly doing more than simply paying lip service to the issue of age and employment, its actions to date suggest that, for the time being at least, it has backed away from fundamental reforms which might have a real effect on older workers' employment prospects.

Legislation proscribing age discrimination has not been ruled out but a government which is keen to maintain good relationships with employers may be reluctant to be seen to be adding to their burden at a time when it is also dealing with new legislation on employment rights and a national minimum wage. But there is no evidence that education campaigns alone have been nor will be particularly effective in overcoming age discrimination. Among UK employers in general there still appears to be little interest in developing policies towards older workers. On the other hand, there is some evidence that legislation elsewhere has been effective in improving the employment prospects of older workers. Without similar legislation in the UK, it is hard to see how the issue will break into the equal opportunities mainstream. Together with pension and social security reform and more opportunities for education and training the introduction of legislation might bring significant benefits for older workers.

The aim of this chapter has not been to diminish the problems (including age discrimination) faced by younger unemployed people but rather to argue for balance in policy making and the presentation of policy. As Young and Schuller (1991) argued, the sheer weight of numbers of people in the third age may ultimately force the government to give older workers a better deal. However, this will be of little comfort to the person who is currently facing involuntary retirement at the age of 55.

References

Arrowsmith, J. and McGoldrick, A. (1996), *Breaking the Barriers: a Survey of Managers' Attitudes to Age and Employment*, Institute of Management, London.

Bytheway, B. (1995), *Ageism*, Open University Press, Buckingham.

Casey, B., and Laczko, F. (1989), 'Early retired or long-term unemployed? The situation of non-working men aged 55-64 from 1976 to 1986', *Work, Employment and Society*, 1, 4, pp. 509-26.

Casey, B. and Wood, S. (1994), 'Great Britain: firm policy, state policy and the employment of older workers', in F. Naschold and B. de Vroom (eds), *Regulating Employment and Welfare: Company and National Policies of Labour Force Participation at the End of Worklife in Industrial Countries*, Walter de Gruyter, Berlin.

Department for Education and Employment (1998) *Action on Age: Report of the Consultation on Age Discrimination in Employment*, Sudbury: DfEE Publications.

Department for Education and Employment (2000) *Design of New Deal 50 Plus*. DfEE, London.

Employers' Forum on Age (1999) *Employer Awareness of the Code of Practice on Age Diversity: Report on a Survey of Senior Decision Makers in Small and Medium Enterprises*. London: EFA.

Frerichs, F. (1995), *Current developments in labour market policy for older workers in the Federal Republic of Germany*, Institute of Gerontology, University of Dortmund.

Guillemard, A-M. (1993), 'Travailleurs vieillessants et marché de travail en Europe', *Travail et Emploi*, 57, pp. 60-79.

Guillemard, A-M, Taylor, P. and Walker, A. (1996), 'Managing an ageing workforce in Britain and France', *The Geneva Papers on Risk and Insurance*, No. 81, pp. 469-97.

Hansard (1996), Official report: Parliamentary debates, Vol. 271, No. 47, c. 618.

Hansard (1998), Official report: Parliamentary debates, Vol., No., c. 1417.

Hayward, B., Taylor, S., Smith, N. and Davies, G. (1997), *Evaluation of the Campaign for Older Workers*, Department for Education and Employment, London.

Income Data Services (1995), 'Two-thirds take pension before 60', *IDS Pensions Bulletin*, Issue No. 83, 1995, pp. 5-8.

Industrial Relations Services (1993), 'Age discrimination', *Industrial Relations Law Bulletin*, no. 472, pp. 12-14.

Industrial Relations Services (1995), 'Managing redundancy', IRS Employment Trends, March, pp. 5-16.

Inland Revenue (1998) *Occupational Pension Schemes: Enhanced Flexibility*, Savings and Investment Division, London.

Itzin, C. and Phillipson, C. (1993), *Age Barriers at Work*, METRA, London.

Jackson, P. and Taylor, P. (1994), 'Factors associated with employment status in later working life', *Work, Employment and Society*, 8 (4), pp. 553-67.

Labour Market Trends (1998), February.

Lyon, P., Hallier, J. and Glover, I. (1998), 'Divestment or investment? The contradictions of HRM in relation to older employees', *Human Resource Management Journal*, Vol. 8, No. 1, pp. 56-66.

Moore, J., Tilson, B. and Whitting, G. (1994), *An International Overview of Employment Policies and Practices Towards Older Workers*, Employment Department, Research Series, No. 29.

Naylor, P. (1997), 'In praise of older workers', *Personnel Management*, Vol. 19, No. 11, pp. 44-48.

O'Meara, D. (1989), *Protecting the Growing Number of Older Workers: the Age Discrimination in Employment Act*, University of Pennsylvania Press.

Performance and Innovation Unit (2000) *Winning the Generation Game: Improving Opportunties for People Aged 50-65 in Work and Community Activity*, The Stationary Office, London.

Potter, J. (1996), 'Redundancies in Great Britain', *Employment Gazette*, Vol. 104, No. 2, pp. 41-48.

Taylor, P. and Walker, A. (1991), *Too Old at 50*, Campaign for Work, London.

Taylor, P. and Walker, A. (1993), 'Dealing with age discrimination in England: the merits of education vs. legislation', *Ageing international*, Vol. 20, No. 3, pp. 36-40.

Taylor, P. and Walker, A. (1994), 'The ageing workforce: employers' attitudes towards older workers', *Work, Employment and Society*, 8, 4, pp. 569-91.

Taylor, P. and Walker, A. (1996a), 'Intergenerational relations in employment: the attitudes of employers and older workers', A. Walker (ed.), *The New Generational Contract*, UCL Press.

Taylor, P. and Walker, A. (1996b), 'Gradual retirement in the UK', in L. Deslen and G. Reday-Mulvey (eds), *Gradual Retirement in the OECD Countries*, Dartmouth, Aldershot.

Taylor, P. and Walker, A. (1998), 'Employers and older workers: attitudes and employment practices', *Ageing and Society*, 18, pp. 641-58.

The Guardian (2000a) 'Tories Go A'courting', 30 May, 21.

The Guardian (2000b) 'Ministers Move to Woo Over-50s', 26 April, 10.

Trinder, C. (1989), *Employment after 55*, National Institute for Economic and Social Research, London.

Ventrell-Monsees, C. (1993), 'How useful are legislative remedies?: America's experience with the ADEA', *Ageing International*, 20 (3), pp. 41-45.

Walker, A. (1985), 'Early retirement: release or refuge from the labour market?', *The Quarterly Journal of Social Affairs*, Vol.1, No.3, pp. 211-229.

Walker, A., Guillemard, A-M. and Alber, J. (1991), *Social and Economic Policies and Older People*, EC, Brussels.

Walker, A. and Taylor, P. (1993), 'Ageism versus productive aging: the challenge of age discrimination in the labour market', in S. Bass, F. Caro, and Y. Chen (eds), *Achieving a Productive Ageing Society*, Auburn House, London.

Warr, P. and Pennington, J. (1993), 'Views about age discrimination and older workers', in P. Taylor, A. Walker, B. Casey, H. Metcalf, J. Lakey., P. Warr and J. Pennington (eds), *Age and Employment: Policies, Attitudes and Practices*, Institute of Personnel Management, London, pp. 75-106.

Weber, T., Whitting, G., Sidaway, J. and Moore, J. (1997), 'Employment policies and practices towards older workers: France, Germany, Spain and Sweden', *Labour Market Trends*, pp. 143-48.

Wirtz, W.W. (1965), *The Older American Worker*, Report of the Secretary of Labor to the Congress under section 715 of the Civil Rights Act of 1964, Washington DC, US Government Printing Office.

Young, M. and Schuller, T. (1991), *Life after Work*, Harper Collins, London.

16 Fitness for work: the effects of ageing and the benefits of exercise

Alan Nichols and Wendy Evangelisti

Introduction

This paper is based upon a workshop session during which the University of Stirling Exercise Group for Older Participants (SUPERS) demonstrated a typical exercise class, designed to achieve and maintain fitness and health as a key feature of an active lifestyle. The demographic rationale for exercise in the older population is given and the benefits of an active lifestyle are outlined. These include economic factors as well as the maintenance of independence designed to enhance longevity and the quality of life. The principal effects of ageing on the body systems are detailed, and the outcomes of exercise are noted. Thereafter, guidelines are offered for fitness teaching with older participants.

Several industrial countries are currently experiencing the effects of the so-called 'Baby Boomer' generation. The postwar explosion in birth rate has been accompanied by improvements in health and welfare care, with a consequent decrease in premature death from infectious disease. Thus the proportion of the population aged over 50 years is rising and will continue to rise for the predictable future. Medical advances are now concentrated on morbidity and death from degenerative diseases, rather than infectious disease, as life expectancy extends towards and perhaps beyond a notional biological limit of 85 years (Spirduso, 1995).

The current socio-economic culture encourages retirement from active employment at the age of 65 years or less. Thus the older population will cease to contribute to the economy, whilst requiring increasing welfare support for perhaps two further decades. A significant factor in the level of support required by the ageing population will be the point at which degenerative disease arrests individual's capacity to maintain their independence in daily life. This will be a factor of biological age rather than chronological age for which ten biological markers have been defined (Evans, 1992).

There is now substantial evidence to confirm that suitable regular exercises can maintain fitness and health in all age groups, including the elderly (Carnegie Trust,

1993). This will in turn enable the elderly to remain economically active, and thereafter to retain their functional independence, for an extended lifespan. Given an active lifestyle, life expectancy will approximate more to the notional biological limit of the human lifespan, without incurring the economic costs currently envisaged for a more dependent and less active population.

The demography of ageing : the ageing population

The demography of the United Kingdom highlights several key facts relating to the age profile of the population. Census figures (HMSO, 1993) indicate that about 21 percent of the population is aged over 60 years, and 31 percent is over 50 years. Currently life expectancy upon retirement at 60 years of age is 13 more years for men, and 19 more years for women. More than half of the population is either retired or not yet in employment, and so does not contribute to the economy. This figure may be expected to increase throughout the coming half century, and the implication of this trend is that welfare costs may be expected to increase proportionally. The proportion of economically non-active (under 15 years and over 65 years) to active (15 to 65 years) members of the populace will increase from currently less than 20 percent, to over 33 percent by 2030 (OECD, 1988). It is however contended that these costs may be alleviated by a healthier, less dependent and consequently more productive elderly population.

Table 16.1 : General population statistics (UK)

Percentage of Annual Population Growth	0.3
Percentage of Economically Active Population	52
Life Expectancy (M)	73 years
Life Expectancy (F)	79 years

Table 16.2 : Percentage and gender of 50+ population (1993)

AGE GROUP	MALE percentage	FEMALE percentage	TOTAL
70+	3.9	6.7	10.6
60-69 years	4.7	5.4	10.1
Sub-Totals	**8.6**	**12.1**	**20.7**
50-59 years	5.3	5.5	10.8
TOTALS	**13.9**	**17.6**	**31.5**

Table 16.3 : Predictions of age increases

AGE GROUP	1991	2011	2031	2051
	Percentage			
75+ years	6	7	8	10
60-74 years	16	16	18	15
TOTALS	**22**	**23**	**26**	**25**

Other significant factors

The current health profile shows good health until 75 years of age, and thereafter a more rapid decline. Good health is maintained while the individual remains functionally independent; when independence is lost, health declines more rapidly, and *vice-versa.* Male life expectancy is lower, but older surviving men (80+) report less ill health (Tinker and Grundy, 1992).

The benefits of fitness: a fitness balance sheet

Shephard (1988) reviewed the reported costs and benefits of an exercising versus a non-exercising population. This may be adapted to illustrate the possible factors by which the benefits associated with a healthy older population may be evaluated.

The costs of illness

A similar analysis can be used to evaluate the costs of morbidity associated with lack of fitness and health.

To the individual

Lost income

Lost independence

Lost capacities

Reduced longevity

Greater expenditure on medication

Greater welfare costs

Lost quality of life

To the employer and state

Costs of provision of hospitals, staff, public health, welfare services, medical education, insurance and research. Loss of productivity, reduced tax revenues, reduced economic activity.

Table 16.4 : Cost and results of fitness to health

COSTS	BENEFITS
PERSONAL FACTORS	
• Extra food intake	• Improved diet (minerals, vitamins, energy)
• Purchase of sports/activity clothing	• Reduced spending on 'junk food', alcohol and so on
• Purchase of sports/activity equipment	• Reduced risk of fall and injury
• Fees: admission a memberships	• New recreation, leisure and social opportunities
• Travel to sports venues	• Better perceived health and less illness
• Time taken with exercise	• Improved quality of life, self-esteem and control
EMPLOYMENT FACTORS	
• Provision of exercise facilities	• Improved productivity and job satisfaction
• Provision of medical care	• Reduced staff turnover and lower absenteeism
• Time allowed for fitness training	• Lower injury rates and lower insurance costs
• Training and sports injuries	• Enhanced corporate image
GOVERNMENT	
• Cost of health and fitness promotion	• Reduced hospital and health care costs
• Provision of fitness facilities	• Reduced benefit costs
• Provision of fitness services	• Reduced geriatric dependency
• Employment costs of fitness staff	• Enhanced employment
• Infrastructure: premises, roads, services	• Economic growth and tax revenues

Source: the authors, using Shephard (1998)

The benefits of exercise

Exercise, functional independence and longevity

Pekkanen et al (1987) argued that activity could prolong life by two years. Exercise can contribute to health, extending functional independence by up to ten years.

Individual benefits

Many researchers and writers have pointed to the benefits that older people derive from regular exercise. They include feeling better, hoping to live longer, reduced fatigue, faster recovery from exertion, greater strength, steadier balance, greater creativity, more energy, better sleep, healthier appetite, better memory, more output, better posture, less illness, enhanced mood, and greater resilience.

Kaman and Patton (1994) and Shephard (1990) reviewed such reported benefits. In our own experience as well as that of many researchers, regular participants report enhanced self-image, and also quote an average of two years reduction in perceived age. There is less personal expenditure on health care and on alcohol and tobacco. Individuals who participate in lifelong regular exercise thus have improved quality of life and less illness, and also an estimated average of ten additional years of functional independence.

Benefits to the state

A 5.5 percent annual reduction in direct health costs of exercising individuals has been calculated, to include the costs of hospitals, doctors, nursing and drugs, as well as lower associated costs, including research, training, public health, medical and care facilities and insurance.

Benefits reported include fourfold reduction in medical consultation time, four days per annum less illness, a 25 percent reduction in heart disease treatment costs, and lower hospital bed occupancy and care time. The cost of additional longevity is balanced by the fact that 33 percent of exercisers die before they require institutional care.

The fitness industry is a significant source of employment, and a significant source of revenue through taxation. Some tax and employment gain is however offset by reduced tobacco and alcohol revenues.

Ageing and physical fitness

Physical capacities decline with age, and ten biological markers associated with ageing have been identified (Evans, 1992). Aerobic capacity, measured by the quantity of oxygen that can be absorbed (Vo_2Max), is lost at a rate of 5ml/kg/min. per decade (0.8 percent per annum) from the age of 30 years. Static strength and dynamic strength both decrease by 40 percent (male) and 20 percent (female) between 35 years and 70 years. Speed of reaction declines by up to 20 percent over the same time span, and flexibility also declines. All of these figures are of course averages.

Table 16.5 : Percentage of people aged 55-74 years who found it difficult to walk 400 metres

Men	55-59 yrs	60-64 yrs	65-69 yrs
Difficulty	12.3	17.0	20.1
Inability	5.0	7.9	9.4
Women			
Difficulty	12.6	15.8	19.9
Inability	5.8	8.0	7.9

Table 16.6 : Percentage of people aged 55-74 years who found it difficult to lift or carry 25 pounds

Men	55-59 yrs	60-64 yrs	65-69 yrs
Difficulty	11.6	15.4	16.8
Inability	3.5	3.8	5.6
Women			
Difficulty	22.9	31.0	33.8
Inability	9.1	8.7	9.3

Source: National Centre for Health Statistics

When considering the benefits of exercise for the elderly, the concepts of functional independence and active life expectancy are central. The aim must be to prolong physical independence, thereby gaining prolonged active life expectancy and thus a better quality of life. This is correlated with longevity, namely quantity of life. An exercise programme should aim to maintain levels above the thresholds of independence for the health related fitness factors. These include aerobic endurance, strength, muscular endurance, and flexibility. If these factors are maintained, it will also be easier to maintain such factors as co-ordination, balance, speed and precision. From such activity, the vital quality of life will be more readily sustained. The employment capacities of a healthy and fit individual will be prolonged as a consequence.

Ageing, exercise and fitness

The respiratory system

Vital capacity (the amount of air inhaled and exhaled) is generally reduced by up to 25 percent, largely as a consequence of stiffening of the various tissues, by 60 years of age. There is increased risk of emphysema or bronchitis.

Physical activity, including breathing exercises, maintains lung function, and so the oxygen supply necessary for exercise.

The blood vessels and blood supply

The blood vessels become less elastic, providing less efficient transport of the oxygen and nutrients needed for exercise, and less efficient removal of the waste products. The blood contains elevated levels of fat, which may be deposited on the walls of the blood vessels. Blood pressure may become elevated, and there may be increased risk of stroke.

Exercise using the large locomotor muscle groups will burn excess blood fats, and so maintain the diameter of the arteries and permeability of the capillaries by precluding the build-up of fat deposits. This in turn will maintain the supply of energy fuels to the muscles, and reduce the tendency to hypertension.

The muscles

Dynamic and static strength is reduced as a consequence of lower protein synthesis and fewer fast-twitch fibres. Speed is lost before endurance. There is a smaller proportion of muscle to other body tissue. This affects respiration (the rib cage and diaphragm), posture (the back and stomach muscles), and the main locomotor muscles of the legs and arms.

Exercise prevents atrophy due to loss of functional fibres. It maintains muscular strength and endurance. It improves muscle tone, with benefits to posture and breathing. The greatest benefits occur in aerobic endurance (Type I fibres) rather than anaerobic speed and strength (Type II fibres). The older body can improve muscle function with training.

The heart

The cardiac output (heart rate times stroke volume) is generally reduced from 30 litres per minute at 20 years, to 19 litres per minute at 60 years. This reduced output will delivers less fuel to the muscles for energy production, and removes the waste products of energy production less effectively. There is increased risk of coronary heart disease.

Exercise maintains cardiac function and the consequent capacity for exercise. The onset of fatigue however ensues earlier, reducing peak levels of activity. The older body has considerable capacity to improve cardio-vascular function with training.

The nervous system

Speed of response is reduced. This affects balance and predisposes falling. Long term memory is retained better than short term memory. The senses require stronger stimulation, and the body will react more slowly to changing conditions including the onset of exercise, and the consequent temperature changes.

The older participant is able to use familiar skills and strategies, but performs best with less complex skills that do not require speed. Care is needed to avoid accidents arising from loss of balance or from clumsiness in co-ordination.

The skeleton

The bone structure loses its mineral content, and thus becomes weaker. This affects the spine and the long bones. Suitable bone loading exercise can counter the loss of bone calcium. Bones already affected by osteoporosis should not be heavily loaded or subjected to high impact.

The joints

Joints may become stiff, unstable and painful, with flexibility reduced and muscle action restricted. Exercise maintains joint flexibility, but care is needed with heavily-used joints.

Body composition

The amount and distribution of body fat, muscle and water changes, although total body weight may remain stable. However the proportion of muscle protein to body fat can be maintained favourably by exercise.

Summary: the effects of exercise on ageing

The biological factors that are associated with ageing, which can be improved by exercise, include:

Muscle mass	Muscle strength	Aerobic capacity
Body fat levels	Blood pressure	Basal metabolic rate
Insulin sensitivity	Thermo-regulation	Ratio of high-density to total cholesterol level

Degenerative diseases that may be alleviated or prevented by regular exercise include:

Coronary heart disease	Stroke	Hypertension
Late onset diabetes	Obesity	Osteo-arthritis
Osteoporosis	Back pain	Chronic lung disease
Urinary incontinence	Cancer	Neuro-motor dysfunction

Anxiety and depression, cognitive function and memory are also alleviated or improved through exercise. Rehabilitation and recovery from injury or illness are also promoted by appropriate exercise. The implications of the above for the maintenance of a productive workforce are self-evident.

Ageing and learning ability

The ability to learn and the level of attainment in physical performance both apparently peak at around 25 years. Loss of physical capacity is displaced by greater experience with age. The long-term memory retains skill patterns developed through past experience. This provides a repertoire of skills, and better conceptual grouping - insights, planning and strategies will improve with age.

Speed

Speed of reaction, speed of movement and speed of adaptation to the needs of exercise generally peak at 22-28 years of age. Slowing with age is due to central neural mechanisms, as well as to loss of peripheral function. Slower reactions may contribute to accidents, and time stress may contribute to clumsiness. Emphasis should be on accuracy rather than speed, with particular attention to safety.

Guidance

Lowered sensory perception requires the use of additional and stronger cues to compensate; when learning new workplace skills, a good demonstration (visual guidance) in conditions of good visibility will be needed. There should be a clear explanation (verbal guidance) with a strong and clear voice, and the guidance may require repetition. It may also be necessary to offer manual guidance, supporting the limbs through the required pattern, and using compensatory movements for particular disabilities.

It will be helpful to relate new movement patterns to already-known skills, and to work from simple skills to complex skills. Previous experience will be important. A rhythmic pattern will often assist learning, and music can be very helpful.

Practice

There should be adequate time to practice slowly; time to repeat and reflect upon the movements, using distributed practice, will be needed before adding new skills or increasing the speed or intensity. Longer and more intensive practice (massed practice) should only be attempted once the skill is thoroughly learned. Training sessions should be carefully graded.

It may be necessary to divide more complex skills into several simpler parts for training and practice, and then to join these together as the parts are mastered. Older participants will generally prefer to concentrate upon accuracy rather than speed. Care should be taken to avoid loss of balance, or undue stress on the joints involved.

Knowledge of results

Skill targets should be attainable. It is essential to inform the participants of their success, and to give a clear explanation of the reasons for failure. Constant encouragement is needed.

Motivation

Age has social expectations, and is conditioned by previous experiences. There will be changing reasons for maintaining employment, and strong motivation may compensate for physical decline. Most vitally, there should be an expectation that new skills can be mastered, and that performance in known skills can be improved.

Summary: teaching employment skills

Regarding the effects of increased age on workplace performance, accuracy rather than skill will be preferred. This gives a longer period of control, more processing time and the chance for greater use of feedback. There will be reduced levels of performance in explosive, speed and power activities. Balance may also decline.

Peak performance in endurance and strength events will reduce by one percent and two percent per annum respectively, starting between ages 20 and 35. Performance will be retained best in self-paced, complex, rhythmic, low-impact, non-explosive skills. Older people tend to achieve success in employment skills that involve self-paced activities, high techniques ones that on experience, non-explosive ones, and social ones.

An exercise programme for fitness maintenance in older participants should include the following:

Extended warm-up	Endurance activities	Strength activities
Extended relaxation, cool-down	Bone loading	Balance
Stretching/flexibility	Co-ordination	Memory tasks

Job performance

The criteria for employment beyond the current expectation of retirement may be assessed by considering the following points:

- Regarding general suitability for employment the maintenance of appropriate health and fitness levels should be assessed by biological rather than chronological evidence of ageing.
- Regarding workplace skills, older employees tend to offer enhanced judgement based on experience but to be relatively easily distracted and less able to discriminate between conflicting sources of information when working under pressure.
- Regarding safety, slower reaction speeds may place older workers at greater risks of accidents such as falling or slipping.
- Regarding compensatory skills, older workers tend to compensate for loss of speed by greater accuracy, and simply complex tasks by reducing the choices available.
- Regarding physical fitness, the ageing processes causes progressive decline in physical fitness, including aerobic capacity, strength, endurance, bone mineral content and speed.

Exercise will usually ameliorate and possibly reverse the effects of ageing on physical fitness and the maintenance of functional independence. Exercise also enhances the perception of quality of life, including cognitive functioning, and consequently ameliorates morbidity and enhances longevity. This in turn contributes to prolonged active life expectancy, to extended functional independence and consequently to enhanced longevity.

References

Carnegie Trust (1993), *Carnegie Inquiry into the Third Age, Final Report: Life, Work and Livelihood in the Third Age*. Carnegie Trust, Dunfermline College: Scotland.

Evans, W.J. (1992), 'Exercise and Ageing', in the *Proceedings of the Second EGREPA Conference on Physical Activity and Health in the Elderly*, University of Stirling, p. 48.

Kaman, R.L. and Patton, R.W. (1994), 'Costs and Benefits of an Active Versus an Inactive Society', in C. Bouchard, R.J. Shephard and T. Stephens (eds), *Physical Activity, Fitness and Health*, Human Kinetics, Champaign, Ill., pp. 134-42.

Organisation for Economic Co-operation and Development (1988), 'Demographic Data File', in *Ageing Populations: Social Policy Implications*, OECD, Paris.

Pekkanen, J., Marti, B., Nissinen, A. and Tuomilehto, J. (1987), 'Reduction of premature mortality by high levels of physical activity: A 20-year follow-up of middle-aged Finnish men', *Lancet* I:1473-1477.

Shephard, R.J. (1990), 'Costs and Benefits of an Exercising Versus a Non-Exercising Society', in C. Bouchard, R.J. Shephard, T. Stephens, J.R. Sutton and B.D. McPherson (eds), *Physical Activity, Fitness and Health*, Human Kinetics, Champaign, Ill., pp. 49-59.

Spirduso, W.W. (1995), *Physical Dimensions of Aging*, Human Kinetics: Champaign, Ill., Ch. 12.

Tinker, A. and Grundy, E. (1992), 'The Demography of Ageing', in *the Proceedings of the Second EGREPA Conference on Physical Activity & Health in the Elderly,* University of Stirling, p. 132.

17 Ageism and unemployment: practical remedies from secondment programmes in small and medium-sized enterprises

Colin Bottomley

> If the concept of age discrimination is to have intellectual validity and consistency then it must, initially, be acknowledged that the use of chronological reference points, basically the birthday, or of "stages" which categorise sections of society by age, is wrong in practice and in principle (Midwinter, 1992).

Secondment programmes with small and medium-sized enterprises

In the context of Midwinter's claim it is appropriate to discuss how and whether secondment programmes initiated by the Scottish Enterprise Foundation, latterly the Department of Entrepreneurship, at the University of Stirling have a role in addressing the issue of ageism at work.

The Scottish Enterprise Foundation (SEF) was set up in 1982 with the express intention of the creation of enterprise in Scotland.

Its original mission was:

> To promote enterprise by the development and dissemination of high quality, innovative programmes and products through education and training activities underpinned by research and development work.

The Foundation's work focused upon (i) the identification and training of potential entrepreneurs; (ii) the development of more effective Scottish-based, independent small and medium-sized enterprises (SMEs); (iii) the development of internationally oriented Scottish SMEs; (iv) the support of policy makers, trainers and advisers in the enterprise development field; and upon (v) the carrying of the 'enterprise' message to those currently in higher education and who will be the wealth creators in the next century.

Consequently, the Foundation worked with SMEs at all stages of development from pre-start through birth, growth and maturity to internationalisation. The Foundation's training and development arm, the Business Development Unit (BDU) provided training and consultancy to small businesses.

A major support programme in its portfolio was the Professional Development Programme, which it offered for some eight years. This programme was designed to provide an inexpensive extra resource to the SME in the form of a currently unemployed but experienced manager or a young, unemployed, inexperienced but enthusiastic, young graduate to undertake a growth development project for the host company. The projects were identified by the owner-managers of the SMEs in discussion with the BDU as being important to their organisations' growth and development.

From the outset the programmes had two major objectives, namely competitively priced support for growth oriented small companies, and assistance to unemployed managers and graduates in their searches for new or first careers.

The programme participants were aged between 21 and 63 with the managers being recruited from a broad spectrum of industrial and commercial backgrounds. The graduate participants were normally relatively young, and from a broad range of academic disciplines. In both cases their background and experience was less important than the enthusiasm to explore career opportunities in SMEs.

Equally, it was essential that they identified the secondment period as a chance to obtain experience at the 'sharp end' of business in an SME to advance their career prospects.

These programmes were normally of 28 to 29 weeks in duration with a training element or skills update being provided at the beginning of each programme, of six to seven weeks in total, prior to the participants being seconded to local SMEs. Participants, naturally, joined the programmes in order to deal with the pressing problem of the lack of a job, whilst SMEs became involved to address growth problems which might not be tackled because of a lack of specific, specialist skills, lack of management time (with existing managers being heavily involved in operational duties) or even lack of inclination. Programmes were discipline-specific or sector-specific and of a general business nature. Indeed, specific variants concentrated on human resource management/development, quality management and export marketing along with general programmes in which the participant was involved in a project from any business discipline. In the latter case, projects addressed issues such as marketing, market research, production planning, purchasing and stock control, financial management, computing applications and administration activities.

The training programme was highly participative, being more akin to a series of extended seminar sessions than traditional teaching. It was intensive with full-time attendance (35 hours per week) being demanded. The training ensured an SME orientation in all the disciplines. The disciplines covered included marketing;

market research; financial management; manufacturing strategy; quality management; personal development; job hunting techniques; and project management.

Instructors were drawn from a pool of full-time academics from the Foundation's staff and independent SME practitioners. A great deal of emphasis was placed on personal development in order to prepare individuals to manage projects in the organisations in which they were placed. Regardless of experience it has been found that all participants benefit from such coaching even if they perceived it to be not entirely necessary. Graduates in particular tend to be ill prepared at undergraduate level for dealing with the world of work and in presenting themselves effectively. Changes in the eligibility rules for joining the programme were made some years ago to exclude anyone who had not been unemployed for more than six months. Consequently, participants tended to be highly de-motivated and lacking in confidence when they were recruited to the Programme. Confidence boosting and enhanced personal development activities became core courses incorporated into the programme.

Whilst on secondment the participants received personal tutor support from staff members who had experience in the business disciplines applicable to the specific projects that the secondees were undertaking. Indeed the relevant parties met as regularly as required in or outwith the host company. Experience indicated that a well-developed tripartite arrangement between the owner-manager, the participant and the tutor led to successful programme outcomes.

Some programmes consisted of managers only, whilst others were designed solely for young graduates. However, it became normal practice to recruit a mix of young graduates and more mature managers. The mix of young and mature proved to be very beneficial as the young benefited substantially from the experience of the older managers whilst the older individuals found the enthusiasm and uncluttered, unbiased approach, of the inexperienced graduates most refreshing.

During the programme, participants received no pay but continued to be in receipt of the unemployment benefits to which they were entitled and travelling expenses. The training was supported in each case by the relevant Local Enterprise Company (LEC), the equivalent of the Training and Enterprise Councils (TECs) which operate in England and Wales. In 1996 the participating companies contributed £3.50 per hour for the full-time services of the participant and support of their tutor.

It was not uncommon for the participant to be offered a permanent position with the host company. On occasions the host company treated the secondment period as an extended interview with the secondee. Indeed, experience indicated that the ability of the owner-manager and the participant to 'rub along' with each other was the vital ingredient in employment being offered. However, there was no compulsion on the company to offer a job nor was there any compulsion for a participant to accept any job that might be offered. The level of job creation in the host companies averaged some 40 percent in each programme with a further 55 percent obtaining jobs in other companies during or immediately after the completion of the programme. In job creation terms the programmes were perceived by charterers and participants as being good value for money.

Given the limited job markets for young graduates and for unemployed managers of a 'certain age' the programme provided an *entreé* into further career opportunities that might not otherwise be available. Clearly, there were always concerns about exploitation and cheap labour and indeed, it is difficult to dismiss such claims. Certainly, some participants expressed real distaste when they found themselves working for 'benefits' whilst being employed alongside paid employees in their host companies and they were also often concerned that they might have an influence on the longer term employment prospects of such colleagues.

Although it was made clear to prospective participants before and during the programme what the implications of participation in the PDP were, their expectations could change once they had joined the programme, and later during their secondments. Individuals needed to see the programme as an investment in their future careers if they wished to join the programme. Otherwise, the potential for disenchantment with the 'cheap labour' secondment process was high.

However, the opportunity to experience direct, 'hands-on', work experience was very productive and stimulating. Whilst SEF continued to seek to support SMEs it did not see any conflict between that objective and 'opening a door' to employment for individuals whose job hunting was severely limited by economic factors and age or inexperience factors. For many, the programme was a last resort in their employment search.

SEF had long-standing battles with successive ministers of employment, trying to persuade them that the payment of a basic salary to secondees would not be expensive, and would prove to be a cost-effective use of taxpayers' money. Sadly, the battle was never won despite many persuasive arguments.

The professional development programme and ageism

It should be stated at this stage that SEF did not set out to deal with the specific problem of ageism when the series of Professional Development Programmes was initiated. Clearly, the term *ageism* may have a broad range of definitions. In the context of this current discussion we utilise a definition that does not directly link to the work environment although the discussion is within the context of work.

For the purposes of this chapter Comfort's (1977, p. 35) definition serves well as a working definition:

> Ageism is the notion that people cease to be people, cease to be the same people or become people of a distinct and inferior kind, by nature of having lived a specified number of years.

The programme was designed with the express intent of supporting SMEs in their growth and development. SMEs have been characterised as being short of resources, mainly, but not exclusively of cash; having multi-functional managers;

lacking specialist staff; being short of promotable manpower; financially vulnerable when managers make mistakes; having owner/managers who concentrate too much on the tasks they enjoy; lacking leverage with financial institutions; having credit control problems and difficulty collecting money owed; having short term planning horizons, emphasising survival, opportunism and fire-fighting; utilizing informal communication and control systems; having limited market shares; evincing close relationships between the profit motive and the efforts of the owner/manager; and tending to be more hostile to government and academic institutions than larger companies.

For the foregoing reasons any assistance to SMEs had to be very cost-effective, and had to take account of the fact the owner-manager is often busy dealing with operational matters and has little time to dedicate to 'training' new staff at any organisational level. Further, the perception of training is often one of cost rather than investment and experience shows that owner-managers are rarely good at all business functions, although as the often sole manager, they have to wear several business 'hats'. The evidence of the SEF over a period of 12 years also indicated that they are not good at recruiting the right people into their organisations. Indeed, owner/managers are prone to recruit people who are almost exactly like themselves, although what they often really need are people with complementary skills and experience.

The PDP attempted therefore to 'smuggle in' training with individuals who had complementary skills, at competitive prices, and offered them in a non-intrusive manner. Unemployed managers, initially, and graduates at a later stage were perceived to be appropriate vehicles for such activities. Sadly, from the very first programme it was never possible to provide any semblance of a salary.

In 1993 the Department of Employment changed the eligibility rules for people joining the programmes. From that time individuals were required to have a period of six months registered unemployment before they could be considered for this subsidised Training for Work activity. Prior to this, individuals need only have been unemployed for one day in order to be considered. This had ensured that the target groups of graduates and managers did not suffer the severely demotivating and demoralising implications of extended periods of unemployment before they became eligible. Therefore, under the new rules when potential candidates enquired about the programme within the six-month qualification period they could not be considered until that six-month period had passed. This was very dispiriting for those individuals who were keen to join the programme but would have to wait much longer before they could be considered.

A number of issues relating to the problem of ageism became apparent to SEF from that time, more particularly as economic recession increased. There was an awareness that a significant number of individuals over the age of 40 were being made redundant and were finding, increasingly, that their job prospects were severely curtailed because of age. Indeed, according to Brents (1986):

> The concept of ageing is as inevitable as physical and mental decline and the subsequent institutionalisation of retirement emerged in the twentieth century

> from workplace conflicts over changes in the production process and worker productivity.

Anecdotal evidence from participants in the PDP confirmed that opinion. However, the situation emerged, over time, that the PDP did indeed address, at least by default, the issues of ageism in redundant experienced managers. From internal research with potential candidates the following reasons for non-recruitment of managers of the over 40 age group were directly articulated or hinted at. Employers ask 'how many years will they work before retirement?'. They feel they cannot afford to invest in short term appointments. Employers 'suspect' people who are willing to work for less than they were paid in their previous jobs. They suspect people with 'no experience' of their sectors. Unemployed managers are seen as potential threats to the existing management team if they are well qualified. The stigma of unemployment is also influential. It was felt that candidates would be 'inflexible' because of an inability or unwillingness to change. Candidates often 'lacked interview skills', especially where they had worked in one industry and one company for many years. Their backgrounds and CVs were sometimes 'unsuitable', and their experience too narrow. They may be seen as overqualified, too experienced and not mobile enough. They may lack information technology skills. They are often seen as less dynamic and less motivated than younger, and presumably hungrier individuals. Finally, it is felt that they will cost too much and leave as soon as a better paid job arises.

Research in this field tends to support this internal survey. With specific reference to ageism Abercrombie, Hill and Turner (1994) argued that:

> Ageism is a contemporary social problem raising questions about exploitation. victimisation and stigmatisation. It is important not to look at the chronological age of individuals to recognise that ageism exists but to look at the criteria in terms of social expectations and values by which one is labelled young, middle-aged or old.

Midwinter (1992) argued that:

> ... discrimination, for good or ill, by the artificial application of ages is damaging and wrong at any time of life and should not solely be regarded as an aspect of older age.

He continued:

> Ageism generates and reinforces a fear and denigration of the ageing process and legitimises the use of chronological age to mark out classes of people.

Although, perhaps relating specifically to ageism amongst middle-aged and older people the former findings are entirely relevant, too, in the writer's experience to the young graduate and professional sectors. Graduates who do not succeed in obtaining gainful employment immediately after graduation are also threatened by an extended period of unemployment. Long gone are the days when large national and multi-national organisations recruited large numbers of graduates from a broad range of disciplines to their in-house graduate management programmes. It is unlikely that those days will ever return. Inevitably, competition for places in large organisations is very high and companies can be and are very selective.

Additionally, the number of graduates seeking work opportunities has increased greatly since the 1970s as policies designed to extend tertiary education have been developed. No longer is a degree of any grade a passport to a job and companies are much more particular about the level and type of degree being offered by interviewees. Even the professions, which have tended to be more all embracing in academic discipline terms, recruit fewer graduates. Consequently, this 'top-slicing' renders many graduates not immediately employable and many have to accept jobs in bars and restaurants, which although not well paid, help to repay loans and keep the wolves from the door. There is also the associated problem of job substitution when graduates take up service sector, semi-skilled jobs that might more normally be acquired by less academically qualified individuals.

The major market for graduate jobs has to include, therefore, the SME sector, which encompasses companies which would not normally and traditionally recruit graduates, and which consists largely of organisations to which graduates would not normally apply for employment.

The SEF's research on graduates being considered for its programmes identified a number of reasons for their lack of success in obtaining gainful employment. These included lack of experience, lack of company interest in recruiting graduates, perceived lack of relevance of particular degrees and skills, poor interpersonal skills, lack of confidence exacerbated by unemployment, lack of experience of interviews, lack of knowledge of the world of work and of the business environment, and overly high expectations engendered by the education system. The foregoing 'characteristics' are alluded to by Duncan (2001) in his chapter in this book.

Further, focus groups of SME owner-managers revealed that they will not recruit graduates because they do not have the time to spend 'training' them and that unless graduates can make immediate impacts on joining their companies they will not entertain them as employees. Indeed, if they have any slight doubt about the ability of graduates to make early impacts they will not take the risk of employing them. Owner-managers have indicated, too, that they believe that they do not get an opportunity to get to know graduate employees over an extended period before they might be considered for recruitment to companies. They would like the opportunity to get to know them first during their undergraduate programmes. They believe that 'fitting in' is of paramount importance when joining an SME. They have indicated, too, that they believe that graduates expect to be considered managers immediately after appointment and do not appreciate the need to 'learn the ropes.' They are unwilling 'to get their hands in the dough' as indicated by the Managing Director of a local, medium sized bakery business. No doubt, too, these beliefs are held in other, larger, organizations. Such views of owner-managers may or may not be correct. However, if these are the perceptions of the owner-managers it is important to be aware that these are reasons that militate against the employment of graduates in many SMEs.

Trends in age levels

Almost 50 percent of the candidates on the PDPs were over 40. This figure did not change significantly over the whole series of programmes regardless of the eligibility rules. However, following the change in eligibility rules the percentage of under twenty-fives rose from 20 to 25 percent. This change was in part because of the conscious decision to offer a graduate-only Programme in the January of each year at a time six months after the previous year's graduation and consequently when a large number of graduates became eligible for the Programme.

The two groups of potential candidates who have been identified as being subject to ageism factors constitute some 70 percent of the participants of the programmes and it became clear that in both situations the need to re-motivate and enhance feelings of self-worth and confidence must be central aspects of the training programmes. Experience indicates that managers in the 40 plus category, who become redundant for the first time since they started working, find the problem of unemployment immensely difficult to deal with. SEF had many examples of managers who have convinced themselves that it will not be difficult, given their experience, to get another job. Indeed, they are prepared to accept a short period of 'holiday and rest' at the outset whilst they re-establish themselves. However, as they start to apply for jobs after the two month 'rest and recuperation period' they very often find that the task of finding a job is very difficult and they find themselves subject to problems of ageism. During this time their motivation, discipline and general demeanour plummet exponentially.

After six months they are getting desperate and after a year they can become very depressed, bitter and acrimonious or alternatively totally depressed and withdrawn. It is difficult to refresh and revitalise these people, but being removed from the isolation of being at home and being amongst a group of others suffering similar problems proves in the majority of cases to be strengthening and a release from many of the pressures, real or imaginary, to which they have been subjected. Indeed, in the 55 plus category it is often found that managers simply stop applying for jobs after six months because they perceive that they have little chance of obtaining any gainful employment. The programme gives a structure to their lives and a discipline that had been missing. In many cases, too, it has removed and relieved the problems of husbands and wives being at home, together, for an extended period. This situation can create strong domestic tensions. In a number of cases managers have felt unable even to maintain their social activities. 'I can't go to the golf club' is one example often quoted by unemployed male managers.

The SEF experience indicated that managers start to feel better about themselves during the training programmes and when they have a real project to 'get their teeth into' they perform well, recover their confidence and feelings of self worth. It has also been identified that participants, who had job hunting assistance from SEF staff, improved their job search activities, submitted better job applications and performed better in interviews. It was not uncommon for people to obtain permanent employment during the programme with their host companies. Indeed, and as noted earlier, some 40 percent of participating managers were offered jobs with their companies. It is not impossible to become 'relatively indispensable'. When managers can offer experience in more than one functional area it is found that they can more easily seal a permanent position with the host company. It is for that reason that the SEF regularly seconded participants to carry out projects in areas in which they would need to use new skills which, with support, from their tutors they could practice in their host companies.

One particularly interesting success story concerned a very experienced 60 year old electrical engineer who had been made redundant. SEF seconded him to a local manufacturing company, which was initially reluctant to take him. His age was not mentioned specifically, but it was clear that this was the hidden agenda. However, the company was eventually persuaded to take a chance with him. Not surprisingly the final outcome was that he was offered a permanent position because of his excellent performance. Although the number of 60 year olds joining the programmes was quite low this case is quite typical of the success of the older group of participants as a consequence of their involvement in the Programme.

The task of creating openings in companies for the older participants was not easy. Indeed, SEF had two full-time industrial liaison staff members who were meeting owner-managers on a continuing basis to discuss how the programme could help them. Sometimes the SMEs were rather particular about who they would accept as secondees and it took great powers of persuasion to convince the owner-managers that the secondees could make real contributions with the help and support of tutors. Despite the low cost of secondments it could be difficult to place an individual if his or her experience was not perceived as immediately relevant.

There is some evidence that managers were very daunted by new challenges in new companies and new industries after periods of unemployment and they did rely on their tutors a great deal, particularly in the early days of their secondments. There was the odd occasion when an individual had just not been able to tackle such a new challenge. In those cases SEF tried to accommodate them elsewhere but it could prove to be quite difficult. It is striking to note that participants would do anything to get on a programme because of their desperation, but still, occasionally, found it difficult to accept a new challenge. It is an understandable and sad reflection that managers can become so isolated during an unemployment period and that there is little in the 'system' to support them apart from the PDPs. Even then, many cannot come to terms with joining such a programme. It was SEF's belief that only 10 percent of unemployed managers were prepared to consider the PDP as a potential way forward, despite the dissemination of the success stories through the SEF newsletter for individuals attending the Employment Service offices.

The problem of owner-manager reluctance to receiving a secondee was especially problematic at the height of recession of the early 1990s, though the position improved subsequently. This improvement may have been associated with the fact that the economic development departments in local authorities started to see the benefits of the secondment process to local businesses and became increasingly willing to subsidise secondments in appropriate cases. Further, as the level of 'laying off' people stabilised owner-managers seemed to be more willing to take the risk of secondments. It is rather ironic that during the recessionary periods when SMEs could really benefit from extra support they were the most reluctant to take up the offer of secondees.

Many managers left the programme because, owing to better interview performance and technique, they obtained permanent positions outwith host companies. Evidence suggested that 50 percent of the participants obtained gainful employment either during the programme or within two months of the completion of their secondments whilst the remaining ten percent probably took a little longer to achieve their objectives. It should be noted that participating managers often accepted positions which paid little less than they had received in their previous employment. In some cases this might have been influenced in part by a willingness to take whatever they could or the redundancy packages that they had also received made that situation a more realistic possibility.

It should be noted that the number of female managers joining the programmes was rather low. This may reflect the low level of female manager unemployment, but is more likely to reflect the traditionally low proportion of women in the so-called managerial categories. What can be stated, though, is that the successful secondment and employment of participating women was high and that those few who joined the programme became significant success stories. The Women's Unit in the SEF also had success with its women-only programmes. In dealing with the issue of unemployed graduates the balance between males and females continued to be skewed towards males although recruitment was actively undertaken for both males and females and regardless of the academic disciplines that the graduates had studied.

Problems of ageism that graduates face were indicated earlier, but it is probably the inability to obtain the opportunity to acquire appropriate work experience, which most regularly militates against their success in gaining employment. How can they get the necessary experience if no employer will give them the chance to prove their abilities? It is also clear from SEF's evidence that the problems of poor interpersonal skills, the inability to interview well, to produce acceptable CVs and to target their job applications were also significant.

During the training programmes it was found that the interpersonal skills development issues proved to be as important to graduates as much as to the participating managers. The SEF had a preference for mixing the two target groups rather than to segregate them. The attendant issues of ageism seem to be better dealt with in mixed groups.

It is clear that the graduates obtained a great deal from the experiences of the managers. This helped them to prepare for the secondment periods as managers could describe the sort of working environment that they might find in industry. For many of the graduates the training programme gave them an intensive and focused insight into management disciplines. As the training was entirely practical in nature and based on casework and practical activities, graduates without business experience found that they had, at least, basic business skills that they could use in their secondments. Clearly, many graduates were very dependent upon their tutors in the early part of the secondment period and felt the need to meet with them on a regular basis. To satisfy that need, tutors were instructed to visit the graduates within the company as often as possible and to maintain links proactively so that the graduates' confidence was maintained. Of course, they, too, found the prospect of undertaking a project rather daunting, and hence the need for relatively intensive tutoring at the outset. However, they were also encouraged to maintain links regularly with their Programme colleagues. They were encouraged to maintain the network that they had become a part of during the training programme. This help was seen to be most beneficial and supportive. Even graduates with business studies degrees found that this support network was very helpful as they, too, had to convert their academic knowledge into practice when they were in their secondments. Turning theory into practice has its problems!

Graduates were somewhat reluctant to subject themselves to the interpersonal development aspects of the training Programme when they initially joined the programme, but they quickly identified the benefits that accrued. Many felt that these activities had been serious omissions in their undergraduate programmes and would have welcomed the opportunity to receive such assistance at an earlier stage.

The SEF identified the fact that graduates produced better job applications, wrote better CVs after exposure to the Programme, and also performed much better in interviews and in more confident ways. Again, evidence suggests that the conversion of these interviews into gainful employment improves significantly as a consequence of joining the programme. The success rate of graduates in obtaining permanent employment in their host companies or elsewhere was found to be rather less than that of the experienced managers. Some 20 to 25 percent of graduates were offered employment by their host companies whilst a further 30 to 40 percent obtained employment elsewhere during or within two months of completing their secondments. A further five percent tended to proceed to postgraduate studies.

It must be stated that graduates were a little more difficult to 'sell' to host companies than managers for many of the reasons articulated earlier. The SEF had to emphasise the skills that graduates had in data collection, problem solving, data analysis and interpretation. Their freshness, objectivity, untainted/unbiased approach to new challenges was emphasised to owner-managers. Clearly, it was important that the tutor support offered was emphasised to owner-managers and it was probably this 'two for the price of one' approach that normally sealed and confirmed the involvement of the SME.

SMEs are more willing to accept the graduate who has very specific skills such as engineering, financial or computing skills where they can identify technical skills that are directly relevant. In other cases it is found that research oriented projects such as market research and quality management are projects in which SMEs are willing to risk a graduate secondment.

Graduates who are flexible in the types of project that they are willing to accept are more likely to be successful in fitting in with their host companies, and like managers they can make themselves 'relatively indispensable' once they are established. Clearly, the support of the tutor often engendered a positive outcome. In the case of graduates, they were simply seeking opportunities to prove themselves. The programme often provided that opportunity, an opportunity that might not be available in other circumstances.

The portfolio ultimately included a number of industry specific and discipline specific programmes, the latest addition being a human resources management/disciplines variant, which proved to be most successful during the piloting process. A further successful development was in the joint venture developments with institutions in other countries where the problems of ageism are also being met by both older, experienced and unemployed managers and young, inexperienced and unemployed graduates.

Conclusions

It is believed that this type of programme continues to provide an important support service both to programme participants and to participating companies. The format still has the potential for development in a broad range of delivery modes and with applications in many industrial sectors and for a broad range of business/management disciplines and in a variety of cultural environments.

It is also argued that it is, as yet, one of the few programmes which has identified and addressed the issues of ageism which confront both young and older individuals and who could otherwise make a substantial contribution to a company in the SME sector. Perhaps government ministers will one day identify the fact that increased support to unemployed graduates and managers and to participating companies can be and is a very cost-effective means of using taxpayers' money. Funding such programmes and providing participants with a modest stipend must be an infinitely better use of public funds than paying subsistence money to unemployed managers and graduates to stay at home.

The SEF, more latterly the Department of Entrepreneurship at the University of Stirling, itself withdrew from offering the Programmes as it had identified the need to concentrate on a more academic developmental role. The PDP provision passed to its sister organisation, the Lothian Management Centre in Edinburgh, which continues to offer the programme successfully to the target sectors. Despite a substantial upsurge in the economy over the recent past, the programme continues to have a place in satisfying the needs of managers who become redundant or need a change of career at a 'certain' age, and fulfils the needs of recent graduates who may find a specific 'first career path' difficult to identify.

The contribution of research into ageism has obviously had an effect on government and has forced government in UK to endeavour to begin to address the issue of age discrimination. As Worsley (1999) indicated:

> ... The publication of the government's Code of Practice on Age Diversity in Employment which sets out guidelines for employers in areas such as recruitment and redundancy, is good news for employees.

Also Ginn and Arber (1996) argued that:

> ... facilitating employment among the older generation, especially women, requires antidiscrimination legislation, incentives and policies aimed at decreasing unemployment for all age groups.

It is difficult to dispute that such policies have an important role, even if they only serve to cause employers to think about their actions in this area. However, it is the writer's belief that, ultimately, such policies are difficult to police. Indeed, Howard (1999) put this in context when she wrote that

> ... age discrimination is not prohibited under British law, although employees can turn to unfair dismissal laws to obtain justice. Laws and regulations that control employers today have not eliminated ageism but have made it more subtle and complex.

Consequently, alternative approaches as described above have a significant role to play. Clearly, there are issues of recruiting both participants and participating companies to the Programmes, but with persistence and sound investment mutual benefits can and do accrue. It is a good use of taxpayers' money in both economic and social terms to support the PDP and similar programmes – they are cost effective and positively outcome related. Enlightened governance in which subtle approaches such as the PDP process provide an alternative to legislation, yet do not replace it, have a part to play in ensuring that the human capital that can contribute to society and the economy has the chance to make that contribution throughout its working life.

Personnel and human resource professionals also have a role to play in this process, and as Ducheyne (1996) contended, these professionals must be involved in '... changing attitudes toward the older worker and in ensuring longer employment'.

It is this mix of approaches that will in the longer run ensure that ageism in the workplace becomes a less significant issue. The writer would wish, though, to commend the approach described in this chapter as a core approach and not simply one that might be considered when the level of unemployment amongst older people as well as recent graduates is at a high level in times of economic depression. It needs to be embedded at all times as a normal, natural opportunity for any manager or graduate seeking a new or different career. Given that jobs for life have become much less likely than in the past the PDP arrangement can provide an appropriate approach as part of the reflective process of selecting career patterns.

References

Abercrombie, N., Hill, S. and Turner, B.S. (1994), *The Penguin Dictionary of Sociology,* Penguin, Hamondsworth.

Brents, B.G. (1986), 'Political Intellectuals, Class Struggle and the Construction of Old Age: The Creation of the Social Security Act of 1935', *Social Science and Medicine*, pp. 1251-60.

Comfort, A. (1977), *A Good Age,* Mitchell Beazely, London.

Ducheyne, D.A.H. (1996), *The Elderly Employee in Perspective. Challenge for Personnel Management,* Tijdschrift voor Sociale Wetenschappen.

Duncan, C. (2001), 'Ageism, early exit, and the rationality of age-based discrimination', in I. Glover, I. and M. Branine (eds), *Ageism in Work and Employment*, Ashgate, Aldershot.

Ginn, J. and Arber, S. (1996), 'Gender and Attitudes to Retirement in Mid-Life', *Ageing and Society*, January 1996.

Howard, L. (1999), 'UK Tales of Woe, Real and Not so Real', *National Underwriter,* Vol. 103, Issue 47, 1999.

Lyon, P., Hallier, J. and Glover I. (1998), 'Divestment or investment? The contradictions of HRM in relation to older employees', *Human Resource Management Journal*, Vol. 18, No. 1, pp. 56-66.

Midwinter, E. (1992), *The Carnegie Enquiry into the Third Age. Citizenship: From Ageism to Participation*, Research Paper No. 8 Carnegie UK Trust 1992.

Worsley, R. (1999), 'The Art of Forgetfulness', *People Management*, Vol. 5, Issue 13, June 1999.

18 Managing the third age workforce: a review and agenda for research

Christine Tillsley and Philip Taylor

Introduction

In this chapter we review progress towards overcoming age discrimination against older workers in the labour market. The first part is concerned with changing demography and patterns of labour market participation among those aged 50 and over. Government and employer policies towards older workers are subsequently reviewed and the significance of the introduction of more 'inclusive' policies towards older workers among some employers and by policy makers is evaluated. We also identify what can be learned from approaches to the ageing of the workforce in other countries. Finally, we critically examine the state of knowledge in this area and identify new avenues for research. In the first instance, the historical context to the discussion is provided.

Background

Evidence from the UK Labour Force Survey (Employment Department 1995; DfEE, 1998) shows that, by the mid-1990s, the effects of the last recession may have compounded the already falling levels of economic activity among older people. For example, economic activity rates among older people have been declining steadily since the 1950s but this trend accelerated during the 1970s and 1980s. Thus by Autumn 1997, three quarters (75 per cent) of men aged between 55 and 59 were either in employment or seeking paid work, compared with 93.0 per cent of this age group in 1975. Whereas eight in ten (82 per cent) men aged between 60 and 64 were economically active in 1975, the figure had fallen to one in two (50 per cent) by 1997.

National economic activity rates tend to mask regional differences. Analysis conducted by Collis and Mallier (1996) showed that, although activity rates for third age men (aged 50 to 69) fell overall by 19 percentage points between 1971 and 1991, there was a marked North-South disparity in the magnitude of this decline. While the rate in the South East fell by 16 percentage points, in Northern

England it dropped by 23 percentage points. This has been ascribed to regional differences in the demand for labour (Gudgin and Schofield, 1993) and to declining jobs in heavy industries, notably mining (MacKay, 1992). In the North and North West of England and in Scotland, higher proportions of men retire between the ages of 56 and 59 than nationally (Smith and Duffy, 1993). In addition, Clark and Anker (1990) have argued that a larger population of older workers in an area tends to lower their job opportunities and wages, thus reducing the proportion of older workers in the labour force.

On a national level, declining labour force participation among those aged 50 and over has been attributed to a number of economic and political factors, and to structural features. Older men have tended to be located in declining industries, under-represented in industries experiencing growth and to be particularly affected by reduced demand for unskilled workers (Jacobs, Kohli and Rein, 1991; Trinder, 1989). Moreover, in periods of recession, older workers have been utilised in early exit strategies to counter the problem of youth unemployment (Kohli, Rein, Guillemard and van Gunsteren, 1991; Trinder, 1989). Once unemployed, they often find it more difficult than younger workers to secure other jobs. Organisational delayering, downsizing of operations and process re-engineering have fragmented the traditional employment relationship and affected the ability of older workers to sustain positions on age-stage career ladders. By using early exit schemes to shed surplus labour employers have effectively institutionalised ageism, delimited work careers and marginalised those employees approaching or in their fifties.

Although levels of economic activity have steadily declined among older men over the past forty years, the rate has fluctuated in accordance with periods of economic expansion and contracted when demands for skills have grown and receded, respectively. During the recessions of the late 1970s and early 1980s, levels of economic activity fell markedly among men aged between 60 and 64: from a rate of 82.3 percent in 1975 to 69 percent in 1981, and subsequently down to 55.4 percent by 1985. Over the following period of economic expansion the rate declined very little, reaching 54.4 percent by 1990 (Taylor and Walker, 1996a, 1996b).

In the 1990s there was concern about the decreasing proportion of older workers in employment and the failure to utilise their skills, knowledge and experience. As the economic dependency ratio shifts and there are increasingly more people outside than inside the workforce, governments and employers are becoming more aware of the need to ensure that resources to meet the social and welfare needs of the young, the sick and the elderly are adequate. The problem is, however, being exacerbated by the increasingly earlier delimitation of the work career. In the late 1950s, older workers were regarded as being beyond the age of sixty; in the late 1990s, the term 'older worker' is being used to encompass those aged 50 and over, and sometimes younger. In the next section we briefly review the responses of successive UK governments to the problems facing older workers. This is followed by a review of the steps taken by governments in other countries.

Domestic responses

Older workers' employment has been an issue of perennial concern to labour market analysts and employment commentators since the 1950s when post-war industrial change and fluctuating employment levels meant than an increasing number of men aged under 65 were involuntarily leaving the labour force. As long ago as 1958 *The Economist* noted that:

> ... the main folly of present trends in unemployment surely lies in the large number of older people who are being dismissed at an age when their transfer to the reserve pool is a sheer waste because no new employer is ever likely to take them on.

Historically, interest in older workers has been linked to the economic cycle. In times of economic expansion when labour and skills have been in short supply, government campaigns have been mobilised to encourage older workers to remain in, or return to, the labour force. Conversely, during periods of economic slump and high unemployment, older workers have been coerced into retirement through financial inducements and ideological arguments. Thus in the early 1950s post-war reconstruction, economic expansion and a shortage of 'prime age' labour led government agencies to promote the positive advantages of employing the over-60s (Jolly et al, 1980). The government machinery, which only twenty years earlier in a period of high unemployment had been emphasising older workers' inefficiency and promoting the benefits of retirement, now extolled the virtues of older workers to employers and encouraged statutory retirement to be deferred. For example, a National Advisory Committee on the Employment of Older Men and Women was established in 1951 to draw attention to labour shortages and to encourage older workers to defer retirement. As Phillipson (1982: 31) asserts:

> In place of the 'virtues of retirement' of the high unemployment 1930s, the 'dangers of retirement' became the *leitmotiv* of the full employment era of the 1950s.

The impact of government responses to the economic cycle on the fortunes of older workers was most evident during the 1980s when faster economic growth, declining unemployment and skill shortages were preceded at the beginning of the decade by economic recession, manufacturing decline, technological change and high unemployment. The government used early retirement as a mechanism for regulating employment access for young and 'prime age' labour. For example, the Job Release Scheme was targeted at those approaching retirement age to offer them financial incentives to relinquish their jobs to younger workers (Casey and Wood, 1994). Earlier retirement became prevalent with the wide use of schemes by larger companies. Exit from the labour force became the socially accepted norm at 60 and even younger. An early retirement culture pervaded much of industry as exit schemes offered a mechanism for easing out employees perceived as being less efficient, removing promotion blockages and for carrying out the more socially acceptable practice of making older rather than younger workers redundant. The supposed shortcomings of older workers were resurrected and they were transformed from being productive members of society into a *near senile gerontocracy*, regarded as hampering both economic growth and the initiatives of young people (Phillipson, 1982: 28). As this recession ended the employment prospects of younger people improved while those of older unemployed people did not (Payne and Payne, 1994).

However, in a few years the government's attitude towards older workers was transformed. From 1989 frequent references have been made by ministers to labour shortages and the loss of skills due to retirement. In contrast to statements made in the early 1980s, the then Secretary of State for Employment, Norman Fowler, referred to the government's desire to 'encourage the elderly to lead healthier lives and work longer' (Sunday Times, 19 January 1989). The government's dramatic change of heart reflected the twin pressures of demographic change and rapid economic growth. Even as the UK economy plunged into recession in the early 1990s the government continued to promote the cause of older workers and to introduce policies aimed at assisting their re-integration. In contrast to countries which have comprehensive (US, Canada) and partial (France, Spain) anti-age discrimination legislation, successive UK governments have used a combination of campaigns and educative initiatives to encourage the recruitment and retention of those in their sixties and, more recently, in their fifties and beyond (Taylor, this volume; Taylor and Walker, 1997). Targeted at employers and older workers these have been the mainstay of government policy towards managing the third age workforce. On the other hand the option of legislation has been consistently ruled out (Taylor, this volume; Taylor and Walker, 1997).

In addition, in 1993 the government established a Ministerial Advisory Group on Older Workers although, at the time of writing, it is not active. Also, in 1989 retirement was one of the most crucial areas to be scrutinised by the House of Commons Employment Committee. The Committee advocated the 'decade of retirement' as a Government objective. But, despite providing the government with the opportunity to reduce overall pension costs, accommodate the changing demography and offset skills shortages, as well as offering a means of encouraging older workers to remain in employment and to reduce their working time gradually, policies to facilitate the flexibilisation of retirement have so far failed to be implemented, although the government has recently published a discussion paper (Inland Revenue, 1998).

The effect of successive governments' policies appears to have been marginal (Hayward, Taylor, Smith and Davies, 1997) and it is arguable whether the problems facing older workers have been accorded the level of attention they deserve. Thus in the early 1990s the government did not resort to the same approach to older workers which had been taken during the previous recession. On the other hand there are areas of legislation and practice where discrimination on age grounds remains. For example, recent government employment policies have had a deliberate emphasis on younger people. The second author discusses these issues in more detail in his contribution to this volume. It is thus our contention that, while there has been a shift in attitudes towards older workers among policy makers, which was largely unaffected by the last recession, the policy situation is now one of confusion with some favouring and some excluding older workers.

Global approaches

The ageing of the population is not just a UK phenomenon but is a challenge facing governments and industry across Europe and beyond. It is estimated that over the next decade, the number of people across the European Union aged between 15 and 29 will fall by 10 million (Walker, 1997). Despite the shifting age composition of the population in Europe and elsewhere, the contraction of young and 'prime age' sub-populations is only just beginning to affect policies and practices towards older workers. Although initiatives are being introduced in some European Union member states, early exit from the labour market by those aged 50 and over remains the norm. In Germany for example, government proposals for gradual retirement have been welcomed widely though it has been acknowledged that financial protection for older workers' incomes, particularly in the move from full- to part-time working, and for improvements in their working conditions are needed if greater progress is to be made (Dury, 1997).

Different models have been adopted at the macro level to manage the third age workforce. In the USA, for example, the enactment of anti-discrimination legislation has, for the past thirty years, offered older workers a level of protection unknown by most of their European counterparts (Moore, Tilson and Whitting, 1994). According to Standing (1986) discussing the impact of the USA's Age Discrimination in Employment Act following its introduction in 1967:

> it is surely no coincidence that from 1969 onwards men aged 55 to 64 no longer had a higher unemployment rate than those aged 25 to 54, and from 1973 onwards had a distinctly lower one.

In Sweden, an active labour market policy, part-time pensions with a high replacement rate and a successful partnership between state and enterprises have afforded older people the opportunity to retain their status and to be productively involved in society later in life than many of their UK counterparts (Wadensjö, 1996; Reday-Mulvey and Delsen, 1996). Meanwhile, in Japan changing employment policies are leading to a reduction in the use of seniority-based payment systems and low mandatory retirement ages (Reday-Mulvey and Delsen, 1996; Takayama, 1996).

As an alternative to the polarities of legislation and voluntarism, the Japanese model offers a structuralist approach. Japan is the most rapidly ageing country in the world: in 1950, three in ten workers were aged between 40 and 59; by 1996 the proportion had grown to one in two (Clark and Ogawa, 1996). In the meantime, the proportion of workers aged under 25 has fallen from one in three of the workforce to one in ten. With the escalating costs of health care, social security and other retirement programmes the government is intent on extending working life by increasing the mandatory retirement age from 60 to 65, encouraging the use of re-employment and employment prolongation after mandatory retirement and improving employment opportunities for older workers (ibid). Personnel and wage policies have been responding to the changing demography by moving away from the traditional commitment to lifetime employment and seniority wage systems to the use of merit pay, assistance with placing retired workers and greater use of policies allowing re-employment after mandatory retirement (ibid). Other forms of transitional experiences include self-employment and assistance with moving to new employment with a subsidiary of the parent company (ibid).

In Japan the widespread use of seniority payment systems has so far prevented the raising of mandatory retirement ages in some sectors, industries and firms because of the expense of retaining workers at the top of their pay scales. By comparison, the use of re-employment and employment prolongation has allowed firms greater flexibility in managing their third age workforces by enabling the retention of selected workers, plus the ability to reduce wage costs for these workers by around ten to twenty per cent. Clark and Ogawa (1996) suggest that the systematic reduction of wages for older workers after mandatory retirement is an important reason for the higher demand for older workers in Japan. On the other hand despite being effective in providing older workers with employment, it could be argued that these programmes devalue the experience of, and contribution made by, older workers by reducing both their status and remuneration levels. Nevertheless, the wide range of options available to older workers may explain why economic activity rates are high: nine in ten men in their late 50s, eight in ten men aged between 60 and 64, and one in two men up to the age of 70 remain in the labour force (Clark and Ogawa, 1996).

With the ageing of the population and the changing composition of the labour force in the UK, industrialists, trade unionists and employers may be forced to re-evaluate their attitudes towards recruiting, retaining and developing employees, regardless of their age. Research evidence concerning employers' policies and practices towards older workers is reviewed in the next section.

Managing the third age workforce: employers' attitudes, policies and practices

Incidence and characteristics of third age management approaches

A decade ago the first author conducted a study into the impact of age on employment (Tillsley, 1990). At that time, around one in ten advertisements placed in the national press carried an age restriction, while in some local labour markets the incidence increased to one in eight of the jobs on offer. At around the same time, one in four of the posts advertised in a professional personnel journal carried an age limit. Recent evidence (Hayward et al 1997) indicates that employers are now reportedly avoiding the use of age-limited job advertisements and, moreover, are focusing on skills rather than qualifications, thus reducing implicit ageism. It may be that this apparent change is no more than a result of different methods of measurement. However, if we accept that the use of explicit age discriminatory practices is presently on the decline then several important questions arise. First, to what extent have employers changed their employment policies and practices? Second, is this change due to socio-political moves towards the inclusion rather than the exclusion of particular groups from the labour force? And third, and alternatively, have economic factors engendered some short-term gains for older workers?

As we have seen, during the late 1980s and early 1990s third age management was largely characterised by the trend in early exit strategies to counter problems of youth unemployment (Kohli et al, 1991). Jobs held by older workers in traditional industries declined, while delayering within many organisations and the move away from pyramidic towards flatter management structures meant the removal of whole tiers of senior management posts traditionally held by older men. Although some sectors of the economy were expanding rapidly during this period, only a small number of firms were recruiting staff beyond state pension age or initiating training programmes for older workers. Despite forecasts of skills shortages due to the demographic downturn in the number of young entrants to the labour market (NEDO, 1989) and an increased interest among policy makers and commentators in the employment of older workers (Taylor and Walker, 1997), the effects were diluted by the recession of the early 1990s.

Overall, UK evidence suggests that where employer activity has occurred, this has usually been concentrated around the recruitment of older workers – the entrance point from the labour market – instead of their utilisation, development and retention within organisations. Among employers there is strong evidence that the incidence of exit schemes targeting older workers was high during the previous recession. Recent research (Arrowsmith and McGoldrick, 1997) found that 87 percent of organisations surveyed which had pursued 'downsizing' strategies had implemented programmes which had affected older workers disproportionately.

Even though there is evidence that some employers introduced policies based on the inclusion of older workers during the late 1980s and early 1990s in response to skills shortages and concern about the demographic timebomb (Trinder, 1989) there is evidence that some policies came under pressure as the UK plunged into recession in the early 1990s (Taylor and Walker, 1998). Nevertheless, we would argue that age discrimination is now on the agendas of some employers even if there is a long way to go before it attains the status accorded other forms of discrimination.

Thus there is little evidence to suggest that there has been a significant change in attitudes and practices towards older workers among UK employers. Some age barriers have gone, but this may only be a temporary situation while the UK is experiencing economic growth. On the other hand, employers appear to be wary of investing in third age workers (Taylor and Walker, 1998). In the following section, we look in more detail at the factors affecting management policies towards older workers.

Factors influencing third age management policies

With regard to the characteristics of employers' policies and practices towards older workers, and the processes by which they evolve and develop these may, to varying degrees be influenced by:

Sectoral and organisational features. Evidence shows that, while age discrimination in employment persists, albeit on a differential basis between public and private sector employers, policies based on the inclusion of older workers are more prevalent in the public sector, and in larger than in smaller employing organisations (Hayward et al, 1997). This is in line with findings from recent research into another equal opportunities issue, namely disability (Honey, 1993; Dench et al, 1996).

Organisational, professional and occupational changes. A factor which plays a significant role in shaping policies towards older workers in organizations is their pervading cultures. The attitudes and assumptions held by senior and middle managers towards older workers – as well as those of their colleagues and peers – are important in determining whether and how policies and practices are implemented (Itzin and Phillipson, 1993; Taylor and Walker, 1998). A good deal has been written about ageism in employment, particularly employers' attitudes towards and perceptions of older workers. Although the term 'older worker' is generally used to refer to those aged 50 and over, it is open to different interpretations. Steinberg et al's (1996) Australian survey conducted among 104 companies in Brisbane found that, while the ages of 51 to 55 denoted 'older worker' for employers, employees tended to select 56 to 60 years of age. Around 35 percent of employers and 14 percent of employees questioned perceived workers aged under 50 as being older.

Stereotypical assumptions about older workers abound – notably perceptions that they are resistant to change and inflexible in their ways (Heaton, 1989; Steinberg et al, (1996), lack the requisite job skills (Thompson, 1991), and have difficulties with training and adapting to new technology (Taylor and Walker, 1994). Thus like race and gender, age is used by 'gatekeepers' within organisations to regulate access to employment and career opportunities. As with other characteristics, age is used as a metaphor for a particular set of attributes, abilities or inabilities to assign positions in organizations, to refuse entry to internal labour markets and to discard workers at certain points in their life cycles through redundancy or early retirement.

Situation and locational factors. Other influences over the development, or otherwise, of third age management strategies are situational and locational factors – such as the sphere of operation, market place and image, and geographic location. There is limited evidence (Thompson, 1991; James, 1994) that the impetus for employers' policies towards older workers has sometimes been local labour market conditions, where the emphasis has been on recruiting older workers in response to labour shortages to fill particular positions in specific locations. This suggests that rather than basing employment decisions on a long-term strategy, employers – for example, in retailing – have tended to recruit to part-time and unskilled jobs from the reserve of older people on an *ad hoc* basis in response to local market requirements. Such policies have thus been implemented on a piecemeal rather than on a universal scale in organizations.

Constructing a research agenda

As we have already seen, much has been written about the relationship between age and labour markets. However, we would argue that there is a long way to go before we understand the issue fully and can make informed recommendations to decision makers. In this section we briefly set out what we consider are weaknesses in the present literature and suggest some new avenues for research.

Methodological issues

Much has been written about age and employment issues, particularly in the 1950s (Logan, 1953; Le Gros Clark, 1959) and 1960s (OECD, 1965), and again in the 1980s (Cooper and Torrington, 1981; Hutchens, 1988; Kohli, Rosenow and Wolf, 1983). Over the past decade much of the debate has centred around age discrimination in the labour market and the consequent barriers to employment (McGoldrick and Arrowsmith, 1992; Trinder et al, 1992; Taylor and Walker, 1993), employers' perceptions of older workers (IPM, 1993 and Pollard, 1997) and on inherent ageism in redundancy and retirement polices and practices (Walker, 1985; Trinder, 1989; Laczko and Phillipson, 1991). Relatively less attention has been paid to the retention, development and management of older employees and their use as valuable resources. Where studies have been conducted, these have tended to be confined to specific sectors of the economy (Itzin and Phillipson, 1993; METRA, 1995) or have drawn upon respondents with certain characteristics, for example, membership of particular organisations (Arrowsmith and McGoldrick, 1996; Lyon and Pollard, 1997). Methodologies adopted in projects have often been concerned with collecting quantitative data and have provided little opportunity for exploring issues – such as career planning for third age workers, re-training, job-redesign, retention beyond state pension age or gradual retirement – in any systematic way.

In addition, as research into age and employment issues has largely been conducted during periods of economic recession, when the emphasis for many organisations has been on 'downsizing', reorganising the production of goods and services, and on streamlining operations, employers' policies have generally been characterised by labour shedding and the selection of those aged 50 and over for early retirement or redundancy (Walker, 1985; Trinder, 1990).

Finally, a major problem has been that studies have been carried out in insufficient depth to draw accurate conclusions about such issues as sectoral, occupational and gender differences and the experiences of different age cohorts.

Another weakness is that most studies have been cross-sectoral in nature and have thus not allowed us to view the development of policies and practices affecting older workers.

Understanding and contextualising ageism in the workplace

There has been little systematic research undertaken to investigate how ageism is constructed and institionalised within organisations. Kohli et al (1983) have asserted that, although considerable work has been undertaken at the macro level, it is essential to understand how strategies of organising life courses of workers are developed and implemented at the level of individual firms. Indeed, more systematic research needs to be undertaken within organisations if we are to understand the key factors, influencing the adoption, or otherwise, of ageist behaviour in the workplace; the extent to which policies and practices adopted by senior managers are a reflection of the internal culture of the organisation; and how ageist attitudes are formulated and transmitted in the workplace.

Another factor which has affected our understanding of employers' policies is that research has tended to examine particular aspects of policies and practices towards older workers, rather than to contextualise these within the broader framework of organisational responses to economic and structural change. Casey, Metcalf and Lakey (1993) went some way to addressing this in their study of employers' approaches towards older workers, highlighting the positive influences which could be exerted over their employment by organisational change, improved utilisation of employees and variability in business demands. However, examples of policies towards older workers were used to substantiate particular points rather than present an holistic examination. Moreover, no analysis of the interplay between the various organisational features and environmental factors was provided, or of the extent to which certain elements may outweigh others.

Barriers to increasing flexibility in retirement

Recent research (Hayward et al, 1997) indicates that some UK employers are introducing measures to make retirement more flexibile. Hayward et al's (1997) survey found that four out of ten employers had increased the flexibility of retirement provisions, notably larger private companies (49 percent) and large public sector organisations (52 per cent). One in ten employers, overall said they had changed or relaxed pension rules, compared with one in four public sector employers. When those employers who used flexible retirement practices were asked about the age span covered, the average minimum age for men to retire was 59 and the average maximum age was 67, while for women the average upper and lower ages for retirement were 65 and 58, respectively. Thus, flexibilisation allowing for later retirement appears to be more a feature of women's employment than men's. More research needs to be undertaken to explore the barriers to flexible retirement which exist within some organisations, and how these might be addressed. Evidence (and Walker, 1994; Taylor and Walker, 1996a, 1996b) suggests that the following factors may be contributory: perceived potential to delay the career progression of younger workers; an emphasis in some organisations on early retirement; negative attitudes towards older workers; the impression among line managers that employees would be uninterested; and pension scheme rules. These need to be explored further.

Effect of employers' retention initiatives on organisational performance

To date, few studies have investigated whether and how employers' retention policies might be changing as some employers recognise that there is a business case for retaining workers over the long term (Taylor and Walker, 1995). Within some organisations, managers appear to have regretted the loss of knowledge and experience when older workers are retired or made redundant. Where downsizing and re-organisations have rendered whole cohorts of older workers 'redundant', the decline in experience and knowledge may have a measurable effect on organisational performance. This may also be true in terms of retaining older workers. Detailed research on the effects on performance, as well as on other areas, of retaining or shedding older workers has yet to be undertaken.

Although some studies have investigated polices towards third age management (Hayward et al, 1997), such as re-training, retention beyond normal retirement ages, job-redesign and gradual retirement, these have tended to be concerned with their incidence rather than their form and effect or, moreover, the context within which they operate. Research into age and employment issues has often had specific concerns and priorities, and thus failed to investigate developing areas fully. In the research conducted by Taylor and Walker (1994), for instance, even where retention strategies were identified by the researchers, these were not explored in any detail because they were not a focus of the study.

The changing nature of organisations and work

Since the 1970s the nature of employment has changed, with the streamlining of operations, re-engineering of processes, the increased use of information technologies and the intensification of work. Meanwhile, the traditional contracting relationships have been changing with the increased use of temporary employment (Casey, Metcalf and Millward, 1997). It has been argued (Arrowsmith and McGoldrick, 1997) that the flexibilisation of work offers the potential for new forms of recruitment and retention among older workers, while technological innovation, new methods of working and changes within the labour process provide scope for training and development. Ostensibly, the growth in fixed-term employment contracts challenges barriers based on age-related assumptions, offering older employees access to second career and post-career jobs – on an equitable basis with younger employees. However, research examining this possibility has yet to be undertaken.

Conclusions

With the changing composition of the labour supply pool in the UK, Europe and beyond employers will, over the next few years, need to radically alter their attitudes, as well as their policies and practices towards older workers. One model is Japan where the proportion of over 50 year olds already outweighs those aged under 25 and government, employers and key agencies are working to improve employment opportunities for older workers. In the UK a comprehensive strategy for dealing with the problems faced by older workers has yet to emerge. The enactment of the Disability Discrimination legislation in 1995 may provide some impetus for employers to reconsider their employment practices towards older workers who develop long-term health problems or disabilities. However, significant improvements in the employment prospects of older workers may only come over the long term.

Are more UK employers orienting towards older workers? We cannot provide a definitive answer but it is our contention that again, relatively little has changed over the past decade. While there have been laudable attempts at increasing the supply of older workers and encouraging employers to address the issue, economic activity rates among older workers have continued to decline and most employers appeared to have remained relatively unmoved by overtures about the demographic 'timebomb' and the issue of ageism. Some employers have recognised the issue and have attempted to introduce policies and practices accordingly. However, the removal of age barriers from parts of the recruitment process, which seems to have been the strategy most adopted by employers, is only a very small step towards overcoming the substantial age barriers which exist in organisations. There are few examples of job redesign, career planning, training and development initiatives and radical new approaches to retirement among employers.

Until more up to date, substative research is undertaken to investigate in detail the ways in which organisations are approaching the management of their third age workforce, it will not be possible to determine those changes in policy and policy making which are enabling employers to meet the challenges they will face in the future. In particular, research needs to be undertaken to investigate how policy towards older workers is made within organisations – both at a general and specific level – and the process by which policies, such as those for age management are devised and implemented. Are they imposed by a central management team, developed via more local sites or championed by individual managers? Within particular occupations and professions there is an emphasis on younger and 'prime age' workers – for example, in those related to media and sales. How is an organisation's policy formulated and applied, particularly under the predominance of internal sub-cultures, such as those of professional and occupational groups?

There is also a need for more research which explores employers' attitudes and practices towards older workers during periods of economic growth and tighter labour markets, which looks at the experiences of different sub-groups of older workers, and for research which examines the extent to which and how the loss of older workers through redundancy and retirement has affected organisations' performance. In addition, more research is required which explores barriers to greater employment flexibility among older workers.

In our review of research in this area we have presented a pessimistic, but we believe, realistic assessment of the situation of older workers in the UK labour market. Progress to date has been slow and it is our contention that there will be relatively little until policy makers recognise that ageism in the labour market is a serious problem requiring urgent attention and radical policy initiatives, such as increasing flexibility in retirement. There are some recent signs that policy makers have begun to alter their attitudes, but for the time-being many older workers will continue to face a bleak future.

References

Arrowsmith, L. and McGoldrick, A. (1996), *Breaking the Barriers*, Institute of Management, London.

Arrowsmith, L. and McGoldrick, A. (1997), 'A flexible future for older workers?', *Personnel Review*, Vol. 26, No. 4, pp. 258-73.

Casey, B., Metcalf, H. and Lakey, J. (1993), 'Human resources strategies in the third age', in IPM (1993), *Age and Employment: Policies, Attitude and Practice*, Institute of Personnel Management, London.

Casey, B., Metcalf, H. and Millward, N. (1997), *Employers' Use of Flexible Labour*, Policy Studies Institute, London.

Casey, B. and Wood, S. (1994), ' Great Britain: Firm Policy, State Policy and the Employment of Older Workers', in F. Naschold and B. de Vroom (eds) *Regulating Employment and Welfare: Company and National Policies of Labour Force Participation at the End of Worklife in Industrial Countries*, Walter de Gruyter, Berlin.

Clark, R. and Anker, R. (1990), 'Labour force participation rates of older persons: an international comparison, *International Labour Review*, No. 129, pp. 255-71.

Clark, R. and Ogawa, N. (1996), 'Human resources policies and older workers in Japan', *The Gerontologist*, Vol. 36, No. 5, pp. 627-636.

Collis, C. and Mallier, T. (1996), 'Third age male activity rates in Britain and its regions', *Regional Studies*, Vol. 30, No. 8, pp. 803-09.

Cooper, C. and Torrington, D. (1981), *After Forty: the Time for Achievement?*, Wiley, London.

Dench, S., Meager, N. and Morris, S. (1996), *The Recruitment and Retention of People with Disabilities*, Institute for Employment Studies, Brighton.

Department of Education and Employment (1998), *Labour Force Survey data* (Autumn 1997 quarter).

Drury, E. (ed.) (1997), *Public Policy Options to Assist Older Workers*, Eurolink Age, London.

The Economist (1958), December, cited in Le Gros Clark, F. (1959) op cit.

Employment Department (1995), *Employment Gazette*, April.

Gudgin, G. and Schofield, A. (1993), 'The emergence of the north-south divide and its projected future', in R. Harrison and M. Hart (eds), *Spatial Policy in a Divided Nation*, Regional Studies Association, London.

Hayward, B., Taylor, S., Smith, N. and Davies, G. (1997), *Evaluation of the Campaign for Older Workers*, The Stationery Office, London.

Heaton, S. (1989), 'The Grey Discrimination', *Industrial Society Magazine*, June.

Honey, S. (1993), *Employers' Attitudes Towards People with Disabilities*, Institute for Manpower Studies, Brighton.

Hutchens, R. (1988), 'Do job opportunities decline with age?', *Industrial Labor Relations Review*, Vol. 42, No. 1, pp. 89-99.

Inland Revenue (1998), *Occupational Pension Schemes: Enhanced Flexibility: A Discussion Paper*, Savings and Investment Division.

IPM (1993), *Age and Employment: Policies, Attitudes and Practice*, Institute of Personnel Management, London.

Itzin, C. and Phillipson, C. (1993), *Age barriers at work,* Metropolitan Authorities Recruitment Agency, Solihull.

Jacobs, K., Kohli, M. and Rein, M. (1991), 'Testing the industry mix hypothesis of early exit', in M. Kohli, M. Rein, A-M. Guillermard and H. van Gunsteren, H. (eds), (1991) (op cit).

James, L. (1994), 'Hot house flowers: a UK retailer's response to older workers', *Investing in Older People at Work: Symposium*, Health Education Authority, London.

Jolly, J. Creigh, S. and Mingay, A. (1980), *Age as a Factor in Employment*, Research Paper no. 11, Department of Employment, HMSO, London.

Kohli, M., Rein, M., Guillemard, A-M., and van Gunsteren, H. (eds) (1991), *Time for Retirement: Comparative Studies of Early Exit from the Labour Force*, Cambridge University Press.

Kohli, M., Rosenow, J. and Wolf, J. (1983), 'The social construction of ageing through work: economic structure and life world', *Ageing and Society*, Vol. 3, pp. 23-42.

Laczko, F. and Phillipson, C. (1991), *Changing Work and Retirement*, Open University, Milton Keynes.

Le Gros Clark, F. (1959), *Age and the Working Lives of Men*, Nuffield Foundation, London.

Logan, W. (1953), 'Work and age: statistical considerations', *British Medical Journal*, 28 November, pp. 245-57.

Lyon, H.P. and Pollard, D. (1997), 'Perceptions of the older employee: is anything really changing?, *Personnel Review*, Vol. 26, No. 4, pp. 245-57.

MacKay, R. (1992), 'Labour market adjustment in Wales', in C. Verhaar, L. Jansma, M. De Goede, J. Vanophem and A. de Vries (eds), *On the Mysteries of Unemployment*, Kluwer Academic, Dordrecht.

McGoldrick, A. and Arrowsmith, J. (1992), 'Age discrimination in recruitment: an analysis of age bias in advertisements'. Paper presented at the conference on *The Employment of Older Workers in the 1990s*, Sheffield University, April.

METRA (1995), *Employment of Older Workers and Age Auditing*, Local Government Management Board, London.

Moore, J., Tilson, B. and Whitting, G. (1994), *An International Overview of Employment Policies and Practices towards Older Workers*, Employment Department Research Series No. 29, Sheffield.

NEDO (1989), *Defusing the Demographic Timebomb*, NEDO, London.

OECD (1965), *Job Redesign and Occupational Training for Older Workers*, OECD, Paris.

Payne, J. and Payne, C. (1994), 'Recession, restructuring and the fate of the unemployed: evidence in the underclass debate', *Sociology*, Vol. 28, No. 1, pp. 1-19.

Phillipson, C. (1982), *Capitalism and the Construction of Old Age*, Macmillan.

Reday-Mulvey, G. and Delsen, L. (1996), 'Gradual retirement in the OECD countries: a summary of the main results', *Geneva Papers on Risk and Insurance*, No. 81, pp. 502-23.

Smith, C. and Duffy, B. (1993), *Retirement in Britain*, Halifax Building Society, Halifax.

Standing, G. (1986), 'Labour flexibility and older worker marginalisation: the need for a new strategy, *International Labour Review*, Vol. 125, No. 3, pp. 329-48.

Steinberg, M., Donald, K., Najman, J. and Skerman, H. (1996), 'Attitudes of employees and employers towards older workers in a climate of anti-discrimination', *Australian Journal on Ageing*, Vol. 15, No. 4, pp. 154-58.

Takayama, N. (1996), 'Gradual retirement in Japan: macro issues and policies', in L. Delsen and G. Reday-Mulvey, (eds) (1996), *Gradual Retirement in the OECD Countries*, Dartmouth, Aldershot.

Taylor, P. and Walker, A. (1994), 'The ageing workforce: employers' attitudes towards older workers', *Work, Employment and Society*, Vol. 8, No. 4, pp. 569-91.

Taylor, P. and Walker, A. (1995), 'Utilising older workers', *Employment Gazette*, April, pp. 141-45.

Taylor, P. and Walker, A. (1996a), 'Gradual Retirement in the United Kingdom', in L. Delsen and G. Reday-Mulvey (eds) (1996), *Gradual Retirement in the OECD Countries*, Dartmouth, Aldershot.

Taylor, P. and Walker, A. (1996b), 'Intergenerational relations in the labour market: the attitudes of employers and older workers', in A. Walker (ed.), *The New Generational Contract*, UCL, London.

Taylor, P. and Walker, A. (1997), 'Age discrimination and public policy', *Personnel Review*, Vol. 26, No. 4, pp. 307-18.

Taylor, P. and Walker, A. (1998), 'Policies and practices towards older workers: a framework for comparative research', *Human Resource Management Journal*, Vol. 8, No. 3, pp. 61-76.

Thompson, M. (1991), *Last in the Queue? Corporate Employment Policies and the Older Worker*, Report No. 209, Institute of Manpower Studies, Brighton.

Tillsley, C. (1990), *The Impact of Age upon Employment*, IRRU papers, No. 33, University of Warwick.

Trinder, C. (1989), *Employment after 55*, National Institute for Economic and Social Research, Discussion Paper No. 166.

Trinder, C., Hulme, G. and McCarthy, U. (1992), *Employment: the Role of Work in the Third Age*, The Carnegie United Kingdom Trust, Dunfermline.

Wadensjö, E. (1996), 'Gradual retirement in Sweden', in L. Delsen and G. Reday-Mulvey (eds), *Gradual Retirement in the OECD Countries*, Dartmouth, Aldershot.

Walker, A. (1985), 'Early retirement: release or refuge from the labour market?', *The Quarterly Journal of Social Affairs*, Vol. 1, No. 3, pp. 211-29.

Walker, A. (1997), *Combatting Age Barriers in Employment*, European Foundation for the Improvement of Living and Working Conditions, Dublin.

Part V
Conclusion

19 Therefore get wisdom

Ian Glover and Mohamed Branine

Silence is the virtue of fools.
(Francis Bacon: *Cogitationes de Natura Rerum,* 5, 9, translated from the Latin).

Introduction

Ageism can be depressing to read and write about. It is not pleasant to contemplate evidence about depressed and at times suicidal young people unable to develop adult identities, about middle aged people unimaginatively employed due to inane age-related prejudice or about energetic mature people on the scrapheap. However we have come to realise that the underlying forces which have made ageism into something of a public issue in the early twenty-first century are on the whole benign ones, since they include greater wealth, longer lives and heightened concern for injustice. We have been converted from worried pessimists to concerned and fascinated optimists.

In this concluding chapter we first note, briefly, the main issues which the preceding chapters, including the first, address. Then we discuss each chapter in turn, extracting from it what for us are the points of argument and the facts most relevant to the understanding of those issues. Finally, and apart from the final concluding paragraph, we draw together all the evidence and issues previously discussed or referred to in a section concerned with future policy and research.

The main issues addressed so far

The first is the value of and the need for thinking about relationships between age, work and employment and all other relevant phenomena, rather than about the narrower and more emotive notion of ageism. Let us use an example to explain this important point.

In the late 1990s a friend of ours in her late fifties was turned down for a chair by a Scottish university after having what she felt had been an excellent interview and series of discussions with potential future colleagues. Two chairs had been on offer, one in finance, marketing or strategy or some combination of these, and one, for which she was a candidate, in organizational behaviour. Five people were interviewed, three for the first post and two for the latter. One of the candidates for the former was about her age, one was about forty and the other was probably, she felt, in her late twenties. The person last referred to was the only internal candidate. The other candidate for the chair in organizational behaviour told her that he was in his early thirties. The candidates heard a hint during their visit to the institution that one appointee would probably be a 'mature' experienced one and the other a much younger one who would have a good track record but who could also learn from such experience while being a long term prospect. They were also told that the decisions would be made immediately after the interviews, in the early evening of the Wednesday set apart for them, and that they would all be telephoned with the result within the next two working days. Our friend was telephoned at 4.55pm on the second of these by the university's director of human resources. She was told that 'unfortunately, the posts have been offered to two of the other candidates'. However one had not so far accepted, after over a day of being advised by telephone message of the offer of a job, and if this person did not accept the offer, it would be offered to our friend. In the event, and a week later, our friend learned that her rival had taken up the offer.

During her visit for her interview our friend had become quite familiar with the other older candidate, and it turned out that this person had been one of the successful ones. He was told shortly after taking up his post that the two best interviewees had been himself and our friend. He had been clearly superior to his two competitors but our friend's younger rival for the organizational behaviour post had been almost as appointable as our friend and had been offered a post because of the institutions' desire to appoint one very experienced older candidate and one significantly younger one. The two unsuccessful, and younger, candidates for the finance/marketing/strategy post had not been as appointable as the other three, particularly the two oldest candidates. Our friend had thus lost out because of her age, but not because of ageism. In fact the director of personnel had commented to her, over lunch on the interview day, that 'we are not an ageist institution'. The appointments were designed to help stimulate research in a large segment of what was a large new university so that a mixture of experience and of long term prospects was required. Our friend was promoted to professor in her own institution a year later. She did not feel that the new university concerned had discriminated unfairly against her on the grounds of her age. It was her experience and achievements, which she could not have had to offer but for her age, that had secured her an interview in the first place. Age had been the main factor in her rejection but it had not been used unfairly in the circumstances. Indeed the interview panel appeared to be slightly prejudiced, if anything, in favour of older candidates.

We tell this story as an example of sensible age-related discrimination in action, of the more or less appropriate use of age in recruitment and selection. We are therefore re-emphasising the main point of our introductory chapter, that it is not age discrimination which is wrong, but rather incompetent age discrimination. The other main issues that have concerned, and concern, us are the commodification versus greening of work and employment, the relevance of the idea of reflexive modernity in a context of high affluence and growing longevity, and the economic practicality and social desirability of policies intended to encourage and support more intelligent forms of age-related discrimination in employment. In other and briefer words, we are interested in the economic, flexible and sympathetic development and use of people at all stages of what we hope will continue to be their increasingly lengthy and varied lives, in ways which whenever possible and useful help make their ages work for and not against them.

How the chapters contribute

The six, seven and four chapters which, respectively, are in Parts Two, Three and Four of the book rarely if ever sit very neatly in them. However we make no apology for the glorious messiness of reality. We believe that each group of chapters offers substantial food for thought about the heading and the phenomena under which it is classified.

Chapters two to seven are thus on the whole concerned with the problem of ageism in work and employment, and with its causes. We located that by Colin Duncan first because it both addresses definitional issues and, even more importantly, the rationality of age-based discrimination as often practised by employers against older employees. Duncan begins by noting how concern about such 'ageism' was first generated by gerontologists in the 1950s and 1960s. They had claimed to have detected a growing 'blame the victim' mentality towards older people. Enforced retirement, poor social provision and low incomes had been the main reasons for this, rather than the biological and psychological decline attributed to them. In the USA the term ageism had begun to be used fairly widely in the 1970s but in the UK it only began 'to enter the popular vocabulary [in] the 1990s in the context of a concern over early exit'. It now applied rather more often to the 'young-old', for example people in their fifties and sixties, than to the normally retired 'old-old'.

Increasingly, ageism had come to be understood as a harmful social, rather than biological, phenomenon. It was not new. Indeed it predated capitalism. Before the invention of printing and the loss of oral traditions associated with the coming of modernity the old were repositories of learning and experience. In industrial societies they had lost this function, just as they had always been characterized by loss of physical strength. Fear of physical decline and the decline of custom in an era of apparently accelerating change had led to a situation in which negative images of old age and the old were widely instilled into people. Relevant attitudes were reinforced by structured dependency: in the era of compulsory retirement old age was seen as a burden, and education, medical and social neglect of the old were officially sanctioned. Although people became more diverse with age (Laslett, 1989) old age was perceived as a kind of affliction or disease and older people were homogenized and dehumanised. They were victims of patronising concern at best and neglect and vilification at worst.

Duncan considers definitions of age and ageism in some depth, notably those of Bytheway (1995). He notes how ambiguous they often are, varying between applications to people of all ages and to the 'old', normally to those who are at least of retirement age. We think that this reflects the tendency of the 1990s and after to realise that ageism is applicable to people of all ages and that it is most helpful to consider it in such a way. Ageism is an intergenerational biological, economic, psychological and social phenomenon as, of course, age itself is. He goes on to ask whether ageism as largely applied to old people is particularly relevant in the context of employment. He argues that it is, insofar as the abilities and experiences of older employees tend to be devalued systematically compared with those of younger people. He also, by contrast, shows how age discrimination in employment begins much younger than most writers on it had admitted. Upper age bars were often set at 'around the 40 age mark' and opportunities for promotion and training often began reducing at about that age, and women suffered the double jeopardy of age and gender based discrimination at virtually all ages. The 'prime age' band in the eyes of most employers was from 25 to 35 and many people under the former age suffered from age discrimination.

Duncan goes on to note how many employers were, in the 1990s, distinguishing between age discrimination based on irrational prejudice and that based on commercial practicalities. He argues, using evidence about early exit from the UK labour force, that the exclusions of many people in their 50s and early 60s from employment had created 'a generation in limbo' (Bosanquet, 1987). In the 1970s and 1980s, in the UK and other developed countries, the large scale early exit from employment of older people, especially that of males, had been much more attributable to 'push' as opposed to 'pull' factors. Push factors meant economic conditions and employer policies, whereas pull ones emphasized the attractiveness of some exit routes. Most authors agreed with Duncan that push factors were much more powerful, and indeed that such pull ones as attractive early retirement schemes were often simply the sugar coating the unpleasant pill of a fundamentally antagonistic process.

Around 1990, however, early exit became much less socially acceptable as a way of coping with mass unemployment and structural change. Governments were realising and becoming more concerned about the costs of early exit in a context of ever-increasing longevity. The recession of the late 1980s which lasted well into the 1990s was affecting many mature and senior middle-class employees in commerce and finance. Such people had rarely if ever experienced loss of employment and they often attributed it to ageism, and did so publicly. The growing debates about ageism of the 1990s tended, however, to ignore the possibility that relevant employer actions were economically rational.

In the key section of his chapter Duncan distinguishes between four types of rationality of employers' policies towards older employees. One type treated them unfavourably and was commercially damaging. The second also treated them unfavourably but was commercially rational. The third was favourable towards them and commercially rational, and the fourth was also favourable, but not commercially rational. Ageism defined as policies or practices with no commercial basis was that of the first and fourth types. Some employer policies could be age-based but neutral or impossible to assess in terms of their commercial effects. It was often thought that most employer policies were of the first type but Duncan disagrees with this.

Nonetheless this view was the 'current orthodoxy'. Both the Conservative governments up to 1997 and most other concerned public bodies such as Age Concern, the Institute of Personnel and Development, trade unions and the Equal Opportunities Commission, felt that age discrimination of all kinds was both commercially damaging and irrational as regards the abilities and motivation of relevant groups of employees. Industrial gerontology had shown for a quarter of a century that such employer beliefs that older employees tend to be less productive, and both less trainable and less worth training given their apparent lack of long term employment prospects, and so on, were largely mistaken. Older employees possessed such virtues as 'stability, low turnover, commitment, [and] responsibility', and they held much of the 'collective memory' of their organizations. In particular they tended to be more knowledgeable about markets and better at handling customers than younger staff. Few employers knew the age compositions of their organizations (Worsley, 1996), and the costs of early retirement packages were sometimes greater than the salaries that had been saved. Such evidence and arguments had been used to support a perception that employers were often irrational and prejudiced about age, or simply out of touch with the choices of their managers and personnel departments.

However, Duncan suggests, early exit and similar age-related policies may be quite rational on business grounds. Older employees might be competent but they were also often genuinely more expensive than younger ones. Their seniority and their tendency to enjoy prerogatives based on it often made them more difficult and expensive to redeploy or to fire than younger counterparts. The latter tended to be more productive mainly because they were paid less, and the costs of their occupational pensions tended to be lower. Unless some way of paying older staff less existed, the temptation to shed them was strong and to do so was often likely to reduce costs and to enhance productivity. The trend towards more flexible working practices also favoured the substitution of younger staff for older ones, because it increasingly made financial sense to employ casual labour for the increasing numbers of narrow static jobs for which workers are interchangeable (Standing, 1986, p. 336). Sometimes older employees were lacking in terms of qualifications and skills and if they were employed in relatively large numbers they could limit promotion opportunities and affect the morale of younger ones. Most employees over 50 were unfamiliar with computers whereas virtually all people under 30 had some familiarity and usually a considerable amount. Other factors working against older employees which Duncan notes are the climate of continual reorganization in the face of competitive pressures in the 1980s and 1990s, the tendency and ability of older workers to resist such changes as decollectivization and culture change initiatives, their general value to the system as part of the 'reserve army of labour', their growing social and political obsolescence in organizational hierarchies which are increasingly characterized as 'young' and dynamic', and so on. We ourselves doubt the validity of some of these points. For example we are not sure that the morale of employees of any age cohort is necessarily more important than that of another. We know that computing skills are easy for older people to learn unless they have been continually discouraged by ageist comments. We also suspect that much of their educated scepticism about recent managerial developments is wholly admirable. However they clearly do have some validity and widespread belief in them gives them power independent of the extent of their basis in fact.

Duncan also notes how it has largely been retailing and hotel and catering sector employers who have discriminated positively in favour of older employees on commercial grounds. These sectors had experienced labour supply problems and employers in them had found older employees to offer some advantages in the form of stability, commitment and interaction with customers. However the number of sectors in which it was convenient and cheap to employ older people in significant numbers was likely to be quite restricted. There was also, however, some evidence that many employers did employ more older staff than was in their interests, mainly from a mixture of habit, culture and other rather arbitrary reasons to do with the actual availability of labour in specific instances.

In general, organizations had very varied age profiles without employee age having many particular or obvious effects on business performance. Different types of employee were often treated differently regarding their ages in the same organizations. Employers tended to be harder on older staff as regards recruitment, deployment and development but to be more generous as regards pay and other rewards associated with seniority. They were ambiguous but not lacking sophistication towards them on the whole, and they also often knew how to exploit or reinforce ageist prejudices for their own commercial advantage. There was little serious evidence of the mixture of commercial irrationality and negative stereotyping of older staff by employers which many writers assumed. Duncan is apparently quite sympathetic towards the interpretation of Guillemard and van Gunsteren (1991). They felt that employers did tend to view older employees in a negative light but that this was fairly rational in business terms. They felt that early exit policies were actually evidence of decline in employer ageism. Retirement was increasingly based on functional criteria rather than on chronological age. Older employees were losing their jobs in an era of intense competition because they were 'less useful or efficient, possibly, *but not necessarily*, as a result of ageing', and not simply because of their ages.

Duncan concludes by arguing that while some employer prejudice against older employees clearly existed, much employer behaviour was quite rational, and indeed evidence of declining employer ageism. Policies which assumed irrational employer ageism could be very counterproductive, reinforcing the labour market disadvantages of older workers by forcing employers to think more rationally than hitherto and thus encouraging them to become even tough-minded towards the continued employment of relatively expensive elders. Any legislation against ageism ought, in logic, to apply to people of all ages. However, and because age-related prejudices were 'deeply ingrained in human nature', and because there was no clearly oppressed group, 'almost everyone might be considered both perpetrator and victim'. There could be enormous scope for challenging employers, and thus considerable employer resistance. In Canada, the only country in which anti-ageism legislation had been framed so as to apply to all age groups, enforcement was poor and 'the Supreme Court has ruled that while compulsory retirement is discriminatory, it is still legal'. Yet if legislation only applied to older people it could also be seen as discriminatory against younger ones, and also even as sexist. The USA's experience of its Age Discrimination Act of 1967 was one of many exceptions being sought and obtained with little in the way of an effective challenge to employer policies based on ageist prejudices being mounted. In the UK attitudes and policies seemed to be fairly volatile and shallow, and concern about future population trends not very strong. This did not augur well for older employees. 'Third agers', the 'young-old' were being encouraged as elsewhere to be 'integrated into society through roles that do not necessarily contain a work element'. This might lead to their distancing themselves from the 'old-old' as had been observed happening both in the USA and in the 'offhand attitude of the Carnegie researchers [of the mid 1990s into the Third Age and its needs] towards fourth agers, indicating an apparent willingness to reinstate the distinctions and inequalities of traditional old age'.

In chapter three Glover and Branine discuss the same issues addressed by Duncan in a more speculative way. Both of these papers use definitions of ageism which see it as something directed at people of any age. However Glover and Branine allow themselves to be somewhat more optimistic than Duncan and they are readier to see ageism as a largely irrational phenomenon, partly because they are less concerned than he is with the attitudes of employers and thus with financial costs of training and employing people. They criticise a number of (what they feel are) academic and popular myths which have helped to underpin ageism and base their relatively optimistic conclusions on their concern for the long term and the point that an on average older but physically younger, fitter and stronger population appears to be both achievable and an opportunity rather than a threat.

Together, and with their differences of emphasis but similar assumptions and concerns, these first two chapters set the scene for the remainder of Part Two and of the book as a whole. They regard ageism as widespread across age groups and employment sectors and varied in its character and effects, and deep-rooted because of its basis in the life cycle, the fear of death, and in valuations of strength, beauty, ability, expertise, wisdom and so on.

Chapter four by Peter Herriot is somewhat more focused on the management rhetoric, especially that of the USA, of the 1990s and the main victim of it, the plateaued middle manager. For Herriot, the hero of management rhetoric of the 1970s was the leader of the great corporation. He (normally it was a he) had been replaced by the worker hero of the Total Quality Management of the 1980s. Then, in the 1990s the 'fashionable hero was the change-maker ... the young thruster who disregards procedures, challenges authority, and gets things done'. The villains had included lazy workers, trade union activists and 'wily Orientals ... [who stole] our ideas'. There had also been, on very many occasions, the middle manager who stifled both inspiration coming from the top and innovation coming from below, acting as wet blankets to protect their own power and their own jobs.

Herriot's main focus is the 'worst villain of all ... the plateaued middle manager'. In order to consider the situation and role of this person he uses attribution theory from social and occupational psychology. Attribution is the 'psychological process of allocating a cause to a person or event'. Some attributions are made to the person under consideration and others to external forces, to other people or other elements of their situations that affect the person. These are usually called internal and external attributions, respectively. Herriot noted how it is the individualistic USA which is the main source of popular management literature, with its use of heroes and villains to explain organizational success and failure. The culture of the USA was 'particularly characterised by internal attributions of causality'. An internal locus of control was a desirable management characteristic in the USA. However, and in fact, plateaued managers were often victims of external events, outside their control. This did not stop them, nonetheless, from getting the blame for their organizations' problems, and from being blamed further when they pointed to the effects of unavoidable and damaging external events.

Herriot reviews a number of studies of the careers of managers in the US and elsewhere and of the arguments and debates surrounding them. Ference, Stoner and Warren (1977) had identified four types of manager: stars, high performers and likely to be promoted; comers, low performers yet still likely to be promoted; solid citizens, low on promotion but high on performance; and deadwood, low on both. The latter two types were plateaued with deadwood being former solid citizens whose performance had declined. Feldman and Weitz (1988) 'extended ... the hint of villainy' by attributing such factors as low motivation, lack of ambition, lack of interest in the job, discontent, stress and burnout to plateaued managers. People with such attributes were unlikely to receive 'further assignments of increased responsibility', and tended to be 'deadwood'. These authors had tended to focus on internal, personal, attributions and reasons for plateauing. Managers had clear senses of being ahead or behind of their career timetables, as defined in terms of grades achieved by certain ages. They tended to see themselves as behind when they were not, 'as judged by actual age-grade distribution', because they underestimated the numbers of older people in particular grades. Whatever the reality the concept of the deadwood plateued manager had entered the academic vocabulary of management in an era when employers were downsizing and cutting costs.

For Herriot, the real reasons for plateauing were not, in general, the shortcomings of individual managers. It was simply impossible for most people to reach the higher or top levels of management: in pyramid-shaped organizations there were simply not enough posts available. Plateauing was also usually the cause of low motivation and performance, not its effect. Herriot and colleagues had shown that the higher people were in hierarchies the longer they stayed in particular jobs, and 'the longer they remain in a job the less satisfied and more bored they become'. Different kinds of business strategy produced different kinds of career structure and levels of opportunity. Higher proportions of deadwood plateaued managers tended to be found in organizations operating relatively unambitiously in relatively static markets. Size of organization had clear effects, too: bigger organizations promoted from within much more often than smaller ones. Tournament mobility was also a very relevant notion. Failure in early promotion rounds, early after taking a first job, tended to be fatal. Politics and patronage were also key influences: being in a favoured function, being at headquarters or on a high profile assignment all helped. Patronage was so important that even to be perceived as having a patron, in the absence of a real one, could be advantageous. For Herriot it was mainly these kinds of influence, or the lack of them, and not inadequate ability or motivation, which led to managers being plateaued.

Herriot, Hirsh and Reilly (1998) had noted some of the functions that managerial rhetoric performed. One was aspirational: here top managers spoke of what was happening as if it consisted of what they wanted to happen, usually by concentrating on some things and playing down or ignoring others. Another was presentational. Situations are interpreted as ones of opportunity and hope, rather than as ones of threat and uncertainty. Finally, rationalisation was used to justify management actions and the results of them by explaining them in the most favourable terms. In short, facts were selected, presented and explained in ways which were most compatible with the pursuit of managerial self-interest. Managerial rhetoric almost always, Herriot argues, favours the new over the 'old' or 'traditional'. Change is good and stability is bad. Resistance to change comes from the 'deadwood'. Flexibility comes from the young. The rhetoric of change is supported by that of culture. Organizational cultures should be unified and not plural, and transformative and new and not stable and old. If older employees are to keep their jobs, they must be ready to change their beliefs and values. The rhetoric of human resource management underpinned all of the above. Human resources were there to be husbanded (as in our 'greening') or 'used up' (as in our 'commodification') in the pursuit of business objectives (Legge, 1995). It was 'entirely justifiable to cut out deadwood and cast it aside in such a context'.

For Herriot the deadwood manager stereotype and the rhetoric surrounding it had given top managers ways of justifying job losses amongst middle managers and professionals, to those of them who survived, which appeared to be needed or which were useful political weapons and virility symbols in the 1980s and 1990s. The survivors, it was suggested, were those who were valued by top management, who formed the 'core' of expertise in a company, and who had long term futures in it. And if change programmes failed, if desired transformational effects were not achieved, the 'deadwood' would be useful scapegoats. More generally still, the insecurity and paranoia of many top managers often led them to attract mediocre individuals to themselves and to perceive helpful comments and useful criticism as personal disloyalty. They often denigrated and excluded 'stars' because their successes reflected badly on themselves and because they wanted to control everything around them. Middle managers, without power bases needed for fighting back, were ideal scapegoats in such situations.

Herriot points out that management by cost cutting, downsizing and by following the advice of management gurus and consultants, treating change, novelty and short run efficiency as ends in themselves, have often failed to enhance profitability, let alone the development of abilities, over the longer term. The deadwood rhetoric was invalid. Many redundant middle managers and professionals were re-employed as consultants, or got equally good jobs with competitors. Management fads were notoriously short-lived. Top managers were conspicuously greedy, disloyal and their rhetoric was belied by the experiences of subordinates. Also workforces were growing older and managers and professionals were increasingly in demand. Top managers would need to regain employee trust, after getting age discrimination a bad name.

In their chapter Ann McGoldrick and James Arrowsmith offer similar kinds of arguments to Herriot but with differences of emphasis as regards types of datum used and the kinds of influence discussed. They explore the roles of objective and organization level conditions and processes, as well as subjective stereotyping, in producing age discrimination. They use two sources of data to illustrate problems faced by older employees. The first is about potential entry to the labour market, with the chapter's authors outlining some of the main findings from surveys of national recruitment advertising reported in four years from 1981 to 1993. The second is about a more intensive view of perceptions of older employees of UK companies. This is based on an Economic and Social Research Council (ESRC) funded study of age and employment conducted with a sample of Institute of Management (IM) members, examining individual experiences and attitudes, as well as relevant employer policies and practices. The account of the results shows how important both managerial stereotyping and various organizational characteristics are as influences on age discrimination.

Specific concerns of this chapter include the following. There is, first, the gap between growing employer, government and public concern with age discrimination and the ongoing and widespread practice of it. The authors emphasize the strength of evidence on the positive attributes of older employees in ways which suggest that there may be plenty of justification for widespread suspicions of the operation of a self-fulfilling prophecy regarding their abilities, motivation, commitment and performance. The surveys of recruitment advertising suggested that discriminatory references to age in job advertisements were more common for managerial and professional posts and careers than for more junior ones, more common in industry than in services and also more common in the private sector than the public one. The use of age limits in advertisements appeared to have increased in the 1980s and to have reduced in the 1990s. The 'golden age' for candidates for employment appeared to be from 28 to 37. Age discriminatory occupations tended to be ones in which direct selling and business generation and other forms of face to face contact relevant to performance were involved. Less discriminatory occupations tended to be technical and other ones with clearly defined skills, qualifications and experiences, ones for which age *as such* need not be quoted in recruitment advertisements. Most upper age bars in advertisements were 'placed prior to the age of 50'.

As regards management attitudes towards older employees, previous studies had suggested fairly widespread prejudice and the use of older employees as 'last resorts' even when jobs were relatively plentiful. External recruitment and selection, rather than in internal labour markets, was where more age discrimination tended to take place. Line managers, in some surveys, seemed to be more prejudiced than their organizational superiors or human resource professionals, and likely to frustrate any 'progressive policy initiatives'. The authors' own ESRC funded study of IM members obtained data from 1,665 individuals. Respondents tended to be male, over 40, and in senior or middle management jobs. In general older employees were regarded as more reliable, committed, conscientious, loyal and conscientious, and more socially competent and more likely to produce high quality work than their younger counterparts. On the other hand they were thought of as less flexible and able to change, with less development potential. Many respondents thought that organizations needed balanced age mixes and that chronological age was not a reliable predictor of abilities: people could be young at sixty and old at thirty, and so on. Employees became 'older', on average, between the ages of 50 and 54, although women tended to become older at slightly younger ages than men.

Respondents reported themselves as less likely to use age discrimination when promoting and (especially) training people than when recruiting and selecting them. Nearly half (44 percent) of the respondents believed that their ages had been unhelpful when they had applied for jobs, and 24 percent indicated that they had suffered in the same way as regards promotion. Female respondents were much less likely to admit to discriminating on the grounds of age and seniority, and older male respondents were more likely than their younger male counterparts as well as their female ones, to admit that they had. Managers in larger organizations were more likely than those in smaller ones to make the relevant admissions.

Regarding the future, the respondents were in general keen to address the issue in their own organizations, tending to regard age discrimination as equally harmful as racial or sexual discrimination, or slightly more so. Most (about two thirds) were in favour of legislation against upper age limits in recruitment advertisements and for relevant forms of comprehensive employment protection. It was regarded as a moral issue by 90 percent of them, as a business one by 73 percent, and as a 'mainstream managerial' one by 62 percent. Views about the nature of age discrimination and its causes, associated problems and possible solutions were very diverse. There was a great deal of ambivalence and paradox in the answers to the more open-ended questions. Age could be a convenient if partial indicator of job relevant attributes like physical strength and fitness, or family circumstances. Respondents were often derisive about ageism in society and in general, but they also felt that age profiles were justifiably seen as relevant for, for example, 'career progression, pension funding and general organizational vitality'. Mature and younger managers alike were criticized for sometimes fearing the experience and abilities of older candidates for jobs. Many respondents felt that younger employees could cope better with long hours, work intensification (and in some cases low pay), than older ones. They tended to be more up to date in 'new and/or rapidly expanding technological fields'. However the discarding of the stability and experience of older employees for cheaper young ones was admitted or noted with little obvious satisfaction or pleasure. McGoldsmith and Arrowsmith conclude by arguing that employers and legislators needed to pay more attention to older employees and older unemployed people in a context of greater longevity, but they do not take sides on the issue of legislation, while making a strong pleas for more thorough and open debate and problem resolution.

The sixth chapter, by Philip Bowers, explores the issue of whether retirement is economically sustainable given relevant changes in demography and employment patterns. He considers the public finance implications of pensions and health care costs and the burden of increased dependency ratios between the proportions of the population in employment and those reliant on them, on future generations. He focuses on the potential effects on equities from positive net cash flows into pension schemes to negative cash flows. What he has to say has important implications for the future of relationships between age and employment.

Bowers begins by noting how the problem of an increasing dependency ratio in the UK is not and will not be as severe as in several other OECD countries. Even so present UK policies looked likely to result in a greater disparity between the incomes of different kinds of retired people, and an unacceptable problem of old age poverty. Partial, rather than delayed, retirement might be the best source of a solution.

Bowers notes how current UK policies designed to effectively reduce the state old age pension are likely to make those entirely dependent on it much poorer. In the future about half of retired people would have occupational pensions with maybe a further 30 percent having private ones. Men were much more likely to have occupational or private pensions than women, and private pensions tended to be very expensive. There was also the related problem of funding long term health care for those elderly people in need of it, which tended to bear much more heavily on those who had been thrifty than on those who had, for whatever reason, not been so. A further problem was the reduced rates of savings prevalent with a well funded elderly population. Pension funds could move into deficit and cease to be sources of savings.

In any society with an 'ageing' population, those in employment either had to pay more to support the retired, or see the latter becoming poorer. Investment in human and physical capital could alleviate this situation by facilitating increased production and thus consumption, but for retired people to have a claim on the national product they needed to have property rights. In an agrarian society, they usually owned land and livestock until their deaths. In industrial ones most employees were unable to save much, although increasing numbers were inheriting property and other forms of capital. Retired people had had to be provided for and the state had stepped in with retirement pensions, first in Bismarck's Germany, then in the UK in the 1900s and in the USA in the 1930s. At first state pensions consisted only of minimum subsistence incomes. The principles of compulsory retirement and that of keeping the burden of state pensions on taxpayers to a minimum combined over time to raise the moral issue of public niggardliness towards senior citizens. Efforts were therefore made in many developed countries in the second half of the last century to raise state pensions to levels significantly above minimum subsistence ones. In the UK, as elsewhere, both public and private sector employees had increasingly built up their own occupational pension schemes throughout the last century, and recent UK government policies have been for the state pension to revert to or even to below the bare minimum with a growing emphasis on individual provision through occupational and personal pension schemes.

Because of greater longevity the threat to UK pension funds in the twenty first century was a real one if, as noted above, nothing like as serious as in several other OECD countries, including the USA. Investment by pension funds of the richer countries in emerging markets was unlikely to be the solution because the latter markets were simply not big enough to meet the demand. Bowers discusses a number of possible scenarios for funding pensions and the lives of older people for the first half of this century. He takes into account such factors as changes in company earnings and investment income, changes in patterns and kinds of saving including those designed to buy property, and changes in the buying and use of life insurance, changes in the form of pension schemes, changes in patterns of employment, changes in economic growth rates, demographic changes, changes in international capital markets, changes in patterns of expenditure and so on, and in the end arrives at the conclusion that retirement 'will be sustainable' in the UK 'with present distributions of income and their continuation'.

Nevertheless, whereas retirement incomes currently consumed about 30 percent of income from work, they would come to consume about 40 percent. Because annual rises in state pensions were being frozen in relation to increases in prices, those whose lives had been relatively poor were being made relatively even more worse off in retirement. For many with occupational pensions and substantial properties and other savings, retirement would be more than comfortable. However it would be 'long and constrained' for many others. Some of these would be capable of working and thus of enhancing their incomes, but there was at present nowhere for them to work. Also it was those without occupational pensions who most needed more resources, yet their care was 'more or less assured by the state [and they] might therefore have least incentive to join in any such co-operative venture' as (say) part-time work 'when newly retired, against a promise of care in the more distant future and with an uncertain need for it'. A 'new set of regulated labour markets where the elderly had privileged access to such jobs, very probably on a part-time basis' might have to be created. Therefore, and instead of 'the complete retirement that dominates at present with our relatively favourable support ratio' the result could eventually be part-time retirement.

The final chapter in Part Two, by Ian Glover, is also concerned with the future as well as with present difficulties and their causes. Its main concern is with the nature of ageism in general and in different parts of the world. It has a strong emphasis on ageism as being something that affects people of all ages, on ageism as an intergenerational phenomenon, and not just as something to do with later life. By the use of examples of often very different forms of ageism from different historical periods as well as from different societies, the author gives an idea of how varied and complicated a phenomenon it is, and of how dubious and uncertain generalisations about it can be.

Rightly or wrongly, however, this does not stop him from making three broad generalizations. One is that overt and aggressive forms of ageism will tend to be less prevalent in societies with cultures of 'tradition and renewal', in which the past and the old are regarded and drawn upon as sources of present and future strength and in which intergenerational relations are mutually supportive. Examples of such countries included those of the 'Latin Catholic South' of Europe, and Japan. The second is the 'external threat and response hypothesis': countries and other human collectivities including employing organizations facing serious threats from outside tend to close ranks and to find roles for people of all ages.

Finally there was the 'security and affluence' hypothesis. Here affluent societies which for whatever reason (such as victory in the Second World War) are resting on their laurels, 'tend to over-value youthfulness hedonistically at the expense of the upbringing of the young and the wisdom and welfare of elders'. Glover goes on to suggest that the contemporary and growing upsurge of interest in ageism has a number of positive features including straightforward growing awareness of and openness towards the issue, and that the present situation in the UK at least, resulting as it does from longer lives and greater health and wealth in general, is more of an opportunity that a threat, even if it has yet rarely addressed or dealt with it as such.

Together the chapters in Part Two addressed the issue of the need for age discrimination to be competent (rather than opposed in all its manifestations), for the issue of commodification versus greening to be discussed along with the notion of reflexive modernity, and some relevant policy issues and implications. Duncan's strong arguments to the effect that not all employer prejudices and behaviour regarding employee age are irrational are evidence of this. Herriot's explanations of the ways in which (mainly incompetent) age discrimination is rationalised as well as manufactured by managerialist academics, managers and employers perform a very similar function from a rather different yet complementary standpoint. The data reported by McGoldrick and Arrowsmith are from relatively large scale surveys of recruitment advertisements and of managers' and employers' experiences, attitudes and polices. They suggest that there is widespread and growing awareness of ageism as an issue and problem, both moral and practical, for employers and employees in particular and for society in general.

Bowers' concerns are clearly for the longer term. He explains how it may be necessary as well as desirable for employment to continue beyond retirement in a situation in which there are many more, and many more older, retired people than in the past. His arguments and ideas fit in very well with the greening thesis of Branine and Glover (1997) whereby many people may live much longer and in general more fulfilling lives than in the past, but with less continuity and rigidity in their patterns of employment. The concerns of Glover and Branine's chapters also address the issue just referred to, particularly that of reflexive modernity, whereby people come to change and develop, as well as merely to rely on and serve, the institutions thrown up by early industrialization.

Part Three is focused on the experience and practice of ageism in work and employment. In chapter eight Adelina Broadbridge explores relationships between age and employment in retailing in the UK. In the first part of her chapter she considers some of the difficulties of defining older employees and of knowing when age discrimination is happening. She also outlines various attitudes towards older employees and the effects that these can have on their career development. She discusses effects of demographic changes on company decisions about the employment of older people, exploring relevant characteristics of retailing with regard to age, and she uses examples to show how some companies have responded to external developments.

In the second part of her chapter Broadbridge uses data from a survey of retailing employers to investigate the career development of managers. From this she concludes that there are no appreciable differences between younger and older managers' perceived abilities to progress their careers, but that on average, the older managers studied had been in their positions three times as long as the younger ones, which may explain why older managers report lack of career progress as the least satisfying feature of their current jobs. This last point of Broadbridge's relates to that of Peter Herriot, in his chapter, about older managers often being unjustifiably dissatisfied with their lack of promotion given the relatively small numbers of higher level positions available in most employing organizations. In general and for her sample, however, Broadbridge found 'no appreciable differences between younger and older retail managers' perceived ability to progress their careers'. She is broadly optimistic about the employment of older managers in retailing on the basis of her findings and related research but concludes by emphasising a need for more qualitative work and for longitudinal studies, so that the specific reasons for the effects of age on the careers and employment of older managers and staff can be understood more fully. We agree very strongly with this last point, and would also emphasise a need for research to focus on individual occupations and sectors because the character of age discrimination varies so much between them. Broadbridge's chapter itself superbly exemplifies the integrity and value of sector-specific management research.

In chapter nine, Karen Rodham develops the arguments of her conference paper, which was concerned with ageism as experienced by young female academics. We ourselves have witnessed, in varying contexts, by no means all of them academic, how both relative youthfulness and relative age serve as apparent surrogates for lack of relevant experience. In other words younger employees are stigmatised as inexperienced and naïve, and older ones are stigmatised as being out of touch with contemporary developments. By contemporary we mean those phenomena which relatively powerful individuals or groups of them whose power derives from their group membership feel most familiar with, however superficial and transitory. Such phenomena include some professional and other concerns and techniques, and management fads. Relevant professional concerns often include ones to do with career advancement.

Rodham's data are ancedotal and were collected in informal conversations with 20 young academics, seven male and 13 female, aged between 27 and 36. At the time of writing Rodham was 28, and is 'white, female, heterosexual and ... employed by a British university'. The respondents came from various academic locations and were employed to teach social scientific, nursing and business and management subjects. Rodham was well aware of the limitations of her sampling and of her own experiences of ageism while also keen 'to address the imbalance on the literature' on ageism, which tended to focus strongly on the problems of older employees. She was interested in the coping strategies used by young academics, as well as in their problems.

She begins her discussion by describing the emphasis on older employers in research into and writing about ageism, as being ageist itself with only a minority of writers even touching on and giving lip service to that experienced by younger people. The immediate experience of being blocked or excluded on the grounds of one's age was virtually the same whatever one's age. She then describes the experience of ageism of younger academics, specific and general. Remarks made by older colleagues about the achievements, like doctorates, of younger ones, tended to denigrate them or to mix praise and disparagement. Achievements were often attributed to luck rather than to effort and seemed to be designed to erode the confidence of younger colleagues. Disparaging comments could come from individuals who were only a few, say less than ten, years older. Three quarters of the respondents found that administrative support tended to be concentrated on more senior colleagues whose demeanour and ascribed status lent them airs of greater importance. Comments by more senior academics seemed to be influenced by external forces such as the growing emphasis on research achievements in appraisals and promotion decisions. Understandably, perhaps, individuals with upwards of 20 years' teaching experience felt threatened by 'youngsters with PhDs' who were shortlisted for promotion when they were not. Length of service rather than actual experience and qualifications tended to be emphasised by such people and in one case a young academic was forcefully informed in an appraisal interview that a senior lectureship would only be likely to be attainable in their mid to late thirties. The idea of serving one's time before becoming promotable appeared to be widespread. Students were also responsible for such ageist comments as 'you don't look old enough to be a lecturer'. Some mature students openly resented being taught by lecturers who were the same ages or younger than themselves. Most students seemed uncertain about being taught by younger academics, who sometimes felt constrained to tell them about the substantial nature of their qualifications and experience.

Rodham uses the three dimensional view of power developed by Lukes (1974) to discuss ways in which relationships between older and younger academics tended to be structured and 'clarified' by the former. Lukes (1974) had focused on ways in which potentially conflictual issues are often 'kept out of politics through the operation of social forces and institutional practices, or through individuals' decisions'. Conflict was often kept latent, when the exclusion of the interests of relevant parties was either not realised or not openly admitted by them. Younger academics, lacking in the status that went with length of service and the position power and resources of senior posts, often chose not to make an issue of ageist comments whilst retaliating in more or less covert ways, often by increasing their academic output and consolidating their positions.

We ourselves have witnessed sharply expressed affront on the part of more senior academics at the conference presentations and published outputs of more junior members of staff. One (relatively) young academic expressed surprise in a meeting in a former polytechnic that his prolific publications had been completely omitted from an official document when the much less prolific ones of senior and other colleagues had been included, and was responded to with, and expected to be mollified by, the statement 'But you've got lots of publications!'. On another, later, occasion, this time in an 'old' university, and well into his own middle age, he cheerfully and enthusiastically informed a rather status-conscious and unproductive senior colleague that he had just made his fifth and last conference presentation of a busy summer vacation period. This caused the senior colleague to erupt, rather incoherently although not without some force, at what he appeared to regard as impertinence. Of a young male colleague of hers who appeared to be conforming in an ageist climate, and who had responded to a query with 'I'm sorry, I am only new, you had better ask "x"', Rodham points out that his behaviour could be interpreted in two ways. He could have been accepting the situation and losing confidence in his own ability. Or he could merely have been feigning an inability to cope, and 'in effect' delegating 'responsibility to older academics ... and appearing to comply with the ageist viewpoint, thereby avoiding conflict'. If the latter was the case a subtle form of retaliation may have been occurring whereby the younger person was cunningly exerting power over older colleagues by conforming to their more superficial expectations. Rodham call this the Fox Syndrome. Another way of interpreting his reply is, of course, 'Don't treat me like a dogsbody just because I am/seem young/junior'.

A second strategy used by younger academics was the Ostrich Syndrome. Here ageist comments and assumptions are ignored on the surface, in order to avoid conflict, by conforming to such expectations as not putting one's job or doctoral title on one's office door. Officially the relevant institution encouraged staff to have their titles put on their doors but there was an informal rule in some departments that to do so was in conflict with the institution's equal opportunities policy(!). The third strategy, part of the chapter's title Rodham calls the Buffalo Stance. In Africa buffalos were 'famous for their keen sense of smell and ... said to know the presence of intruders at 500 metres'. Here younger staff met ageist assumptions and comments head on. Ageism was no more justified than, and was as harmful as, racism or sexism, and it needed to be openly confronted, contradicted and otherwise opposed. Rodham ends with a strong plea for ageism against younger people to be brought fully on to the agenda so that harmful unconscious prejudices are handled as openly as those against older ones. She prefers the Buffalo Stance and we admire her for it while also feeling that the Fox Syndrome can also be helpful to use alongside it on occasions, partly in order to confuse and tease opponents. Are we being ageist or realistic in suggesting this?

Chapter ten consists of an interview with David Jenkins, a very successful and thoughtful management consultant in the eighth decade of his life, with wide ranging experience of postwar British management including a short spell early in his career of working directly under the extremely energetic and able General Ismay, who had worked very intimately with Churchill throughout the Second World War. From the interviews it is clear that Jenkins has a very sharp, lively and practical outlook combined with strong healthy scepticism about philosophical and political speculation. These characteristics lend particular weight to Jenkins' iconoclastic derision for the thoughtlessness and indeed ignorance of many managers rejecting the potential of mature employees, and to his special contempt for personnel or human resource departments which incompetently and lazily use age in deselecting candidates for employment, development, promotion and so on. Jenkins' thinking is notable for its focus on specific tasks and situations, as perhaps might be expected from someone with degrees in history and law and a background often in line management as well as in self-employment.

He is particularly suspicious of arms' length types of management often associated with management fads like quality, re-engineering and human resource management, with arrogant assumptions about the relevance of different kinds of formal qualifications and the apparent irrelevance of varied practical experience, of the use and abuse of young so-called high-fliers, and of lack of imagination in the practice of employment in general. Some of Jenkins' views are contradictory, at least on the surface, and as regards such rather general notions as apprenticeships, career, redundancy, mediocrity, and ageing and ageism. However this simply reflects his focus on and respect for the variety and complexity of the real world. He is very definite and clear about ageism: for Jenkins competence, which includes integrity, is everything. Age as such is of marginal relevance to the demands of most tasks but it is abused as a specious but politically convenient surrogate for ability.

A rather more intellectually detached approach than those of the last three chapter authors is used by Jenny Hamilton in chapter eleven. She is concerned with the issue of legislation against age discrimination and she outlines the approach taken in South Australia. She reviews relevant issues and literature and describes the background to the legislation with which she is concerned, and explores the scope of its anti-age discrimination provisions and enforcement mechanisms, and then explains the approach of the relevant courts to the legislation. She finds age discrimination illogical, unjust, a way of frustrating legitimate personal aspirations, and economically dubious, particularly in the context of increasing longevity. She asks whether legislation is the best way of tackling the problem given employer scepticism about employment regulation. She suggests, however, that if age discrimination, unlike that against race, gender and disability, is not tackled by law, the public may conclude that it is relatively unimportant. Thus she emphasises the 'powerful symbolic function of law'. It gives legitimacy to the concerns of those abused and affected by discrimination and it provides a structure within which harmful behaviour can be challenged. She notes how several countries such as Australia, Canada and the USA had legislation in place and suggests that their experience might be useful for informing and even for guiding British choices about the nature, scope, organization and enforcement of any legislation.

Hamilton chooses to examine South Australian anti-discrimination legislation on age partly because it has similarities to UK sex and race legislation. Debates surrounding its introduction in South Australia had been similar to those surrounding its possible introduction in the UK. Both Australia and the UK had also experienced declining birth rates and people living longer and healthier lives. Both had witnessed the automation of many semi-skilled and skilled jobs, and delayering and reductions in numbers of middle management positions in many organizations and sectors. Legislation had been involved in Australia mainly because of a perceived need to manage a rapidly changing economy and labour pool more flexibly and effectively.

South Australia had been the first State in Australia to introduce any form of anti-discrimination legislation, in 1975 with its Sex Discrimination Act. In 1991 it had also led the field as regards age discrimination with an amendment, making it unlawful, to the South Australian Equal Opportunity Act of 1984. Other Australian States and then the Federal Government followed suit quite quickly and by 1996 its Workplace Relations Act had made unlawful the dismissal of any employee on grounds of age. Currently in South Australia employment discrimination was forbidden on the grounds, not only of age, but also on the grounds of 'sex, marital status, race, physical disability, intellectual impairment, sexuality, pregnancy and sexual harassment.' Before the 1991 amendment to the 1984 Equal Opportunities Act regarding age was passed the Commission for Equal Opportunity in South Australia had received hundreds of complaints about age discrimination in employment and with regard to 'access to goods and service, education, accommodation and clubs'. Political support for the age-related amendment to the 1984 Act was bi-partisan and public and political support for it was generally strong, although not uncontroversial with employers being in the van of the critics.

The scope of the legislation is such that it covers discrimination in most public areas of life, with a strong focus on employment of virtually all kinds and for all of its stages from advertising vacancies to termination. In 1993 the imposition by an employer of a standard age for retirement was made illegal on the ground that 'to force a perfectly healthy individual to retire on the basis that they had reached a certain age was ... discriminatory'. The 'provision of goods and services including accommodation and membership of clubs and associations, access to education, the sale of land, and the conferral of qualifications' were also covered. The Act applies to people of all ages but although it is wide-ranging there are nonetheless some exceptions which are concerned with social policy considerations. These include certain factors to do with children and other young people, charities and projects set up for the benefit of members of particular age groups, certain types of employer of young people, genuine requirements that job holders be of particular ages, the ability to perform particular tasks without endangering others and the ability to respond adequately to certain types of emergency. Hamilton suggests that elements of some of these exceptions tend towards the ageist and implies that they are sometimes likely to give rise to controversy.

Both direct and indirect discrimination are prohibited. The former simply means instances of employers treating someone in a protected group less favourably than others. The key test is: would someone have received the same treatment but for their age? Indirect discrimination happens when a requirement is imposed which, while superficially fair, results in a member of the relevant group being treated less favourably while not being necessary for the job to be performed. For example an employer could require someone to have a newer kind of qualification than others which also equip people to perform relevant tasks, with the effect that fewer older people will be able to comply.

Hamilton goes on to explain how the Australian legislation has a potentially wider scope than UK law on racial and sexual discrimination. In Australia if the intended effect of some general or particular stipulation for holding a job is to discriminate and if it does indeed operate against the interest of a complainant then it is defined as discriminatory. The relevant UK laws are narrower in their approach to employer requirements or stipulations and less likely to favour complainants. Hamilton notes how both the UK and South Australian approaches tend to be weaker in the area of indirect as opposed to direct discrimination, that they focus on individual instead of group instances of discrimination, and that they fail to recognise entrenched and structured discrimination such as the widespread under-representation of certain age groups in sections of the media. Beyond UK age and sex discrimination legislation, that of South Australia on age also prohibits characterisation, meaning the use of presumed characteristics of a group – the presumed inflexibility of older people or the presumed immaturity of younger ones for example – to discriminate against members of it. A provision in favour of positive discrimination was debated at the draft stage but was not accepted.

Hamilton explains how the Australian Equality of Opportunity Commission, rather than in the UK an Industrial Tribunal followed by the Employment Appeals Tribunal and then the civil appeal courts, handles complaints in South Australia. In the latter instances a Commission member first tries to settle the matter informally. If this fails, a 'compulsory confidential conciliation conference' is called. This can reach settlements involving apologies, agreements about what was denied, compensation, reinstatement, and policy and/or procedural changes. If no agreement is reached at this stage the matter is no longer confidential and it can be referred, for judicial determination, to the Equal Opportunity Tribunal. In practice five percent or less of cases reach the Tribunal, with most being resolved in conciliation or withdrawn by complainants, or declined by the Commission. However the power of the Tribunal to award unlimited compensation and to order changes designed to preclude further complaints is considerable.

Hamilton feels that the South Australian legislation has probably been successful because the numbers of complaints made to the Commissioner for Equal Opportunity fell significantly after its introduction. Most complaints made were about age discrimination in selection for promotion and training, and about 'losing employment to younger persons'. Most complaints were made by men over 44: Hamilton felt that this could have been either because men had higher expectations than women or because they simply experience more discrimination. Younger women, aged 15 to 24, and especially those working in retailing, were more likely to lodge complaints than younger men.

Hamilton then explores a few instances of the application of the South Australian legislation in a little depth, showing it to be reasonably if not completely effective in fulfilling its purpose. In her chapter's conclusion she asks whether South Australia's relatively integrated approach to anti-discrimination legislation has advantages over the UK's more piecemeal one. She feels that it does have insofar as the application of general principles of justice and so on are more readily comparable with a less fragmented approach, insofar as it makes it easier to compare the effects on complainants of different forms of discrimination, insofar as to existence of one monitoring body rather than several facilitates a more coordinated and effective state approach to discrimination in general, and so on. She concludes with a number of points about the details of legislation concerning compulsory retirement, the need for careful drafting of laws, the roles and the effects of exceptions, and conflicts between administrative and economic contingencies on the one hand and moral and political ones on the other. She argues, rightly in our opinion, that the South Australian example has clear relevance to the UK situation, and that the law is part of the cultural heritage of a nation and one of the systems which teaches people about socially and commercially acceptable behaviour. Ultimately, she argues, the case for or against legislation on discrimination is about whether the set of rules which constitute the law should 'actively influence cultural change (rather than ... [be] passively reflecting it)'.

We ourselves (see below) are broadly and with certain reservations in favour of legislation. We are attracted by the relative freshness of the Australian approach which seems to us to exemplify Rodham's Buffalo Stance by confronting the unconscionable head on, without the sort of often disingenuous prevarication and dissimulation common to many other cultures.

In chapter twelve Darren Smith addresses some of the stereotypes which exist concerning older versus younger employees in New Zealand businesses. Partly on the basis of data obtained from members of the New Zealand Institute of Personnel Management (the IPMNZ) he argues that the ages and the sexes of respondents affected how they perceived the attributes of older and younger employees. In general, IPMNZ members viewed older employees as being more reliable and socially skilled, more experienced and more loyal than their younger counterparts. However they were thought of as being less accepting of new technology, less adaptable to change, less suited to learning quickly and less interested in training. Smith draws attention to similar attitudes held by Institute of Personnel and Development (IPD) members in the UK.

Smith starts by noting how the average New Zealander is growing older and how, in 1992, age discrimination was outlawed in New Zealand. As in other countries, the legislation covers people of all employable ages and allows for exemptions. He goes on to review a wide range of data and literature on age, work performance and employment. It showed that while age is not in general a valid predictor of performance, the performance of older employees tends to be rated lower than that of younger ones even when the performance of older employees was superior. Young employees tended to be favoured in selection decisions for lower status jobs. Older employees tended to be regarded as less creative and productive and less interested in change than younger ones, but as more stable, trustworthy and reliable. Older employees tended to suffer from negative stereotyping as regards performance and to be treated unfavourably and unfairly as a consequence.

Smith knew that negative stereotypes of older employees existed in New Zealand, and that little was known about their composition. Past research into effects of age stereotypes on performance evaluation had been largely concerned only with managerial and professional employees. Smith's study was concerned with the stereotypes held by managers in New Zealand about older non-managerial employees. His respondents consisted of 106 members of the IPMNZ, aged between 25 and 64 with 67 percent being between 36 and 50 and with nearly two thirds of them being male and the other third or so female. A mail questionnaire was used and it was designed to focus on two factors, Work Effectiveness and Stability, from Rosen and Jerdee's (1976) four work-related characteristics, the other two being Interpersonal Skills and Adaptability.

It was found that older IPMNZ members regarded older non-managerial employees as being more interpersonally skilled than younger ones, and that the IPMNZ sample as a whole saw the former as being more loyal to their employers. The 'loyalty' of older employees was often noted and emphasized in surveys of others' perceptions of them. However the possibility that older employees may have little choice but to be loyal to their employers, and its relevance, are rarely explored. Male respondents, more so than female ones, tended to rate older employees as being more effective at their work than younger ones. Male respondents tended to view older employees as having more useful experience than younger ones, and female respondents felt that older employees were more able to learn quickly than younger ones. Smith noted how his female respondents had more first-hand experience of ageism than his male ones, who however had been in their current positions longer. His older respondents tended, more than their younger counterparts, to regard older employees as more competent at their work than younger ones, and to regard them as being less likely to take things easy at work. Older respondents were also more likely to think of older employees as being more interpersonally skilled than younger employees. Almost three fifths of the respondents felt that there was a problem with age discrimination in New Zealand. Respondents who were male were more likely to think this than the female ones, but older and younger ones alike were equally likely to do so.

Smith compared his responses with those obtained from a sample of UK IPD members. Differences were not very pronounced although the UK respondents did tend to regard older employees as less adaptable and flexible than their New Zealand counterparts, and similarly the UK respondents felt that older employees thought before they acted more than the New Zealand ones did, whereas the New Zealand respondents tended to see older employees as being more effective in their jobs. The attitudes found by Smith in New Zealand were however broadly similar to those found in the UK and the USA. He felt that such findings imply that older employees should be put in charge of teams more often, that they should be trained in less group-centred and school-like ways than those used with younger people, and that managers were too often unaware of the potential for development of older staff. Smith also stresses the tendency for experienced people to be able to understand the nature, role and value of experience much more effectively than less experienced ones. His evaluations also suggest, as of course do intuition and commonsense not to mention experience itself, that younger people tend to be more subjective about the qualities of older ones than older ones are about their qualities. Smith is uncertain as to why more male IPMNZ members than female ones felt that ageism was a problem for personnel practice and business. He speculates about this at some length and remains uncertain and we think that he is right to do so. He suggests that more positive perceptions of older employees in his New Zealand sample compared with those of the British one may be attributable to greater stress on equality and less on power distance than in New Zealand.

From New Zealand we move in chapter thirteen to the European Union (EU) where David Parson and Lesley Mayne consider the issue of ageism in the social policies and labour markets of EU member states. They use evidence from a research project which is based on an annual survey of employers' human resource management (HRM) polices and practices in organizations employing over 200 people, so as to make comparisons between a number of EU countries. They argue that national level public and political interest in ageism has yet to be translated into effective action by most employers. Part of the problem was lack of research into employers' policies and innovations. They record the main facts about stabilizing levels of population across the EU, about longer lives and so far slight upwards trends in state retirement ages. They also note how this upward trend 'conflicts with what is happening in the labour market itself', with earlier exit being a progressive trend throughout the last century across Europe. Earlier exit was partly a product of age discrimination, partly one of private and occupational pensions helping to fill the gap years between retirement and the payment of state pensions, and partly one of public policies which sometimes subsidised early exit. Falling demand for labour underpinned all of these influences of course.

In the UK there was now, in the mid-late 1990s, a hiatus between a need for employers to adapt to and use a 'greying' workforce, and often 'ill-influenced and short-sighted' employment and HRM attitudes and practices. Across the EU and in OECD countries outside the EU like the USA far fewer men aged over 54 were in employment in 1990 than in 1971. Sweden was something of an exception, where activity rates for men over 50 had been protected more and eroded less. However, and while an ever higher population of the EU-12 workforce was aged 50 or over, pension funds were starting to be put under pressure, public and government attitudes towards ageism and regarding the possibility of an active third age were changing, early retirement was becoming a costlier option for employers, and there was a good chance that any re-emergence of labour shortages would lead to increased demand for the skills of mature employees to be retained and developed.

The authors then describe and report the findings of their own and colleagues' survey of organizational HRM policies and practices of organizations employing over 200 people in Belgium, Denmark, Finland, France, the former East Germany, the former West Germany, Ireland, Italy, The Netherlands, Norway, Spain, Sweden, Switzerland, Turkey and the UK. The answers reported by the authors draw on parts of this large-scale survey. The data reported are for 1995 and came from over 6,000 organizations, of which nearly 5,000 employed 200 or more people. They are probably over-representative of larger organizations and come from 'all sectors of employment'.

In the UK three fifths of employers collected data on their own organizations' age structures, with 36 percent of these having employees with average ages between 41 and 50. Over 90 percent of the UK organizations had equal opportunity or diversity policies and of these 79 percent were written ones. Nonetheless only a tenth of the organizations targeted older people in their recruitment processes. There was a fairly small but significant tendency for organizations to decrease rather than increase their numbers of older recruits. Only 10 percent had recruited past state retirement age and this was most likely to have been for manual and clerical positions. No organizations intended to recruit past state retirement age in the future. Fewer than 10 percent had introduced methods designed to increase recruitment or retention of older employees in the last three years. There were some differences in policy and practice between sectors and in terms of organizational size as measured by numbers employed. Larger organizations and those in the public sector were the most likely to have written equal opportunity or diversity policies. Manufacturing was more likely than the public sector, and especially services, to employ older staff. Organizations with over 1,000 employees tended to contain more people under 30 than those with fewer than 1,000 employees. There was a small tendency for numbers of older recruits to have decreased in the last three years.

Across the EU a policy of discouraging the exclusion of older people from the labour market and of making the most of their experience had begun to be advocated, with little obvious effect, especially as regards practical details. A 1994 report of research into employment practices in 22 countries contained no evidence to the effect that legislation against ageism can be successful. In the main survey reported here it was found that over 50 percent of all organizations across Europe collected data on the ages of their employees. The same figure was over 80 percent in Belgium, western Germany, France and the Netherlands. The average ages of workforces were very varied with Ireland and Italy having the youngest ones and Denmark, Finland, France, eastern Germany, Norway and Sweden having the oldest. Breakdowns of these data by organization size and sector produced very little if anything in the way of surprising results. Relatively few employers targeted over 50s when recruiting. The countries in which the highest populations of organizations did this were France, Spain and the UK with (only) 13, 12 and 10 percent of employers respectively doing so. In general service and public sector employers are more likely to target over 50s than those in manufacturing. An interesting exception was the UK public sector. While over 90 percent of the employers in it had written equal opportunities polices, they were less likely to target over 50s than UK manufacturing employers.

As for countries, Norwegian employers were by far the most likely to increase recruitment of over 50s with nearly 40 percent of them doing so. Apart from those in Italy and Turkey very few organizations recruited people past state retirement age. The practice was quite varied by country in terms of types of people recruited. In Norway they tended to be professional and technical and in Germany and Denmark they tended to be manual. There was evidence in some countries of genuine attempts to use different methods to aid the recruitment and retention of older employees. The most popular method was phased retirement. Re-entry programmes for older workers were very rare. The Swiss were by far the most likely to remove age criteria for training and the Dutch similarly 'stood alone' in introducing retraining programmes. UK employers were the most likely to remove age criteria from advertising. Flexible working time as a recruitment/retention method for older staff was most likely to be used in the Netherlands, Switzerland, Norway and Denmark. The country most likely to use a combination of different methods was Switzerland. Most other countries concentrated on one method. The Netherlands concentrated on retraining, France and Denmark on phased retirement, and so on, but in general the levels of use of all methods were low.

Parsons and Mayne cited widespread political and lay concern across Europe about the 'demographic imperative' of a 'greying workforce' along with a general lack of consistent employer action. In the early 1990s in the UK and in the context of recession, many employers had to cut costs and downsized, often dramatically. In doing so they were losing skills that they would need for any upturn and which they really seemed to need for their present survival. Numbers of young people were much smaller than for a long time so that recruitment and skill problems were likely to persist or get worse in the future. The 'cures' of downsizing to cut costs or of buying expensive skills in often seemed worse than the disease. The skills of older employees needed to be retained and developed, not ignored or junked. While we can see some counter-arguments having some validity – such as ones about demographics not being quite as 'imperative' as Parsons and Mayne suggest and about the need to invest in the longer term future – we find all these points broadly convincing.

In chapter fourteen, the final of Part Four, we return to New Zealand with Graham Elkin. He begins by noting how the country has an ageing workforce and a growing economy, along with full employment and some skill shortages. To maintain and improve its standard of living, New Zealand needs to change its attitudes towards employing older people. By 2031 nearly a fifth of New Zealand's population is likely to be over 65, more than double the proportion in 1951. And in 1951 there were seven people of working age to each over 65, whereas in 2031 the ratio is likely to have fallen to three to one. Regarding the ratio of people actually working to those over 65 there is likely to be a rise from 24 over 65s to every 100 employees to 45 for every 100 in 2031. Elkin feels that this has strong implications for demands on the time of employed people with ailing or very old relatives, for pensions and for provision of residential care.

In the 1950s New Zealand had had one of the world's highest standards of living but from then until the 1990s economic growth rates were low, probably because of over-regulation of the economy, including protectionism. In the 1980s there was considerable deregulation and liberalisation and growth of GDP rose markedly. Unemployment rose for a few years and then declined steadily. In the longer term full or even over-full employment was in prospect. This was part of the background to the growing proportion of dependent older people whose needs had to be met. One way of doing this, and of responding 'to the labour market pressures that full employment may bring' would be to extend working life. This could be seen as imposing an unwanted burden on older people or it could be seen as the ending of age discrimination against people in their sixties. With many women unable to work because of elder care responsibilities and with large-scale immigration unlikely to be adopted as policy, and with large-scale substitutions of technology for labour also unlikely, the only remaining major source of labour is likely to be fit older people, under and over the statutory retirement age.

Elkin notes evidence of the usual kinds of prejudice against older worker – they are thought of as reliable plodders – and in doing so uses the evidence reported by Darren Smith in his chapter in this book. He refers to business reasons given by Peter Worsley (1996) for employers having older elements in their workforce: accumulated experience, skill and knowledge; an 'extra' source of labour and skill; the fact that many of them consist of the best, most competent, people available; the increasing age and maturity of the average customer; their collective, tacit, memory; and the fact that customers and others are likely to perceive employers as good ones if they see that they have reasonably mature and otherwise diverse workforces. Elkin cites several prominent UK examples of employers of mature staff. He goes on to discuss the problem of middle aged people being unable to work, or finding employment difficult, because of their elder care responsibilities. New Zealand (and Australian) employers were well behind US and other overseas ones in helping employees to cope with elder care. He goes on to make an original, fascinating and creative suggestion that child care facilities might be made cross-generational. Elderly people, those over 65 in Elkin's terms, might usefully be employed in child care centres, giving affection, knowledge and skills in return for a greater sense of usefulness. In New Zealand this would be very compatible with Maori family traditions. The development of mutual care groups of the retired is another idea of Elkin's.

He goes on to argue that traditional notions of career and stability of employment are increasingly illusory and irrelevant and in need of transcendence. Too many people were still chosen for jobs and promoted (or not) in them using very traditional assumptions about career and identity depending on particular employers. Too few workplaces were still not family-friendly enough and too few employers recognised and used adequately the diversity of employees' backgrounds, abilities, commitments, choices and careers. More radically flexible approaches to age, work, employment, citizenship and the life course were needed in an era in which the 'age for discarding people has been rapidly falling' with damaging effects on the self-esteem of many mature people. Unfortunately, perhaps, much of New Zealand culture was youth-oriented, coming from the time when young Britons and others settled in the country, and from the sporting traditions of the All Blacks, the Silver Fern and so on. However there were grounds for hope in a possible fusion with very different Maori and/or Pacific Island traditions of respect for the wisdom of older people. We find this a very thoughtful, wide-ranging and constructive paper. As with many Highlanders and Islanders in the UK, perhaps distance is another source of wisdom in New Zealand, which is also of course relatively sparsely populated and also a very long way, culturally and emotionally as well as geographically, from major centres of population and activity.

What do these chapters on the experience and practice of age discrimination tell us? Most tell us at least something about all of the issues identified in the first main section of this chapter. Broadbridge offers, among other things such as a strong review of relevant literature, very solid and encouraging evidence on the practicality of making workforces and management structures more diverse and flexible in terms of employee age. Rodham's chapter tells us exactly what it feels like to be demeaned and at times infantilised by not very mature behaviour on the part of a generation which grew up believing in the cult of youth and/or which is threatened by a more demanding professional environment than the one which they entered when its members were younger. She also explains to some effect why direct, honest and open confrontation of abusive behaviour has more integrity and may often be more effective than other approaches, even if the use of more devious ones is at times unavoidable. Jenkins' interview is notable for its forceful contempt, deeply rooted in very varied and relevant experiences, for the incompetent management of employment and work. For Jenkins age discrimination is a form of sub-optimising behaviour rooted in the lack of ability, commitment and ultimately, moral fibre, of its perpetrators.

In Part Four the chapters on possible remedies for age discrimination and on the longer term prospects have a strong practical policy emphasis. Together with the chapters in Parts Two and Three they have things to say which to varying degrees belong in the other Parts of the book but of all the Parts, Part Four is probably the most focused on its specific concerns.

In chapter fifteen Philip Taylor, who is one of the UK's most experienced ageism researchers, focuses on ageism in the public policy context. First he reviews developments in public policies towards older employees over the last twenty plus years and shows that despite growing awareness among policy makers little has changed among attitudes and practices towards older employees and their employment prospects. He discusses the feasibility of the legislative versus the educative approach and then suggests ways in which public policies on age discrimination and older employees might develop, identifying areas where problems might arise.

Taylor begins by noting the main facts of growth of unemployment at each end of the age scale, and of growing longevity. He discusses the vulnerability of older people in the labour market and argues that early retirement is very often a euphemism for unemployment of a kind which is often stigmatised and psychologically unpleasant. Taylor goes on to discuss employers' policies, attitudes and practices. Most UK employers in the 1990s were seen to have done little or nothing to alter predominantly ageist policies towards older employees. Employers, and line and personnel managers had the usual attitude towards older employees: they are more experienced and reliable but less flexible and less worth developing than younger counterparts. Young and Schuller had identified three 'age classes' and listed them in order of status with those of prime working age coming first, followed by the young, and then by the old. The ages of these classes were not fixed and indeed Taylor points out that the state had 'played an important role in extending the length of time many people will spend in the third age class'.

In the 1970s and 1980s, and at times when full-time employment was contracting and large numbers of young people were entering the labour market, governments had sought to get older people to leave the labour market by taking early retirement. Youth unemployment was a major priority and financial incentives were given to older people to retire early, and Job Centre staff discouraged older people from seeking work. In the 1990s however there was an 'apparent' shift in policy in favour of them. Fewer younger people had been entering labour markets in the second half of the 1980s, when there was also significant economic growth. Among the various government measures designed to favour older employees from the later 1980s onwards there was the abolition of the earnings rule which had penalised those who earned more than £75 per week after reaching the state pension age, and the lifting from 59 to 63 of the age limit for access to the main government training programme for the long-term unemployed. However the latter change was ineffectual. Conservative governments up to 1997 preferred exhortation and publicity over legislation on age discrimination. However in 1994 an industrial tribunal did class as unfair the dismissals of three employees in their early sixties on the grounds that it was wrong to make people redundant on the grounds of age. Research commissioned by the government and published by the Department of Employment in 1994 appeared to show that legislation against age discrimination neither improved the prospects of employment of older people nor actually caused them to be employed more often or for longer. Others including Taylor himself had opposed this interpretation.

The last Conservative government had also commissioned a detailed review of the legislation versus education issue, one which used results of surveys of employer attitudes and practices, and of the 1993 'Getting-On' government campaign designed to make them more enlightened. Taylor criticises the methods used in the research which seemed to have been prejudiced in favour of employers expressing preferences for education over legislation. Yet although most employers felt that legislation would not work in practice, 'an even larger minority felt that legislation might improve the employment prospects of older workers'. A 'large majority' also felt that there should be legislation on age discrimination given that it existed in other areas. Taylor argues that education and persuasion, the Conservatives' voluntary approach, has done little to improve the prospects of older people. Crucially, nearly 90 percent of a sample of employers thought that they would never mention age in their equal opportunities statements, and there were sound reasons for thinking that the methods used by the Government and its associated researchers to elicit relevant employer attitudes were producing underestimates of the true extent of age discrimination. Further, an 'option of education campaigns [had been] tried and rejected over 30 years ago, prior to the introduction ... in 1967' of the USA's anti-age discrimination legislation. An early retirement culture was now firmly entrenched in the UK. Early retirement was simply 'easier and more palatable to employers and trade unions' than the alternatives.

After its election in 1997 the Labour government had dropped its commitment to legislation, favouring voluntary persuasion 'while not ruling out the [future] possibility of legislation'. After consultation a non-statutory voluntary code of practice was launched in the Spring of 1999. Taylor doubts whether it has reached relevant decision-makers and whether anyone will take any notice. Decentralized personnel management involving line managers in employment decisions more than hitherto was one of several factors making for lack of employer concern and action. Job Centres were also recently told not to take vacancies with upper age limits. Before that Job Centre staff had simply been told 'to dissuade employers from specifying age limits in advertisements placed in job centres'.

Since the 1970s pension reform had risen up the policy agenda, especially that of the Labour Party. Many groups were advocating flexibility in the age of retirement and gradual retirement. UK employers had so far only occasionally encouraged gradual retirement whereas governments in other European countries had introduced a variety of schemes. UK tax laws governing occupational pension schemes were currently designed to inhibit or prevent gradual retirement, to prevent abuse of relevant tax concessions. In 1998 the Inland Revenue had produced a consultation document which was about enhancing the flexibility of occupational pension schemes, but so far the government had not taken any action. Currently the government is also, through its voluntary New Deal 50 plus programme for those over 50 who have been unemployed for six or more months, encouraging older unemployed people to return to work. The programme gives employment advice, training grants and employment advice. Taylor points out that in France and Germany and in the UK over ten years ago similar schemes had not achieved much due to lack of employee and/or employer enthusiasm. More encouragingly, perhaps, and even if the scale of relevant efforts is hitherto small, some other recent UK government activities regarding older people had included, among other things, an interest being taken in their employment prospects.

Taylor goes on to consider possible developments in public policy. Voluntary persuasion of employers seemed to have failed. Legal remedies were unquestionably no simple matter, especially as regarding scope, exceptions, and even possible deleterious unintended consequences. Overall, Taylor feels that the advantages to be gained from having legislation in place would outweigh any disadvantages. However legislation would not be the whole solution. The state and occupational pension schemes, with their fixed pension ages, underpinned many barriers to the employment, training and development of older people. The government needed to take a wide-ranging look at these and other relevant institutionalised forms of ageism and to identify examples and to encourage the development and spread of more imaginative approaches to employment and retirement.

A report from the Cabinet Office's Performance and Innovation Unit (2000) on government policies for older people had made a number of recommendations on their role in society, and on their employment, on working practices, or pensions and on retirement. Some of these are rather vague and unambitious and the whole package is not powerful. Taylor emphasises the need for widespread cultural change in the face of deeply rooted ageism. He describes how the issue lags behind those of race and gender. One relatively favourable feature of the general context was apparent concern among older people about pensions, health and an apparent 'youth' bias in Government policies in general. The Conservatives had been trying to capitalise on this. Taylor notes how the last Conservative government had, after great public pressure, introduced legislation against discrimination on grounds of disability. It was very possible that both major parties would compete for the '"grey" vote at the next general election by promising to legislate on age discrimination'. Employers' organizations would resist such proposals vigorously. However the rights of older people would figure prominently in UK policy debates for the foreseeable future.

Taylor concludes by noting how although the present Labour government was taking the issue of older employees seriously insofar as it was taking some action, it had so far 'backed away from fundamental reforms which might have a real impact on older workers' employment prospects'. The government wanted to maintain good relationships with employers and was thus reluctant to legislate on age. Yet only a combination of legislation, 'pension and social security reform and more opportunities for education and training', and more persuasion and public debate, would be likely to do much for older employees. Younger people faced many problems including serious age discrimination too, but the balance of government concern was still skewed towards them. The growing weight of numbers of third agers would almost certainly force governments to give them a better deal, but in the meantime many older people were confronted with involuntary retirement and all the problems that went with it.

Taylor's thoughtful depiction of the current position is very justifiably pessimistic for the short term but also more optimistic about what is likely to follow. The next two chapters in Part Four, because of their specific concerns, are more upbeat, but equally realistic. In chapter sixteen Alan Nicholls and Wendy Evangelisti argue for fitness for work in a society in which almost all employers may eventually seek to employ healthier and fitter people regardless of age. After discussing the relevant demographic facts and the functional benefits of fitness they discuss the costs of illness and then go on to emphasize the value of exercise and the usually underrated capacity of people to learn in later life. Nicholls and Evangelisti outline the costs and (the greater) benefits of exercise for older people in some detail.

They then go on to evaluate the costs of illness associated with lack of fitness and health, to individuals, to employers and to the state. They suggest that while activity can prolong life by two years, exercise can enhance health and extend financial independence by up to ten. They explain why this is the case in some detail. For example exercise burns excess blood fats and maintains the diameter of the arteries, reducing the risk of stroke, hypertension and so on. Exercise prevents muscle atrophy and improves muscle tone and function, helping posture, breathing and endurance. Exercise also maintains cardiac function, counters loss of bone calcium and maintains joint flexibility. It helps to prevent all forms of heart disease, obesity, back problems, cancer, urinary incontinence, osteoporosis, osteo-arthritis, chronic lung disease and neuro-motor dysfunction. It also has many cognitive, psychological and social benefits. Older people learn in different ways from younger ones, and the authors explain how in relation to both employment and exercise.

They end, first, by spelling out the effects of increased age on workplace performance. Older people appear to perform best in 'deep and slow' ways whereas younger people are 'more shallow and fast'. These attributes are complementary: a strong argument for age diversity in employment. The parable of the tortoise and the hare is also relevant. Second, they make a number of points about employment beyond the usual ages(s) of retirement. In summarised form, they are: exercise improves strength, fitness, independence, life expectancy and last but not least, mood; biological rather than chronological age is the best indicator of fitness for employment; and older people tend to be high on accuracy, judgement and the ability to simplify complex tasks but to be physically slower and slightly more at risk from accidents, and to be relatively easily distracted, especially when working under pressure.

Therefore the main message of this chapter is a very important one for us and for all readers of this book. A so-called 'ageing' population is only likely to be a burden if it fails to keep itself fit. The extended life span which has been achieved since the nineteenth century is a product of improved standards of living, including health. Therefore it seems, and is, ridiculous to suggest that it is beyond human wit for people who are healthier, more durable and long-lasting and more knowledgeable than people have been at any time in recorded history cannot stay healthy and fit for most of their lives.

Chapter seventeen, by Colin Bottomley, offers evidence of successful and thought-provoking practical action against ageism and unemployment. He describes a secondment-training programme that helps people to gain employment in small and medium-sized enterprises (SMEs). In 1982 the Scottish Enterprise Foundation (SEF) was set up to help create enterprise in Scotland by identifying and nurturing programmes of education, training and research, by helping SMEs to develop, and to do so through active links with others with similar concerns in government and the public sector, business and higher education. The SEF's training and development arm is its Business Development Unit (BDU). Since the late 1980s the BDU has run a Professional Development Programme. This uses experienced but currently unemployed managers and young, unemployed, but enthusiastic, graduates to undertake growth development projects in host companies. Projects are defined in discussion with between the BDU and individual owner-managers. They all have the twin aims of providing inexpensive support to the SMEs involved and help to the unemployed managers and graduates in their pursuit of new careers or first ones. Programme participants are aged from their early twenties to their early sixties. The managers come from a wide range of sectoral backgrounds and the graduates, who tend to be much younger, have studied a wide range of academic subjects. Enthusiasm for SMEs matters more than type of background.

The programmes last for between six and seven months, with the first six or seven weeks being used for pre-secondment training and/or skills updating. They offer the SMEs specific skills, and/or the time and inclination for developmental and innovative work. Programmes can be specific to disciplines, sectors and/or of a general business nature. The training programme is intensive and highly participative with the needs of SMEs emphasized very strongly whatever the focus, such as financial management, job hunting techniques or export marketing, of the moment. Instructors consist of full-time SEF academic staff and independent SME practitioners. Personnel development, self-presentation (especially of the graduates) and project management skills are coached. All participants have to have had at least six months' employment, and each has an academic tutor who forms a tripartite team along with the SME owner-manager and the participant. All programmes contain mixtures of young graduates and older managers, who respectively offer each other relatively fresh and open outlooks and experience. Participants are unpaid but continue to receive unemployment benefits plus travel expenses. Local Enterprise Companies (LECs, equivalent to Training and Enterprise Councils, TECs, in England and Wales) support the training along with the participating companies.

About 40 percent of the participants find jobs with their host companies and a further 55 percent find other jobs during or immediately after completing the programme. Most participants are very enthusiastic about the whole venture although a minority resent, to varying degrees, being 'cheap labour'. The programmes do overcome the age and inexperience factors which make employment difficult for the participants, who tend to find their experiences stimulating and productive. The SEF has long tried to persuade employment ministers to allow secondees to be paid basic salaries but it has yet to succeed.

The main original focus of the Professional Development Programme was the need of the SMEs involved for more resources, especially of management ones. Programmes need to be non-intrusive and cost-effective in the eyes of owner-managers. They tend to supply skills and attitudes which complement rather than imitate those of owner-managers. By default more than anything else the Programme has addressed the problem of the ageism faced by redundant managers over 40 and that faced by inexperienced graduates who tend to lack the most attractive kinds of background in employers' eyes. The unemployed managers tend to be regarded with some suspicion by the SME owner-managers, partly because of ageist prejudices and partly because their backgrounds are not obviously suitable. The graduates tend not to be confident high-fliers attractive to blue chip companies or other similar employers and if they become aware of its relevance to them they tend to be drawn to the SME sector out of necessity. However many SME owner-managers still regard graduates as too costly to train and/or to 'fit in' and/or likely to be disruptive *prima donnas*. They tend to have such partly ageist views about them as believing they want to be managers immediately on starting work, and that they do not want to 'get their hands dirty'. All of the ageist perceptions referred to in this paragraph are of course likely to have at least some basis in reality, and it may be that in most cases SME owner-managers are too busy and pressurised to risk testing them without the kinds of benefit given by the Programme.

The Programme also appears to work wonders for the often very badly damaged or otherwise relatively low self-esteem and motivation levels of participants. Some became 'relatively indispensable' in their host companies and/or far more competent job applicants and interviewees. SEF staff often have to give participants much support, often after going to great lengths to get SMEs to accept them. Bottomley goes on to discuss many other features and aspects of the Programme. He re-emphasizes the value of young unemployed graduates and older unemployed managers learning from each other, for instance, and he stresses the usefulness of networking amongst participants and tutors during their Programmes. Two powerful lessons can be learnt from Bottomley's chapter. One concerns the value of proactive and creative activity in the face of defensiveness and prejudice. The other concerns the nature of ageism in employment matters: some of it is not irrational insofar as experience underpins it. Many young people *are* immature and it would, of course, be amazing if that was not the case. By the same token many older people *are* discouraged and tired or complacent and some are unacceptably conservative. When employers perceive such things accurately and respond sensibly, they become examples of *good* age discriminators.

Chapter eighteen concludes Part Four. Christine Tillsley and Philip Taylor critically review some of the literature on age discrimination and propose an agenda for research. They focus initially on relevant demographic and labour market phenomena regarding 'third age' people of 50 and older. Problems of unemployment amongst third age men are seen to be generally more acute in parts of the UK than elsewhere. Relevant structural, policy and social influences are discussed accordingly. In the past, until the 1990s, older employees had been encouraged to leave the workforce in recessions and to return to it in times of expansion. Exit of elders had accelerated in the early to mid 1980s and an early retirement culture had grown up. However from the later 1980s onwards rapid economic growth and demographic changes had begun to combine with the beginnings of changing, and more positive and proactive, approaches to the value and employment of older people, to push governments in what is in many respects an entirely new direction. This takes account of the lengthening life span, of longer and healthier lives, and seeks to develop and enact, if not a cult of age, experience and wisdom to oppose the cult of youth, beauty and strength, a vision of much more valued, numerous and involved third agers.

However effective action had so far been a different matter. Legislation on age discrimination, more flexible and gradual retirement, changes in education, training and social welfare have yet to be adequately designed and linked up, let alone implemented. In general confusion reigned amongst policy makers, 'some favouring and some excluding older workers'.

Population 'ageing' was a 'problem' facing governments 'across Europe and beyond'. In the USA the legislation against age discrimination of 1967 had been fairly effective. Elsewhere a mixture of confusion, and to a smaller degree, useful responses tended to be the norm. There were positive developments in Germany, Sweden, and especially, Japan, the world's most 'rapidly ageing' country. In Japan, the extremes of legislation and voluntarism were being avoided in favour of a 'structuralist' approach. The mandatory retirement age had gone up from 60 to 65 and many measures to prolong working life, often after mandatory retirement, were being implemented. One in two men aged 65 to 70 were employed in Japan, eight in ten from 60 to 64, and nine in ten in their late 50s. Problems with seniority-based payment systems and the reduced pay of employees over 65 remained and existed but Japan clearly offers the UK an example of the direction in which it should be moving in this context.

Tillsley and Taylor then review the results of research into relevant employer attitudes, policies and practices. They noted some evidence of decline of explicit age discriminatory practices, as with job advertisements, since 1990. Employers still tended to target older staff when downsizing but more of them were targeting such people when they were recruiting than in the past. However more positive action by employers tended to be restricted to recruitment: there was little if any emphasis on deployment, development and retention. Age discrimination was now on the agenda of some employers but it had nothing like the priority accorded to other forms of discrimination. Most employers were still very wary of investing in third age people. Larger employees, and public sector ones, appeared to be somewhat more enlightened towards them than smaller, and private sector, ones. Stereotyping of older people as inflexible and under-skilled was still widespread. They were still treated as part of the 'reserve army of labour', even by the most enlightened employers. They were classic victims of employers' short termism.

Tillsley and Taylor go on to identify gaps in the literature and research. More needed to be learnt about how older employees were managed and developed and much of the existing research into employment matters tended to be quantitative and large scale with little if any effort being made to explore phenomena and issues in depth. Studies also tended to have been conducted during recessions and not at other times. There was little if any longitudinal work and there was a general lack of depth and detail.

More specifically little was known about how ageist attitudes and behaviour developed in employing organisations and thus about their specific origins and nature. There was a need to understand all organizational policies and practices in their economic and political contexts so that all of the factors underpinning employment ageism could be understood. More also needed to be done to understand UK employers' tendencies to make retirement more flexible, and to explore 'whether and how' there might be 'a business case for retaining workers over the long term'. Studies of employers' retention policies were so far mainly concerned with their incidence and general features rather than with their details and how they evolved. There had been growing flexibilisation of employment in the 1990s but studies of it had rarely explored its relationship with the age composition of workforces. The authors conclude by arguing that progress in the UK in the employment of older staff and in the development of more age diverse workforces had been slow against the backcloth of a growing need for progress and change. Without research designed to develop understanding of why this had been the case further progress might be difficult.

The four chapters in Part Four collectively tell us that there is no real reason why people of all ages cannot make very substantial contributions to the economic life of the UK. In the future most older people are likely to be experienced, skilled, knowledgeable and fit for work, and given relevant employment, encouragement and support, capable of co-operating extremely well with younger counterparts. Some of the barriers to their productive employment were to do with laws governing pensions and taxation but these could usually be circumvented or changed. Many other barriers consisted of little more than custom and practice, even if some of the problematic underlying attitudes were widespread and often deeply rooted.

Future policy and research

Much of what needs to be written here has been spelt out or implied by the chapter authors. Employment needs to become more open-minded, flexible, diverse and creative than it is and has been. So, accordingly, do the development and provision of education and training, internal promotions, welfare payments and pensions. Many specific points about research are implicit in the coverage of the chapters. Very obviously the experiences of other countries which are facing the same issues, in the same ways, as the UK, are highly relevant. Jenny Hamilton's chapter on South Australian legislation and the points made about Japanese patterns of employment and retirement by Tillsley and Taylor are massively useful pointers here.

Many very important contributions have been made by gerontologists and by writers on youth employment and unemployment. These need to be brought together more often, and students of HRM in particular and of management in general have done very little so far to understand age-employment relationships, and need to do much more.

Here some of our own recent writings are pertinent. On some relevant aspects of HRM Lyon, Hallier and Glover (1998) contrasted its ostensibly developmental rhetoric with the widespread involuntary retirement of many older employees. HRM writers had placed a strong emphasis on strategic investment in employees as a vital component of business policy. In reality HRM policies tended to be financially driven with most older employees defined as peripheral and as unworthy of development. Employers' wanted their organizations to have strong cultures and for their workforces to be adaptable. Older employees are often assumed to have loyalties and attitudes which pre-date 'most employers' introduction of goals, values and practices associated with HRM'. The 'length and diversity of their work histories' acted against them in the eyes of 'new broom' managements. On greenfield sites the latter often preferred younger and inexperienced workforces for their tendencies to be compliant and uncritical. Long-standing managerial prejudices against older employees, with terms like 'over the hill' and 'past their sell-by date' in common use, underpinned more recent behaviour.

HRM rhetoric tended to legitimise existing attitudes. That, indeed, was its wider and true purpose, in a context of disruptive and volatile socio-economic changes. HRM's 'aim is ... to legitimise employers' demands for greater employee loyalty and accountability at a time of diminishing work opportunities and employment protection' (pp. 59-60). HRM became vital to the 'appearance ... of long term investment in key employees', who tended to be young, partly through the exclusion of older ones. This was usually done quite openly in order to reassure younger employees of their priority status. Many methods were used to persuade or coerce older employees to leave, from references to the needs of younger colleagues with greater family commitments to threats to reduce early retirement terms if the employees concerned will not retire 'voluntarily'. Employer behaviour reinforced and was reinforced by widespread ageist prejudices. HRM was 'long-termist' in one sense: 'it valorises youthfulness and invests in the future on the basis of potential rather than track record' (p. 60). The authors are fairly unconvinced, at least for the time being, by arguments about changing public attitudes backed by long term demographic imperatives. They regard short run economic and business exigencies as more powerful. In reality many employers were not very interested in any sort of long term investment in employees of any age.

Students of management tend to fall into two camps: mainstream and critical. Mainstream management research and writing has largely ignored ageism in work and employment. Branine and Glover (1997) argued that age is a major factor in management and organization, affecting divisions of labour and many other aspects of how people are employed. They pointed to connections between the cult of youth and the short termism of much contemporary managerial behaviour. They pointed out that 'beliefs about age, work and employment are about structures of power and domination, socialization and moral values, and experience and fact' (p. 237). They were concerned with assumptions about the nature of human ability, competence and potential, and of innovation, tradition and progress. Attitudes towards the development of 'human capital' varied across countries, sectors and organizations, often with major practical ramifications for management. Age profiles of organizations often varied, or failed to, in ways which reflected their roles and needs as, for example, 'star', 'cash cow', 'question mark' or 'dog' companies. Sometimes assumptions about occupations and careers were age-based, privileging the routinized charisma of gilded youth or that of presumptively wise elders. Different kinds of management control, like bureaucratic, output and cultural control, seemed variously more attractive than others to younger or older employees. In sales and marketing younger people seem, to some managements, more suited to (some) front stage roles involving customer contact, whereas older employees could sometimes have more to offer in backstage roles like market research. Many people assumed that engineers and scientists were 'obsolescent' after 40, although in our opinion there is little solid evidence to support the assumption. The main point made in our 1997 paper is that there is usually very little that is simultaneously explicit, realistic and systematic about management behaviour with regard to age and employment and that almost all management researchers had done very little to point this out or to offer useful help.

Critical writers on management include labour process thinkers and researchers. These adopt a left of centre or liberal humanistic/emancipatory stance but they have almost entirely ignored ageism as a source of exploitation and oppression (Glover and Branine, 1997). Perhaps this is not so remarkable: who wants to identify with 'losers', especially old ones, when you are knocking on the gates of power? Labour process researchers had however written a great deal about labour exploitation in general and about racial and sexual discrimination in particular. Glover and Branine's paper explores the importance of links between ageism and such social and economic phenomena as life cycles, divisions of labour, managerialism and industrialization.

Our own policy preferences are for legislation of the US and South Australian types *and* for voluntary measures. These are not mutually exclusive and indeed in the USA for example legislation exists to signify and legitimise desired standards as much as anything else. We also strongly favour the current Japanese approach of combining gradual and flexible retirement with the provision and development of employment for older people. We do not believe that anyone should be required to 'make way' in the workplace for someone else because of reasons to do with age. To say that someone should be denied opportunity either because they look young and less mature, or because they are older and have 'had their life', is unconscionable. We are far more in sympathy with the view that a person's life is worth what they feel and want it to be worth and not what someone else thinks it is worth. More importantly we are opposed to all forms of social exclusion based on factors over which its victims have no control. Also we valorize wisdom as perhaps the second most valuable human quality, second only to benevolence and co-equal with determination and perseverance. We see no reason whatever why in many circumstances people in their sixties, seventies and eighties and so on should not be considered for promotion or new opportunities and be treated just as favourably as much younger fellow candidates. We believe that the vast majority of people are capable of development until final physical decline becomes acute and irreversible. We also have no objections whatever to the notion of seventeen or eighteen year olds being top job holders, at least not in principle, which means that we would enjoy witnessing and not be emotionally biased against such phenomena.

Thus we have come to believe that it is very important to distinguish between good and bad age discrimination. We have substantial experience, and not only as people being taught or as teachers and researchers, of working very harmoniously with people of radically different ages from ourselves. We know from experience that age diversity is infinitely superior to any alternative as regards learning about and performing complex tasks.

Final ideas and suggestions

We are pleased that the diverse contributors to this volume all sing with more or less the same tune, that they regard the unfair use of their ages against people as wasteful and as a matter for serious public concern in the present context. We feel that this fact adds genuine weight to all of the main points that are made in the book. Yet at the same time our subject remains a fairly new one with many details remaining implicit and half understood and even muddled. Therefore, and at the severe risk of repeating ourselves beyond the point at which repetition is usefully adding emphasis, we will make a number of final points, in the form of ideas and suggestions, in an attempt to round out and round off what have at times been a number of fairly new and raw arguments.

First, there are several references in this book to the development of new forms of employment, in Japan for example, for retired people. These help to keep older people active and productive. While we broadly approve of such developments we also see dangers in them, dangers of ghettoizing and homogenizing the activities and the roles of elders in what could come to resemble new versions of the workhouses of Victorian times and earlier. In the UK context many pensioners own their properties and have few charges on their incomes, and some part-time earnings are useful supplements to their pensions and productive in the widest sense. However anything which excludes reasonably experienced adults from opportunities to share in decision making, economic, social and political, and which helps, however implicitly, to infantilise them, is worth resisting. Because no one can know what someone will think up next, it is never very satisfactory to tell them that they have had their say. As we have suggested if someone in the eighth decade of their life, or older, is competent to contribute to the work of an organization at any level including the highest ones, it is unreasonable and unfair to everyone to exclude them from doing so.

Second, we have not explained our choice of the title of this chapter. It comes from the book of Proverbs in the Christian Bible, although it is a sentiment expressed throughout all the world's great religions and by many others. 'Wisdom is the principal thing. Therefore get wisdom, and with all thy getting get understanding' is the original text. We expect that readers will need no further explanation of its present relevance.

Third, we offer a tentative set of preliminary practical guidelines for thought and practice. These are, first, that a much higher proportion of labour forces in developed countries is becoming chronologically old by historic standards, and it will be increasingly capable of bringing a wide range of experience, knowledge, information, skills, as well as wisdom, to workplaces. Second, age diverse workforces tend to be more competent ones than those which are similarly aged, and also more likely to engender constructive social interaction of all kinds. Third, a very wide and increasing variety of tasks, some mundane, some very complex indeed, need performing in advanced industrial societies. Fourth, and in situations in which there is 'greening' of work and employment, the more physically threatening forms of work should tend to be performed by those with the most robust immune systems and constitutions, that is people who are biologically young from all social backgrounds. Fifth, it is increasingly realised that intellectual ability and potential are spread throughout human populations much more widely than was assumed in less affluent and democratic times, and that the most intelligent people are not simply and largely upper middle class white males in their mid twenties! Sixth, emotional resilience and tolerance, while far from being attributes unique to elders, do tend to grow with age, and thus occupations and tasks requiring balance, detachment, objectivity and lengthy and deep experience and so on, should be staffed and performed with significant and adequate numbers of mature (but not necessarily merely chronologically old) people. Finally, people are the sum totals of their experiences and therefore all employers should always as a matter of course take the whole of a person's life into account when considering if and how to employ them. They should not stigmatise adversity when it has apparently retarded the advancement of someone: instead they should look upon evidence of rising above adversity in a favourable light. Contemporary ageism devalues courage and persistence as well as wisdom.

Our fourth main suggestion is that the more creative and flexible approaches to employment and related phenomena that we are advocating do not preclude reconsideration being given to the notions and institutions and practices of apprenticeship and vocation. If a set of tasks is difficult it is criminal to pretend otherwise, and mature learning is a personal and interpersonal matter, and it is rightly and necessarily protracted, and it is also 'poetry'. Anyone who has had the privilege of being taught by exceptionally competent people knows this, and realises the crucial degrees to which competent human societies rely on such learning. To trivialise the notion of apprenticeship is destructive and naive, just as denying the importance of the altruistic dedicated service to humanity embodied in the concept of vocation is. However the notion of a 70 year old apprentice learning from a 30 year old master is one which we find delightful: it embodies appropriate respect taken to almost its logical conclusion. Also in the context of this fourth point, we are attracted strongly by Colin Bottomley's faith in SMEs as vehicles for constructive social change. Their tasks and roles in economic life are often vital and their potential varies from the useful to the infinite. They tend to offer more authenticity and more experience of life's crueller truths than life in larger organizations, and even to be more fun.

Fifth, we re-emphasize our belief in holistic thinking about age, work and employment. Ageism is multigenerational and intergenerational and it transcends generations. It thus goes deep: its roots are historic and of course permanently and profoundly connected to the fact of human mortality. We cannot remember or find out who said that 'the world belongs to the dead' but there is a massively powerful sense in which it does, and always will. The twentieth century cult of youth of many Western societies and their tendency for younger people to be neglected by their parents and to form peer groups from whence they take their standards of behaviour have been sources of moral concern in recent years. A few months ago a colleague whose parents' work had ensured that he did not live in one country for more than two or three years when he was young told us that 'I never had a group of "mates" of my own age. I did have many friends of different ages and backgrounds though. As I've grown older I've come to recognize the value of having such a wide range of friends. I hope that it has made me more tolerant and understanding, and it has certainly made life more interesting'. This seems to us to exemplify the value of non-ageist or anti-ageist ways of living. Getting one's standards of behaviour from 'mates' on the street corner or in the pub or club does not seem not particularly adult. Similarly we mistrust organizations whose leadership is visibly self-confessedly old or young. Neither the expression 'we are a young company' or evidence of rule by what used in the 1960s student protests to be called 'senile gerontocracies', is particularly impressive. Also on our belief in a holistic approach to our subject we reiterate what Philip Taylor has long and most sensibly emphasized: the importance of 'joined up government' regarding age, economic development, education and training, employment, health, welfare and retirement. The context of such policies is probably, by the way and in opposition to the conventional wisdom of management gurus, one in which the pace of change in the world may well be starting to *decelerate* (Ackroyd, Glover, Currie and Bull, 2000).

Sixth, we re-assert, following points made in Ian Glover's chapter, our faith in the notion of reflexive modernity for understanding our arguments. Overcoming contemporary ageism is all about transcending the quick fixes of early industrialization and the relatively rigid organizational mechanisms designed to inhibit the abuses and excesses of unprecedentedly rapid economic development. Fixed age categories are crude and restrictive things as long as we continue to inhabit affluent and sophisticated societies, and we are in a position to leave them behind, at least until the next major environmental, military or political cataclysm.

Seventh, we are interested in some of the terminology and assumptions used to discuss age, work and employment, and relevant policies. For example we suspect that the terms 'the elderly' and 'older workers' will be used, respectively, about far fewer people, and much less often, in the future. Genuinely elderly people will tend to be fourth-agers, those approaching death because they are very ill and/or very feeble. Most people over 50 or 60 including most of those now called elderly will simply be called older people. They will increasingly be active and assertive citizens for whom a term with strong connotations of physical decline will be inaccurate and irrelevant. The term older worker implicitly accepts the notion that career advancement is inappropriate for the vast majority of mature people, that they have had their chances and failed to take them, and that they are incapable of truly demanding, energetic and creative full time work, and incapable of learning too. Both the term and the notion will we believe increasingly be interpreted as patronizing and inflexible, as implying premature, unnecessary and irrelevant foreclosure of options 'on behalf of' mature people. We also hope that the rather odd and partly self-contradictory term 'an ageing population' will pass from use, with terms like longer-living and healthier, and perhaps our neologisms 'juvenating' and 'juvenation' being used instead. We suspect that if debates about our subject become more thoughtful and better-informed, as we expect they will, that some of the less intelligent forms of political correctness will be exposed and become less prevalent. Relationships between age, work and employment are more complicated than those between gender or race and work and employment, and this fact should encourage more thoughtful approaches to the subjects of prejudice and discrimination. Regarding assumptions needed to underpin helpful policy developments, we suggest that some deep and hard thinking is needed in order to generate effective and just policy guidelines for the following: the role of apprenticeship, broadly defined, and its relationships with education, employment and citizenship; the employment of the many individuals whom we have called chronological misfits on various occasions, and the philosophies needed by employers if such people, those who for whatever reason do not fit readily into career structures and organizational hierarchies, are to be employed to most effect; and phased retirement, an inevitably moveable and complicated feast which needs to be underpinned as far as possible by principles of economic and social justice.

Finally, we reiterate, once more and unashamedly so, the book's main point. All ageism is bad, but age discrimination should always be good.

Postscript

This chapter was last checked in on a beautiful late summer's day in 2000 in the bay window of a hotel room overlooking the harbour of Kirkwall, Orkney. Now the final checks to the book are being done in the depths of a Scottish Central Belt winter, numerous IT glitches and several months later. Although the weather is worse, some things offer cause for guarded opinions. Since 2000 ended we have learnt that the UK government plans to end compulsory retirement and to legislate against age discrimination, and that in the USA, the average age at which people retire has begun to rise.

References

Ackroyd, S., Glover, I., Currie, W. and Bull, S. (2000), 'The Triumph of Markets over Hierarchies: Information Systems Specialists in the Current Context', in I. Glover and M. Hughes (eds.), *Professions at Bay*, Ashgate, Aldershot.

Bosanquet, N. (1987), *A Generation in Limbo: Government, the Economy and the 55-65 Age Group in Britain*, Public Policy Centre, London.

Branine, M. and Glover, I. (1997), 'Ageism in Work and Employment: Thinking about Connections', *Personnel Review*, Vol. 26, No. 4, pp. 233-44.

Bytheway, B. (1995), *Ageism*, Open University Press, Buckingham.

Feldman, D.C. and Weitz, B.A. (1988), 'Career plateaus reconsidered', *Journal of Management*, Vol. 14, No. 1, pp. 69-90.

Ference, T.P., Stoner, J.A.F. and Warren, E.K. (1977), 'Managing the career plateau', *Academy of Management Journal*, Vol. 2, pp. 602-12.

Glover, I. and Branine, M. (1997), 'Ageism and the labour process: towards a research agenda', *Personnel Review*, Vol. 26, No. 4, pp. 274-92.

Guillemard, A.M. and van Gunsteren, H. (1991), 'Pathways and their prospects: a comparative interpretation of the meaning of early exit', in M. Kohli, M. Rein, A. Guillemard and H. van Gunsteren (eds), *Time for Retirement: Comparative Studies of Early Exit from the Labour Force*, Cambridge University Press, Cambridge.

Herriot, P., Hirsh, W. and Reilly, P. (1988), *Trust and Transformation: Managing the Employment Relationship*, Wiley, Chichester.

Laslett, P. (1989), *A Fresh Map of Life: the Emergence of the Third Age*, Weidenfeld and Nicholson, London.

Legge, K. (1995), *Human Resource Management: Rhetorics and Realities*, Macmillan, Basingstoke.

Lukes, S. (1974), *Power: a Radical View*, Macmillan, London.

Lyon, P. Hallier, J. and Glover, I. (1998), 'Divestment or investment? The contradictions of HRM in relation to older employees', *Human Resource Management Journal*, Vol. 8, No. 1, pp. 56-66.

Standing, G. (1986), 'Labour flexibility and older worker marginalisation: the need for a new strategy', *International Labour Review*, Vol. 125, No. 3, pp. 329-48.

Worsley, R. (1996), *Age and Employment: Why Employers Should Think Again about Older Workers*, Ace, London.

Index

For Product Safety Concerns and Information please contact our EU representative GPSR@taylorandfrancis.com Taylor & Francis Verlag GmbH, Kaufingerstraße 24, 80331 München, Germany

Batch number: 10725973

Printed by Printforce, the Netherlands